CW01150460

CATHY FREEMAN
A Journey Just Begun

CATHY FREEMAN

A Journey Just Begun

ADRIAN McGREGOR

RANDOM HOUSE
AUSTRALIA

Random House Australia Pty Ltd
20 Alfred Street, Milsons Point, NSW 2061
http://www.randomhouse.com.au

Sydney New York Toronto
London Auckland Johannesburg
and agencies throughout the world

First published 1998
Copyright © Adrian McGregor 1998

All rights reserved. No part of this publication may be reproduced,
stored in a retrieval system, or transmitted in any form or by
any means, electronic, mechanical, photocopying, recording
or otherwise, without the prior written permission of the Publisher.

National Library of Australia
Cataloguing-in-Publication Data

McGregor, Adrian.
   The Cathy Freeman Story.

   ISBN 0 091 83649 2.

   1. Freeman, Cathy, 1973–. 2. Runners (Sports) - Australia
   - Biography. 3. Aborigines, Australian - Women - Biography.
   I. Title

796.42092

Design by Yolande Grey
Typeset by Asset Typesetting Pty Ltd, Sydney
Printed by Griffin Press Pty Ltd, Adelaide

Extract quoted on page 21 is from *Under the Act* by Willie Thaiday,
N.Q. Black Publishing, Townsville, 1981.

Every effort has been made to identify individual photographers
and permission holders, but for some photographs this has not
been possible. The publishers would be pleased to hear from any
copyright holders who have not been acknowledged.

10 9 8 7 6 5 4 3 2 1

*To my beloved late sister
Anne-Marie, the first to help
me realise that I have to
make the most of who I am every day.*

Cathy Freeman, 1998

CONTENTS

	Preface	ix
1	Meeting Cathy. 1997–98	1
2	Big Shot and Twinkle Toes. 1936–93	8
3	Cecelia's Story. 1939–98	15
4	Wonder Girl. Primary School, 1983–86	31
5	Speaking Out. 1984	43
6	Welcome Stranger. High School, 1987–90	50
7	Rookie's Gold. Commonwealth Games, 1990	65
8	Our Own Little Flo Jo. Melbourne, 1991	81
9	Lessons in Lactic. Pre-Olympics, 1992	99
10	Stargazing. Barcelona Olympics, 1992	110
11	A Sad Homecoming. Stuttgart Worlds, 1993–94	121
12	No Big Cat Fight. Pre-Commonwealth Games, 1993–94	143
13	Black is for the People. Commonwealth Games, 1994	162
14	Winning Yet Losing. Post-Commonwealth Games, 1994	180
15	Mickey Mouse Meets. Pre-Worlds, 1995	193
16	A Tin Medal. Worlds, Gothenburg, 1995	208
17	A Woman and Three Men. Atlanta, 1996	226
18	La Gazelle. Pre-Olympics, 1996	243
19	F-L-A-G. Atlanta Olympics, 1996	252
20	Roll the Dice. Atlanta Olympics, 1996	267
21	Whoopin' Mary-Jo's Butt. Post-Olympics, 1996	276
22	Time Heals. Pre-Worlds, 1997	287
23	Conchita in El Paso. Pre-Worlds, 1997	301
24	First Among Billions. Worlds, Athens, 1997	319
25	Towards Sydney 2000	339
	Short List of Honours	353
	Index	355

Preface

Cathy Freeman's story ranks as one of the most revealing biographies ever written about a sportsperson whose career is still active. When I first discussed the idea with Cathy and her long-time partner, and manager, Nick Bideau, they were a couple. By the time I began my research, they were no longer together, even though Bideau remained her manager. That I was able to proceed was due to the grace with which Cathy accepted that her private relationships would have to come under the spotlight, so closely were her personal and professional lives intertwined.

Cathy Freeman's life is so filled with training, travelling, racing and obligations to media and her sponsors, that windows of time for her to slow down and explore her memory and feelings are difficult to snare. For these reasons, and others, producing this book has not been easy, for subject, manager and biographer.

That is has emerged, thanks are due to Cathy herself for allowing her life to be explored so thoroughly. This is an authorised biography, in that it has been written with Cathy's assistance. But as is quickly obvious upon reading, Cathy has not censored herself, or attempted to censor me.

CATHY FREEMAN—A JOURNEY JUST BEGUN

The biography would not have been written without the generous assistance of Nick Bideau whose journalistic training, and memory of places, times and events, was crucial. Occasionally this biography may make uncomfortable reading for Bideau, but his long-time dedication to Cathy's professional success and personal wellbeing extended to this book too.

Team Freeman—Peter Fortune, Maurie Plant and Peter Jess —all made themselves readily available, as did her back-up squad of Garry Miritis, Dr Peter Fuller, Mark McGrath and Jeff Simons. Melbourne Track Club's Zoe Jess and Athletics Australia's Brian Roe and Damien Booth were extremely helpful, as was Mike Danila from Cathy's school days.

On the family front, special mention is due to Cathy's mother Cecelia, whose own childhood partly emerged here, and to Cathy's stepfather Bruce Barber. Cathy's friends Alexander Bodecker and Peta Powell were always up front.

Up north, Tolibah Fisher, Lillian Grey and John Talbot lent a generous hand while, down south, Kelvin Doyle made sense of Cathy's photographic album in her absence. Janice Saunders' detailed scrapbooks were invaluable, as was her luxury limo guided tour of Mackay.

In the early stages of research I am indebted to Qantas for flights north and south, and to Brian Breingan, librarian at Queensland Newspapers, a friend of many years. Robyn Smith made transcription look easy.

In production, I am grateful to Helen Dash for her preliminary reading and sound suggestions, to Gail Intas for her insight, Julia Taylor for her osprey-eyed editing, Kim Swivel for patient hours on the phone and Random House's Jane Palfreyman for her unflagging support. Finally I'd like to thank editor Margaret Sullivan who did the hard yards at the start of this project but, regrettably, heard the call of Ireland.

Adrian McGregor, 1998

1.
MEETING CATHY.
1997–98

The first morning I awoke in the house where Cathy Freeman once lived—in Miller Street, Richmond, an inner-city suburb of Melbourne, my eye caught upon a black and white sticker pasted to a mirror beside the bed. I rose and saw a number and name which galvanised me from mere methodical sports author to excited Olympic pilgrim. The number and word were '48.60, Atlanta.' Cathy had typed the famous prediction on a sticky label ages before the 1996 Olympics, as an affirmation of the time she wanted to run in the 400m final.

Cathy thought she was typing the time that black Frenchwoman, the elegant Marie-José Pérec, had run to win the 400m gold medal at the Barcelona Olympics in 1992. She believed she'd have to aim to run at least that fast in Atlanta. But she got it wrong. Pérec ran slower, 48.83 seconds in Barcelona. But what matter? The power of the mind. In Atlanta, Cathy ran what she typed, or near enough, 48.63s. To gaze at that time, still there, to see her grand ambition—it was then a whole second faster than she had ever run before—was to become caught in a sepia hiatus of history. As I stood there I saw her once more in slow motion, in Atlanta, pushing herself to the edge, and beyond.

CATHY FREEMAN—A JOURNEY JUST BEGUN

Above the number was another sticker with the words 'World's Greatest Athlete'. They were the words Cathy had copied from an old sticker that her mother had given her as a teenager, a legend to paste on her bedroom wall to seep into her daughter's subconscious. And it had worked.

I wandered through the house where our conversations, the journey through her life, were about to begin. The house is owned by Cathy's manager and erstwhile partner, former Melbourne sports journalist Nick Bideau, and the rooms are still redolent with her presence. Videotapes of her races are stacked behind the television; scores of tarnished silver cups, oddly shaped trophies and inscribed medals fill a glass cabinet, together with Yothu Yindi CDs; a bookcase is lined with such titles as *The Bid: How Australia Won the 2000 Games, Winning Without Drugs, Winning Women, Aboriginal Myths* and *Murawina (Black Women)*.

The floors of cupboards are filled with orphaned track and training shoes and, in the laundry, the washing machine is waist deep in discarded Freeman posters, tracksuits, cold-weather jackets, multi-coloured anoraks, cotton T-shirts, lycra shorts and sponsors' bags.

Freeman has a carefully crafted media image, designed to avoid any controversy which could cloud her sparkling public persona for sponsors and advertisers. I am uncertain, therefore, of the true nature of the young woman who is about to entrust me with her memories. Too young for her life's story? She has been in the media's headlines for nearly 10 years—since she was 16—an entire career for many sportspeople. She may be young, but she inhabits a large sporting space.

A door knock disturbs my reverie and suddenly she's there, dark glowing skin, bobbed dark brown hair, wide smile, white teeth and round brown eyes. We're a little awkward and she promises to try her hardest with her memory, though she's a little weary, having come from a strenuous weights session at the Victorian Institute of Sport.

As I deploy my recording paraphernalia, Cathy, subject of

MEETING CATHY

a thousand interviews, watches unfazed. In conversation she laughs often, frowns when perplexed, yawns unabashedly and lets silences sit. What becomes evident, as an hour passes, is that she has no photographic memory of the progression of races in her career, or the times, or even the places. She has always delegated that, first to her family, then to her support crew, the people I will call Team Freeman.

They in turn tell me about the mental delete button which she uses to block any input which might disturb her internal attention to the singular sensation of running. She employs the erase switch in different ways, from ignoring political controversy, or the performances of most of her rivals, to her legendary capacity to curl up and sleep, even if she's in the back seat of a car speeding along narrow, twisting mountain roads in Scandinavia. What she does retain are vivid images and emotions about occasions, and these are the rich lodes I become privileged to discover.

Listen, for instance, to her breathlessly chasing down Nigerian Mary Onyali in the final few metres of the 200m final at the Commonwealth Games in Victoria, Canada in 1994: 'It happens quickly. You start to feel good, and you feel yourself lift and come out of yourself. Like you feel you're high above the ground and something happens to you, and you lift to another level. You lift and you just feel like magic. You feel, wow! It's a great feeling, just amazing.' Her voice soars, her face is luminous. 'It's more than just running, it's … flying! You want to win so much and whoever's got the biggest heart, whoever's the most honest with themselves on the day, wins.' That day it was Cathy, by a mere 0.1s.

Freeman lets her running do the talking and it's impressive. Training partner Patrick Seal has spent hours with her in the gathering dusk on the ochre-coloured tartan track of Melbourne's Olympic Park. 'Running beside her, she's like whispering death,' he says. 'You don't hear her. I lead out and though I'm a lot taller, her stride is nearly as long as mine. When she wants to go past, you first see her feet in your peripheral vision, then she's past so quickly you almost lose your equilibrium. It's pretty daunting training with her. I'm always running scared.'

Her main 400m rival in Australia has been four times national champion, Perth's graceful Renee Poetschka. 'We'd come off the bend neck and neck,' says Renee. 'And I'd be putting in a really good effort until in the last 50m she would effortlessly ease away. And I'd go, "Oh no, she's done it to me again!" She's so fluent and smooth. It's amazing, she's such a light, lithe young thing. I've got 10cm in height on her, longer legs, and still she does it. It annoys me, I want to know her secret!'

No secret. Running has loomed in Freeman's life long since before she can remember, and quickened in her childish legs in games of tiggy or catch-and-kiss around the house with her brothers. Cathy's primary school athletics was a succession of audacious displays, in which her prodigious talent confounded opponents and produced victories without apparent effort.

Cathy attended St Joseph's Primary School, Mackay, for four years, from when she was aged five to nine, yet she holds not a single athletic record there. 'She only ran to win,' says St Joseph's sports co-ordinator Bessie Bauldry, half in frustration and half in fond memory. 'She didn't want to show off. In the high jump, as soon as the last girl in her age group went out, bang! Cathy would knock the bar off next jump, even though she'd been clearing it by a good six inches beforehand.' The same with sprinting, only ever doing just enough to win. One day Bauldry decided to test eight-year-old Freeman. She raced her in training against the nine-year-olds, and Freeman won; then against the 10-year-olds, same result; finally against the 11-year-olds, Cathy was stretched, but still won, just. Now Bauldry knew what an exceptional athlete she had on her hands.

Cathy remembers her first race because she almost missed it. She had on her athletics uniform—a long yellow pinafore with slits down the side, and blue pants underneath, and was rushing through the schoolyard to run for her school house, named Gold. 'I ran into a piece of wire sticking out from a steel post in the schoolyard and hurt my eye,' she says. 'It was watering, but I had to run, so I ran with one eye closed.' Of course she won. It was the 80m dash for eight-year-olds at St Joseph's in 1981.

She didn't just win. 'She won by metres, way out in front of the rest of the girls,' says her mother, Cecelia. 'I didn't take too much notice at the time.' But Bessie Bauldry took notice, and soon discovered an enduring facet of Cathy's attitude to athletics. 'She wouldn't come to training unless I actually went to get her,' says Bauldry. 'She knew the starting time but she'd never be there. I'd tell other children to go and find her and they'd say, "She won't come, Miss." So I'd have to leave training and go and find her in the library or toilets or wherever she was hiding. She wasn't like other children, she wasn't keen to train.'

Perhaps training is too strong a term for primary school athletics. Bauldry encouraged the children to join in practice because they invariably found it enjoyable, not because it was essential to their future success. Cathy couldn't be bothered training as a child because she could do what she wanted without practice—win.

Bessie Bauldry discreetly discovered that the Freeman family was not flush with funds, so, when Cathy qualified from St Joseph's for the Mackay district athletics, Bauldry bought her the correct school T-shirt. When she qualified from there to the Pioneer zone, and then to the Dawson Valley titles, the school paid her entry fees. And when she qualified for the state titles in Brisbane, Bauldry iced a cake and raffled it, selling two dollar tickets until she had enough to send Cathy and two other girls to Brisbane.

That was Freeman's first flight. 'It was night-time when we landed in Brisbane,' says Cathy. 'I had a window seat and out there in the darkness I could see all the city lights. It was so big, the lights seemed to stretch forever.' Cathy was billeted with a family in what, to her, was a huge, rich house, in Aspley. 'I had my first pair of spikes, blue Pumas, and I didn't know that you weren't supposed to wear them around the house,' she says. 'And this lady got very upset and said, "Oh Catherine, I think you'd better take them off, dear, before you tear up the carpet." I think I already had.'

Cathy duly won the 80m gold medal, her first state title. Two teaching sisters from St Joseph's picked her up from Mackay airport that evening and drove her home to where her mother sat waiting for her on a tiny porch under the night sky. 'When the sisters told Mum I'd won a gold medal, she smothered me with hugs and kisses,' says Cathy. The next day, at assembly, she was applauded and showed off her medal. First lesson of athletics: winning equals rewards. 'That's how it all began,' says Cathy. When the Freemans moved to Hughenden in 1983, Bessie Bauldry was so worried about Cathy's shy nature that she wrote ahead to the Hughenden head teacher advising of the newcomer's talents.

Cathy enrolled in St Francis Primary School, Hughenden, where Sister Geraldine Kearney scarcely needed any prompting to note Cathy's ability. 'She ran everywhere,' Kearney said, when interviewed years later. 'Her grace and style were obvious. Others would run their hearts out but she'd be lengths ahead.' Kearney also foresaw Cathy's failings. 'If it had been left to her, I don't think she would have pushed herself,' she said. 'She didn't have enough tickets on herself.' She still doesn't; it's one of her endearing qualities. But it didn't seem to slow her progress through her early school years as she sprinted, hurdled and high jumped her way to national titles, effortlessly breaking the hearts of less talented girls.

At the Queensland age titles in 1983, Cathy, 10, high jump winner from the north Queensland zone, walked over to the competition area, threw down her run-up marker and said, 'I think I'll jump from here.' Vanessa Gray, from Condamine

MEETING CATHY

in south-west Queensland, the top high jumper in her zone, was astonished. 'We'd been stretching, measuring our run-up and doing the right stuff, and she'd just come from some sprint event,' says Vanessa. 'She didn't even have jumping spikes, she wore her running spikes. We didn't take her seriously. Then, when her turn came to jump she ran straight at the bar, and did this amazing 90-degree twist in the air and sailed high over. We all just stared and thought, "O-mi-god!" It was very funny actually, because I used to train hours every day with my mum, and Cathy just launched herself way over.'

Vanessa's mother, Lyn Gray, was impressed and amused by Cathy's astonishing athleticism. 'When she ran, her long straggly legs would go whizzing around,' she says. 'And to high jump she just used to run up to the bar and go phhhht! It was so easy for her, much to everyone's disgust. But no-one disliked her, she was a lovely, lovely girl.'

Cathy's athleticism is in her blood, passed down through generations unknown—if only the oral history of her Aboriginal clans and tribes could tell us more. But it emerged, to our certainty, in her grandfather, Frank 'Big Shot' Fisher, and he passed it on to his son, Norman 'Twinkle Toes' Freeman, who passed it on to his daughter, Cathy Freeman, who became the champion of the world.

2.
BIG SHOT AND TWINKLE TOES.
1936–93

In 1954, after full-time in the touring Great Britain rugby league team's match against Wide Bay in Maryborough, an Aborigine attempted to enter the tourists' dressing-rooms. When he couldn't get past the doorman, the Aborigine, Frank Fisher, appealed to a friend, Percy Iszlaub, a front-rower in the Wide Bay team and long-time mayor of Wondai Shire Council. 'Perc, can you get me in,' said Fisher. 'I've got a boomerang here I want to give to Nat Silcock to take home to his dad. I played against his father when Great Britain toured in 1936.'

Iszlaub smuggled Fisher through the door and introduced him to Silcock who greeted him with surprised pleasure when he heard Fisher's mission. 'It's wonderful that I met you, my father often spoke about you,' said Silcock. 'He said that the best player they met on the whole tour was a five-eighth at Maryborough called Frank Fisher. Never seen such a gifted and talented player, he said.' Frank Fisher was Cathy Freeman's paternal grandfather.

After the match, over a drink, Fisher told Iszlaub that back in 1936 he had been extremely worried about marking the Great Britain five-eighth, legendary Welshman A. J. (Gus)

Risman. 'So I used my speed to move up on him quickly,' said Fisher. 'I played safe, nothing flash, just dropped around his hips, and never missed a tackle all night.' Risman was so impressed that he is reported to have invited Fisher to come to England to play club football. Iszlaub had his hand on the bar and Fisher placed his own next to it. 'You know, Perc, if this had been that colour,' said Fisher, pointing from his arm to Iszlaub's, 'I reckon I could have played for Australia.'

Frank's people belonged to Birri Gubba, a traditional language that embraced 18 Aboriginal groups in the Burdekin River basin, from the Whitsundays in the north, west to Charters Towers, south to Clermont and east to Marlborough on the central coast of Queensland. He was one of 11 children in the Fisher family which the Queensland government moved from their tribal grounds to the Aboriginal mission at Cherbourg.

Frank scored a try against the 1936 British tourists and, in the team photograph, appears to be the only Aboriginal face in the local side. He lived in Cherbourg and for digs on that Maryborough trip in 1936 he bunked down with a friend, an Aboriginal tracker, at Maryborough police station. Cherbourg, an all-Aboriginal team, had a fine record in those days, once defeating, at their height, the famous Galloping Clydesdales from Toowoomba. Cherbourg's team often rode hundreds of kilometres to matches in the back of an open truck, and some then played the match in bare feet.

In his prime Frank was a big man for a five-eighth, over 95kg (about 15 stone) which was as heavy as Wally Lewis, Australia's champion rugby league five-eighth of the modern era. Frank's son Norman Tolibah (Tolly) Fisher says his father was either making it happen on the field or was part of it happening. And just as Wally Lewis was known as King Wally for his total domination of matches, Frank was also known locally as The King. He was barrel-chested, with thick thighs, and was, according to Tolly, 'as strong as a scrub bull'.

Iszlaub, who played against Fisher, says Frank delighted in sleight-of-hand. 'His favourite deception was a fake scissors move where he rolled the ball behind his back as his teammate crossed behind him, but instead of passing it, he held on,' says Iszlaub. 'If his opponent hesitated, Frank was through the gap with speed I have seen matched since only by St George's Reg Gasnier in the 1960s and the Broncos' Steve Renouf today.'

Percy Iszlaub avers that Frank Fisher was also an excellent sprinter, winning many of the district titles in near even time—professional running argot for 10 seconds for 100 yards. 'Had he been properly coached, good judges believe Frank could have reduced his times to near those of the great A.B. Postle, who ran in carnivals around here,' says Iszlaub. Toowoomba-born Arthur Postle was a professional sprinter who set world records for the 50 yards (5.2s), 60 yards (6s), 75 yards (7.2s) and 200 yards (19s) between 1906 and 1912. When Iszlaub queried Fisher about his sprinting, Fisher confessed, 'Yeah, I could go, Perc, but I didn't like the hanging around, waiting for the heats to get through to the final. I preferred the intensity of rugby league.'

Swampy Fisher, one of Frank's brothers, still lives at Cherbourg and attests that Frank was a good cricketer as well. 'He looked after his body as a young man,' says Swampy. 'He was a right-hand batter, and had a real hawk-eye in slips. He once played with Eddie Gilbert in a Wide Bay team with some white boys.'

Eddie Gilbert—the name conjures controversy from Australia's cricketing past. An Aboriginal from Cherbourg, Gilbert was an opening bowler whose awesome pace saw him selected to play for Queensland. As a boy, Percy Iszlaub lived on a farm outside Wondai and remembers, one Sunday morning, cycling home with the paper and seeing Gilbert bowling in a local match. 'They were playing on a concrete wicket with a canvas Kippax mat laid over the top,' says Iszlaub. 'There was no-one in front of the wicket, not a single fieldsman.'

BIG SHOT AND TWINKLE TOES

Gilbert stunned cricket's establishment when he bowled the great Donald Bradman for a duck in a Sheffield Shield match at the Gabba in Brisbane in 1931. Bradman wrote later, 'I unhesitatingly class this short burst as faster than anything seen from Larwood or anyone else.' But Bradman also added, 'The players all thought his action decidedly suspect.' Gilbert never played for Australia, whether because he was simply never selected on merit—which was unlikely—or because of the allegation that he was a 'chucker'—which was unfounded—or, as his supporters allege, because the selectors 'drew the colour bar'.

Swampy and Tolly Fisher both assert that the colour bar blocked Frank from higher honours. Percy Iszlaub agrees it is possible, but adds that it was made doubly difficult because of where Fisher lived. 'If you didn't play in one of the Bulimba Cup teams—that's Brisbane, Toowoomba or Ipswich—you had great difficulty in representing your state, no matter who you were,' he says.

Fisher played effectively until he was 40 and ran on in his last match, for Wondai against Kingaroy, at Kingaroy football ground, at the remarkable age of 50. Swampy Fisher tells the story that Frank then retired to coach Cherbourg and one evening berated Jack 'Champ' Malone for being late to training. 'You can't talk to me like that, I'm Champ Malone,' said the indignant player. To which Frank replied, 'You might be bloody Champ, but I'm the big shot here and I run this football team.' And the name Big Shot stuck with Frank ever after.

When Fisher died in 1980, aged 75, the local paper's obituary to him was headlined: KING FISHER IS GONE. In 1996 a new bridge was named after him in Cherbourg, and Tolly's dedication to his father, on a small metal plaque beside the bridge, reads: 'Frank "Big Shot" Fisher, a pioneer in his own right, rugby league was his domain and forte, 'twas to enlighten and strengthen many a path of life's highway.'

CATHY FREEMAN—A JOURNEY JUST BEGUN

In 1940, Frank Fisher and Geraldine Roy, a young Aboriginal woman from Fraser Island then living at Woorabinda mission, had a son, Norman. Soon after, Geraldine married Claude 'Charlie' Freeman and Norman was brought up in Woorabinda as Norman Charles Freeman—Cathy Freeman's father. Norman regarded himself as a Woorabinda Freeman, son of Claude, a ringer renowned for his horsemanship.

If Frank Fisher was brilliant on the field, Norman Freeman was equally mercurial. But off-field, where Frank held down a job for many years with the Queensland Forestry Department, his son Norman was far more itinerant and easygoing in lifestyle. His nickname was Fringey, after Fringe Island, next to Palm Island where the Freemans spent some years when Norman was growing up. He was Fringey by name and Fringey by nature, never conforming too long in regular life. The Freemans eventually left Palm Island and moved back to Woorabinda where young Norman quickly made his name as a rugby league player.

He was first publicly noticed in the early 1960s, when he came down from Ayr with the Burdekin rugby league team to play Mackay, on the central Queensland coast. Gar Houston, who called more than 200 matches for local radio 4MK Mackay, says Freeman destroyed Mackay almost single-handedly. He sat amazed at this young Aboriginal centre who was lightning off the mark, could step off either foot, shed tackles and kicked goals from unbelievable distances.

Not only that, Norman Freeman was somewhat of a showman. In an era when a celebration on the field was confined to a manly clap on a teammate's shoulder, Norman played up to the crowd after scoring, which was often. He'd throw both arms in the air in a victory salute, trot to the sideline, smile and wave and generally carry on. The crowd loved him.

He also sledged opponents, provoked blues, but cleverly always kept his own temper and would duly be awarded the ensuing penalty. Once, playing for Mackay against Townsville, he outpaced two defenders and had only the canny fullback, Wally Tallis, father of 1998 Test forward, Gorden Tallis, to beat. Norman cheekily yelled out to Tallis, a tall, gangly man, 'Hey, Wally, open your legs and I'll nip between 'em!' Wally duly nailed him.

Norman became known as 'Twinkle Toes' and deserved the name, says Terry Hayes, chief rugby league writer for the *Mackay Mercury* in that era. 'He was a picturesque footballer, had a flair about him,' says Hayes. 'He often played centre, but at fullback he loved fielding an opposition kick and when confronted by a ring of defenders, he'd use his acceleration to slip between them, leave them standing.' Shades of his dad, Frank 'Big Shot' Fisher.

Norman played mostly with the Magpies club in Mackay. In 1967 he was their leading pointscorer and played in their 1971 premiership winning side. Magpies president John Talbot recalls a match where, with a minute to go, and the Magpies behind by a point, the opposition drop-kicked out from beneath their posts. Freeman caught the ball 55m out and drop-kicked it straight back between the posts to win the game. (A field goal was worth two points then.) 'He could do anything like that,' says Talbot. 'People used to shake their heads in disbelief.'

I spoke briefly to Norman in 1993, over the telephone from Woorabinda, and he told me, 'Yeah, they reckon I was quick, but I played football with my head not my feet.' He did indeed, and more so as he got older. He would tell younger players, 'I'll open the gaps, you go through them.' Even in the twilight of his career, he played in the All Blacks versus All Whites charity game, held in Barcaldine for many years. Kangaroo stars, like Rod Reddy and Ted Goodwin, were often guest players for the All Whites, but it was the All Blacks' Freeman the crowd always came to see bamboozle everyone.

Norman also played for Mackay in the Foley Shield—

cradle of many Test players—against Burdekin and Townsville. Gar Houston, who saw Elton Rasmussen and the Laird brothers graduate from the Shield to play for Queensland, rates Norman every bit their equal. 'He could have played for the state easily, but he wasn't a great trainer,' says Houston. 'He lacked the discipline to go further.'

One season Norman travelled with the Mackay team to play against Burdekin, his former stamping ground, hopped off the bus with the team to be met by some of his mates from old times. He started yakking, went to the pub, started partying and missed the match. He was like that, Norman, a devil to rely on, but likable, well spoken, and able to spin a yarn or play the guitar with equal charm. He could sit in a pub broke for a week and never go short of a beer.

Cathy says it is a joy for her to run into friends who knew her father and hear a new story about Norman the nonconformist. Such as from Skip, one of Norman's mates from Rockhampton, who hitchhiked around the north with him, free as a pair of galahs. When they were hungry, they'd raid a farmer's poultry pen and, over an open fire, burn the feathers off and eat barbecued chicken for dinner.

Then there was the time, after a night out, Norman caught a $3 taxi ride home but had only $2.90 in his pocket. 'Hang on,' he said to the cabbie, went inside and came back with a milk bottle, refundable at any shop for 10c. And the driver accepted it, because he was Norman Freeman—Fringey Freeman, footballer extraordinaire.

But they were his declining years. He is remembered as a superb footballer, as fleet of foot as his father, Frank Fisher, and, in an Australia of greater equality, who knows what heights of sporting recognition father and son might have reached? What we do know is that Norman Freeman married Cecelia Sibley, a young woman from Palm Island and that in 1973 they had a daughter, Catherine Freeman, in whom all that athletic heritage became manifest in the most magnificent manner.

3.
CECELIA'S STORY.
1939–98

Cathy Freeman is very close to her mother, Cecelia, a bond that has grown in strength rather than been diminished by their continued separation since Cathy went to boarding school aged 14. But then, separation is nothing new to Cecelia, indeed it existed as a sadness in her life from when she was a child. She rarely spoke about her past as Cathy grew up but her daughter sensed hardships and injustices. She would know much, but not all, of Cecelia's story which now unfolds.

Cecelia Agnes Sibley was born in 1939 on Palm Island, about 60km north of Townsville in north Queensland. Palm tolls a sad story in the history of Queensland's treatment of indigenous people over the past 100 years. Successive Queensland governments used Palm Island as a white supervised government mission and penal colony, enacting laws directly responsible for the Stolen Children generations.

Before World War II the eugenics movement, a racist concept committed to policies to improve the genetic stock of a nation's offspring, was strong worldwide. In Australia, the Queensland, Northern Territory and Western Australian governments saw that while Aboriginal numbers were slowly decreasing there was, in their eyes, a rising population of politically and biologically dangerous children with Aboriginal mothers and non-Aboriginal fathers—'mixed bloods' as they were referred to. Policies were instituted to take these children, particularly girls, from their mothers and bring them up in non-Aboriginal communities. The assumption was they would be raised in status, marry white males and become absorbed into the white population.

Hitler's pogrom against the Jews, and the Nazi Holocaust, so totally discredited eugenics and race-based policies that after the war the rationale for continuing the practice in Australia changed. It became justified as cultural assimilation, raising educational standards and encouraging the adoption of the Australian way of life.

On Palm Island, Stolen Children were separated into male and female dormitories, forbidden to speak any Aboriginal language, and sent to schools to learn non-Aboriginal culture. Respected author of Aboriginal histories, Henry Reynolds, saw the last of these dormitories on Palm Island in 1969. 'The girls' dorm had been knocked down, but the boys' was still there,' he says. 'It was a large, timber, two-storey, Queensland-type building with wire mesh enclosing the windows. The system was just coming to an end.' Reynolds says the aim was to break the link between parent and child. 'They grew up without knowledge of their culture, without normal relations with their parents, with no normal family life,' he says. 'Whole generations were institutionalised, which caused family dysfunctions for generations to come.'

Aboriginal families deemed to be troublesome by police, or who merely questioned government policies, were punished by being sent to Palm. The government would also evict from Palm to other white supervised missions, at Cherbourg and Woorabinda, to break up clans and families. Separate and move, divide and disintegrate; it was a constant threat in many Aboriginal families' lives.

Cecelia is the daughter of Alice Mero and George Sibley.

CECELIA'S STORY

Alice's father was a Syrian migrant, Willie Assad, and her mother was Dora Brook of the Kuku-Yalanji tribe, near Tully. Being slightly fair, Alice was taken and sent to Palm Island when she was eight years old. She spoke her tribal language fluently, but on Palm she was assigned to Aboriginal foster parents from a different tribe and then, when she became an adolescent, was put in the dormitory. No-one spoke her dialect and she gradually lost it.

Breaking down tribal languages and culture was inherent in the assimilation policy: to speak only English and live in communities in a quasi-European culture. Alice took her name from her foster father, George Mero. When Alice was a teenager her mother, Dora Brook, was sent to Palm too, but it was too late for mother and daughter to restore their original bond. They became two more tragic casualties of the Stolen Generations.

The landmark Human Rights and Equal Opportunity Commission report, *Bringing Them Home*, delivered in 1997, estimates that up to 100,000 such children were taken from their Aboriginal mothers. The report recommended that compensation be paid to all members of the Stolen Generations for racial discrimination, deprivation of liberty, pain and suffering, disruption of family life, loss of cultural and native title rights, labour exploitation and economic loss. Cathy Freeman's mother and grandmother suffered all of that. The report further recommended that family members and descendants of those taken away qualify as claimants. Alice Mero was one of the Stolen Children, and her daughter, Cecelia, almost certainly qualifies as one of the claimants. Cathy adored Alice Sibley, her grandmother, whom she knew for many years growing up in Mackay and refers to as Nanna Sibley. Of all Cathy's close relatives, Nanna was probably more in touch with her Aboriginality than anyone. She knew enough to scare Cathy with ghost stories about the kadaicha man, the Aborigine empowered to avenge tribal grievances by pointing the bone at the wrongdoer.

CATHY FREEMAN—A JOURNEY JUST BEGUN

George Sibley, Cathy's maternal grandfather, was born in Mt Molloy, in the Kuranda ranges above Cairns, in 1918, and accompanied his family when they were sent to Palm Island in 1925. The Sibley family tree can be traced back to 1870, a predominantly Aboriginal line descended from tribes in far north Queensland, Tully to Daintree, Bloomfield to Cooktown. Included in the tree are two non-indigenous great-great-grandfathers of Cathy's—George Charles Sibley, a settler from Dorset, England and Tommy Ah Sam, a gold prospector from Kwang-Tung province in China.

On Palm Island, young George Sibley and Alice Mero had two children, the elder, Cecelia, being Cathy's mum. Cecelia never knew her father as a child because George Sibley left the island about a year after she was born. Alice Mero then married his brother Sonny Sibley and they had eight children.

Away from the island, George's trail took him from mission to mission, Bamaga to Cherbourg, always being moved on by white authorities, primarily because he was a man who stood up for himself. He was tall, around 180cm (6 foot), and in a photograph of the 1939 Palm Island amateur boxing squad, he is a square-shouldered, lean-limbed 20-year-old. He was not of the class to be a 10-round main event fighter, but much better than a mere prelim pug. On the mainland he joined the famous Jimmy Sharman boxing troupe which travelled around country shows. For several years he could be seen at the Brisbane Exhibition, standing with other boxers, in boots and boxing gown, arms akimbo, glowering from a podium. One of the boxers beat a bass drum which resounded excitingly around the showgrounds while a spruiker challenged foolhardy lairs in the audience to earn a quid fighting one of the Sharman boys inside the marquee. Just as often Sharman would have a 'plant' in the crowd who would challenge to fight, and so the crowd paid to watch a sham fight between the two Sharman employees. George, a welterweight, travelled around Queensland fighting under the name of Salvargi.

CECELIA'S STORY

George disappears then from contemporary view until he re-emerges in 1953 on Thursday Island working as a deckhand on boats fishing for trochus shells. He was 35, past his prime, but not too old to fight the main event as part of the island's celebrations to mark—incongruously on this isolated tropical isle—the coronation of Queen Elizabeth II.

John Cockatoo, of Cairns, saw that fight. Cockatoo, whose sons and grandsons played AFL in Melbourne, was manager of a Presbyterian hostel on TI in those days. The boxing ring that night was set up on the main football oval. 'It was a big night all right, they had a bazaar, tables and food, and the whole island turned up, would have been a couple of thousand,' says Cockatoo. Sibley, though not in the best condition (his training diet consisted of damper, corned beef and a few beers), was chosen because of his record as a fighter. His opponent, a Malay called Tony Sabatina, was the better boxer and far fitter. 'But George was a slugger. He just went at it for round after round, and wore the other bloke down with his stamina,' says Cockatoo. 'He won by a point, which pleased the crowd because they all knew him, he was their favourite.'

Some 15 years later, Cockatoo met him again when Sibley was working as a railway fettler on a flying gang out of Cloncurry. 'He was a serious sort of bloke,' says Cockatoo. 'Very modest, never talked about his boxing days and his face was hardly marked. He was never given any argument either because everyone knew his boxing reputation and steered clear.' In his last years George, a severe diabetic, returned to Palm Island, where he died in 1992. His photograph appears in Professor Colin Tatz's book, *Obstacle Race*, about Aborigines in sport. He is pictured in the ring and his fight second is Jack Hassen, Australian lightweight champion from 1949–51. Hassen was born on Palm Island and is related, by marriage, to Alice Sibley, Cathy Freeman's grandmother.

Cecelia's childhood on Palm, with mum Alice and

stepfather Sonny Sibley, was idyllic despite having no electricity, no telephone, no books, no newspapers, a radio of sorts and one double bed for her and her siblings. She says she enjoyed attending a Catholic school run by American nuns, the Franciscan Missionaries of Mary. Cecelia and a crowd of other Aboriginal children, who lived in segregated government dormitories, gathered in front of the dormitory matron's office each morning to be escorted by a black policeman about 8km to school. Sometimes they'd walk by the sea and, if the tide was out, would crack oysters on the way, or get soaked splashing each other and be given fresh, dry clothes by the nuns.

After school Cecelia often returned past her grandmother's house, Annie Ah Sam—George Sibley's mother—where four huge painted Chinese vases stood on the verandah. Annie Ah Sam grew orange and lemon trees, and all sorts of tropical fruit—custard apples, paw paws and mangoes. She'd feed Cecelia and her cousins fruit, as well as scones or damper sweetened with margarine and syrup. The syrup was supplied by the government, ladled out to families in billies from a huge wooden barrel. Occasionally relatives fished for turtles, and Cecelia's mother, Alice, would host a family feast by steaming it in its own juices with vegetables.

Growing up, Cecelia remembers the Freeman clan, who moved to Palm for several years, walking past her weatherboard house every Friday night on their way to the old-time dance in the local hall. 'Norman's mother and stepfather, Gerry and Claude, loved dancing,' she says. 'It's funny, Norman's path and mine must have crossed a bit, but I don't remember him particularly.' The Freemans eventually moved back to Woorabinda mission on the mainland, the base community for the greater Freeman clan.

The Sibleys were soon to follow. Cecelia left school aged 15, taught herself typing and worked in the Department of Native Affairs office on Palm as the switchboard operator. 'It wasn't hard, there was only one line to the mainland,' says

Cecelia, laughing. They were tranquil days but she began to notice that life for adults on Palm was not the idyll it was for kids.

Aborigines needed permits to go on holidays, to visit relatives, even to leave the island to shop in Townsville. If they weren't back by the nominated permit time, police brought them back. Those who elected to leave the island for another mission had their permits stamped and forwarded to the next director, sometimes with wholly unsubstantiated and defamatory remarks about the person's character. The mission director, superintendent, administrator or protector (never was a title more Orwellian) had absolute power.

Willie Thaiday, an elder on Palm, wrote in his damning book, *Under the Act*, published in 1981:

> We got to do everything what suit the Superintendent, not us, and every Super got the law in his own mouth. What he say is law and the government allow them to make the rules. We know it is wrong but still you can't say nothing because the moment you say something they throw you in gaol. If they say you go to gaol you can't say what for and you don't know when you come out. I saw some boys, two or three of them, who spent 18 months without court.

From her office, Cecelia once heard an Aboriginal yardman address her white boss by his christian name, instead of 'Mr', and saw the trouble he got into. 'There was an air of oppression because you had to look up to all these white people,' says Cecelia.

Sonny Sibley, Willie Thaiday and several others organised a strike against the superintendent, R.H. Bartlam, accusing him of docking the islanders' wages for alleged mistakes. Bartlam insisted the island women scrub the hospital floors or clean white officials' houses and if they refused they were gaoled. The women wanted to stay home to look after their children. One girl who ran away from her dormitory was punished by being put in gaol, shaved bald and forced to wear a bag dress—an ordinary hessian sack with the corners snipped out. The strike was a rare, and entirely symbolic, challenge to white authority.

One night, soon after, Willie told Sonny, 'This night is too still. Must be something gonna happen.' Said Sonny, 'No, everything's all right. Nothing gonna happen.' At 4 a.m. armed police raided the homes of Sibley, Thaiday and five others. 'Don't move, Willie, or you'll get hurt,' a policeman warned Thaiday. Handcuffed, they were marched to the beach and bundled into a military patrol boat. They had only the clothes they wore. Police met them at Townsville wharf and later handed them their destinations—Thaiday and Sibley to Woorabinda. Sonny's papers were marked that he was a strike ringleader.

Their families were in shock. Superintendent Bartlam called Cecelia into his office. 'Your family's being sent to Woorabinda, but you don't have to go,' he said. 'You haven't done anything wrong.' Cecelia relayed this to her mother, Alice, who wept at the thought of her family being broken up. It was a nightmare for a Stolen Generation child. 'Anyway, there was no question about it,' says Cecelia. 'I went with my family.'

The *Townsville Bulletin* reported on 14 June 1957 that seven handcuffed Aborigines were brought ashore by police at Townsville after having been transported by RAAF crash launch from Palm Island. They were Sonny and Willie and friends. Five days later, the *Bulletin* reported, 'Twenty-five Palm Island Aborigines left Townsville under police escort on the Brisbane mail train last night.' They were the families.

There was no winter on Palm, but there was 600km south at Woorabinda. The train stopped at Rockhampton, the families were unloaded and driven two hours in the back of an open truck to be dropped at the Woorabinda mission at midnight. They huddled, shivering, in blankets, no beds or furniture, in an old house on the river bank until sunrise.

CECELIA'S STORY

After a year or so Sonny, a marked man with the administration, left. He told Alice he would get work out in the community, but ended up in Western Australia. Cecelia didn't see him again for another four years. 'Sonny leaving affected me a lot,' says Cecelia. 'We got sent to Woorabinda because of what Sonny did, then he left and we had to stay.' Long-suffering Alice, her second partner gone, worked as a machinist to support her children. 'She was a very, very strong woman,' says Cecelia. 'She rarely spoke about her childhood. I believe it was too painful for her. And when she did I could see the anguish in her eyes. Yet I never heard her utter one bad word against the government. She just rose above all the pain she encountered in her life.'

Cecelia began spending her weekends horse-riding with her future husband, a handsome, dashing fellow who was already making a name for himself as a footballer—Norman Freeman. On Palm, resourceful families owned boats, but at Woorabinda it was horses and Norman owned a chestnut mare called April.

The pair struck up a long, intermittent relationship, interrupted by Norman travelling the state playing football, driving trucks, or working as a surveyor's chainman. Cecelia gained an exemption from the permit system and left Woorabinda to stay with her aunty in Innisfail where, aged 21, for the first time as an adult, she met her father, George Sibley. 'I had mixed emotions, seeing him,' says Cecelia, thoughtfully. 'I'd grown up not really knowing him as my father.' From there she took a job in Kuranda and in 1961 moved to Cairns.

Cecelia had a son, Gavin, in 1961, and then in 1966, a year after she and Norman married, Anne-Marie was born in Emerald hospital. It was a difficult birth and when Cecelia saw the anxious reactions of medical staff, she thought her daughter was stillborn. Half an hour later her doctor said there would be something wrong with Anne-Marie but they weren't sure what it would be. Mother and daughter were sent to Rockhampton for specialist treatment and it was discovered that Anne-Marie had cerebral palsy. Even today, Cecelia cannot talk about Anne-Marie at length without becoming tearful. 'She couldn't walk, but she could crawl and make noises and knew Norman, myself and Gavin,' says Cecelia. 'But the more she tried to talk the more the muscles in her mouth and tongue would spasm. We loved her, and Gavin particularly was good, he was very close to her.'

Every day in Australia three babies are born with a degree of cerebral palsy. It can be caused by brain damage during the birth and, once damaged, the brain is unable to repair itself. Patients often suffer uncontrollable muscle spasms and although Anne-Marie did not spasm, her body gradually stiffened as she grew into childhood. Anne-Marie's frustration can't be comprehended because, from the Freeman family's long hours of experience with her, she appeared to have an unimpaired intelligence. The agony for Anne-Marie would have been to be trapped inside her body, unable to communicate with her family or the outside world. 'To look at her, you wouldn't think anything was wrong,' says Cecelia. 'She didn't have that vacant stare, in fact she communicated with her eyes.'

The most effective help for severe cerebral palsy comes from teams of nurses, physiotherapists, occupational therapists, social workers and volunteers, who devote themselves to making a sufferer's lifestyle as normal as possible. It was this full-time assistance that Cecelia's doctor had long recommended for Anne-Marie, but which Cecelia had resisted, unwilling to abandon her daughter, as she had been once abandoned herself by her father and stepfather.

When Anne-Marie turned seven, growing bigger and becoming more difficult to manage, events came to a head. Cecelia fell pregnant again and the strain was endangering her health. Yet she was nearly eight months pregnant before her doctor convinced Cecelia that Anne-Marie should enter a special home in Townsville, and then later in

CECELIA'S STORY

Rockhampton. 'I didn't want to let her go. I put it off until I couldn't cope any more,' says Cecelia, sadly. 'We took her there and I cried and cried all the way home in the train. It broke my heart to leave her and I cried myself into exhaustion.' Anne-Marie lived another 17 years in the home in Rockhampton, visited regularly by her family, and not a visit ended without Cecelia, and later Cathy too, departing amid torrents of tears. Leaving Anne-Marie was agony enough, but for Cecelia it was also one more instance of a family member being lost to an institution.

On 16 February 1973, Catherine Astrid Salome Freeman was born. 'I had Yasmin in mind, but as soon as I saw her, the name Catherine came into my head,' says Cecelia. 'Astrid was from Norman's first cousin.' Salome? 'Well, we were living in a block of flats in Mackay at the time and this old Torres Strait Island woman behind us called Salome used to tell me, "Now you make sure you name the baby after me." So I did, just to please the old lady.'

After Catherine, came Norman in 1974 and Garth in 1976. The family was close, despite the 16-year age stretch between Gavin and Garth. Norman wasn't a father to show the children great affection but, says Cecelia, 'I could tell how much he loved them by the way he touched them and spoke to them.'

He dressed the boys up in his club's colours to watch him play and made a great fuss about them at the football ground. 'He was a brilliant player,' says Cecelia. 'Once he got the ball, they couldn't catch him. Ever seen a crab running? Well, that's how he was, change directions, here, there.' Football was Norman's life. 'He'd get up on match day, very early, and polish his boots,' says Cecelia. 'He'd polish them until they shone, and get his gear ready. Then we'd get the paper the next day because he was always being written up.'

But something was wrong. Norman complained of feeling dizzy and a blood test revealed he had severe diabetes. The news floored Norman physically and psychologically. He was such a healthy man, his fitness was his pride. He'd never been sick. 'It's funny,' says Cecelia. 'We both didn't pick he was sick, but once they put a name to his condition he started to sink. He'd always loved a drink, but it wasn't a problem, it wasn't affecting our marriage. But as the sickness got worse, so did the drinking. And that did affect us.'

Cecelia attended barbecues with the other footballers' wives after matches. 'I'd socialise with the other women out in the beer garden while the men were at the bar,' she says. 'But thank God I didn't get caught up with drinking, didn't get bogged down. It got to the stage where I didn't want to take the kids to the barbecue because Norman would drink too much. He knew it was getting closer to the time when he wouldn't be able to play, the love of his life. And he couldn't cope with it. His decline was terrible to watch.'

One of Catherine's early memories is of coming home and finding all the glass from framed photographs smashed. 'Mum and Dad were arguing so I hid behind a lounge chair,' she told me. Cecelia remembers that. 'He smashed them up in frustration,' she says. 'Rather than hit me he smashed things. In the end it got too much and when I saw a Friday night binge coming I'd pack the kids up and we'd go over to Mum's for the weekend.' This, too, Cathy remembers. 'I'd be really upset because I wanted to see my father and I didn't understand why I couldn't,' she says.

In 1978, Norman left and returned to his Freeman clan in Woorabinda. Cecelia saw it coming, but children never do. Eldest boy Gavin adored his father, and Cathy was the apple of her father's eye. She was angry. However illogically, both children blamed the remaining parent for the loss of the departed one. Cathy was just five.

Cecelia, as had her mother before her, found a job to support her children. She became a cleaner at Mackay North State High. Says Cathy, 'Early in the morning she'd go up, before anybody got there, and clean up. Then she'd come

CECELIA'S STORY

home for breakfast, make us lunch, and after school we'd go down to the high school with her and she'd clean it again.'

Says Cecelia, 'Catherine was such a little darling. Gavin never came, so she was the eldest and while the younger ones played, sliding down some grassy slopes on cardboard boxes, Catherine would come in and help me sweep or stack chairs.' Cecelia enjoyed low rent in an Aboriginal co-operative house but her wage was scarcely enough for food. Cecelia fed the children and then herself. Or sometimes just the children.

The final act in the saga of the Freeman family's early personal struggles then unfolded. In 1979, Bruce Barber, a railway guard from Brisbane, broke up with his wife and moved north for a new start. He knew friends in Mackay and through them met Cecelia. He was stationed at Coppabella, several hours drive inland from Mackay, but came down to the coast on weekends to visit his friends. One weekend the friends were away on holidays and Bruce, searching for an overnight bunk, knocked on Cecelia's door. After a cautious courtship he became the lodger that stayed. Barber belonged to the Baha'i faith, a gentle, pantheistic religion which features, as central tenets, equality of gender and race. The faith's high morality put into doctrine feelings which Cecelia had longed to express.

'I'd grown up a Catholic and when we went to church the white people sat in the front and the black people sat right up the back,' she says. 'I knew in my heart it wasn't right. And the more I read about Baha'i, it was as if someone had pulled blinkers off my eyes.'

Barber is a shortish, bearded man, laconic, persistent and patient. He needed to be. Though Norman now lived at Woorabinda, he occasionally visited the family, which he still regarded as his own. 'He could never get that out of his head,' says Cecelia. When Bruce arrived on the scene, Gavin, 17, who had assumed the father role for the younger children, took off for Woorabinda. 'You better come and see what's going on, Dad,' he warned Norman.

Says Cecelia, 'Norman was very, very hurt. It never dawned on him that I would become involved with someone else. Not that I was looking. Bruce just turned up at the door with a friend. I was wary because I had no intention of becoming involved with another man.' The children resented Bruce. When they opened the front door to him, they'd call out, 'It's that white bloke for you, Mum.' And when he moved in to stay, Cathy stood at her bedroom door and snarled to brother Garth, 'What's this bloke doing here?'

The family's acceptance of Bruce Barber into the family proceeded cautiously, however, Cecelia fretted that perhaps the stress of Norman leaving and Bruce arriving was affecting Cathy. One morning, Cathy, aged seven, came to breakfast with a strangely crooked smile. Alarmed, Cecelia called out, 'Catherine! What's the matter with you?' Cathy had Bell's palsy, a disease which paralyses the nerves in the face. For the mother of a daughter with cerebral palsy, any paralysis meant panic stations. A few days in hospital and Cathy recovered. The contrast between Anne-Marie and her palsy and Cathy and her usual good health remained a constant in Cecelia's memory. 'They looked very much alike, and Anne-Marie had that same charisma that Catherine has,' says Cecelia. One day, years hence, Cathy baulked at training, telling her mother she wanted to give up athletics. Cecelia admonished her, 'You've got two good legs and two good arms, now you use them.' Cecelia had a firm compact with herself. 'It was as if God gave me Catherine and her wonderful gift to compensate for the heavy cross I had to bear with Anne-Marie,' she says.

One day Bruce called the children together and announced to them, 'I want to marry your mother.' Cathy was furious. Bruce Barber was the usurper. When her father originally left, Cathy had written to him telling him that she was still his little girl and that she loved him. At Christmas she'd visit Woorabinda and go horse-riding with him. So when the family drove out in their blue Holden Kingswood,

CECELIA'S STORY

Cecelia in the front beside Bruce driving, Cathy, sitting in the back, would hook her foot under the seat and kick her mother. 'I didn't like it, the fact that she sat next to him,' she says.

To make a clean start, Bruce and Cecelia obtained divorces and then drove the family down to Woorabinda to inform Norman of their marriage plans. Old bonds ran deep. Cathy saw her mother sit beside Norman on a river bank, kiss him and tenderly offer, 'If you don't want me to, if you want us to come here to Woorabinda, we will. This is still your family.' But Norman replied, 'No, you'll never come here to live.' Cecelia repeated her offer. 'No, you'll be right in Mackay,' said Norman.

Says Cecelia, 'I'll never, ever forget the look on his face, the deep feeling of loss. But I don't think he wanted the children to see what he was doing with his life.' For years Cathy blamed her mother for losing her father, but apologises for that now. Yet she can still appreciate her father's selflessness. 'He did have a bit to do with the course that my life took,' she says. 'Simply by his decision to let go.'

The Freemans and their athletics were an arduous undertaking but Bruce Barber didn't see it that way. 'As far as I was concerned, if you loved that woman, you took her and everything that came with her,' he says. His dedication gradually won over the children, particularly Cathy who initially was so distrustful. 'In one sense, Cathy was right about me,' says Bruce. 'Adults fail to realise that we should consult more with children when we make decisions affecting them. Such as marrying their mother.' The children came to believe that Bruce cared for them, according to Cecelia. 'They accepted discipline from him,' she says. 'Mind you, they only got reprimanded by him when it was warranted.'

Norman resented Bruce at first, but after he saw that the children were being looked after, he relented. He told a friend, 'They'll be fine. He's a good bloke, Bruce. He's a

CATHY FREEMAN—A JOURNEY JUST BEGUN

Baha'i.' Bruce and Cecelia were married in 1982. Cathy was aged nine. One Baha'i belief is that, as a moral sentiment, you should aspire to your highest potential. Bruce Barber was about to project that belief on to his talented stepdaughter who would one day carve a swathe through the ranks of the nation's athletic titles.

4.
WONDER GIRL.
PRIMARY SCHOOL, 1983–86

At the national age athletic titles in Melbourne in 1984, Cathy, aged 11, and her teammate, Vanessa Gray, ganged up on the NSW girls and psyched them out in the high jump. It was sheer interstate rivalry. 'When I cleared the bar she'd leap all around the place. You know Cathy, she was loony tunes,' says Vanessa. 'And when she went over I'd get really excited too. We bumped the NSW girls out and after that basically it became Cathy and me jumping against each other, which wasn't much of a competition because I knew she would always beat me.' Which Freeman duly did, on a countback after they deadheated on 1.53m (5 foot 1 inch), a new national age record. They were good friends and had fun with a newspaper photographer identifying themselves afterwards. 'Well, we're both wearing maroon uniforms, but she's black,' said Vanessa. 'And she's white,' chimed in Cathy, giggling her trademark helpless laugh.

By 1984 north Queensland newspapers were referring to Freeman as the 'wonder girl' from Mackay. She took the state age sprint double, 100m (13.51s), 200m (26.72s) and the high jump (1.45m) that year, and at the Pacific Schools Games in Melbourne she won her first national titles: the 200m gold, the high jump gold, and silver in the 100m.

After those titles, her stepfather, Bruce Barber, ever on the lookout, contacted the Australian Institute of Sport in Canberra, with the result that Cathy was invited to spend a week there under the eye of sprint coach Norm Osborne. The whole family were with her on holidays that trip, so they camped in a caravan park near the AIS while Cathy met Australian athletes preparing for the Los Angeles Olympics, a few weeks off.

The following year, 1985, although Cathy and Vanessa were the same age, 12, Cathy had graduated to high school while Vanessa was still in primary. Secondary students were not allowed to compete against primary so, with Cathy and Lyn Gray cheering from the sidelines, Vanessa won the nationals with a record leap. 'It was great to have Cathy sitting nearby because I'm such a stressed person and she isn't, she was always relaxed,' says Vanessa.

Cathy blitzed the Queensland age titles that year, winning the 100m in a personal best of 13.4s, the 200m, the high jump, and came third in the 400m, a new event for her. But constant school changes played havoc with her form for the nationals in Brisbane where she ran second in the 200m and third in the 400m. Her approach to athletics was still decidedly nonchalant. She would eat a Mars bar while waiting for a sprint final, and once, as she turned flat-chat into the straight in a national age 200m, pulled down her singlet at the front because it had ridden up under her competition top.

Those early years were not all plain sailing. In 1983, when Bruce Barber was transferred to Hughenden, the family moved with him. Cathy was unhappy to leave her friends and relations, and the sea, for this small, dry, dusty town, 500km due west of Mackay as the crow flies. Once there she was consistently and inexplicably defeated by a tall local girl and seemed about to miss the state titles—until Bruce's sleuthing discovered the school had made a mistake in Cathy's age and had her competing a year ahead of her correct group. Then Bruce heard that someone had protested against Freeman contesting the state championships because she hadn't attended a state school for at least 15 days before the titles. This had indeed been an archaic rule, made obsolete seven years earlier. There were other minor incidents too, Bruce says, of medals or ribbons not awarded.

He's adamant that there were instances of discrimination against Freeman. They are difficult, at such a distance, to prove and Cathy cannot recall any prejudice against her as an Aboriginal. She can recall the disdainful looks some mothers gave her after she trounced their daughters, but there may be other reasons for this. It may have been because Cathy won with such insouciance, or perhaps because whenever she changed schools she disturbed established athletic pecking orders. 'Yeah, some mothers used to give me funny looks,' says Cathy. 'I'm not stupid, I'm pretty good at picking up on how people feel. I hadn't thought about the black thing, though. I thought it was just because I'd beaten their daughters.'

It was at Hughenden that Bruce, sitting on a log watching Cathy train, had his vision of her as an Olympian. 'She reminded me of a champion racehorse,' he says. 'Just the symmetry of her movement.' Bruce was watching her on the school oval one afternoon, after school. 'I was just running, around and around and around, 12 laps of a 400m dirt track, no shoes,' says Cathy. 'Bruce had no instructions. We didn't know what we were doing.' Cathy had just run third in the state 100m, and the national titles were six weeks away. Bruce decided for himself—'I don't know anything about style, or technique but at least I can try to get her fit.'

He wrote to state school sporting officials for a training program. He then found that for the next six weeks he always seemed to be off duty from his job as a guard with the Queensland railways every afternoon, which enabled him to supervise Cathy's progam. Even railway roster clerks were starting to hear about Cathy Freeman.

Bruce soon had Cathy running a four-lap warm-up, followed by exercises, stretches, sprints, starts and a four-lap warm down. He must have been doing something right. The state team attended a camp at Caboolture, on the outskirts of Brisbane, en route to Melbourne for the nationals. In 10 days, at team trials, Cathy beat the girl who ran second in the state titles, and then beat the winner.

That Cathy, and young brother Norman, who was proving every bit as talented as his sister, were able to compete at school carnivals around Australia was entirely due to Bruce's tireless fundraising activities. He started off selling lamingtons door-to-door and graduated to raffles of, not so much meat trays, as meat doors—whole doors laden with $300 worth of meat. A friendly butcher provided the meat free. His fee: when Cathy wins gold tell her to come and say hello.

Bruce sat at a small table in Mackay's main street every Saturday morning selling raffle tickets. 'Two coppers arrived one day, and I didn't have a licence,' he says. 'I had a little placard with Cathy and Norman's photos on it and their achievements. They read it and said, "That's OK. We'll buy a couple, thanks."'

He made leathergoods and sold them at markets, raffled a 44-gallon drum of petrol and even organised a country and western dance night from which he made $400 to pay for Cathy's interstate accommodation. 'He was unbelievable,' says Cathy. 'I'd hear him tell Mum, "I'm walking out to do this or that," and next thing we'd have our travel money.'

Darby McCarthy, the former champion Aboriginal jockey, knew all about the family's hardship, having visited them at their Mackay home. He was on the National Indigenous Sports Award board—together with such Aboriginal luminaries as Pastor Sir Doug Nicholls, the late Sugar Ray Robinson, basketballer Danny Morseu and Charlie Perkins.

The board chose the 1986 award winners and various board members were plumping for their choice from basketballers, AIS athletes and kids from strong sports associations. Says McCarthy, 'We broke for lunch and it was such a tussle that we passed over the juniors and voted on the seniors. Next day I grabbed Charlie Perkins and said, "Charlie, when we first set these awards up, it was for people who had no money. This girl is 13. At the last state awards, her mother asked me permission to raffle chooks on the night. I've been to their house, she needs help." Charlie finally said, "OK, Darby, we'll give it to Cathy."'

But what really opened Australia to the family were Bruce's railway passes which granted them free train travel—four passes per year inside Queensland, and one interstate pass. Year after year, Bruce and Cecelia organised their annual holidays around the state or national titles.

Rail travel could be slow, however, and once it took the family five days to rail from Mackay to Adelaide. They travelled by night in ordinary sit-up seats, with Cathy, Norman and Garth at their feet in sleeping bags. 'I hate kids racing up and down in trains screaming and yelling,' says Bruce. 'And those kids were very active. So our logic was to travel by night and let them run crazy during the day. Every place we stopped—in Sydney it would be the Domain or Manly beach—we'd let them go berserk. Then we'd walk them miles through museums and art galleries and, by the time we boarded the train and they had dinner that night, they were just about ready to sleep.'

Cathy loved the train journeys, still does, loves everything from the sway, the rat-a-tat-tat, the whistle, even the cramped toilets. 'After every nationals we'd have a holiday in that city,' she says. 'In Sydney we stayed in a yukky small apartment in Kings Cross and I saw drug syringes in the gutter outside. But from there we were able to walk to the Opera House, the Harbour Bridge and Circular Quay to catch the ferry to Manly.'

Despite Bruce and Cecelia's best efforts, athletics was keeping the family poor. Eventually, in 1987, Cecelia wrote out a profile of Catherine and Norman's impressive records and posted it to, among others, the Aboriginal and Torres Strait Islander Commission, asking for financial assistance. Nothing eventuated but, visiting Canberra for a carnival soon after, they stormed ATSIC's offices and emerged as the first recipients of a pilot program which awarded $8000 each to Cathy and Norman.

Marrying Cecelia brought Bruce into contact with the great diaspora of Aboriginal life which he previously only knew from the media. 'In Australia, 99 per cent of what is said about Aboriginals is negative,' he says. 'But I discovered things which really opened my eyes, about their culture, their beliefs. We arrived in Brisbane once and this Aboriginal friend put us up and next morning cooked us a real nice breakfast. Later I found out she was broke and that was the last food in the house. They are an extraordinarily generous people.'

He was also uniquely placed within the Freemans to detect discrimination to which the family might be inured through familiarity. 'People won't discriminate to Cecelia's face, but I hear because people don't know I'm her husband,' he says. And he's witnessed the more blatant occasions, such as once when they were waiting to board a train at Melbourne's Flinders Street station.

Cecelia takes up the story. 'Cathy was about 13, and she was lying along one of the bench seats in her tracksuit,' she says. 'She'd been racing and she was tired. Anyway, there were lots of other seats available when these two ladies walked up and started shouting, "Get up! Get off! You lazy ... we need to sit down." Bruce jumped up and said, "What do you think you're doing?" They didn't connect him with us and said, "This is no place to be lying down, and it's none of your business anyway." Ohhh! Bruce saw red. He said, "It is my business, this happens to be my daughter. There's plenty of seats over there, now go and sit down, and leave us alone."'

Another occasion, this time in Sydney, Cecelia and Cathy were standing by a flower stall at the markets waiting for Bruce to return from shopping. Says Cecelia, 'When the owner saw that we weren't buying anything she came out and said, "Can you move along? Move along, please." I said, "Why? We can stand here if we want to." She didn't want a couple of Aboriginals standing by her stall. It didn't happen that often, that stuff, then it would, out of the blue.'

Late in 1984, the family now back in Mackay, Cathy joined the Slade Point athletic club and began to compete in earnest. Aged 11 she ran third in the prestigious Campbell Miles trophy for the women's open 100m at the north Queensland titles. Three years later she became the youngest runner ever to win it.

Slade Point was based at Melaleuca Park—now Cathy Freeman Athletic Park—a picturesque oval within a javelin's throw of a tropical sea looking out towards the Whitsunday Islands. In the fiercest Mackay heat, Melaleuca remains cooled by sea breezes, and shaded by huge paperbark and umbrella trees. The soil is sandy, the track is grass, the lanes marked with sump oil. A tiny grandstand squats under the trees. Here Cathy happily donned her white shorts with red stripe, and red and white v-top, and ran and whiled away the hours at Sunday meets. 'I don't ever remember thinking to myself, "Oh, this is a drag, I don't want to do it,"' says Cathy. But brother Norman definitely didn't want to. 'He didn't like running 200m,' says Cathy. 'So he'd hide behind the trees and pull strips off the paperbarks.'

The first time the club coach, Lyle Daniel, saw Freeman run he took one look at her and said, 'That girl should be running the 400m not the 100m.' It was a comment echoed by other astute observers for years, but as a junior Cathy wasn't interested in running deadly 400m distances. She had the rhythm, and the long, loping stride, but not the strength.

Nor, as it turns out, would it necessarily have been a good habit for Freeman to acquire, since modern 400m races are run at a fast clip, with little time for loping.

Three women, former club president Janice Saunders, journalist Penny Pollock and coach Sue Evetts, are owed a debt of gratitude for their transport services, picking Cathy up from her home in Mackay and driving her to meets. Says Saunders, 'Initially Cathy wasn't that interested in athletics. Often when Penny or Sue went to collect her, she would be off riding her bike around town.' Says Evetts, 'If she wasn't at home I'd wait or call back. If she didn't want to go, I'd nag her until she did. My patience wore thin sometimes, but thank God we persevered.' The women's patience had much to do with their recognition that in Cathy there resided the glint of a champion. Their enthusiasm, as athletics fans, was to be reflected in later years by other coaches who found themselves in the presence of a rare gift. Opposed against their exuberance, Cathy's laidback attitude to training could be mistaken for indifference. The women couldn't get mad at her anyway. 'She didn't have a mean bone in her body,' says Saunders. 'I never saw her bad-tempered. If she lost a race, she lost. Finish.'

When I recounted that story to Penny Pollock, she said, 'My husband is killing himself laughing remembering a meet we took Cathy to at Sarina, about 30km south of Mackay. She lay in the back of the car most of the afternoon until we said, "Look, you've got to come and have at least one run." She crawled out of the car and jogged around in a race, and there must be half the girls in Sarina club who can now boast they once beat the great Cathy Freeman.'

Cathy's march through the age titles faltered only once, when, aged 13, she went down with glandular fever, followed on quickly by shingles. Her parents pulled her out of athletics for the 1986 season. 'She had brought her 100m time down from 13.4s in 1984 to 12.6s in 1986,' says Bruce. 'But the glandular fever knocked her. She couldn't run for a month. She took two whole years to work back down to those times again.'

Bruce was Cathy's greatest advocate. 'Even when Cathy was only 14 he was quite sure she was going to run in the 1990 Commonwealth Games,' says Penny Pollock. 'He'd tell that to anyone who'd listen, he drove us mad telling us, actually. But he was a good father to her. And I've got a lot of time for the mum, too.' Bruce would second that. 'Right from the day she was born, Cecelia has had her back to the wall, yet she kept her family together. That's why she rates so highly in my estimation.' The pair became, indeed, the quintessential battlers, materially poor, but rich in love and dedication, which they lavished on their children.

Those years in Mackay, principally at 10 Burston Street, Cathy recalls as her happiest in childhood. She would buy the house if she could, she told her mother. It's a steel-roofed, low-set cream bungalow with aluminium sliding windows, double car-port, and a tiny balcony on which Cecelia sat, waiting for her precious daughter to return from her athletics trips. The house has a large front and backyard, a chainwire fence, but only an unmade footpath outside. In summer Mackay is a fecund riot of vegetation, and Cathy's house was surrounded by palm, mango and fiddlewood trees, tipuana and poinciana, and native bottlebrush shrubs. Behind the house a large hill leads to a peak crowded with communication antennas.

The people who lived further up the hill were rich, says Cathy. 'They had brick houses, fancy fences, nice gardens and big wooden doors,' she says. 'I thought that anyone who had a car, a telephone or a carpet was rich.' These were happy days in Mackay for Cathy, her large extended family of cousins, uncles and aunts close at hand, all gathering at Christmas for beach barbecues and singing—they were islanders after all, Palm Islanders.

A Torres Strait Islander family lived behind them, but essentially it was a white neighbourhood. Cecelia never sat

Cathy down to talk to her about racism, or the Stolen Children, or land claims. 'I just thought the children didn't need to know all those things at that age,' she says. 'It would have filled them with resentment and all that negative sort of emotion.' All she told them was that if they ever got called names, never to respond. That would just lower themselves to their tormentor's level. Just ignore it and walk away.

Cecelia's life had been one in which her great motivation was to break free from the cycle of Aboriginal deprivation her mother had endured. As an adult, she chose to live in town suburbs, never wanting to subject her children to the debilitating life as she knew it on the missions. Even her second marriage to non-indigenous Bruce Barber carried an element of her escape from the penury of her past. She never denied her Aboriginality, but she rejected its accompanying poverty. In later years, as her family grew and left, she became more confident in her own Aboriginal identity. Her anxiety subsided about her difficult past and Cecelia began reaching out to Aborigines through community centres. She became a justice of the peace and was asked on to committees for Aboriginal health, child care and education. She became an invaluable conduit to government departments. How could they doubt her? She had seen it all. But back in those Mackay days, survival was all. Cecelia was a peaceful and compliant Aboriginal citizen.

Yet the children were already learning their own code to cope with the chagrin of being black in a white society. Cathy explained it to me one day. During interviews, as a journalist and for this book, I must have asked her a dozen times about racism and largely drawn a blank. What I hadn't divined was that a sense of discrimination can come from within as well as from the outside. This was Cathy's surprising soliloquy:

'You have to remember that the black people I grew up with, my family, friends and relatives were very shy,' she says. 'They had low self-esteem. Because they were like that, I was like that, too. I thought it was normal. The first day

Norman and I went to high school in Mackay, we were too shy to put our bikes with all the other bikes. We ended up leaving them on the other side of the street. In Queensland, if you go among the young black people, there's a saying, "Oh, *shame*!" If you felt too shy to walk across to the other side of the hall at school to get some food, and you asked someone to walk over with you, it was "Oh, *shame*!" When we walked into new places we were just totally intimidated because we felt that, being black, we had no right to be there. In a group we felt better, but individually we lacked confidence.

'It's weird, but we felt bad about being black. And when someone was too embarrassed to do something because they were black, we'd go, "Oh, *shame*!" We never wanted to stand out. It was a sort of black world–white world, and we were too ashamed to go mixing with people in the white world. That was our mentality. I think it was a carryover from our ancestors, being institutionalised, like my nanna. That's why a lot of people stay on missions and don't venture into the mainstream. Like, even my mum, as I was growing up, if I was going out with someone, she'd ask, "Is he black, or is he white?" That would be the first thing. As though, if he's white, it's different.'

This was a stunning revelation from Freeman who, in her public image, has always conveyed a sense of assurance in her own scattered, conversational way. It meant that, as a teenage girl, her self-image was little different to any other street Aborigine who runs with their black pack as a form of security against the seemingly impenetrable world of white Australia. Only Freeman's special gift, her running, enabled her to break the shackles.

Cathy wishes her mother had educated her about race relations, spoken more about her childhood on Palm Island and Woorabinda. 'Older people who were brought up on missions, who were controlled, don't talk about it much,' she says. 'Although Mum does talk about it now, as I get older.'

At school, Cathy learnt that European exploration discovered Australia. Cecelia couldn't help; she didn't know much herself. At the time Cathy didn't think: 'Hang on, what about our side of the story?' She was too unworldly to make the connection, she says. 'As a child I was always in my own space. I used to wake up and see around me the people who loved me, my family, and I did the things that I liked doing. But when I think back now, yeah, it's unfair. The education system was very ignorant back then.'

Cecelia's protectiveness extended also to Cathy's teenage freedoms. 'I stayed home all the time,' says Cathy. 'I'd ask to sleep over at a friend's place and, I don't know if Mum was wary of strangers or not, but I wasn't allowed to. Nor to go roller-skating with my friends on Friday nights. I'd get upset, but in the end I'd accept it. I'd sit in my room and play music.'

Cecelia puts Cathy's passivity down to her placid, loving nature. 'She rarely put on a tantrum, whereas the boys were the exact opposite,' she says. 'Catherine didn't like life to be unhappy, didn't want to see the bad side. She wanted it to be all rosy. Maybe if she'd rebelled, we would have said, "All right, you can go, but be back by such-and-such a time."'

Cathy did explode once. 'I took off, rode my bike into town to go to the football with my friends,' she says. 'I rode like I was possessed for 10km. When I got home later I got the biggest smacking, which was fair enough, I suppose.' Later, at high school, Cathy developed older friends, boys who'd go nightclubbing and drinking. 'They were a pretty wild bunch,' she says. 'Mum made sure that one of my brothers came out with me. She was just scared for me, I guess.'

Cecelia agrees. Yes, she was over-protective. She'd lost one daughter, Anne-Marie, and she'd become super cautious about Cathy. As well, Cecelia had memories of Palm Island, where young Aboriginal girls were molested by white and black men, but the complaints were swept under the carpet. Unfortunately, Cecelia, despite her vigilance, was not able to entirely protect Cathy.

5.
Speaking Out.
1984

One morning Cathy bounced cheerily into Miller Street for our daily interview, sipped a glass of water—she was always rehydrating after track or weight training sessions—plonked herself on the lounge, and prepared to be interrogated. We had grown used to each other's company by now and with each new revelation she made I would concede little snippets of my life—as the biographer must—to maintain a mutual sense of balance. We communicated well, considering I was 30 years her senior, though occasionally she would be amazed at my ignorance of her modernity and would rock with laughter, saying, 'Oh, Adrian, you're such a dag sometimes.'

This day I intended to ask her about the season of 1996, and the wonderful drama of the Atlanta Olympics. 'This is probably one of the most significant moments in your life up until now,' I said. I saw something click in her mind. 'Turn the tape off,' she said, seriously. 'No,' I said. 'Just talk, we'll decide what to do with it later. I can wipe the tape or give it to you.' She paused, settled, and took a deep breath.

Among the many moves that Bruce Barber's job as a railway guard entailed, one was to Coppabella, 136km west of Mackay, through which huge coal trains hauled to and from the mines at Moranbah. The majority of people who lived there worked on the coal trains and Bruce would sometimes take the children down to ride one of the multiple engines which drew the coal trucks. The railway ran about 400m from Cathy's home and through the night the intermittent movement of rolling stock lulled her to sleep. It was 1984 and Cathy was 11.

One afternoon, after school, a man known to the family called in at her home and chatted casually to her. Cathy trusted him and was pleasant. On some pretext he lured Cathy into a downstairs room where he placed his hand on her buttocks. 'I freaked out and ran,' says Cathy. 'It frightened the wits out of me. I didn't complain because I didn't want to upset anyone. I just wanted to forget about it, and I did for a long time.' But it left her apprehensive. He occasionally returned to the house but usually either Cecelia or Bruce was there. The school bus dropped her a kilometre from home and if she recognised the man's car approaching as she walked, she thought, 'Oh God!' and became panicky. Her anxiety remained, but nothing further happened.

Until about three months later, when a second, more serious, incident occurred. The man was visiting Bruce and Cecelia, and Cathy had a cousin staying overnight on a mattress on her bedroom floor. That evening after the two girls went to bed and turned the light out, Cathy heard someone in the bathroom next to her bedroom. Then she heard her door open and saw the man there in the dark. She heard him approach across the room and felt him sit on the side of her bed. He then sexually molested her with his hand and made her place her hand upon himself. The shock that this was to Cathy makes her wince even today. She simply had no idea, had no concept, of the act of sexual molestation. The air of innocence she emanates today, even as an adult, has its genesis in her complete naivety back then. As devastating as was the physical contact, the mental assault was its equal. 'I had my eyes shut but I was awake,

awake through this whole thing but petrified,' says Cathy. 'I couldn't move, couldn't call out. I don't know why I didn't yell out for my parents, don't know why I pretended to be asleep, don't know why I didn't jump up and scream. I don't understand myself. I was just a shy little girl. I didn't really know what was going on. I just wanted him to go away.'

In the still of the night with the train trucks rumbling in the distance, Cathy lay in frozen silence, enduring indignities, desperately detaching her mind from the scene, from the room, until the man eventually rose and left. She thinks the incident lasted only a few minutes. To Cathy, everything was a blur after that. Somehow she fell back to sleep. 'The next morning I just thought I'd had a bad dream, a nightmare,' says Cathy. 'Or part of me hoped I'd had a bad dream. I remember feeling, I don't know, confused. And disillusioned.'

When Cathy was pubescent, about 10, her mother spoke to her briefly about the facts of life and warned her never to let anyone touch her sexually. And nor had she, but this had occurred in her own home, in her own bed, by someone known to her. Another cousin of Cathy's later confided that she too was scared of the man, and knew not to be left alone with him, to stick close to her mother if he was around.

'Everything changed, the way I saw the world changed,' says Cathy. 'It was tougher, and sadder. And it affected me in little ways. It definitely affected the way I saw men. It taught me the difference between a good man and a bad man, to learn pretty quickly about men and what they should and shouldn't want. And it made me alert to things, like walking into a newsagent and seeing a man looking at a girlie magazine and turning the page upside down and looking at it every which way.'

Some time later, Cathy saw the man again at a barbecue and stood horrified, heart palpitating, unable to move. 'Everyone expected me to be friendly, you know how I am, to move about kissing and hugging everyone, friends and family, but I couldn't do anything,' says Cathy. 'They were calling to me to come over here, come there and it was so painfully obvious to everyone around me that something was wrong. I looked at him and knew I couldn't go near him. It affected me. I can see now how it stays with you, even though you don't know what it's done to you.'

What it does is damage. Sue Featherstone, 50, an Aboriginal counsellor at Gallang Place in Brisbane, generously agreed to speak to me about the incident without knowing the identity of the woman concerned. Such assaults were common in Aboriginal communities and rarely talked about, she said. 'The family, and the child, understands that a complaint might send the offender, a friend or a relative, often a breadwinner, to gaol,' she says. 'The last thing they want, under any circumstances, is for the police to be involved. That usually means trouble for everyone.

'Young girls are shy and naive, it's part of their charm. They don't want to make a scene, or draw attention to themselves. They will go into denial. You never want to cause your mother grief, because she's usually had enough already. So the girl becomes an adult before her time, she protects her family. The victim becomes the nurturer. It's a terrible irony.'

Featherstone says girls who have their status as a child invaded have an important development stage in their lives damaged. This in turn can produce problems with adult relationships later on. 'Instead of being nurtured by her family over the incident, the girl has to nurture herself,' she says. 'When, as an adult, she tries to heal that deficit through a loving partner, it doesn't work. Her partner can't possibly repair her childhood wound, no matter how much affection they provide.'

And, finally, depending upon the severity of the assault, the child's self-esteem can be scarred. 'Look at the wrong messages such an incident teaches a child—that they are of such little value that an adult male requires no consent from them to touch them sexually; that they are worthy only of physical sex, with no affection required,' says Featherstone. 'It goes on and on. Don't ever underestimate the impact.'

Featherstone said such assaults are only now becoming more talked about in indigenous circles. 'It's only in the last couple of years we've been able to get our people to talk about domestic violence,' she says. 'The rest is down the track a little. For your friend to speak out as she has is very brave, and almost certainly beneficial to her.'

Cathy's memory is that she never spoke to her parents about the incident and has clung to an anger which she directed primarily at her mother for somehow not safeguarding her from the assault, though she now understands that Cecelia was over-protective rather than the opposite, and was not to blame. She also believes that her cousin on the floor beside her must have known what was happening, but was equally terrified.

Yet, extraordinarily, Bruce recalls accidentally intercepting the man emerging from Cathy's bedroom that evening and questioning him. Because of the man's suspicious behaviour, Bruce ordered him out of the house. The next morning Bruce spoke to the two girls and then called in the police. The police interviewed both girls but Cathy, ashamed of the incident and her part in it—though terrified and unwilling—denied that there had been any physical contact, a typical reaction in such cases. Cathy told them that he had exposed himself and nothing more. She couldn't bear to admit what had taken place. Already the child was assuming guilt for her own behaviour even though an adult's power and authority gave her no choice. No charges were ever laid because, in Queensland before 1989, indecent exposure in a private home was not an offence.

Cathy had blocked out all memory of the police involvement until I reminded her, and she sat with an air of amazement as I recounted Bruce's prompt action. Now she does remember the police, and the man's wife in tears. Bruce, in turn, had no idea of the serious nature of the assault until

I repeated Cathy's allegations. The family's silence had been complete for over 10 years. It was typical of a silence about child abuse that has enshrouded Australia and which only now is being lifted by Royal Commissions into paedophilia and special inquiries into child abuse. Children do not accuse adults because they fear they will not be believed. Because the majority of offenders are known to the family, incidents are hushed to avoid embarrassment. Consequently psychological counselling for the child is not provided.

Cathy courageously chose to reveal the traumatic episode here because she suspects such assaults happen just as often in indigenous families as in non-indigenous, yet little attention is paid to the former. It's the same with domestic violence, she says. 'Did you see that New Zealand film, *Once Were Warriors*? We need Aboriginal films like that because it's more like a documentary; it's a cultural education for everyone to see.' In the film a young girl, about Cathy's age, is raped in her bed by a friend of her father's during a drunken party. Later, severely depressed, the daughter commits suicide after which her account of her silent ordeal is discovered in her diary.

Cathy's own message is that such assaults are not the sole province of white Australia. She blames herself for the silence which shrouded the incident, as it was happening, and in the aftermath. 'I'm strong enough to deal with it now, but because I said nothing then, he could have gone on and done it to other girls,' she says. 'So speaking out isn't just for me, it's to help other girls out there, and young boys too, anyone who's been molested. It's to help them deal with this stuff. The lesson is, if it happens to you, don't be afraid, you're not to blame, tell your parents. And parents should get help for their children so it minimises the mental damage. Sadly, we do have men like him out there, but staying silent doesn't help.'

Cathy sat quietly after she had poured out her story. 'Ah, you've become my confessor,' she said at length, looking me directly in the eye. 'It doesn't get much more personal, does it?' No, it didn't. I was very moved by the story with which I had been entrusted. I thought about how she had waited all those hours of our sessions with that secret in her heart, how she must have wondered whether she could ever share it with me.

I told Cathy that I would take advice on the legal implications of her story and that nothing would leave that loungeroom until she wanted it to. She calmly assured me that she didn't intend to pursue the matter further. 'Obviously I still have negative feelings about it all, but I don't feel that angry, I don't feel that it has particularly hindered my growth,' she said. 'Too many wonderful things have happened to me to focus on the bad things. I've dealt with it now. And if speaking out saves one person from going through what I did, then it will all have been worthwhile.'

And part of dealing with it was to get it out in the open, even though she knew the pain it might cause her friends, and distress to her family. She was aware, as a secondary element in the matter, of the risk that publicity associated with the incident might overwhelm her otherwise happy childhood, and subsequent triumphant athletic carrer. 'But my life is more than a sports book, isn't it?' said Cathy. 'So that's the way it has to be, and that's how I want it to be.'

6.
WELCOME STRANGER.
HIGH SCHOOL, 1987–90

'For most coaches, it never happens,' says Romanian coach Mike Danila. 'To coach Cathy Freeman, I was over the moon. Every coach is dreaming about this thing, like you are prospecting for gold and you find a big nugget. There are many prospectors all over the world, but very few find the Welcome Stranger nugget. This is the feeling when you find someone like Cathy. In all my coaching years I hadn't seen a talent like hers.'

Danila's alliance with Cathy in 1989 at Kooralbyn International School, inland from the Gold Coast, was the key that first locked her harum-scarum talent into a reasonably disciplined training regime and gave Cathy a taste of a future she had only vaguely dreamed about. And for that, once more, Cathy can thank her parents.

Late in 1987, Bruce and Cecelia visited Cathy's school, Pioneer High, in Mackay, to meet the vocational guidance officer. He had interviewed Cathy the previous day and was disturbed by her responses. He had asked Cathy what she wanted to do when she left school and Cathy had said, 'I want to win gold medals at the Olympic Games.' But what about after the medals and the Olympic Games? 'I don't care,' said Cathy.

WELCOME STRANGER

The officer found that, far from being concerned, the Barbers were in cahoots with Cathy. With no real competition in north Queensland, they felt her running was going nowhere. They had been casting about for a scholarship at a southern Queensland school with a good track record, so to speak. They had heard about Paul Faithful, in Toowoomba, who had coached one of Cathy's idols, Glynis Nunn, heptathlon gold medallist at the Los Angeles Olympics in 1984. A few days after the interview, Pioneer High's headmaster rang the Barbers to say he had arranged a scholarship at the exclusive girls' school, Fairholme College in Toowoomba.

Fairholme, established in 1917 as a gift to the Presbyterian Church, sits on a bluff of the Great Dividing Range, 130km west of Brisbane. In winter the temperature drops to near zero, and that's without the chill factor of the westerlies which sweep off the inland western plateau. Damp mists shroud the escarpment and the six-hectare school grounds in an eerie quiet. It is at once a romantic and yet austere setting, worthy of an Antipodean Brontë novel. When Cathy arrived in early 1988 she was one of only three black students in a school enrolment of 600, most of whom were from farming and grazing families in northern NSW and south-west Queensland. Some were the fourth generation of their family to attend.

Boarders at Fairholme, except for those on scholarships—known as college council fee remissions for financial hardship—were paying solid fees for their high-quality tuition. By 1998 the figure was $12,000 a year. The school produces such good results that you could count on one hand the students who don't go on to tertiary study. Cathy, from warm, coastal Mackay, and no great shakes as a scholar, couldn't have entered a more contrasting, and alien, environment. It was the climatic equivalent of her mother being transferred from balmy Palm to wintry Woorabinda at about the same age, 40 years earlier. Worse, for Cecelia it was the departure of her second daughter from her house.

And once more there were overtones of a family member being cast out to an institution, even if it was a highly respected boarding school. It was such a dreadful wrench that she and Bruce immediately began plans to move south to Brisbane.

A tearful Cathy rang home the first night and was on the phone for an hour. She was homesick and, night after night, cried herself to sleep. Thereafter she rang once a week and mother and daughter would both be in tears. 'I told Bruce I was going down,' says Cecelia. 'I told him to get me a ticket, I'm bringing her home.' Bruce dug his heels in. 'No, you're not,' he said. 'Let her go, give her a chance to stand on her own two feet.' Her two fast feet, he meant. Bruce Barber arrived in the Freeman family's life as a healing force, assisting Cecelia to hold the children together as a unit, yet even he felt that Cathy's talent must have its day, whatever the emotional cost.

Cathy was a cultural shock for Fairholme, too. The week before leaving Mackay she had a work experience stint at a hairdressing salon and on the last day arrived home with startling grey streaks through her dark brown hair. 'You should have seen the look on the Fairholme headmaster's face when we first walked in,' says Cathy. 'The first thing that had to change was my hair.'

Being from a working-class family at such a school, Cathy fell in with some north Queensland country girls with a bit of spirit, who dyed the principal's cat green, snuck out to meet boys and were inattentive in class. Once, much to Cathy's embarrassment, a boy sent her some flowers. She wasn't interested in him but it earned her the nickname 'Flowers' which her friends gleefully yelled out to her when she raced at athletics carnivals.

Cathy observed the ways of middle-class girls, everything from make-up to debating. 'Just little things, like the way they'd use special soap and brushes to clean their skin,' says Cathy. 'They were really articulate too and a part of me wished I was more like them.' She followed the school team to debating competitions and saw how they used palm cards and thought on their feet, skills she would eventually employ herself once her own fame demanded it. 'These girls were going to be women who would be really significant in society,' says Cathy admiringly—forgetting that she had become one herself.

Fairholme was Cathy's adolescent introduction to middle-class Australia, a process of assimilation which has never ceased since. She saw the Jaguars and Mercedes pull up to collect daughters, saw the privileges and comforts that comparative wealth brought, the opportunities available to pursue career interests. She came to understand that society rewards those who conform to the norm. It is quite likely, second only to her mother's example, that at Fairholme were sown the seeds of conservatism that she attached to her Aboriginality for the next few years.

'We'd talk about the colour of our skins, though never in a nasty manner,' says Vanessa Gray, Cathy's high jumping friend from primary who was already at Fairholme. 'We'd even tell Aboriginal jokes and Cathy used to laugh. Whether it worried her internally I don't know. I don't think she considered herself different. She was just one of us.' School sports master John Sessarago thought the same thing. 'Whatever the media said, in athletic circles she was never referred to as an Aboriginal,' he says. 'I don't think she ever thought of herself as different, either. She was just another Fairholme girl.'

Yet on special weekends, as a boarder, she was allowed to stay outside the school, and her favourite house parent was Uncle Darby—former champion jockey Darby McCarthy. Cathy would spend the weekend with McCarthy's two daughters, both a little younger than her, sitting on their beds watching television and eating chocolates, happy with her Aboriginal friends. McCarthy, who had retired in Toowoomba, was the supporter who went in to bat for

Cathy in the national junior sports awards in 1986. He had subsequently chaperoned Cathy, and a young Aboriginal friend—a niece of former boxing great Tony Mundine—to the Brisbane dinner where she received her award.

In summer, Toowoomba has fresh, clean air, but in winter the mornings snatch the breath away. 'We had to get up early for cross-country runs,' said Cathy. 'I ran five kilometres, never won, nowhere near it. We'd wear tracksuits, gloves, beanies, scarves, anything to keep warm,' she says. 'But the wind would blow right through you.' Cathy developed exercise-induced asthma from those chill morning runs, and even today carries an inhaler in case she feels short of breath. 'Dressing for school I'd pull my socks up to my knees, and wear my tracksuit pants under my tartan skirt to keep warm,' says Cathy. 'I'd pull the tracksuit legs up over my knees so you couldn't see I was wearing them.'

Couldn't see them but, as Kylie Stafford says, nor could you walk with your legs together either, with these rolled pants bulging underneath. Like Cathy, Kylie was on a scholarship. 'We were there for sports,' says Kylie, pointedly. 'No matter what you called it, hardship or whatever. As long as we did well at sports, it was fine. Cathy wasn't at all scholastic, I'm not going to lie. I know, I used to sit next to her. She was a nice person, relaxed, do anything for you. But she was lonely and because she was so talented everyone tried to mollycoddle her. She couldn't have cared less either way, she more or less withdrew into herself.'

Vanessa Gray says the same. 'She was in her own world. Didn't concentrate in class, just stared into space a lot. And during study breaks she'd fidget the whole time, or get off her chair. I think Cathy found something she was good at, running, and she didn't need to be good at anything else.' Sports officer Sessarago taught younger grades at Fairholme and occasionally Cathy would wander down to his class. 'You could have almost put her in my class, she giggled as much as the kids,' he says, kindly.

WELCOME STRANGER

Kylie Stafford was deposed by Cathy's arrival at Fairholme. Through grades 8, 9 and 10, Kylie had been the school 100m, 200m, 400m, hurdles and long jump champion. She was looking forward to completing grades 11 and 12 undefeated, a unique achievement. 'I would have had a 100 per cent record my whole school career,' she says. Until the advent of Freeman. 'It was an interhouse rivalry thing,' says Kylie. 'Cathy was in Black, I was in Stephens. Black was strong in grade 10, where Cathy should have been, and weak in grade 11. So they bumped Cathy up against me in grade 11, which was illegal, because I read the rule book after the carnival.

'I had been the strongest in grade 11 but I knew I couldn't beat Cathy, so to preserve my undefeated record I asked to be bumped up to grade 12, because I knew I could have won the senior year even though they were older than me. But the school wouldn't allow it. I was fuming. You have no idea how annoyed I was. I ran second behind Cathy in the 100, 200 and 400—not a lot in it, about a metre each time. I could have touched her back. I did beat her in the hurdles, though, because Cathy couldn't hurdle then, never been taught. She was like one of those Toyota chickens when they jump in the air, her legs went everywhere. It was quite amusing. And she took about 50 stutter steps between each hurdle. So I finally got something on the dear girl.'

Stafford had suffered the same fate as Vanessa Gray, who was now sports captain at Fairholme. 'It was hard on Vanessa,' says Stafford. 'She'd had to compete against Cathy all through primary at state titles, and suddenly she turns up at Fairholme, of all places. She sort of broke Vanessa's heart sometimes because Vanessa trained very hard, whereas Cathy was just a natural.'

Vanessa, now a physical education teacher, laughed when I asked how she felt about her bogeyperson enrolling at Fairholme. 'To tell you the honest truth, I don't think any of us were too pleased when Cathy turned up,' she says. 'We knew our winning days were over. But nobody disliked her, you couldn't.' What frustrated other girls, she says, was the ease with which Freeman won. 'She had this long stride, which made her look, when she raced, as though she wasn't really going fast. My grandmother used to say that the only reason she won was that her stride was three times longer than everyone else's.'

For all her teenage innocence and charm, Cathy occasionally annoyed her friends. 'You'd organise to do something, like relay training, and she wouldn't turn up,' says Vanessa. 'And she always depended on someone, friends, to get her out of bed to train, because she couldn't remember what time to get up. Even at athletics carnivals. She would be entered in every event and she'd need someone to organise her to be there. In the end, if she didn't turn up where she was supposed to, no-one batted an eyelid. That was just Cathy.'

Sports master Sessarago saw that Cathy didn't train much, but didn't need to. 'Without training, she could go to the state secondary schools in 1989 and set four records against kids who trained a lot,' he says. 'At that stage she was a better high jumper than sprinter, she had such explosive power and strength.' Cathy jumped 1.72m, a state record for the under-16 that year. 'Don't get me wrong, she trained, did a bit of power work, few sprints, some weights,' says Sessarago. 'But her program wasn't as heavy as it could have been.'

However laidback Freeman appeared to others, it masked a deep-seated need, in the absence of any other personal skills, to win at athletics. Vanessa Gray's mother, Lyn, recalls Vanessa scoring a rare high jump win over Cathy once in a school competition. 'From then on, Cathy trained seriously. She didn't like getting beaten,' said Lyn. John Sessarago confirmed that, inwardly, Freeman was not a glad loser. 'She got beaten at a regional carnival in Harristown once and she wouldn't go and get her second-placed ribbon,' he says. 'We had to literally drag her to the podium. That was the only time I got cross with her. So that attitude, hating to lose, was already there.'

Mid-year the athletics team watched the 1988 Seoul Olympics on television and after Carl Lewis and Florence Griffith-Joyner scooped the medals pool, Sessarago turned to Cathy and said, 'Freeman, you could be up there with those guys if you wanted to.' The idea stuck in her head. Later Sessarago gave her a framed black and white photograph of herself high jumping, with a quote written on it from F.D. Roosevelt: 'The only limit to our realisation of tomorrow will be our doubts of today.'

Later that year she and brother Norman, whose running was also being noticed by national sports officials, were chosen for an International Athletics Exchange tour to the US which took in the Mt Sacramento relays in California. It was her first trip overseas and her first inkling of the rewards that athletics held. 'At Mt Sac we were at the track when a whole bunch of us saw Carl Lewis and we just went crazy,' says Cathy. She had her photograph taken with the approachable Lewis, the beginning of encounters which led to a friendship in later years. Says Cathy, 'Then someone said that Flo Jo was around so we went screaming off down the warm-up track and she was just sitting there.' Cathy asked her what was the hardest thing in becoming a champion. Flo Jo replied that it was getting out of bed every morning, knowing she had to train. It wasn't until years later, when Cathy began training so hard it hurt, that she understood Flo Jo's remark. Despite all the drug rumours, Flo Jo looked normal and feminine to Cathy, not muscly like on television. 'We all peeked at her long fingernails,' she says. 'They're her trademark. But it's quite common over in the States with black women. They look like ugly claws.'

Cathy was billeted with a white family in Los Angeles and one day, while walking with her billet, they were approached by a black youth on the street. 'He suddenly pulled this pocket knife out and sort of flicked it,' says Cathy. 'My billet said, "Hey, what are you doing? It's me!" So she obviously knew him. It happened too quickly for me to be scared, but ahhh! Made you think.' It was also an education for this Fairholme girl to see how US teenagers interacted. 'I couldn't get over how fast the boys were in terms of coming on to girls,' says Cathy. 'They called out "Hey, girl!" and "Hey, you fine thing!" and I'm thinking, "I'm not walking near them. I'm going another way." They were so fast.'

In Australia, Cathy's black male friends were more shy than her white male friends. But in the US the blacks were the opposite, loud, proud and strong, and they took it onto the track with them. 'I could smell their aggression,' she says. 'You could almost taste it. It was intense and competitive. Like nothing I'd ever seen before. It would have been intimidating to be a white athlete competing against them. It made an impression on me. That whole culture of America, so much more emotional, so much more passionate than back home.'

The team visited Disneyland, where Cathy caught up with Norman who'd been on a slightly different tour. He'd spent all his pocket money, could he have a loan? Kid brothers! When Cathy returned to Fairholme all that her friends wanted to hear about was how she touched Carl Lewis's strong, brown back. Sessarago noticed a definite change in Cathy's motivation. He sent a video of her high jumping to Athletics Australia's national event coaches for evaluation. And took her to Queensland University for a weekend's high-performance testing.

'The physiologists said she was quite incredible in the dimensions of what she could do,' says Sessarago. She also proved a natural at other sports, a smooth stylist as a swimmer, represented the school in netball and made the state team in touch football. 'She was a handy winger,' says Sessarago. 'Didn't have much of a step, but could really fly given an overlap.'

Paul Faithful, the coach Cathy had ostensibly gone to Fairholme to be near, had little input into her development. Ken Stafford drove his daughter Kylie and Cathy to Faithful's club, Garden City, in Toowoomba, for training twice a week and down to the QEII stadium in Brisbane for competitions. 'I don't think Paul took me very seriously,' says Cathy. 'I didn't get any one-on-one coaching. I guess the opportunity just wasn't there.'

Faithful, as manager of state school teams, had known of Cathy for years. 'She had all the talent in the world, but she wasn't particularly dedicated,' he says. 'You couldn't make a prediction about her because you couldn't be sure whether she'd train.' But that year, at the Pacific Schools Games, Faithful saw a race that stuck in his mind. 'She ran an under-16 400m and she was absolutely brilliant,' he says. 'She had them shot to pieces after 300m but she'd probably run about 10 races in a couple of days and she fell in a hole and finished second. I always felt after that run that 400m would be her go.'

As 1989 dawned, with Cathy about to turn 16, her scholarship with Fairholme became tenuous and once more the Barbers were in search of a landing ground for her. Cathy's brother, Norman, had been awarded a scholarship to St Joseph's Nudgee College, Brisbane, where Mike Danila was athletics coach. In the winter holidays Danila conducted coaching clinics up and down the Queensland coast, and Norman and Cathy attended in Mackay.

Soon after, Danila took the job as coach at Kooralbyn International School, and asked the headmaster, Chris Madden, if he could bring some talent with him, specifically Cathy, on a half-scholarship. Bruce Barber, who has a poker player's steel, said a full scholarship would be acceptable. 'We'll have to wait until next month's board meeting to approve that,' Madden told Danila. 'Too late, we'll lose her,' said Danila. 'OK, full scholarship,' said Madden. 'On a three-month trial. But it's going on your head. If you prove to be wrong, we'll both lose our jobs.'

Then they all informed Cathy of the fait accompli. 'I always went with what my mum wanted,' says Cathy. 'But I was sort of frazzled, leaving another school, even though I didn't have any really close friends there. I was shy when I arrived at Fairholme and I think boarding school helped me come out of my shell a bit. And the company I kept, the people I listened to, helped me. I don't regret Fairholme. Adapting to new schools, new people, different cultures, prepared me so well for the life I eventually chose.'

Departing Fairholme was a mutually happy occasion. At assembly the deputy principal asked everyone to wish Cathy well, which they did. 'It was really cool of her to do that,' says Cathy. Says Vanessa Gray, 'Fairholme was a great school, but it just wasn't Cathy.'

On 6 August 1989, Mike Danila did the round trip, drove from Kooralbyn to Acacia Ridge, in Brisbane, where the Barbers had moved, to pick up Cathy's bags, headed for Toowoomba to collect Cathy, and drove back down to Kooralbyn. As an ardent athletics coach, he couldn't have been more content had Flo Jo herself been sitting beside him.

Kooralbyn International School, built in 1985, is an unusual concept, an independent, non-government, non-profit, privately owned school run by a board of governors. It is built amid old dairy farms on the picturesque eastern foothills of the Teviot Range, an hour's drive south-west of Brisbane. The setting is naturally peaceful, and only a short walk to the newly built Kooralbyn Valley Resort, a 4.5 star, country-theme hotel with a golf course, polo fields, pony trails and bushwalking.

The school sits on 50 hectares, and has its own four-lane grass running track, not unlike Melaleuca Park in Mackay, even down to the small, open stand for spectators to watch events. The school is co-educational, has 250 high school students, about half of whom board, and 30 per cent of whom are from overseas. Its fees were similar to Fairholme's for boarders, which meant that in two years, in modern terms, Bruce Barber had negotiated scholarships worth $24,000 for Cathy.

Danila was so excited he would have had Cathy training that Sunday evening. 'I could hardly wait for Monday,' he says. 'I had a squad of 15 athletes and at 3.30 p.m. they were getting changed and having a drink and Cathy, being new at the school, was still talking to everyone. I waited 10 minutes and then walked up to her and said, 'Cathy, what about training?' And she said, 'Oh, are we today?' It was like the question was a surprise. So clearly she was not used to training.'

To respect track time was a matter dear to Danila's heart. 'She was not very disciplined at first,' he says. 'But every week, every month she got better. And as she improved she became more confident that what I am telling her is right and will make her successful. She started believing in me very strongly.' Says Cathy, 'We were very different but I adored him. His whole European attitude. I was so casual and he was so intense, and very passionate about track and field. He kept things interesting, kept us laughing all the time. It was fun. We were always doing new things. He didn't like me having boyfriends, didn't want me riding horses or running cross-country, as I had at Fairholme. "Sprinters do not run across hills," he told me. The training was hard and we trained in a group but he always gave me a little extra attention, made me feel that I was going to do big things one day.'

As a young man, Danila was in the top echelon of 400–800m runners in Romania but did not make any representative squads. Instead, he graduated from university in physical education in 1979 and began coaching full time. In 1987 he was chosen to take the Romanian team to the World Student Games in Zagreb, Yugoslavia. It was the opportunity he had awaited. At home he had been suffering under the reign of President Ceaucescu. 'I was not permitted to travel, we had food shortages, oppression was getting worse,' he says. 'Zagreb was my first chance to get out of the country. I escaped to Vienna, asked for asylum and waited seven months for a visa to Australia. Would you believe, in that time, one night I had a dream of coming to Australia and coaching an Aborigine.'

Danila had arranged for his squad to use the spa and pool at the adjacent Kooralbyn resort. The indoor, tiled spa resembles a Roman bath, and the squad sat around the edges in great luxury while Danila lectured them on keeping trim, forgoing junk food and getting good rest. One day in the spa he warned Cathy, 'You better practise your signature.' What for? asked Cathy. 'Because soon you start having to write down hundreds of signatures.' The squad all laughed and chiacked her, but this was just a few weeks before the trials for the 1990 Commonwealth Games in Auckland.

After the homogeneous climes of Fairholme, Kooralbyn's multicultural aspect excited Cathy. 'There were heaps of Asians and black people—Papua New Guineans, Pacific Islanders—and a German, a Cuban, and a French guy, Laurent, who was sort of my boyfriend,' she says. 'It was great. I was a lot happier because the black students made me feel less isolated. And the students were different. Fairholme was elitist and they all seemed to come from the upper class.'

It was interesting: while I talked to Cathy about Fairholme, she didn't criticise the school once, but as soon as we moved on to Kooralbyn, she changed and voiced her doubts about her Toowoomba time. As if she was reliving the whole experience. But she was realistic as well. 'Fairholme was tough because I was a bad student, didn't study, didn't prepare and my marks were really poor,' she says. 'But at Kooralbyn I passed my maths exam because I'd already been through it at Fairholme. The standard of education up there was just so high. I regret not taking my education a lot more seriously.'

On the athletics front, in the space of a few months Cathy had experienced the up-front, in-your-face enthusiasm of American athletics at Mt Sac, and now she was encountering the intensity of a true European track zealot. Training four days a week, Cathy improved rapidly and, in September 1989, Danila took the wheel for the hour's drive in the school's 20-seater school bus to QEII in Brisbane for the season's first competition. Her best time for 100m before Kooralbyn was 12.6s. At QEII she won by four metres in 11.9s. 'It was a big barrier, getting under 12 seconds,' says Danila. His faith in Freeman was vindicated.

The following day, Sunday, returning to QEII for the 200m, Danila stopped the bus at Beaudesert en route and bought the morning newspaper. 'I had tears in my eyes as I read the reports of the previous day,' says Danila. 'It said that Freeman had cleaned up the 100m field and was expected to do well in the 200m. When I saw this I showed it to Cathy. She couldn't believe what kind of an echo her run the previous day would have.'

In an ensuing competition, in November 1989, Cathy improved, running 11.67s electronically—about 11.5s hand-timed. Since arriving at Kooralbyn, Cathy had improved by almost a second over 100m. It was accepted that she had come off a very slow starting base, but Danila began to think that which he had previously not dared—about entering Cathy in the Commonwealth Games trials in Sydney in early December.

Danila rang an Adelaide friend, Fletcher McEwen, an unoffical statistician of Australian athletics. 'I'm coaching this girl Freeman,' Danila began telling McEwen. 'Oh, yes, she ran 11.67s the other day,' said McEwen. Danila was encouraged that Cathy's time had been noted. Could she run in the Games trials? She could, said McEwen. 'The top 20 in the country are usually encouraged to enter and that time ranks her about sixth or seventh over 100m.' Kooralbyn school encouraged Danila, too. All systems go, except no-one had asked Cathy. She was apprehensive. 'Oh, do you think I'm good enough?' she asked Danila.

The week before the trials Cathy ran in an old-fashioned

100 yard race in Brisbane and defeated Kathy Sambell, one of her opponents for the Sydney trials, by 0.1s in 11 seconds flat. It was a timely boost for the southern challenge. In Sydney she ran her heat, semi-final and, still aged 16, made the final against Australia's top sprinters, including Queensland's world-class sprinter, Kerry Johnson.

In the final, her first real race against open-class athletes, Cathy ran the race of her short career to deadheat third with Sambell in 11.42s, behind Kerry Johnson and Monique Dunstan. She had qualified for the 4 x 100m Australian relay team to compete in the Commonwealth Games in Auckland in January 1990.

Melbourne track and field journalist, Nick Bideau, had been warned by Kerry Johnson that Freeman was one to watch. So he did. 'I'd been to meets in America and Europe, but I saw something in Cathy that I'd rarely seen in Australia—someone who flows over the ground,' he says. 'She was smooth and light on her feet, she didn't labour. You see it in someone like Darren Clark. You see it and think, "There's a good runner."' Nick wandered over and asked Freeman what made her run. 'I have a sister, Anne-Marie, who has cerebral palsy,' she said. 'And my mother told me I had two good arms and two good legs, so use them.' Bideau was suitably impressed. It was different to the rambling replies he usually received from young runners. Late the following week Cathy was back home in Brisbane when her parents bought the paper and read out her name in the Commonwealth Games team. It was, as Cathy said, 'like a nice dream coming true.'

7.
Rookie's Gold.
Commonwealth Games, 1990

Cathy Freeman and Kerry Johnson had a problem. They kept dropping the baton in practice. Since Kerry was to run the anchor leg of the women's 4 x 100m relay at the Commonwealth Games in Auckland in a few weeks, and Cathy was to hand her the baton, it didn't augur well. 'Always in a race, we were fine,' says Johnson. 'But in training we just couldn't get it in my hand. We couldn't work it out. There was great concern that in the Games we'd stuff up the change.'

When they arrived in Auckland the Australian girls struck up a friendship with the English team who, on their collective individual times, were favourites for the race. 'We went for a light jog around the warm-up track passing the baton and we even dropped it doing that,' said Johnson. 'The English girls were killing themselves laughing. They thought the race would be a lay down misère.'

This glitch eventually threatened Cathy's place in the relay, but she had already survived an earlier challenge to her right to run. Athletics Australia had originally nominated 70 as their likely team number to the Commonwealth Games Association but the selectors had chosen 85. Only Kerry Johnson had qualified individually for the 100m, but the women sprinters had been assured that the first four home in the 100m trial were in the relay. Newspapers listed the names of 15 athletes who were likely to be cut and Freeman, 16, was included in most of them. Nick Bideau was among the journalists who turned the threatened omissions into a cause célèbre for Australian athletics.

'You know they called us Arthur's girls over there, don't you?' says Kathy Sambell. 'Because it was Arthur Tunstall who wanted to cut us from the team.' She was partly right. It was Tunstall, secretary-treasurer of the Commonwealth Games Association since 1969, but he was backed by the rest of the Games executive committee, a majority of whom thought the standards of the athletics team were not high enough to justify their numbers. As the issue gathered momentum the federal government's Minister for Sport, Graham Richardson, rang Tunstall and summoned him and Athletics Australia general manager, Neil King, to Canberra.

According to Tunstall, Richardson returned to his office from the Lower House chamber in Parliament House where Tunstall was waiting and said, 'Did you hear that in there? I'm getting attacked over this athletics business and I don't like it. You're going to have to change your mind.' Tunstall replied, 'I'm sorry, it was the committee which made the decision and they won't change their mind.' Richardson told Tunstall he'd have to convince them. 'There's the phone, call your people up. I'll be back in an hour.' When he returned Tunstall told him, 'I told you, I rang and they won't budge.' Two of the hardest nuts in Australian public life were butting heads. The Games Association was autonomous but, Richardson knew, given the mounting public outcry, that the committee might soon be looking for a way to save face. 'Will you accept an independent arbiter, a referee?' he asked Tunstall. 'I'll tell you who it's going to be—John Coates.'

Tunstall told me, 'I knew then we were beaten, because Coates is a good mate of Richardson's. I knew what he'd do.' Coates, an experienced Olympic executive, proved also a friend of athletics and Cathy and Co survived. Monique Dunstan, 19, in tears when the cuts were first mooted, was overjoyed. Says Kathy Sambell, 'I honestly believe that if Cathy had been cut, we might never have seen her again. You've got to give people a chance to prove themselves.' Perhaps, although a year later Freeman showed she was made of sterner stuff than to cave in over missing a selection.

Since all four relay runners were from Queensland, coach Nancy Atterton flew to Brisbane to blend them into a unit. At QEII stadium she called out to Cathy, 'Stand on the extra 10m line please.' Cathy looked blank. 'Hello,' Atterton thought, 'I've got a raw one here!' The relay baton exchange box is 20 metres long, but there is an extra 10m mark at the back of the box from which runners can take off, provided they only accept the baton inside the box.

Atterton wrote a program of practice for the four and they spent 10 days in intensive training, becoming good friends. 'But Kerry and Cathy, they still couldn't get it right,' says Monique Dunstan. 'It was an actual nightmare. We thought, "Oh my goodness."'

When they were chosen to compete in a pre-Games meet in Hobart, Johnson received a phone call from a worried Cecelia Barber, Cathy's mother. 'She was worried. She couldn't afford to pay for Cathy to go to Hobart,' says Johnson. 'I told her it was all right, we were the Games team, all expenses were paid.' In Hobart, Cathy and Kerry got it right, smooth as silk, and they surprisingly downed the fancied English team. Sportswriter Nick Bideau interviewed Cathy again. 'You girls have got a good chance of winning,' he said encouragingly. She listened politely. 'I was starting to meet a lot of people, you know, they come and go,' says Cathy. 'I didn't think any further about meeting Nick.'

In camp in Sydney, a week before the Games, the three relay girls took young Cathy under their wing, waking her for breakfast and taking her to team activities. 'One morning we forgot her,' says Johnson, amusedly. 'When we came back in the afternoon to go training we knocked on her door and she was still sleepy, she had scarcely stirred the whole day!' At training, Cathy, who has an extravagant back-kick, took off with the baton and spiked Kathy Sambell. 'My shin peeled open like a banana,' says Sambell graphically. 'We got a real fright.' It was not as serious as first thought but management brows furrowed about the team.

To be 16, in her first Games, and only a relay to run, was a recipe for fun for Cathy. She was so little known that the official Australian team manual had no details other than her name. Coach Mike Danila gained accreditation to the Games village and tirelessly rounded up celebrities to introduce to his charge. Cathy had her photograph taken with Jamaican speed queen, Merlene Ottey, who won the Games 100 and 200m double, and then with the Nigerian twins Davidson and Osmond Ezinwa who were both world-class sprinters. UK fast men Linford Christie and Colin Jackson—gold in the 100m and 110m hurdles respectively in Auckland—good-naturedly flirted with Cathy in the dining room. Some jiving black Canadian runners waltzed over and exclaimed, 'Hey, a black Aussie, a black whitey, just like us, how 'bout that.'

Darren Clark, who went on to win the 400m gold, came and sat on the end of her bunk, grabbed a stocking hanging out of a clothes drawer, pulled it over his head and asked Cathy if she could throw a boomerang! 'I had watched him run fourth in Seoul in 1988 on television, and here he was clowning around with me,' says Cathy in wonderment.

At a team meeting she spied Debbie and Deek, two tough competitors she really admired. She'd seen their two come-from-behind golds, Rob de Castella in the marathon in the Commonwealth Games in Brisbane in 1982, Debbie Flintoff-King in the 400m hurdles in the Olympic Games in Seoul, in 1984. It was all exciting but Cathy had too much time on her hands. Since there were no heats, the relay was Cathy's one race and it was on the last day of the Games, so she had 10 days to fill in. By some official illogicality, only Kerry

ROOKIE'S GOLD

Johnson was entered in the 100m even though Australia could have entered three runners. The reason given to the other three girls was fear of injury to them before the big relay, but, as Monique Dunstan says, for the athletes the contrary was true. They all could have used the hit-out.

Cathy grew bored. She made up a song about her boyfriend back home and drove roomie Dunstan to distraction with it. And she slept. Says Glynis Nunn, who was recovering from illness, 'I had glandular fever and she was sleeping more than I was.' For something to do, Cathy attended every village function she could. At one she even met Prince Andrew. 'I got really excited, I don't know why,' she says, pragmatically. She listened to tapes, and hung around the village's bank of computers on which you could look up performance statistics. Sambell thought Freeman was keen on stats when, in truth, Cathy was checking out the computer messages, some romantic, which athletes could send one another.

None of this was harmful, but her dining room binges could have been. 'It's true, I ate and ate, chocolate cake and muffins,' she confesses. 'I put on heaps of weight, I just pigged out.' She even stashed some mini-cheesecakes in her unit's fridge. Mike Danila met her in the village towards the end of the first week and just stared. 'My God, you have put on so much weight. Your legs.' She had put on about 3kg.

Cathy was unconcerned. She knew she'd still run fast, given the chance. But sitting in the unit's loungeroom the next day she overheard snatches of a conversation which made her teenage heart sink. Kerry Johnson, in a back bedroom, was declaring, 'No! No way. If she doesn't run, I don't run.' Management had got cold feet. Cathy's inexperience had been raised at an executive meeting and the possibility was canvassed of experienced heptathlete Jane Flemming replacing her.

The actual source of this concern remains unknown. Jane Flemming strenuously denies lobbying for the berth. 'I'm glad you raised that,' Flemming tells me fiercely, 'because that's something I've been accused of doing. I never, ever spoke to anyone about it. My coach Craig Hilliard told them, "Go with the girls chosen. Jane has enough on her plate." I had the heptathlon, hurdles and long jump to deal with. I competed on five days of track and field. I had no idea what was going on.' She won gold in the heptathlon and long jump.

Relay coach Nancy Atterton clears Hilliard too, adamant that he did not speak at the meeting in question. 'He kept right out of it,' she says. 'It was just a general management question.' Yet team assistant manager in Auckland, Margaret Mahony, says management accepted the advice of coaches, not the reverse. 'Not that I think Nancy wanted to drop Cathy. She was very fond of her.'

Atterton says she argued at the meeting that Flemming had not trained with the relay. Says Atterton, 'I was worried about Cathy in Brisbane but once I set the wheels in motion to fix that, I was happy.' Yet Atterton felt compelled to approach Johnson and Sambell and tell them there was talk about replacing Freeman with Flemming.

'Kerry said she wouldn't run, and I did too,' says Sambell. 'We were the four picked. Cathy was the rookie but she earned her place fair and square. None of us, apart from Kerry, was experienced. I'd only made my international debut the previous year.'

Johnson believes Atterton was concerned about the relay, though Johnson wasn't herself. 'I just knew Cathy would do it right, because in a race she pulls it together, that's one of her strong features,' says Johnson. 'She's relaxed until the moment comes. Then she turns it on.' Atterton returned to management and informed them: if Flemming was in, the others were out. For Atterton, all bases were covered.

All this drama for one spot in a relay race! Australia had a mindset in that era—in which it was becoming increasingly harder to win individual Olympic golds in track and field—to concentrate on relays. But management were also forever haunted by the memory of past relay foul-ups, starting with Marjorie Jackson's dropped baton when Australia's 4 x 100m team were certain gold medallists in the 1952 Olympics in Helsinki.

The morning of Saturday, 3 February 1990, the last day of the Games, Johnson, the relay leader, gathered her crew together. Cathy listened attentively, eternally grateful for Johnson's intervention on her behalf. 'She was like a mother figure to me,' says Cathy. Johnson, who had already won two Games silvers, behind Merlene Ottey in the 100 and 200m, was an athlete of the world class to which Cathy aspired. Johnson's pep talk was more like a powder room chat than a gung-ho call for confidence. 'I think we'll win this today,' she told them. 'So make sure you take your make-up bags with you so we can all look good on the podium!' Then, as they walked onto the track, a last confab: 'You all have to do your bit, you can't leave all the work to me at the end,' she said. 'If something goes wrong, we'll have a little cry about it, we'll all go home, but we'll be good friends at the end of the day.' And so they were and still are.

At the start, reality hit Cathy. One race, one chance. 'My mind was all over the place,' says Cathy. 'I looked at the English, at the Canadians and thought, "Oh my God, this is it, Freeman!"' Dunstan led off, to Sambell, a slick change; to Freeman, a fraction slow. 'I was supposed to sprint during the actual changeover, but I just jogged to make sure my hand was out there for the baton,' says Cathy. 'I wanted to be safe rather than technically perfect.' Then she ran, ran with her characteristic fire, as though igniting down a trail of fuel. 'She was so competitive,' says Bideau, who covered the race for the Melbourne *Herald Sun*. 'She was young, inexperienced and overweight for an elite sprinter, didn't matter. When she raced you could see the tiger in her.'

Dunstan saw that when Freeman came to Johnson, Australia was in front. Kerry knew it, too. 'Cathy had run a really good leg because you can pick out positions on the track as they come around,' she says. Nervous, but not afraid, Johnson stretched out her hand and felt the baton slap into her palm. 'I just knew Cathy'd do it right,' she says. Elated, Johnson absolutely pelted for home for the gold, Australia in 43.87s, England second in 44.15s. Dunstan raced back around the track to greet an excited Johnson. Cathy saw them hugging so figured they'd won, until an official carrying a red protest flag crossed into her lane. She held her breath—and, thank goodness, he kept walking, just crossing the track. A spectator handed Sambell the green and gold boxing kangaroo flag made famous by Alan Bond's America's Cup victory in 1983. Kathy and Cathy jogged back with it together. Sambell still has it. Nobody complained that it was not the Australian flag.

'We did our victory lap, and when we got in front of the Royal box, we had to curtsy and I nearly tripped,' says Cathy, laughing. 'Because I was looking at Bob Hawke, who was looking at me and saying something to the Queen.' Perhaps Hawke was saying: there's Australia's first Commonwealth Games Aboriginal track and field gold medallist. Back in Brisbane, Cecelia, watching television all by herself, was in tears, shouting and screaming. Then suddenly the whole neighbourhood was on her doorstep. Cathy would have rung her except they had no phone.

In the post-race media conference, Cathy recovered sufficiently from her giggles to mention her sister Anne-Marie, and to speak from her heart. 'Being Aboriginal means everything to me. I feel for my people all the time,' she said. 'A lot of my friends have the talent but lack the opportunity.' With their lipstick on and hair combed they mounted the victory dais, Cathy's eyes glistening with tears as the medal was placed around her neck. Soon after, in the Games closing ceremony, Johnson comically fell off the same dais, but disastrously sprained her ankle and left the Games in a wheelchair. Because they nearly didn't even get to the Games, and because they were the last gold medal of Australia's record haul, the four captured the public's imagination. At Sydney airport a large crowd waited for them, waving newspaper front pages with their photograph.

Swimmer Hayley Lewis, the star of the pool, had been chosen to meet the Queen, and Jane Flemming's two golds should have been the track and field highlight. Yet the relay girls were the athletes in demand, and Cathy's Aboriginality set in train a fame which has steamed ahead ever since. Kathy Sambell said a few months later that she felt Freeman was being separated from the other three relay runners by an imaginary barrier. 'We shouldn't be separated into three white athletes and one Aboriginal,' said Sambell. 'We should all just be athletes because being black or white doesn't mean anything on the track.' Cathy couldn't agree more, but the media deluge was indicating otherwise.

The race was Saturday, Cathy arrived home on Monday. At 3 p.m., while the family was at a neighbour's house watching a video replay of the closing ceremony, Bruce slipped out to ring his work. The office told him they'd been trying to contact him. Anne-Marie, 24, had died from an acute asthma attack in Rockhampton. 'I just lost it,' says Cathy. 'It was weird, one moment we were on such a high, and then we were down.' At short notice Bruce tried in vain to book the family north by rail. But Cathy's name was starting to carry weight. Every train journey retains four empty seats for the Railways Commissioner—Cathy and her family could have them.

Anne-Marie's death opened past pains. Cecelia, and Norman Freeman, both blamed themselves for Anne-Marie's disability, as parents do. The hurt was too much for Norman, who did not visit Anne-Marie as regularly as the rest of the family. Cathy's birth had meant Anne-Marie's enforced departure from her family, and as Cathy grew older she too carried her own small guilt. An extraordinary crowd, several hundred mourners, including people from Woorabinda and hospital staff who had only met her once or twice, attended her funeral.

'She radiated a special kind of love,' says Cathy. 'She had these big brown eyes that the nurses said were always the focal point in a room full of people. She knew we were family. We talked to her and even though she couldn't talk, she knew what the hell was going on. I know it's no good saying should have, would have, but if only they'd had computers for her, so that she could have spelt out what she was feeling.' The family had always visited Anne-Marie twice a year, but it was a harrowing time for all. Says Cathy, 'Mum used to break down and cry all the way home after we had to leave. That was really tough.'

Cathy brought her gold medal with her, to be buried with Anne-Marie, but before the funeral Cecelia advised against it. She'd earned it and maybe she would want to show it to her grandchildren one day. Instead Cathy placed her Auckland victory flower posy there. And at the cemetery Cathy tearfully promised, aloud, that all her future running was dedicated to Anne-Marie. It sounds over-emotional, but that was the effect this unusual disabled girl had. Norman Freeman attended the funeral and afterwards spent a quiet moment with Cathy, praising her performance in Auckland. He cautioned her against letting television and fame change her. 'Don't think you're too old to get a beltin',' he said affectionately.

Back home Cathy received a short note of commiseration from journalist Nick Bideau. He'd read how Cathy, in attending the funeral, had missed the Games team's ticker-tape parade through Sydney. Missed that and a civic reception in Brisbane and a gala homecoming to Kooralbyn Valley. But the Aboriginal community in Brisbane honoured her with a gift of a traditional dot painting at a ceremony attended by Test rugby league player Sam Backo, and Jeffrey Dynevor, the first Aborigine to win a Commonwealth Games gold medal, in boxing in Perth in 1962.

Kooralbyn School welcomed her back anyway with a big ovation in the assembly hall and locked her gold medal in the headmaster's safe. A few days later, at the school track where usually 15 athletes trained, Cathy began her warm-up and, like Pied Piper, about 50 other students suddenly joined in behind her. 'Some with a little bit of talent, some with no talent at all,' says coach Mike Danila. 'I couldn't believe it. But after a week I have only 30, after two weeks only 20.' Even staff came just to watch her train.

During training, towards the end of the session, everyone gets to be tired, says Danila. 'But not Cathy,' he says. 'She was almost as fresh at finish like she was at start. Because she got endurance, I knew she could run 400, but it is not necessary to kill with this event too early, because it would go against her speed.' But he upped her training to five days a week and introduced variety into her schedule, teaching her to hurdle.

With her high jump spring and sprint speed, she was soon on song over the hurdles under the valley's blue skies, accompanied by the tuneless carking of Kooralbyn's crows. After two months she ran a close second in the state schools 100m hurdles to Sunshine Coast hurdler Kym Pope, who won in 14.64s. A month later she reversed that result in the national age titles in Melbourne, scampering over in 14.26s to Pope's 14.39s. Not bad for a converted 'Toyota chook'!

At those state titles she suffered a mild asthma attack just before the start of the 200m, but had forgotten her inhaler. As she entered the straight she struggled for breath, but won anyway. She didn't consider pulling out before the start or pulling up during the race? 'No,' she says, shaking her head quizzically. She loved it too much. A photograph of her winning the state open 100m final shows how much she loved it. As she crosses the finishing line, her eyes squeezed shut, mouth open in effort, she punches the air in triumph. Life was good for Cathy Freeman.

With the phone at Kooralbyn ringing endlessly for her, the school arranged for Brisbane agent Ian Guiver, of Celebrity Sports Marketing, to become her manager, whereupon she joined such stellar names as Ian Healy, Craig McDermott, Michael Lynagh and Leroy Loggins. All this was not lost on Norman Freeman at Woorabinda and, though not well, he made the trip down to Brisbane to watch Cathy and Norman run at QEII one weekend. Afterwards, as he and the family descended the stairs, he rested his hands lightly on Cecelia's shoulders. 'He was proud and I think he just wanted to let me know it,' says Cecelia. 'I could see he still had all his old feelings for them, all the love for them was still there.'

At the national titles in Melbourne, in March 1990, Cathy, now 17, was surprisingly pipped (11.77s) by NSW sprinter Fiona Blair (11.76s) in the under-18 100m. This was to become a Freeman trademark. With every step up, she needed bigger fish to fry and, lacking motivation, would just as likely lose less important races. More successful was young brother Norman, who had moved schools to join Cathy at Kooralbyn. He won gold in the under-16 100m hurdles, silver in the 200m and bronze in the 100m.

The following weekend, at Olympic Park, Cathy took on the flamboyant Jane Flemming in the Open 100m but narrowly lost, 11.70s to Flemming's 11.64s. 'Jane told me I would have won if I'd dipped at the line a bit better,' a puffing Cathy told journalists afterwards. 'I'll have to practise that.' Cathy then bounced back the next day to become the first Aborigine to win an open Australian track title, spanking the field in the 200m in 23.59s. At a wind-up party afterwards, Flemming sat talking to Cathy for an hour about her family, her running, school, rock concerts and music in general. They did not discuss the rumours of Flemming's alleged relay takeover manoeuvres in Auckland.

Cathy had beaten an unwell Kerry Johnson—who did not contest the nationals—over 200m at an Australian Institute of Sport meet in Brisbane earlier in the season. Thus Cathy's victory at the nationals took her to the top of the Mobil grand prix series for women's 200m. The prize money of $1500 was to be presented at a gala evening at the Grand Hyatt on Monday night. She had nothing to wear.

Journalist Nick Bideau, having written a feature about the brother–sister team, Cathy and Norman Freeman, was contacted by sports goods giant Nike, asking him to invite Cathy around to accept a gift of some athletic gear. He picked her up from her Carlton motel and, at Nike, was struck once more by her polite, unaffected manner. 'She didn't say, "Thanks for the gear, see you later,"' says Bideau. 'She wanted to look around, meet people, ask questions.' Afterwards Bideau drove her to Prahran where he paid for an outfit she chose to wear that evening. Why did he pay for it? 'Because she didn't have any money,' says Bideau. Obvious. 'Raelene Boyle presented me with the award,' says Cathy. 'I was excited to meet her for the first time, I hugged and hugged her. I was truly honoured.'

On 19 July 1990, Cathy left with the Australian squad for the world junior championships in Plovdiv, Bulgaria, where the meltdown of the eastern European political barriers was playing havoc with the titles. In a warm-up for the juniors, Cathy made the final of the 200m at the English AAA (Amateur Athletic Association) championships in Birmingham, and once more ran into Nick Bideau who was covering the tour for News Ltd newspapers. 'We had become quite friendly since Melbourne,' says Cathy. 'So we hung out together. It was all innocent but it became the big gossip thing of the juniors.'

That Australian junior team heralded a marvellous era in Australian athletics over the next decade, containing as it did, Cathy, plus high jumper Tim Forsyth, 17 (1992 Olympic bronze medallist), javelin thrower Joanna Stone, 17 (1997 worlds silver), sprinter Damien Marsh, 19 (1995 IAAF grand prix champion), 400m hurdler Rohan Robinson, 18 (1996 Olympic finalist), discus thrower Lisa-Marie Vizaniari, 19 (1996 Olympic finalist) and 110m hurdler Kyle Vander-Kuyp, 19 (1996 Olympic finalist). At Plovdiv Cathy, 17, came fifth in the 200m final, even though the titles are open to athletes up to the age of 20. Renee Poetschka was a member of the 4 x 400m relay which won gold and Australia finished fifth overall in the medal tally. There was one other significant result at those juniors: the 400m was won by Nigerian Fatima Yusuf in the quick time of 50.62s. Four years later she and Cathy were to be engaged in an epic duel for Commonwealth gold.

In September 1990, Cathy was once more in Melbourne, this time as part of the city's bid for the 1996 Olympics. She had flown south twice earlier in the year for rehearsals, with her manager Ian Guiver as chaperone. Each time she looked up friend Nick Bideau. 'She asked if she could go out with Nick and I agreed, provided she was back by a certain time, and she was,' says Guiver.

In Tokyo for the decision, with Guiver unable to enter the Olympic inner sanctums, Brisbane Lord Mayor Sallyanne Atkinson, with four daughters herself, kept a motherly eye on Cathy. Atkinson, experienced from Brisbane's bid for the Olympics when Barcelona won, says it was a tough week. 'Cathy looks poised and sophisticated today but, aged 17, she was still a thin, shy, overwhelmed teenager amid a lot of tough heavyweights,' she says. For the final sales pitch, Cathy was on the podium with Prime Minister Bob Hawke, Australian Olympic Council executive Kevan Gosper, Victorian Premier Joan Kirner, Moscow swimming gold medallist Michelle Ford and Atkinson.

Gosper introduced Freeman, who looked stunning in a bright red dress, and asked her if she was hoping to compete in both Barcelona and the 1996 Olympics. 'Yes, I am,' said Cathy. She had learnt her lines and which words to emphasise. 'For a young Australian athlete there is an enormous *thrill* in competing in Europe and America,' she said. 'Barcelona would be a great adventure for *me*. But *Melbourne* would be an adventure for the *rest of the world*.'

It was only a short speech, but an Indian IOC delegate

approached her afterwards and said how much it had moved him. It didn't move sufficient other IOC members, however, as Atlanta surprisingly topped Athens for 1996. Says Cathy, 'The funny thing is, the mayor of Atlanta came up and said to me quietly, "Don't worry, Sydney 2000." I just stared. I'll never forget it. It made me think, "Yeah, this bidding …"' Cathy then had to ward off foreign delegates who, mistaking her for an African-American, wanted to hug and congratulate her for Atlanta's great victory. 'Sorry, I'm Australian,' she told them tartly.

On the flight home, sitting in the 747's upper deck bubble, the bid team drowned their disappointment while Cathy curled up on a lounge and slept. Next day, 19 September, the Melbourne *Sun*'s 1.5 million daily readers were treated to a huge front-page photograph of Hawke planting a kiss on Freeman's cheek. She had completely overshadowed Michelle Ford, who had addressed the IOC in French.

Freeman's profile spiralled. She was about to graduate from school: what next? 'Not once did I ever consider getting a degree from university,' says Cathy. 'I didn't do the right subjects and I wasn't interested. People go to university to get degrees for careers to earn money. I wanted to do it through athletics.' But not, at that stage, if she had to train too hard. On her last day of school Cathy and a friend decided they would skip training and hide under their beds when staff came looking for them. Says Danila, 'I said, "Where's Cathy? It's time for training. Everyone can miss training but not Cathy."' He suspected they were hiding in the high grass on hills overlooking the track, having a laugh at his expense, so he traipsed around calling out. Finally, disgusted, he rushed back down the hill, straight into a barbed-wire fence, gashing his leg so badly he needed an anti-tetanus injection. Says Cathy, 'We thought we were really clever, but I felt guilty so we surfaced. And there he was, so angry, with blood dripping from his leg. He made us feel that bad we went and trained anyway.' Cathy's school days were over and in early 1991

Ian Guiver negotiated a two-year deal which enabled her to transfer from the school to the Kooralbyn Valley Resort. She would be tutored in hotel management, health and fitness, and remain close to both coach Danila and her family in Brisbane. 'It was worth $25,000 a year, a big figure in those days,' says Guiver. 'Then along came Nick.'

8.
OUR OWN LITTLE FLO JO.
MELBOURNE, 1991

On New Year's Day 1991, Nick Bideau, 30, driving a florid red hire car, came whipping through the winding turns and giddying hills towards Kooralbyn International School. He'd been sitting around in Melbourne, bored, when spontaneously, and precipitously, he jumped on a flight to Brisbane. Even as he drove south he was telling himself, 'This is dangerous. She's much younger than me. She's already well known. I shouldn't do this.' But he didn't turn around. He enjoyed Cathy Freeman's company and he knew she had fun with him. For her part, Cathy had regularly rung him reverse charges from Kooralbyn.

So, past the Kooralbyn equestrian stables, through the empty school grounds, under the jacaranda trees Nick drove, to the sports oval, where Cathy, alone in her rural world, was stretching prior to afternoon training. 'I was in a really happy mood, thinking about my childhood and people I'd known in Mackay,' says Cathy. 'I had this big grin on my face when this shiny red car came through the school gates. I'm looking and looking and thinking, "Who's this?" Until it pulls up and it's Nick! I had no idea he was coming. But I was really happy to see him. We were both so excited. He said he'd been doing 140 on the highway. It was very romantic. A classic scene of the Prince Charming kind.'

Says Nick, 'She was sitting on this grass oval, not a soul around. I said to her, "There's more to life than this. If you want to be a good athlete, come to Melbourne where there's proper tracks, good facilities and the best runners to train with."' His arrival wasn't all serendipity. Nick had questioned her closely on her training schedules, and he had been to Kooralbyn once before. In October 1990, Nick had visited his sister in Darwin, and stopped off in Brisbane on his way home. He had driven to Kooralbyn, picked up Catherine and returned to Brisbane where they had lunch with Cecelia in the city. Bideau uses three names, Catherine to her face, Cathy in the third person, and occasionally Freeman when he's talking about her professionally.

Cecelia, Bruce, the whole family eyed Nick suspiciously. Says Cathy, 'My elder brother, Gavin, said, "He must want something," insinuating, you know ... He was being protective. It was the age difference mainly. I was still a teenager.' Nick was unconcerned. 'I don't blame them,' he says. 'But I wasn't going to hurt her. I just sensed her career needed guidance, and I knew I could help. It's one of the things I get a thrill out of in life. And she was great company, she made me laugh all the time.'

Cathy trusted Nick—a newspaper reporter—enough to tell him she'd been selected Young Australian of the Year, not announced publicly until Australia Day, 26 January, at the Sydney Opera House. For the third time in a year—her Commonwealth Games gold, the Melbourne Olympic bid and now Young Oz—she had to respond to questions about the Aboriginal condition. 'It's important for my people that we get up and make a future for ourselves,' she said. 'The opportunities are there, I've proven it. I'm an example.'

Academics argue that black sporting success also blinds people to the basic inequalities of race; that not all Aborigines can be Cathy Freeman, so don't throw her up as a typical success. But Cathy's words were pro-active, guilt-freeing; the sort of tone that white Australia likes to hear. She was her own best public relations propagandist. Yet at other times she was more sanguine. At the investiture at Government House in Kirribilli, she was pushed into the background, as though her usefulness as a political gesture was past. 'I had three strikes against me—I was black, I was female and I was young,' she told me back then. 'I suppose I was better off than Stevie Wonder, though—I wasn't blind and I wasn't poor.'

She says the best part of the day was meeting Australian of the Year, the late Professor Fred Hollows, with whom she had an instant rapport. 'He was a saint, but also a bit of a devil at the same time,' she says. 'He was rough, a hard worker, swore a bit, always told it how it was, but he loved his family and had an absolute heart of gold.' There was an extra dimension. One of Fred's link men with Aborigines, Clarrie Grogan, was Cathy's great-uncle. Uncle Clarrie, a much repected elder, was also related to Newcastle rugby league winger Brett Grogan. Clarrie appeared on the 'Midday Show' on the Nine Network, playing the gum leaf and recounting Aboriginal history. When he died a few years later the 'Midday Show' announced his passing. Hollows and his wife Gabi invited Cathy to their home and Fred made plans for Cathy to travel with his eye surgery team into the outback. 'But he was busy, and then it got a bit late,' says Cathy grimly. 'The last thing he said to me was, "Keep running, Cathy." He was one of my all-time top blokes.'

And still the fame came. Jeff McMullen of '60 Minutes' spent a week with her preparing a program. Asked what she thought of her coach, Mike Danila, she replied, 'Good but tough, tough, tough.' In truth, back in Kooralbyn, Cathy was feeling the isolation, especially when Danila left for a coaching stint in Fiji. 'I felt I needed a change,' says Cathy. 'I guess I started making those sort of decisions, to move on, at an early age without consciously knowing it.'

When Danila returned he saw that Cathy had put on weight over the Christmas break. It is important to remember that an overweight athlete still looks svelte to the untrained eye. Cathy was not overweight in the normal sense of the word. Danila complained to Bideau when he visited once, 'I tell Cathy she needs to lose weight, to stop eating, but she won't.' Bideau laughed and replied, 'That might work in Romania, but it doesn't work like that here. You don't say "Stop eating!" and they stop. Here, people are free to do as they please. You have to find another way.' In due course Bideau himself found the way, and if there was a university chair in studying methods to motivate Freeman to achieve her potential, Bideau held it.

Cathy normally raced, rather than trained, herself into shape. But at the Queensland titles on 10 February 1991, six days before she turned 18, her relay mate, Monique Dunstan, tipped her out in the 100m, clocking 11.68s to Cathy's 11.81s. Cathy backed up to win the 400m and admitted ruefully afterwards, 'Maybe the 400m will be my specialist event now.' Not quite yet. In the nationals at Sydney Athletic Field a month later, defending her 200m title, Cathy showed she had courage if not fitness. She told Bideau before the race, 'I'm going to qualify for the world championships here.' Bideau, like Danila, looked at her and thought, 'Phew! There's no way you're fit enough for that.' Cathy led into the straight with Esther Paolo, of Perth, challenging. Ten metres to go, Cathy was falling apart but wouldn't give in, threw herself over the line and deadheated first with Paolo in 23.50s.

Unfortunately she hadn't quite perfected Jane Flemming's dip, dived through the air and landed heavily on her chest and head. In the post-race interview she appeared dazed and on the track doctor's advice, Bideau called a cab and took her to casualty at the Prince of Wales hospital in Randwick. They kept her under observation for four hours, and she was sufficiently concussed to withdraw from the 100m the following day.

Freeman's desperate dive was a glimpse of the will to win that a world or Olympic champion must possess. 'When she was beaten, she still wouldn't lose,' says Bideau, admiringly. 'She had that fight in her.' But her times were going backwards: same race, 23.36s in 1990, 23.50 in 1991. That night, in Steve Moneghetti's hotel room, they watched her on '60 Minutes' as, with her photogenic features and wide, wide laugh, she charmed the lenses and reporter McMullen.

Back at the Kooralbyn Valley Resort, her job seemed small beer after the dizzying heights to which she had so swiftly climbed. 'Actually, it was too much, too soon,' she says in retrospect. 'For what I'd achieved, I got way too much attention.' She fell out with the resort management and turned her gaze upon the vision of a different future which Nick Bideau had drawn for her—in Melbourne, the athletic headquarters of Australia.

Mike Danila and manager Ian Guiver saw it coming when Cathy announced, 'I'm going to Melbourne.' Danila had several other national age champions in his squad, but Cathy was easily his biggest star. He was sad to lose her, but his career was at Kooralbyn. Guiver, who had set up a trust for her, with her parents as directors, had signed Cathy to a three-year contract. But if she wanted to withdraw it was her choice, he said generously.

That just left the family. Says Bruce Barber, 'When we heard of this relationship with Nick we tried to break it up, because he was a lot older than her. Also the way he went about things, writing letters, and turning up at Kooralbyn without informing us first. No, we didn't get off to a good start. Although I will say this now, with hindsight, that everything that he did was for her benefit.' Did Bideau try to explain that his motives were genuine? 'Bruce didn't give him a chance,' says Cecelia. She, too, acknowledges her initial misgivings but says that if Cathy hadn't gone, she would not have the life she now enjoys. 'To me it was the shock of it all,' she says. 'It felt like I was losing my other daughter. I cried, but she just went.'

And Cathy? 'Looking back it must have been hard for Mum,' she says. 'She would have been still grieving for Anne-Marie. And now her little girl was leaving. I listen to my Mum but, at the end of the day, I was always going to do what I was going to do. She begged me not to go, but I just stood there looking at her and didn't let it affect me.' Bideau witnessed this trauma in the Acacia Ridge home, distressed by his role in the tableau, but mightily impressed by Cathy's stony determination.

'They kept telling me to tell her not to go, but I said I wasn't going to tell her what to do,' says Bideau. 'Besides I thought it would be right for her. I told them I'd help however I could.' Cecelia later pleaded with Ian Guiver to intercede. Guiver told her, 'Cecelia, I don't think you're going to win this one and the last thing you want is to become alienated from your daughter.'

What gave Cathy confidence was that Nanna—her grandmother Alice Sibley who was held in great regard by the whole family—liked Bideau. He had accompanied Cathy to Mackay on one of her Young Australian of the Year trips especially to meet Alice Sibley. 'Nanna loved him, they got on really well,' says Cathy. 'And I trusted Nanna.'

Having established that she could stay with Bideau initially in Melbourne, Cathy flew with an Australian squad to the Mt Sac relays, California, in late April 1991. The 4 x 100m relay team needed to run a qualifying time for the world championships to be held in Tokyo that August. The worlds are held every second year to give track and field athletes competition between Olympics. As a specialist track and field event, the qualifying standards are often a little tougher than for the Olympics. To squad mate, Monique Dunstan, it seemed Cathy was drifting from athletics. 'On that trip she seemed to lose a lot of her oomph compared with the previous year,' says Dunstan. But Freeman was in

1936. Cathy's paternal grandfather, Frank Fisher (centre with ball), with the Cherbourg rugby league team. The touring Great Britain team said they had never seen such a talented player.

Left: 1936. Frank Fisher, known as 'Big Shot'. A charismatic man, he was a champion sprinter and, according to his son, 'as strong as a scrub bull'.
Right: 1950. George Sibley (sitting), Cathy's maternal grandfather. He fought all around Queensland with the Jimmy Sharman boxing troupe. His sparring partner here is the great Jack Hassen, former Australian lightweight champion. (*Photo*: courtesy of Alick Jackomos)

1973. Cathy's father, Norman Freeman (back row, second from left), in the Magpies rugby league team, Mackay. Norman, 33 here, was nicknamed 'Twinkle Toes' for his elusive running and speed.

Left: 1937. Annie Ah Sam, Cathy's great-grandmother—George Sibley's mother. Her mother, Maggie, was a member of the Kundijn tribe, from north-east of Croydon, and her father, Tommy Ah Sam, was a gold prospector from Kwang-Tung province in China.
Right: 1990. Alice Sibley, Cathy's grandmother—Cecelia's mother—a member of the Stolen Generation. Her mother was Dora Brook, of the Kuku-Yalanji tribe, near Tully. Her father was Syrian migrant, Willie Assad.

1973. Catherine Astrid Salome Freeman—at her christening with Cecelia, Norman and big brother Gavin. Salome was the name of an old Torres Strait woman, a neighbour of Cecelia's.

1974. Balmy days for Cecelia and Norman in Mackay, years before he was diagnosed as a diabetic. He so prided himself on his strong health, the discovery devastated him.

1979. Cathy, aged 6, with her sister Anne-Marie, 15, and Cecelia. Anne-Marie was born with cerebral palsy but could communicate basic needs. It broke the family's heart not to have her at home.

1980. Peas in a pod. The three youngest Freemans—Cathy, 7; Garth (left) 4; and Norman, 6. Cathy and Norman, both equally shy and athletic, were close during their school years.

1983. Cathy, 10, in her St Francis, Hughenden, school uniform. It was on the school's dusty oval that Cathy's stepfather, Bruce Barber, watching her train, first had his vision of her as an Olympian.

1983. Sydney. Cathy, 10, all skinny legs and arms in lane eight for her first national championships. She came third in the 100m.

1986. Anne-Marie, 22, with a trophy for horse-riding. With her large brown eyes and cheerful mien she looked not unlike Cathy, and made an impact upon all who met her.

1984. Melbourne. Cathy, 11, at the Pacific Schools Games. With her distinctive long stride, she won her first national titles—the 200m and high jump, and came second in the 100m.

1990. Auckland. In the Commonwealth Games village, with the amusing Ezinwa twins, Davidson (left) and Osmond, world-class sprinters from Nigeria. They later became Cathy's friends on the Euro-circuit.

1990. Auckland. In the Games village with an idol, Jamaican Merlene Ottey, already one of the most prolific medallists in women's sprinting. A few years later Cathy was racing her in Europe.

1990. Auckland. The nearly-didn't-make-it gold medal winning 4 x 100m relay team. Left to right, Monique Dunstan, Kerry Johnson, Kathy Sambell and Cathy.

1990. Kooralbyn. At the International School Cathy, gold medal and her Romanian-born school coach, Mike Danila. He knew her potential and wanted to take her to stardom.

1992. Seoul. Cathy with her silver medal in the 200m at the world junior titles. Bronze medallist Merlene Fraser, of Jamaica, became a well-known senior runner, not so the winner, Hu C, of China.

1991. Prime Minister Bob Hawke is delighted to award Young Australian of the Year to Cathy on 26 January 1991. Cathy knew Hawke from when they were both on the Melbourne bid for the 1996 Olympics.

1991. Australia Day. Cecelia and Bruce Barber join Cathy, 18, for the evening's celebrations. Bruce worked tirelessly to assist Cathy's career.

1991. Sydney. Anything to win. After leading in the straight, Cathy deadheats first with Esther Paolo, of Perth, in the national 200m final.

Her dip on the line turns into a dive as she stumbles in her desperation to hold off Paolo. Watching this, sportswriter Nick Bideau saw a champion's true grit.

Prone, she looks up to check the result. She hit her head so hard in her fall that she later developed slight concussion and had to withdraw from the 100m the next day.

1992. The enigmatic Norman Freeman, 17, who had all the speed of his father and grandfather. Champion English sprinter Linford Christie wanted to take Norman overseas to train. Norman preferred footy.

Left: 1990. Woorabinda. Cathy with her father, Norman, after she won her Commonwealth Games relay gold in Auckland. Norman, though immensely proud of her, warned her not to get a big head.
Right: 1993. Cathy, 20, in her Balarinji running one-piece. Balarinji was Cathy's first sponsor. The synergy was astonishing, as both athlete and sponsor thrived.

1991. Raelene Boyle remains Australia's premier sprinter of the last 20 years and coached Cathy for a short time. The partnership did not last, the friendship did.

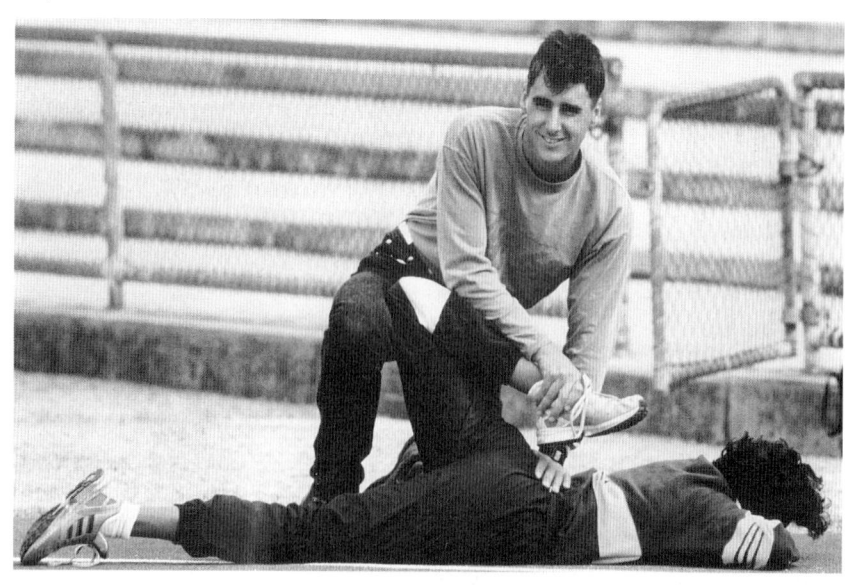

1991. Melbourne. Cathy's then partner and manager, Nick Bideau, stretches her quadricep muscles at Olympic Park. Cathy is so flexible her heels almost flick her bottom as she runs.

1991. Alice Springs. With eye surgeon Fred Hollows, who was Australian of the Year when Cathy was Young Australian of the Year. Cathy said he was a bit of a devil with a heart of gold.

Left: 1992. Cathy's father, good-natured Norman 'Fringey' Freeman in his later years. He continued to inspire powerful emotions in Cathy even after his death.
Right: 1993. Cathy has three brothers and enjoys belonging to an extended family. Here she and Nick Bideau pose with Gavin jnr, eldest son of her eldest brother, Gavin snr.

1992. Barcelona. The women's 4 x 400m relay at the Olympic Games, left to right: Cathy, Susan Andrews, Renee Poetschka and Michelle Lock. No medal but all delighted to have reached the final and run seventh.
(*Photo:* courtesy of Sporting Pix)

1992. Barcelona. The 4 x 400m relay. Cathy, 19, beautifully relaxed compared to the Canadian runner inside her. She was fast but clearly still physically immature.
(*Photo:* courtesy of Sporting Pix)

1992. Near Geraldton, Western Australia. After the Olympics, back to the bush and a professional gift race. To Aboriginal kids, Cathy was more famous than any film star.

1993. Cathy, 20, goes national as cover story of *The Age*'s Good Weekend colour magazine. The photographer brought the unusual outfit along for the shoot. (*Photo:* courtesy of *The Age*)

1993. Woorabinda. Wandering alone at her father's graveside. She wrote to him, rang him, visited him, but was in England when he died.

1995. Mackay. A memorial rugby league match in her father's honour. Note his picture on her jersey. She made the Queensland schoolgirls' touch football side herself.

1993. With her Nanna, Alice Sibley. Cathy was very close to her, but heard only snippets of Alice's bitter childhood experiences.

good spirits, according to Kathy Sambell. 'I have this enduring vision in my head,' she says. 'She was pampering her skin and we walked into her room and there, staring back at us, was a white clay face mask with Cathy's eyes peeping out and her mouth wide open laughing. She looked like the black and white minstrel show. I just wish I'd taken a photo.'

Cathy rang Bideau from Los Angeles and, instead of returning to Brisbane, flew directly to Melbourne, staying at his South Yarra apartment. She had already given him her belongings from Kooralbyn. A few days later, Cathy answered the telephone—a reporter from the *Truth* newspaper welcoming her to Melbourne. 'He was asking me these questions,' says Cathy. 'I was chatting away and at the end I said, "Hey, you are my friend, aren't you?" That's how naive I was.'

Former Olympic long jumper, Gary Honey, called Nick and warned him that a *Truth* reporter had rung and was trying to build a story about Nick and Cathy. That weekend Nick walked to the newsagent expecting to have to search for some small story, only to be confronted by the *Truth*'s front page banner headline: OLYMPIC STAR LOVE TURMOIL! He flustered as he fumbled for coins to buy the paper. 'It was one of those moments when I wanted to buy every newspaper in the shop,' says Nick.

His friend, accountant Peter Jess, advised Bideau to say nothing. Said Jess, 'The moment you say something, whatever you say will put the heat back into it. Let it roll and it will die.' It did and Bideau employed this policy from then on, never feed the flames, let controversy starve from lack of fuel. But the publicity was what Bideau had most feared. 'When I started with Cathy I knew I had better take it seriously, because there were big players out there watching,' he says. 'Bob Hawke was a fan, the Olympic committee loved her, Athletics Australia were asking questions, you could just sense it. I couldn't afford to make a mistake. I was treading on eggshells.

'Actually, I thought that by the time she turned 20, and she'd been overseas, met other athletes, she would have that many options, what would she be interested in me for? That's how I expected it to go, that she'd take off. All I knew then was that I wasn't going to let her down. But the *Truth* story was good, because it taught me never to be in the media with her again.' It had another beneficial side effect, for Cathy. 'It was funny,' she says. 'I think the headline shocked the people on the Australia Day council because I wasn't asked to do many engagements for them after that.'

She was chosen in the 4 x 100m relay squad for the Tokyo worlds and, on the strength of this, appeared on Bruce McAvaney's 'Sportsworld' with Raelene Boyle. After the show, Bideau and McAvaney co-opted Boyle, triple Olympic silver medallist behind juiced-up East Germans in the 1970s, to train Freeman. Bideau knew Boyle wouldn't take it on permanently, but he also knew her presence would keep other coaches from Cathy's doorstep until he could suss out a long-term coach. 'I had my life in order, I was studying horticulture and working with Prahran council,' says Boyle. 'I didn't have the time but I said I'd do it as an interim thing. Cathy was totally out of condition so I set a program to get her fit for the world champs.' Within weeks, rifts appeared. Cathy wanted to take the day off to go horse-riding, to go shopping, to get her hair done. She had $300 worth of extensions put in to make it look longer, and was late to the track. Boyle found herself sitting around Olympic Park, waiting. 'One thing in my career, I was never late for training,' says Boyle firmly. 'I had spent 20 years at the track and I didn't want it over again.'

In desperation she called the AFL's only Aboriginal umpire, Glenn James, who organised some of the faster young umpires, two of whom ran the 1997 grand final, to train with Cathy at Olympic Park. James's daughter Seona was close to Cathy's age, and the family took Cathy out for a meal to help her settle into Melbourne.

But she had no family, no job, no close friends and no money. Bideau became her benefactor and remained so until her talent blossomed and fame brought her sponsorships and financial independence. But for now, under the stress of the move south, the publicity, and a bitterly cold spell, Cathy's health collapsed.

She was admitted to the Royal Women's Hospital for a week with a bacterial infection. Her only other visitor besides Bideau was Boyle. When she recovered she moved into a house which Bideau had bought in Miller Street, Richmond, the house where Cathy and I met to talk. She had lost weight, but it was not a healthy weight loss, she looked wan, small and thin.

One morning, about six weeks after Boyle began coaching Cathy, Raelene called in for a heart-to-heart reality chat. She would no longer coach Freeman, she said. First she put Cathy's Commonwealth relay gold in perspective. 'You've gained great accolades for that, it carries some weight but in world terms, it's pretty meaningless.' Then she put her to rights about potential. 'You've got a lot of ability, but so what? So did I. Those who win Olympic gold are just as talented as you, but they work hard too. Unless you're prepared to do that, you'll go nowhere. If you get serious, I think you could be Olympic semi-finalist material, which would be a pretty good achievement.' It was a tough message, but Raelene knew she had to pull Freeman into gear. 'She was still trying to find her place in the scheme of things back then,' says Boyle. 'Cathy enjoyed the company of the elite, liked to rub shoulders with the Dawn Frasers, the Carl Lewises, leading the star life, but she hadn't really earned it.'

For Cathy, Boyle's words were unforgettable. 'She's a tough, frank woman, Raelene, very sensitive, but she got her message across,' says Cathy. 'She said that if I ever wanted to be somebody I had to stop being as casual as I was. It was one of the most important conversations I've ever had. We both had lumps in our throats when she finished. She was great, she was great, Boyley.' But Cathy had one final, painful, lesson to learn.

She had scraped into the relay squad of six runners, from which four would be chosen for the relay in Tokyo but felt her form improved in a training camp in Darwin. She told Bideau several times, 'I'm really looking forward to getting there and running.' Kathy Sambell, competing for a place in the relay, says now, 'I don't know whether Cathy would admit it, but she wasn't running well.' Monique Dunstan agrees that Cathy seemed to have lost a little heart for running, but Dunstan was annoyed at the last minute selection process anyway. 'It was just ridiculous, never knowing until the eleventh hour,' she says. 'How can a team prepare when they don't know the team?'

In Tokyo, coach Nancy Atterton omitted Freeman from the relay, naming Kerry Johnson, Sambell, Dunstan and Melissa Moore. That day Bideau walked up to the team's headquarters in the elegant Takinawa Prince hotel, and wandered past the exquisite ikebana arrangements in the lobby, sensing disappointment. There, amid the richly upholstered chairs, he found a disconsolate Freeman. 'I'm not running,' said Cathy. 'I'm not in the team.' Then as tears welled up, 'Don't they understand how good I can be?' It was the first time Nick had ever heard Cathy acclaim her own ability. He was astonished that Freeman assumed others accepted that she was the future of Australian running. Cathy told Nick vehemently, 'That's the last time, the very last time I'm going to be in a team just for the relay. From now on I'll be in for my own event.' It was a watershed promise, the like of which she was to make several more times in her career, and she lived up to every one. Bideau shrugs his shoulders. 'They didn't understand her, she didn't understand them,' he says.

Atterton says she would put the same team on the track tomorrow in the same circumstances. 'Quite frankly, at that time Cathy had lost total direction,' she says. 'Either she wasn't well or she'd lost application. I'm very surprised Cathy didn't know she wasn't going to run, that she wasn't in the top four.' Assistant manager Margaret Mahony, a good friend to Freeman, supports Atterton. 'It was a foregone conclusion,' she says. 'I think Cathy knew she wasn't running well.'

Freeman won't lie down. 'Some people can see an athlete's inner ability, and Nancy just didn't have a head for it,' she says. 'Anyone who has watched me knows I run above myself in competition. Maybe they were right, maybe I wasn't fit.' 'Well, they all agree you weren't in form,' I ventured to Cathy. 'Yeah, but I went on to win a world championship being out of form, too,' says Cathy.

Atterton doesn't back off, either. 'You get an athlete of Cathy's calibre, who everyone bends over backwards to help,' she says. 'They can't understand that anybody will ever take a negative approach to them, whether they're running well or otherwise. Being dropped was entirely of Cathy's own making. But I said to myself then, "This will either make or break her," and it damn well made her. All she had to do was get her mind on the job.'

In truth, the runner most hardly done by was young Sydney sprinter, Melinda Gainsford, who was probably the second fastest in Australia behind Kerry Johnson at that stage. 'That year the senior winner at the nationals ran 11.61s and I won the juniors in 11.62s,' says Melinda. 'They took six girls away but they didn't take me. Their excuse was that I didn't run the seniors, but that was a poor excuse because they've always taken juniors for relays in the past and still do.' That omission fired Gainsford up. 'I thought, "OK, fine, if I'm going to make a team I'll make sure there's no shadow of a doubt."' So the relay selectors inadvertently gave the two girls who were to dominate Australian sprinting for the next decade, identical motivation for their careers ahead.

For 10 days Freeman sat, utterly frustrated, sick of watching day after day of athletics without setting foot on the track herself. It was Auckland revisited, only worse. It was a super meet, as Carl Lewis set a world record in the 100m, and Mike Powell broke the longstanding long jump world record. The Aussie women's 4 x 100m relay came eighth in the final. Despite, or perhaps because of, all her awards and honours, Cathy had gone from being a Commonwealth Games relay gold medallist to a mere relay reserve in 18 months. 'I took it personally. I was hurt, yeah,' she says, quietly. 'And ooohh, it made me so much more determined, that whole thing.'

After the worlds, Bideau remembered a coach who he thought might suit Freeman—Peter Fortune, who had coached the 1984 Australian 400m champion Gary Minihan. But Fortune, an avuncular Victorian public servant, had wound down his coaching and was now racing touring cars. He was not keen to re-enter athletics. Bideau consulted his friend, Chris Wardlaw—Steve Moneghetti's coach—who knew Fortune well, and at Wardlaw's request, Fortune agreed to meet Freeman. Bideau felt confident. In person, Freeman is irresistible. 'I've always had a problem saying no,' says Fortune ruefully. What swung him was that maybe one athlete wouldn't be so bad. And she was an interesting case, with her social justice implications. 'When we met, she was quite outgoing,' he says. 'She looked me over and—this impressed me—at the door she sealed it with a hug, which said sort of, "I'm accepting you as my coach."' Wardlaw was pleased at his own matchmaking. 'Fort's got a marvellous way of teaching young athletes to relax in their running,' he says. 'He doesn't knock the stuffing out of them training.' Sure sounded like Cathy's sort of coach.

Domestically, Cathy and Nick gradually settled in to a life together. Nick had met few Aborigines in his life, though he had admired their sporting figureheads, such as Lionel Rose and Evonne Goolagong-Cawley. He found Cathy to be uninterested in material gains and to share without regard for herself. 'Nick's funny with money. He didn't like me giving handouts, or spending it on this or that,' she says. Nick found her to be sensation oriented—'I don't feel good,' she'd regularly say to him at training, which could mean she felt off-colour, or that she didn't feel good *about* something. He was always discovering something new about her. One night, after lights out, he started to say something and she said, 'Shoosh, not now, I'm praying.' Her mother is Baha'i, but her father, Norman, and her Nanna were Catholic. She never prayed for success and, as she grew older, her faith broadened to embrace a universal belief in God. She could not enlighten Bideau about Aboriginal spirituality because she had been culturally disenfranchised by white schools herself.

Did it occur to her that a time would come when an older, sophisticated journalist, and a young, inexperienced athlete would grow apart? 'It didn't matter,' she says. 'We were happy together. I think about the future, but I live each day.' She also recognised that Bideau played many different roles as her partner, not the least of which was that he networked and could make things happen for her. 'When a girl goes without her natural father, you want to replace him,' she says. 'It's easy to see that Nick was my father, my older brother, my best friend, my manager and so on.' She's high maintenance, mate, Bideau's friends said doubtfully, watching Cathy ring the changes in Bideau's life.

Cathy had never learnt to cook, and so became inculcated into Bideau's stir fries, vegetable salads and fruit, backed by Nick's ascetic health philosophy which may best be summarised as any food is too much. He sat amazed as Cathy would declare herself on a diet and then order a huge piece of carrot cake. 'It's a health food, good for you,' she'd tell him. He'd reply, 'That icing sugar and cream on top, that good for you, too?'

Cathy in turn grew used to the friends Nick constantly had as boarders—Fitzroy footballer Brett Stephens, long jumper David Culbert, marathoner Garry Henry. 'I spent a lot more time in the company of men than women,' she says. 'I put up with their jokes and their conversations about sport. It was good in one way, I learnt a lot about men. But it was, yeah, what about the girl? Because us girls *are* different.'

It was through the Fitzroy connection that she met her best friend, Peta Powell, a computer consultant, who was to prove a sanctuary away from athletics in years to come. Powell, a 54s-plus 400m runner began picking Cathy up to take her training when Raelene Boyle was still her coach. 'She'd often have an excuse not to go,' says Powell. 'She wasn't a very motivated person in those days.' Cathy invited Powell to train with her, and when asked how Peter Fortune would react, Cathy said, 'If I want you to train with me, you'll be training with me.' And Powell did. Says Powell, 'That's when I first knew she had her own voice, though you didn't hear it much in those early days.'

It is relevant to note that even in those days, Nick and Cathy had their conflicts. 'Me and my boyfriend used to think we should just walk away and leave them to it,' says Powell. 'And sometimes we did.' Peter Jess concurs. 'They fought from the outset,' he says. 'It was like a war zone sometimes. Half the time I was sent in for light relief, or if it wasn't me it was Fortune. I used to feel exhausted.'

One night Nick came home very late after a big night out and, at 3 a.m., found Cathy in a nearby park feeding possums. 'I was just a kid who got jealous,' says Cathy, laughing with embarrassment. But it reminded her of her father—excessive alcohol equalled unreliability, leading to arguments and suffering. 'You've been drinking,' she'd say, if Nick had a beer after work. Says Nick, 'Occasionally I forgot about the extra responsibility I had.' He modified his single man's habits. And encouraged her independence.

He gave her a few driving lessons, she took a few more from an instructor, and then Nick pushed a protesting

Freeman out of the door to get her licence. 'No, no,' said Cathy. 'I can't do this, there are heaps of things I haven't done. I haven't even reverse parked yet!' Nick had seen enough of her skill to know she could already drive better than most people on the road. 'Go, go,' said Nick. 'You can do it.' She got it, and was thrilled. Says Nick, 'I used to love that sort of achievement as much as she did.' He suggested she find a job. She did, and organised herself to start work in a sandwich bar in Brunswick. That impressed Bideau, Young Australian of the Year, willing to start work in a sandwich bar. But a sprinter, on her feet all day? Not likely! Nick knew John Toleman, a former professional distance runner, who owned a store called Sportsworld in Cheltenham. Toleman had once managed John Smith, an American sprinter who, when he retired, became Marie-José Pérec's coach. Toleman, a larger than life character with a roguish humour, gave Cathy a job and became one of her most ardent supporters. Cathy caught the train to Cheltenham, worked for four hours, and came back to train that evening. Then in early 1992, Australia Post offered her a place in their Olympic Job Opportunities Program.

It was no sinecure. Cathy stood behind the counter in the GPO serving people, thus encountering her first adult racial ignorance as people refused to queue to be served by her. Other times, even in major hotels, she and Nick would enter a lift and find other guests hovering, waiting for the next lift to arrive. 'See that?' she'd nudge Bideau. 'They wouldn't get into a lift with a black person.' Nick never noticed, but he believed her. Says Cathy, 'I wasn't paranoid. I could smell it a mile away. I used to think, "What's wrong? I'm not bad, am I?" I tried not to let it affect me, even though I wanted to burst into tears sometimes, because that's how I felt.'

One weekend Bideau took Freeman to a charity football match and then on to a hotel in North Carlton. Suddenly, after a few drinks, Dickie Merton, a controversial figure in Melbourne football and horseracing circles, climbed up on a bar stool and called out, 'Hang on everyone, I want to pay tribute to Australia's own little Flo Jo, a great champion, *Cathy Freeman*!' He proposed a toast as Nick and Cathy shrank several sizes with embarrassment. She still hadn't won an individual international race, but it was almost as though Australia was willing her to succeed.

Her encounter with her accountant, pony-tailed Melbourne sports eccentric, Peter Jess, couldn't have been more paradoxical—he was a more fierce critic of white Australia than she was. 'She may not embrace it as I do, but she understands that the history of Australia is a nonsense because it's only written from a 200-year-old perspective,' he says. Jess also saw Cathy's relationship with Bideau differently. 'In one sense Nick was a latter day Pygmalion, teaching her a whole range of life skills that she didn't have,' he says. 'But to me, Cathy found Nick, no question. She's a stunning lady. Very mentally tough. Catherine reminds me of a sleek panther—you can't hear it, you can't see it, until it's upon you ... and then it's got you. I'm just in awe of her power. I perceive her as an indigenous Boadicea. She's from one of the few true warrior classes that we have.'

Because Cathy was so young when Ian Guiver set up Catherine Freeman Sports in Brisbane, Cecelia and Bruce were sole directors and shareholders, with a licence to operate the company. Jess established a separate structure with control handed to Cathy, which caused Cecelia and Bruce great angst. Could they trust Bideau and Jess? Cathy obviously did.

To round off Cathy's Melbourne attachments, Bideau introduced her to Garry Miritis, sports masseur to many of the country's top athletes, and international visitors too, such as Olympic 100m champion Donovan Bailey. She still visits Miritis twice a week for preventative massage. Freeman was supple, built like a greyhound, says Miritis, and exceptionally strong for someone of her size.

One day, in November 1991, Cathy, Nick and Brett

Stephens were running 100m sprints on the tan track beside the river in Melbourne's Botanical Gardens. Picnickers at barbecues watched amused as the slim, light-stepping girl gave the blokes a good start and flew past them with a few metres to go. Stephens resolved to fix Cathy's wagon. They'd race her up the track on Anderson Street hill where strength counted, not speed, or so they thought. Says Cathy, 'Oh, those men, they couldn't sprint over short distances, and more important, they were even worse uphill.'

The first few runs Cathy started first, the lads caught her halfway and they stayed together to the top. The last of six, Brett tells Nick, 'We've got her covered here, mate, we'll belt her.' But Nick had run with her plenty of times and knew better. Says Nick, 'Stephens took off, I followed but he left me for dead, and then came Cathy. At the top she was 20m in front of him and 25m in front of me. She was running for 35s up a 220m hill and I thought, "Gee, she's got some lactic tolerance, this girl."' The major ingredient for running the 400m.

Another day, a friend of Bideau's, 1976 Montreal 1500m Olympic champion, John Walker, watched Cathy walk back down after running each hill sprint. Walker called out, 'What are you doing walking back down? Jog back if you really want to get fit.' On the way home Cathy told Nick wonderingly, 'That Walker, he's a wooden man, isn't he!' Nick laughed. Walker—veteran of 100 sub-four minute miles—in 1990, aged 38, could still run 3m 55s for the mile.

The first grand prix meeting of the 1991–92 season, an Olympic year, was scheduled in Hobart and Bideau asked national competitions manager Brian Roe to include Freeman in the 400m. 'Nick, we don't have these races for you to use as training races for young girl athletes,' Roe told Bideau. 'If she's good enough she can compete.' Roe was about to leave Olympic Park but Nick appealed to him, 'Before you go home, stay and watch this four by four, she's running a leg.' Roe sighed and agreed.

CATHY FREEMAN—A JOURNEY JUST BEGUN

Cathy anchored her club's 4 x 400m relay and was handed the baton some 25 metres behind the leader, Danielle Perpoli, who now runs for Italy. Cathy flew after Perpoli, ran her down and won with a 52s-plus lap. Bideau turned to an impressed Roe and said, 'I told you this girl's a good runner. Now what about that Hobart 400m?' Roe pursed his lips and replied, mock-thoughtfully, 'Yeees, well, I'll see if I can fit her in somewhere!'

9.
LESSONS IN LACTIC. PRE-OLYMPICS, 1992

Cathy was nervous. She was keen. She was jumpy. She was anxious, excited, all that. But so was her coach, Peter Fortune. He was shaking. He wasn't quite sure whether she was making him nervous or he'd transferred his nerves to her. They were in Adelaide in early March for the trials for the 1992 Barcelona Olympics and the 400m was a few minutes away. Three of her rivals for selection, Sharon Stewart, Michelle Lock and Renee Poetschka, who was returning from injury, were in the field. Nick Bideau had asked Freeman earlier in the day how she intended to run the race. Said Cathy, 'I'm going to go out hard today.' Bideau thought to himself that was fine because now he'd see what she could really run. But he tempered his thoughts immediately with a caution to Cathy, 'Don't go out too hard, will you?'

When Nick saw Fortune later that day he warned him to be careful with Cathy in the warm-up. 'Keep her calm,' he said. 'She wants to go out hard here. Make sure she doesn't go mad.' But Cathy wasn't listening to Nick or Fortune. 'I was fired up, so fired up,' she says. 'My expectations in my head far exceeded what I could physically do.'

Away. Cathy burst through the first 200m in 23.30s. The crowd went 'Whoooo ...' On television, commentator Bruce McAvaney exclaimed, 'Gee, Freeman has blown them away in lane four.' She had a 15m lead on the field as she approached the 300m mark. 'She's either going to run a world record or this will be the blow-up of the century,' said Bideau out loud. Cathy sped into the top of the straight and hit the wall. She didn't tie up or dramatically shorten stride as do most athletes. Her stride simply slowed as she wound down like a clockwork doll with an expended spring.

Her graphic description matches the doll analogy: 'You're heavy and your mind's wanting you to go and you can't,' she says. 'Your arms feel this big, and your legs feel that big, like they're made out of lead, or cement. You're focused on trying to keep moving and getting to the finish line but you're fighting against something that's dragging you down into the ground. You're in pain but what hurts the most is when you realise ... oh no, the result. I knew I could have won that race.'

First Stewart ran past her, 51.32s, then Lock, 51.94s. Cathy stumbled in third, 52.20s. Poetschka, still finding fitness, finished fifth. In the stands Cathy's friends sat stunned. Chris Wardlaw, remarked to Bideau, 'Mate, you could smell the lactic acid from the stands.' Wardlaw, sitting with his wife, Carmel, overheard a woman behind them say scornfully, 'See, I knew she'd never be any good!' Freeman attracted jealousy in those early days, or racist remarks that she would 'turn black' or 'go walkabout', meaning she would waste everyone's effort by walking away from her career before she had reached her potential.

Wardlaw, however, was quite moved by Cathy's effort. He told Carmel, 'What we have just seen is someone who is prepared to do anything to win.' Whenever they remember that race, Carmel tells Chris amusedly, 'That woman must be spitting chips today.' John Landy, the great miler of the

LESSONS IN LACTIC

1950s, also saw beyond Freeman's burnout, and told her later, 'You have 49 seconds stamped all over you.'

To understand what overtook Cathy requires a brief physiological explanation. Athletes have two energy sources, their aerobic and anaerobic systems. The aerobic system delivers clean and renewable energy by extracting oxygen from the air via the lungs and burning it with glucose in the blood. The by-products of this are harmless—water and exhaled carbon dioxide. Marathon runners primarily employ their aerobic system which is why they can run for several hours.

The anaerobic system is the body's evolutionary fight or flight emergency standby which enables humans to expend a great amount of energy quickly, over a short period. It doesn't require oxygen as a fuel. It has as its pure energy source glycogen which already exists in the muscles. There is sufficient glycogen immediately available for 5–10 seconds of absolute all-out sprinting. A 100m sprinter exhausts this source in one race. Interestingly, sprinters take two breaths over 100m, one at 'Set', at the start of the race, and another around the 30m mark. But these breaths have nothing to do with supplying energy—the race is over before that oxygen can be converted into aerobic fuel.

As a 400m runner, Cathy uses primarily her anaerobic energy system. The drawback with burning glycogen for energy is that it is not quickly renewable and nor is it clean. The first 80–100m depletes Cathy's instantly available glycogen and then she's on borrowed time. Her anaerobic system—which will, in fact, supply extra energy by breaking down stored muscle glycogen—will last only a further 10 seconds to two minutes, depending on the demands made upon it. Using glycogen as a fuel, the muscles excrete lactic acid which is an irritative, causes pain and is produced much faster than the blood flow can wash it away. So if a sprinter continues to push ahead, they are on a fast one-way path to intolerable tissue pain from lactic acid diffusion, followed swiftly by drastically diminished muscle efficiency—the leaden legs Cathy describes. Further debilitation occurs because what little energy the muscles obtain from the aerobic system is exhausted by the speed with which it is being consumed. The blood flow carrying the oxygen can't match the demand and so the muscles go into oxygen debt as well.

The absolutely crucial lesson for Cathy was to learn to expend her anaerobic energy at such a rate that it did not fail her before the finish. To run that razor's edge, she had to know her body, train to recognise and tolerate her lactic acid limits, and judge her entire race speed to within tenths of a second. To misjudge it was to reach the 300–350m mark and know, as she did, that she would not complete the race at optimum speed—to put it mildly.

To assist her to withstand the onset of lactic acid pain, the body produces endorphins, natural narcotics which dampen perceptions of pain. This, too, is an evolutionary response, enabling humans to continue to function despite being wounded or injured. But for athletes, nothing will stop lactic acid stopping them. Renee Poetschka talks about the 'big white polar bear' that climbs on her back between the 300–350m mark as she pushes her anaerobic energy supply to the limit. Others talk colourfully of the piano or refrigerator that lands on them at the same spot. Moreover, there is not instant relief from lactic acid pain when the race finishes. The acid continues to circulate, causing tissues to ache wherever it lodges—lungs, limbs and large muscles. Dual 400m Olympic finalist, Darren Clark, says that in severe instances he's experienced pain for up to seven minutes afterwards. He says, laughing, 'It's at its worst just when the television interviewer comes to talk to you.'

Coach Peter Fortune regards Cathy's Adelaide blow-up as inexperience on everyone's behalf. 'I was pretty new to it at that stage,' he says. 'Cathy was so keyed up before the start that I thought she didn't want to be spoken to ... so I didn't.'

LESSONS IN LACTIC

Subsequently he worked out that Freeman was subject to a minor pattern of psychological over-arousal, of blasting out and forgetting how to pace herself. 'From that point on I tried very hard to project the image, at least, of being very laidback before a race,' he says. 'But the race wasn't totally negative. It showed what a terrific competitor she is.'

Fortune's reluctance to meddle in Cathy's pre-race psyche was consistent with the philosophy he adopted from the outset—to coach her, not control her. 'She had a bloke to manage her—Nick,' he says. 'I wanted her to enjoy coming to training, not to be ordered to. And I think she responded well to that approach. A controlling coach wouldn't have lasted the six years with her that I did.'

His softly, softly attitude was evident the first night he met Freeman for training at Olympic Park earlier that season. When he arrived, she was jogging, not on the main training track, but around the perimeter of the entire complex. 'Shall we go inside to the track now?' he said. When Cathy hesitated, Fortune sensed some discomfort, and quickly added, 'Well, it's just general running, why don't we go over the road to the footy grass and run there?' 'Yes, that would be good,' said Cathy.

Her self-esteem had been shaken by the relay drama in Tokyo. She had gone from relay gold medallist to relay reject, and felt she might be an object of ridicule in the eyes of other athletes inside Olympic Park. Freeman was exhibiting an amusing contradiction of the shy. The reason they're embarrassed by attention is that they're so self-centred they think everyone is looking at them.

Next visit to Olympic Park they graduated to the inside tartan track and Cathy saw that although most of the athletes were serious, few of them were trying to be champions. There were recreational runners, joggers, businessmen shedding lunch waists, club stalwarts and young children. It was a social milieu all of its own, rather like Melaleuca Park back in Mackay—with the addendum that Olympic Park was redolent with grand athletic history. This is where, in the national titles on 10 March 1956, Ron Clarke tripped and fell in the mile. John Landy stopped, went back and helped Clarke up before turning and chasing the field. Despite losing five seconds going back, and disrupting his rhythm, Landy won in an amazing 4min 4.25s. Seven years later, Ron Clarke set his first world record here, the 10,000m, on 18 December 1963, having walked to the ground from nearby Richmond where he worked as an accountant. Raelene Boyle and Rob de Castella trained here. Steve Ovett, Sebastian Coe and John Walker ran here, with crowds of up to 30,000 in the days before drugs made people doubt the sport's integrity.

For the first time in her life, Cathy began to train hard. Back in 1990, her sprint mentor Kerry Johnson had remarked without malice that Freeman was a lazy trainer. Cathy goes along with that. 'I made my first national team when I was 16, and didn't start training seriously until I was 19,' she says. 'At 16 I was just going along for the joy ride.' Peter Fortune was pleased with her enthusiasm. 'I can't say what she was like before I met her, but I didn't find her a lazy trainer in my time.'

That year, to avoid England's winter, Commonwealth and European 100m champion Linford Christie, the man most favoured to succeed Carl Lewis in Barcelona, trained in Melbourne. One day he and circuit agent Maurie Plant were leaving the track when Christie stopped to watch Freeman speed by. 'Take a good look,' said Plant knowingly. Soon Christie was giving Cathy starts in sprint training and running her down. 'If he misjudged, she'd run like a scared rabbit and he wouldn't be able to catch her,' says Bideau. Cathy liked Christie, his self-confidence, the way he took on the Americans. 'He was cocky, but he was down to earth too, never too grand for anybody,' says Cathy. 'I enjoyed those evenings training.' Enjoyed being acknowledged by the man who would soon become the biggest star of all—the fastest man on earth.

LESSONS IN LACTIC

Cathy wasn't the only Freeman to impress Christie. Norman, the 100m and 200m national under-17 champion two years earlier, had moved to Melbourne, playing Australian Rules football, training with Cathy and looking fit. One night the national 100m champion Shane Naylor was watching when Bideau joked to him, 'How about we line you up with Norman and have a race?' Naylor replied, mock serious, 'Gees, no way, he might beat me!' Christie offered to take Norman to England with him and Bideau toyed with the idea of using Norman as Cathy's training partner in Europe if she made the team for the Barcelona Olympics. 'Then I thought, no, he's at school here, with a part-time job, playing footy, it's a normal life,' says Bideau. 'Whereas over there it would be a constant media story, him and Cathy.'

Victorian sprint coach Norm Osborne, who had once cast an eye over Cathy at the AIS in Canberra, saw Norman training and instantly picked the difference. 'He didn't have the same attitude as Cathy,' he says. 'He had the talent, and might easily have been a top runner. But he might not too, so you can't blame him for doing whatever he enjoyed.' Which, like his grandfather and father before him, was playing football, in Brisbane and eventually back in Mackay.

Originally Fortune thought Freeman should favour the 200m, even though he knew that she had a natural 400m runner's rhythm. 'She had good leg speed, though not as quick as some,' he says. 'Her start and acceleration were not great, because she was so small. But she has a wonderful ability to maintain, and actually almost increase, her base speed.'

Cathy's results quickly reflected her resolve. In February 1992 she won the Victorian 100m and 200m and then entered the 400m. It was her first genuine tilt over the one lap and the favourite was Sharon Stewart. As always, Cathy gave it a go, led into the straight, was challenged by Stewart with 50m to go, but dug in and held on to win. As she crossed the line she punched the air, the salute she gives when she's really pumped. She'd beaten a runner she wasn't expected to and had run 52.06s, more than a second faster than her previous best. 'That was a real buzz,' says Nick Bideau. 'Gives me goose bumps just thinking about it because it was a sign of what was to come.'

Her immediate target was to run qualifying times of 52s for the 400m and 23.24s for the 200m for the Barcelona Olympics. With good form and good conditions Melinda Gainsford and Melissa Moore had already run the 200m time in Sydney. Cathy headed for Perth, the second last grand prix of the season, but ran so poorly in the 100m—she didn't even break 12s—that Bideau, standing in the infield, stared and wondered, 'What was that?' Intervention strategy seemed necessary for the 400m. 'There's a big tailwind down the back straight,' he told Cathy. 'Run quickly and it will get you to 150m to go inside qualifying time. Then, when you head into the wind in the straight, dig in, you'll have plenty left.' She did just that, rode the wind, dug in, and ran 51.53s, the season's fastest time in Australia. And a Barcelona qualifier. The contrast between her 100m and 400m then became clear. Cathy knew the 100m was only a warm-up for the 400m, an illustration of how her performance could vary dramatically depending on what the result meant to her.

Nick rang Cecelia in Brisbane on his mobile and gave her the good news. Cathy visited some Baha'i friends and then returned to the Scarborough Beach motel where Nick and Peter Fortune were staying. When Cathy heard that Nick had phoned Cecelia she was angry. She wanted to tell her mum the news, it was her thrill to deliver. They argued and Cathy rushed out of the room, tripped on the stairs and sprained her ankle. Says Cathy, 'Nick came racing after me, and me being really stubborn, just kept running and I hurt it even more.'

Back in Melbourne for the NEC meet a week later, Bideau questioned Olympic selector Brian Roe: how important was it that Freeman run the 200m? 'Unless she definitely can't, I want her to run,' said Roe. It was the showcase grand prix, in front of her home crowd. In Melbourne, 1976 national 1500m champion, Dr Peter Fuller, gave Cathy a painkilling injection, strapped the ankle rigid, and had Cathy bounce up and down on her toes. No pain. Peter Fuller, a sports medicine doctor, was to become another valued member of the peripheral back-up team integral to Cathy's career. Wherever Nick and Cathy travelled in the world, if they were in doubt about Cathy's health, they rang Fuller. That night Melinda Gainsford, in great shape, powered through like a runaway train, but Cathy, with one deadened ankle, ran second 23.09s, another Barcelona qualifier.

Sighs of relief. And even though, soon after, she blew up in that dramatic 400m in Adelaide in the selection trials, she ran second to Gainsford again in the 200m, cementing her spot there for the Olympics. Yet she really looked more world class in the 400m and so the Freeman boffins, Bideau and Fortune, opted for the 400m and 4 x 400m relay, rather than the 200m and 4 x 100m relay.

Off track, in March, Cathy, 19, enrolled in Australian history and politics at Melbourne University, with no serious intention of completing a degree. She was astounded at her first tutorial to witness the lecturer's learned opinions suddenly interrupted by a class of assertive students. 'That meant to me that people were free to express themselves, and that was cool, I liked that part,' she says.

Bideau noticed that Cathy was inquisitive and perceptive. 'She had never been trained to clear think, problem solve, that type of thing,' he says. 'But she could tell me a hundred things about people we met which I would never think. She's poorly educated because, like a lot of sportspeople, she never took much notice. But if she's interested, she asks questions and remembers it all.'

One item she did garner at university, from people she met in the Aboriginal unit, was a large Aboriginal flag. At school she had admired its colours—black for the people, red for the earth, yellow for the sun—and became attached to its symbolism, her own personal connection with the Aboriginal nation. She put it in her suitcase as she packed for Barcelona. Peter Fortune, too, packed his bags, travelling privately, his costs assisted by Cathy's early sponsorships. Her very first sponsor was Balarinji designs, a small clothing company owned by Aboriginal John Moriarty and his wife Ros. John, a victim in the Stolen Children Generation, had approached Cathy at the national championships in Adelaide that year. The offer was only $2000, but as Ros says, 'We just gave it to her because we thought she was a darling.' In return Cathy ran in startling Balarinji designed bodysuits in Aboriginal motifs. The synergy must have worked because four years later Cathy was an international name, and the company was turning over $11.5 million annually, with two Qantas 747s painted in its designs.

Her second sponsor was Nike, but Bideau, who had gradually become her part-time manager, didn't lock Freeman into anything other than a small emolument. He advised her to hold off until she had more in her hand than four fingers—namely a Games medal—to bargain with. Bideau knew Nike. Unless Cathy could back up her contract with results they could drop off and it might be a long wait before they knocked on her door again. But accountant Peter Jess had no such qualms. He told the principals of Oakley sunglasses, 'You better get on board here, this girl is going to be an absolute superstar. If you don't get a loyalty program going now, you won't be able to afford her later.' So Oakley did.

Before they flew out, Nick and Cathy saw a profile on Michelle Lock on 'Sports Sunday' and were amused at the manner in which her coach, Kelvin Giles, yelled at her during training. Giles, who was also fitness coach of the Brisbane Broncos rugby league team, was urging Lock, 'C'mon, you're not tough enough!' Bideau thought to himself, 'Freeman wouldn't last five minutes with that treatment; she'd tell him where to go.' Cathy never responded well to negative reinforcement and the rare times that Bideau tried it, the plan backfired.

Once Cathy was chosen for Barcelona, Cecelia, in Brisbane, decided she wanted to see her daughter's historic run. She visited her father, the old boxer George Sibley, then living in a nursing home on Palm Island. He got around like a down and out, but she knew he had been frugal with his savings. She spoke to him with nursing sisters present. 'Your granddaughter, Catherine, is running in the Olympic Games, and I'd like to go,' Cecelia told him. 'Can you help me?' She took a deep breath. 'I need $4000.'

She was encouraged when he did not dismiss her request outright. 'Do you understand what I'm asking? Are you proud of Catherine?' she asked. Old George's eyes lit up, 'Oh, yeah, yes I am.' So Cecelia concluded, 'Don't answer me now, think about it. I'll give you a week, and I'll ring you from Brisbane.' She did and asked again, 'Well, what do you think, Dad, can you help me?' And the answer came firmly down the line to his eldest daughter, 'Yes, I can.' The words, as much as the gift, 53 years after George left her as a child, went far in healing Cecelia's own sense of childhood rejection. She was off to Barcelona to see George's granddaughter run.

10.

STARGAZING.
BARCELONA OLYMPICS, 1992

As the Australian team gathered for the English AAA titles in Birmingham on 28 June 1992, it suddenly dawned on Cathy Freeman's coach, Peter Fortune, that Cathy was no certainty to run in the Barcelona Olympics, after all. The vicissitudes of Australian athletics had struck again. Fortune had heard that the 1992 national champion Sharon Stewart, and 1991 champion Renee Poetschka, now recovered from injury, were virtually pre-selected for Barcelona. 'Maybe it was my naivety, but it was only then I realised how precarious Cathy's situation was,' says Fortune. 'The runners' form in Europe was really about who was going to get the third Olympic berth.' Nick Bideau took one look at Michelle Lock's lean, muscled body and told Cathy, 'Whoa! That girl's in good shape. She's going to be tough to beat.' And to think, just weeks ago they had both laughed at Kelvin Giles!

So it all started right then, with that race, the British AAAs. No wonder Lock and Giles were looking hyped-up. Bideau, working as a journalist, had been distracted by having to write stories about complaints from British officials about Australian long jumper David Culbert's 'wobbly bits' in his skin-tight lycra body suit. But Nick urgently alerted

Cathy: 'You have to beat Lock here; be even better if you could win this race.'

Cathy didn't panic, nor even concentrate on Lock. 'It fired me up a bit, the news about Michelle, but I ran my own race,' she says, in a PB (personal best) of 51.14s, just closing out a fast-finishing Lock. European circuit agent, Maurie Plant from Melbourne, observed to Andy Norman, at that time the most powerful meet promoter in Europe, 'Take a good look at this girl. Raw talent.'

It was in Birmingham that Cathy began her strong friendship with Australian high jumper Tim Forsyth. 'I had just found out that my great-grandfather had died, and I was very, very close to him,' says Forsyth. 'The one thing I wanted was for him to see me at the Olympic Games, that's all we ever spoke about. When I was a tiny little kid we used to go and see him and he'd hold a stick up and I'd run and jump it. Once I'd done a few and become quite good at it, he'd go inside and get a teaspoon of butter and put sugar on it. And that was my reward.

'So I was fairly devastated and I remember Cathy being so understanding and such a good person to talk to, because she lost her sister and had already been through it all. Everything that she said actually meant something. Not like when people, who haven't really experienced it, say things like, "Don't worry, he's in a happier place." Her words really stuck with me.'

Cathy's next track test was Oslo, Norway, where the field included the talented but physically fragile Poetschka, who had made the semi-finals in the world titles in 1991, and two of the women who became Cathy's great rivals over the next decade, American Jearl Miles and Bahamian Pauline Davis. Ultimately Cathy became friendly with both runners, or as friendly as arch-competitors can be. Davis asked Bideau, 'What's with this Freeman? Is she black or white or what?' Bideau said she was an Australian Aborigine. 'What's an Aborigine?' asked Davis. Bideau explained, adding that

Cathy had other ancestors as well, English and Chinese and ... 'She looks mostly black to me!' quoth Davis.

In later seasons Davis decided to upgrade Cathy's appearance, taking her shopping for make-up and clothes. 'She wore racy gear and she wanted me to buy outfits that, you know, don't leave much to the imagination,' says Cathy, laughing shyly. 'Those Caribbean women are a lot more confident than Australian black women.' Kenyans, too, wanted to know how come black face but straight hair? Don't see too many black faces without curly hair, hairdressers would comment to Cathy inquisitively. Before she had even set foot on her first European grand prix track she was being noticed as exotic.

Oslo, ah Oslo. There is something about these Scandinavian tracks, the long, still Arctic evenings, the tradition of the sport, the track erudition of the crowd, that appeals to Australians. In Oslo, in 1965, Ron Clarke from Melbourne became the first man to run under 28 minutes for 10,000m, an astonishing feat at the time. And just across the fiords, in Turku, Finland, in 1954, another Melbourne man, John Landy, became the second man to run a mile under four minutes, breaking Roger Bannister's world record.

Oslo is a small track, with only six lanes instead of the customary eight, and Cathy was given lane six, the very outside lane where the stagger meant she would be running blind, unable initially to see the runners behind her. This was Cathy's first big European meet and Bideau was afraid that with no runners in view as a speed guide, Cathy might do an Adelaide and bolt out. He asked his mate, his competition resource, Maurie Plant, to see if Cathy could be allocated another lane. But television had already been given the start list, so lane six it was. Bideau and Fortune impressed upon her: just keep up with the others, they're good runners. Don't take off like a maniac.

Cathy was lying on the floor in the warm-up room, stretching, when the double-agent act, Andy Norman, a portly former policeman, and burly Plant, advanced upon her. 'Freeman, Miss Freeman? You're running in lane six,' said Norman in stentorian tones, towering above her. Norman was then the biggest meet promoter in Europe and what he said now was in full view of the other athletes. 'Don't worry about these Americans over here. They've just come from their Olympic trials, they'll be tired. You just go out hard and keep going.' That was it. Nick rolled his eyes at Fortune. Maurie had invited Andy to meet Cathy to give her confidence, but Andy's advice was the exact opposite of the instructions they'd just given her.

Cathy wisely followed Bideau's advice. Miles and Davis passed her in the running but she came back at them in the straight to pick up third, ahead of Poetschka. She had now beaten both Poetschka and Lock—Barcelona beckoned. 'Then Lock ran 50.9s somewhere in Germany,' says Cathy. 'I was really annoyed she had run faster than me. I remember hearing the news and it made me even more determined.' But in a 400m in London, a week later, Cathy faded to finish seventh in 51.75s behind American sprinter Gwen Torrence, who normally ran the 100 and 200m double. 'I was watching the race instead of running it,' said Cathy thoughtfully afterwards. 'I lost concentration watching Gwen. I thought, "Oh good, I'm in with the big guns here."'

In between races Cathy was busy being a tourist, the girl from Mackay catching the London Underground, walking around Trafalgar Square, shopping in Oxford Street, strolling beside the Thames. She had passed through London on her way to the world juniors in Bulgaria in 1990, but this was her first extended stay. Only after years of basing herself in London did the novelty of sightseeing eventually wear off.

Selection day, 8 July 1992, and Freeman achieved another milestone in her career: the first Aboriginal woman selected to compete in the Olympic Games. The three for the 400m were Stewart, Poetschka and Freeman. Lock was in tears, Giles was furious; the foyer of the Australian team's Bromley

Court hotel was filled with media crews interviewing distressed athletes omitted amid a huge selection drama. 'I really felt for them, but what could I say?' says Cathy. She put space between herself and the politics by moving out of the team hotel for a few days, staying with Bideau at the home of his London friends, Carol and Graham Richardson, members of the Croydon Athletics Club. She returned to an unsettled team ready to move into camp in Frankfurt, Germany. Tensions eased when Stewart withdrew from the Olympics injured, replaced by a relieved, and deserving, Lock.

The constant racing in Europe, and the need to keep fresh for each race, had interfered with Cathy's training. She had no huge background of track work and was losing fitness quickly. Maurie Plant rang Bideau to say there was a 300m race at Gateshead in England, the perfect distance for Freeman who was not yet strong enough for successive world-class 400m races. Cathy flew over from Frankfurt and ran a close second to the tall Jamaican, Grace Jackson, who was silver medallist to Florence Griffith-Joyner in the 200m in Seoul in 1988. Plant rang Bideau excitedly: 'She ran well, almost knocked Jackson off. Nearly ran her down.'

This was the genesis of Team Freeman, athlete Cathy, manager Bideau, coach Fortune and circuit agent Plant. Though others—training partners, masseurs, sponsors, and financial advisers—also swung into her orbit occasionally, the three principals combined over the next five years to guide Freeman to the zenith of world athletics. Other athletes may have organised similar back-ups but few observers doubted Freeman's advantage with her team.

In Barcelona, Cathy and Nick were strolling around the city centre when Cathy suddenly asked, 'What do you think it would take to win here?' He knew the defending champion, Russia's Olga Bryzgina, had run 48.65s in Seoul in 1988, and newcomer Marie-José Pérec had run 49.13s to win the worlds in Tokyo in 1991. 'Oh, about 48-something,

I reckon,' he said. Said Cathy, 'Um, do you think I can run that?' Nick looked quizzical: 'Look, probably not, you're not strong enough yet.' Cathy: 'Well, how do you know? What if I tried really hard?' Said Nick, becoming uneasy, 'Well, if you tried really hard, you might run a great PB, but I'd be really surprised if you ran 48-something.'

What's going on? Bideau wondered. Coming from a girl who hadn't yet broken 51 seconds, where 48-whatever would be near enough to an 18m improvement around 400m for Cathy. He was damping her ambition in case she flew out at 48s pace for 300m and blew up, as in Adelaide. But instantly it hit him, 'Gosh, she's thinking big!' He regretted his pessimism. What was he doing, telling her she couldn't run something, if she thought she could? Most athletes would never be so ambitious, would not risk setting themselves up for certain disappointment. But not Cathy. He quickly relented, 'Catherine, you might just do it, you never know.'

Cathy says now that realistically she didn't think she had a chance of winning. 'I mean, there's always a part of me that ... but I didn't think, "Yeah, I can do this." I never thought that. I was just curious as to what it would take.' But with Freeman, you did never really know.

At her first Olympics, and no-one expecting her to do other than her best, Cathy resolved to enjoy herself. Wearing exotic-coloured tops and black lycra shorts, her blonde-streaked hair hitched high on her head by a scarf, she listed her brushes with fame as Boris Becker, Charles Barkley and Phylicia Rashad, the actress who plays Bill Cosby's wife. She dragged Tim Forsyth along to a Nike press conference entitled 'Men Who Fly!' featuring Michael Jordan and Sergey Bubka. And she wanted to see the Dream Team, the US pro basket-ballers, but knew it would drain too much nervous energy watching an entire match. She just had time for a quick congratulations to Kieren Perkins on his 1500m gold.

Freeman didn't just teenage stargaze. She was absorbing

all she saw and heard, and she was learning from the best. If by chance she overheard Carl Lewis's opinion on starting, she would never forget it, whereas Peter Fortune could tell her the same thing a dozen times before she'd take it in. With permission from her roomie, bespectacled, world record-breaking walker Kerry Saxby, Cathy draped her Aboriginal flag in their bedroom. Sometimes she ran wearing black, red and yellow wristbands, her minor statement of who she was. She loved the village but not their unit's position, right over an athletes' bus station. The girls solved that by closing the soundproof windows and turning on a fan.

During one television interview, Cathy motioned to the village food hall and said, 'The food is great, you can identify with it. It's food you can buy in Australia, you don't have to be frightened of getting food poisoning. It's nutritious, it's fresh, it's really good. I'm going training so I'm off to get some fruit.' Could this be the same muffin-munching Freeman from Auckland in 1990?

Olympic opening ceremonies extend for hours and are so tiring that athletes with serious medal chances rarely march. Cathy decided to march knowing that it was probably the last time in her career when she would have the opportunity.

'It was an amazing high,' says Cathy. 'The crowd just lifted you, the feeling was electric. I was marching in the first row, it was unforgettable.' As race day approached she grew excited and nervous, and with good reason. When she was called for her heat, who should be there but Marie-José Pérec. They ran easily, finishing down the straight together, Cathy easing to let Pérec finish ahead. Both went through to the next round. One hurdle passed.

Next day Cathy kept looking for her mother who still had not yet arrived from Australia. Channel Seven's 'Real Life' program was following Cecelia and was interviewing her outside the Olympic stadium when the Australian team bus happened by. Cathy screamed from the window, 'Mum, Mum, there's Mum!' Their tearful meeting was filmed for television, and even now Cathy says, 'I was so happy to see her, so happy.' But for Bideau, however heartwarming the scene, it was a distraction of an Olympic athlete's focus. He could be a wooden man, Bideau.

Then he discovered from whence Cathy inherited her optimism. 'If Cathy wins gold, we're going to have a big party,' Cecelia told Nick. He did a double take. Like daughter, like mother! 'She's not going to win gold,' he said, amazed. Cecelia argued, 'Well, how do you know? She might.' In the face of an enthusiastic mother, Nick stayed calm. 'She can't win. If she makes the final it will be fantastic,' he explained. 'Please don't go around saying that to Catherine. The last thing she needs is to have people expecting too much of her.' Cecelia was happy anyway. 'Oh, no, no, I wouldn't. We're proud of her whatever she does.'

Second round. Cecelia sat in the stands and, as Cathy filed out, Cecelia pulled from her bag a tiny, child-size paper Aboriginal flag. 'I felt a bit sheepish with this dinky little flag,' says Cecelia. 'Then this lady next to me pulled out an Australian flag exactly the same size and we laughed and began waving them both.'

Bideau told Cathy that this was it, no easy races at the Olympics, she had to give it everything. But Cathy ran a poor tactical race, left herself too much ground to make up in the straight and finished full of running, fifth in 51.52s. The English girl, Sandra Douglas, who finished fourth, in 51.41s, Cathy had easily defeated in the AAAs final only a few weeks earlier. But only the first four went through to the semi-final so Douglas went through and not Cathy. In the wash-up, Cathy ran the 13th fastest time, yet missed the 16-strong semi-finals field. Didn't matter, she was out. Lock and Poetschka both cruised through to the semis without having to break 52s. That's track and field.

It didn't devastate Cathy, nothing that a large hug from Cecelia couldn't ease, but it upset her sufficiently to prompt another of her heartfelt resolutions: 'That's the last time I miss making the semi-finals.' And it was. Bideau, expecting her to make the semi-final, had not entered her in the 200m heats on the same day, even though she was eligible. 'If I'd been on top of everything, I would have rung the head coach,' says Bideau ruefully. 'She could have run the 200m, would have been one more time around the Olympic stadium in front of 80,000 people. More experience for her.' He, too, was on a learning curve.

Cathy watched the final and if she needed any convincing that Pérec was the new 400m queen, Marie-José's 48.82s for gold provided it, the world's best for four years and the fastest ever by a non-eastern European bloc athlete. Seventh, in 50.19s, was a Jamaican runner, Sandie Richards, who Cathy would come to know well in later seasons. There were other thrills ahead, namely Tim Forsyth's bronze medal in the high jump. 'I caught him in the lift going out and wished him luck,' says Cathy. 'He looked so relaxed. And when he won bronze, David Culbert wrote in shaving cream across Tim's unit window, "F—ing Legend!" One memory I have of Timmy is that he celebrated so much he couldn't even walk down this tiny hill without hanging on to a tree.'

Nancy Atterton wanted Cathy in the 4 x 100m relay. With Melinda Gainsford, who had made the semi-finals in the 100m and 200m, Australia had a strong team. But Cathy had trained for the 400m and ran in the 4 x 400m, which came seventh in the final. 'She'd really had enough,' says Peter Fortune. 'She'd had no chance to strengthen up and she was very thin.'

Back in Australia Cathy was invited to a handicap race in Kalgoorlie which she accepted because she could also speak to an Aboriginal group there. Among her own she was already a superstar, having conquered the wide, white Australian world of sport. Aborigines are famous in sport everywhere in Australia, but already Freeman had eclipsed them all in her era. Only Lionel Rose and Evonne Goolagong-Cawley from past years matched her.

Her presence among the elderly was remarkable. 'Some of them cry, the older people,' says Cathy. 'They cry on my shoulder and they shake me and hug me and they look like they're never going to let go.' It was a bit overwhelming for Cathy, still a teenager. Bideau, standing back, watched it all. 'One group of old ladies couldn't take their eyes off her,' he says. 'They stayed back until they got a chance and then they grabbed her. They love her, because she looks even more glamorous than they'd ever imagined from television, and yet she's one of them. They recognise themselves in her, and she was a gem. It really lifted them.'

Cathy and Tim Forsyth were made captains of the Australian team to the world juniors in Seoul in September 1992. On tour, the two babes of Barcelona—Forsyth is six months younger than Cathy—once more renewed their friendship. It emerged that, extraordinarily, Forsyth perceived Cathy to be the bigger star of the pair, even though his performance at Barcelona far outranked hers. Yet it was true that only Perkins and Steve Moneghetti received more fan mail than Cathy at the Olympics. 'She had so much notoriety,' says Forsyth. 'When you see people on television you think they have a lot of confidence, even arrogance. But when I got to know her I found she was no more confident than the rest of us. She got such a lot of press back then, it was premature. It may have hurt her in a way; wasn't necessarily a good thing for her running.'

In Seoul she ran second in the 200m in 23.20s, close to her best even though she had done little training since Barcelona. But the aura of the Olympics, any Olympics, galvanises Freeman, and she was thrilled just to run on the track where the 1988 Seoul Olympics were held. Back home, Team Freeman prepared a plan for 1993, the post-Olympic year, but a year which culminated in the world championships in Stuttgart in August. Simple. Freeman had to get stronger and faster. Who was the toughest runner in Australia for Freeman to beat? It wasn't Poetschka, it wasn't Lock. It was Melinda

CATHY FREEMAN—A JOURNEY JUST BEGUN

Gainsford. In Barcelona, Channel Seven had sent a camera crew around the village on a tour guided by Cathy and Melinda. They were staying in the same six-girl apartment and laughed and chatted with each other on camera. They seemed eminently friendly. But 1993 was about to put a strain on that.

11.
A Sad Homecoming.
Stuttgart Worlds, 1993–94

It's about 2 a.m. at Silvers nightclub in Toorak, Melbourne, in early 1993, and a fine mist of perspiration gleams upon Cathy's forehead as she rocks energetically but effortlessly to the rhythms of rapper Ice-T. A sleeveless white dress clings damply to her slim figure, and her red-tinted dark brown hair falls loosely towards her bare back. On the packed danced floor I lean forward and shout, 'Does Fort know you're here?'

Cathy throws back her head and laughs delightedly, mouth wide open. Her coach Peter Fortune is the furthest person from her mind as an ultraviolet strobe sweeps across her like a lighthouse beam, fluorescing her white dress and large, gleaming teeth. She likes the buzz at Silvers even though she once overheard a drunk slur, 'Don't tell me they let Abos in here!' Or as Ice-T raps ironically in his song, 'There goes the f—ing neighbourhood.'

Cathy is no longer the 16-year-old schoolgirl of the Auckland Games, or even the ingenue Barcelona Olympian. She was 56kg in New Zealand, full-faced, fat-thighed and didn't give a damn. Now she's 52kg, hard-bellied, lean of mien, with the dawning confidence of a young woman. She does

100 stomach curls and push-ups daily because that's what Debbie Flintoff-King did to win her Seoul 400m hurdle gold medal. She's so naturally athletic that she seems to glide on the dance floor. As friend Liz Dixon says during a break from the floor, 'I've always said, "If you're an athlete and you're black, you can be happy." It's in her genes.'

Training at Olympic Park, other athletes now pause to admire as she sets off. In sprinting lexicon there are drivers like Donovan Bailey and floaters like Carl Lewis. Cathy floats, glides, a gift few athletes possess but all covet. Her abnormally long stride produces such an exaggerated back-kick her heels seem almost to touch her bottom. Earlier in the evening she had stumbled at the start of her heat in a professional 100m handicap at Prahran. At the gun she bounced out towards an adjacent lane and almost over-balanced correcting her direction. Officials later found she had hammered her blocks in on a slight angle. 'All I saw was the ground coming up,' she says breathlessly. Instead of qualifying for the final she gets a consolation cosmetic package. 'Bet this is for white skin, not black skin,' she says, pursing her mouth to apply the lippie. 'Well, I'm out of the final, let's go dancing.'

Her slim, fit figure owed itself to a conversation in November, the previous year, when Nick Bideau told Peter Fortune he wanted Cathy to train twice a day. His theory was that it would be less stressful for her to train shorter sessions more frequently. Fortune demurred. 'She's still a young girl,' he said. 'She might be,' insisted Bideau, 'but she wants to become a strong woman.' In Cathy's favour was that she had the time, the enthusiasm and the resilience. 'A lot of athletes her age, you wouldn't do it,' says Fortune. 'I still think she was too young, but I went along with it.' He wrote out a twice-a-day regime, double running sessions, though later he moved away from this to a morning weights session and evening running. Cathy was excited by it, the idea of maturing into adult regimes.

A SAD HOMECOMING

The other strategic change for 1993 was to concentrate on 200m, which was the grand prix sprint event for prize money that season. Cathy ran few 400m races that year. She needed more speed and to get that she needed to take on Melinda Gainsford, who dominated the 100m and 200m in 1992. Bideau knew his athlete. Freeman was never much motivated to run against the clock, but she could zero in on a competitor. Fortune concurred. 'Cathy has a simple approach to the sport in many ways,' he says. 'One way is to say to her, "If you beat her, you will improve."' The danger was that in focusing on one other athlete, failure would have meant a debilitating season for Freeman, and a damaging loss of confidence. They were risky stakes.

Not in Cathy's mind. She had been the track's wunderkind since she was 16 and suddenly Melinda Gainsford was the name on everyone's lips. Cathy said to her best friend Peta Powell, 'What's so special about this girl? She may have talent, but I want to meet her on the track.'

In mid-January Cathy checked her speed by entering the Australian 100 yards championship in Hobart, winning in a smart 10.62s; she ran 11s for 100 yards in 1990. She was on target and the target was Melinda. Freeman's first true test came in the Sydney grand prix meet on the Australia Day weekend. As she prepared for the 200m, Linford Christie happened to be playing with national coach Keith Connor's small son in Cathy's lane. She walked up to Christie, ruffled his hair like a naughty child and said firmly, 'Linford, get off the track. I have to run now.' Cathy meant business, and ran like it, 22.62s, a whopping PB compared to her previous best of 23.09s. It would have beaten Raelene Boyle's Australian junior record of 22.74s except that Cathy turned 20 the following month. Gainsford trailed five metres behind in 23.23s. Maurie Plant turned to Bideau, nodded knowingly and said abruptly, 'Nick, that's victory!' Watching Freeman run was like a narcotic to these addicts.

'Yeah, I felt so good that day,' says Cathy. 'Melinda was

shocked, I know, because her boyfriend was there and he hugged her. She was a bit upset, she didn't expect it.' Gainsford's 1992 crown as Australian sprint queen was under challenge. But these were early days. Cathy won all three sprints, 100m, 200m and 400m at the Victorian state titles, before heading for another tilt at Gainsford in Adelaide on 14 February.

Cathy took on Jane Flemming, as well as Gainsford, over 100m, the first time she had raced Flemming since, as a 17-year-old, Jane out-dipped her on the tape in the 1990 national 100m. Bideau told Cathy, 'Flemming's a good starter, beat her out of the blocks and you'll beat Gainsford. Mel doesn't start well. She's really strong through 30–60m, but if you're in front she could tie up,' he said. And so it was. Cathy, never renowned as a lightning starter, flew out of the blocks, Gainsford gained mid-race but couldn't close Cathy down—11.43s, a PB for Freeman, Gainsford half a metre back in 11.48s, and Flemming well beaten in 11.65s.

A short while after the race Bideau went looking for Cathy. Nowhere to be seen. Freeman had been summoned for a drug test and, instead of waiting until after the athlete's last event, as the rules state, an inexperienced—and thoughtless—official had requested a urine specimen immediately. Cathy, the young black girl used to obeying white officialdom, complied. 'I was really annoyed,' says Bideau. 'Instead of resting and focusing on the 200m, she's in with some drug bureaucrat! She was definitely a bit lethargic when she came out for the 200m, plus, having won the 100m, I think she just expected she would win.'

In Sydney, Cathy had matched Melinda for early speed and then ran away from her. This time, in Adelaide, Gainsford had a three-metre lead coming off the bend and Cathy, stretching out desperately in the straight, just caught her on the line—dead-heat in 22.73s. Heptathlete and hurdler, Jane Flemming, perhaps with the female Athlete of the Year award in mind, suggested Melinda go and check the photo-finish. If

A SAD HOMECOMING

Cathy lost just once over 200m during the season her chances for the much coveted Athlete of the Year honour, and $10,000 prize money, were over. First place would go to Flemming who was unbeatable over the hurdles. 'I did check the photo, and it was exactly right,' says Gainsford.

Bideau was developing a new appreciation of the task he had set Cathy. 'I was impressed with Gainsford,' he says. 'I give her credit. She knuckled down and fought back, she didn't take it lying down. She's always had really strong fighting qualities.' Over to Melbourne for the NEC showdown on 25 February, the grand prix of the year, 15,000 crowd at Olympic Park, hometown girl Freeman favoured for the 200m but Gainsford had closed the gap. Cathy's PB was 22.62s, Gainsford's 22.68s—a mere 50cm difference at the tape. This was athletics excitement such as is seen only at the big international GPs in Europe. To build focus for the 200m, Cathy conceded the 100m to Gainsford who won easily, pushing the tension a notch higher. The crowd was abuzz, Gainsford's back, yep, they nodded.

'It was a terrific atmosphere,' says Fortune. 'Cathy raises her competitive instincts when she feels people watching her. It hypes her up. I could tell because she'd start demanding positive reinforcement. She'd say, "Talk to me about this," or "Can I win it?" and she'd want me to say, "Of course you can." I'm not a particularly motivating type and I was aware I shouldn't go over the top myself either, so I'd just say, "Yeah, yeah, you can go well."'

Gainsford was keen, but Cathy was mean. She shadowed Melinda to the turn, edged ahead into the straight and then strode away magnificently over the last 30m, giving her rare, right-fist air punch as she crossed the line. Nick checked the clock: 22.54s, another PB, Gainsford second in 22.66s, improving but still a metre or so behind.

This was painful for Melinda. She hadn't run at all badly. Publicly she said the tough racing was good for them both, but privately each wanted to be the big fish. Reports emerged of Melinda returning to the warm-up area and bursting out in tears of anger to her coach, Jackie Byrnes, 'Why is this happening? What's going on?' Gainsford says she never shows her hurt in public. 'If I'm upset no-one sees it,' she says. 'I don't think anyone really needs to see it. I won't do it until I get home.' But, I suggest to her, wouldn't her coach Jackie Byrnes see it? 'Oh well,' and she laughs self-consciously. 'Jackie may see it slightly, and later my husband. No-one likes to get beaten and I think what happens is the way you use it. You can't let it get you down, you can't let it take control, you just have to work harder to succeed. That's when our rivalry really started that year, when Cathy and I raced each other all season.' In their thrilling duels, they lifted women's sprinting in Australia to a level not seen since Raelene Boyle raced Denise Boyd in the late 1970s.

Nick Bideau chose that moment, when her potential was being noticed beyond the track, to begin serious negotiations with Nike. At his first approach they showed him the door—too much, they weren't paying her that, they said. Nick then broke the figure down into performance-linked bonuses. How about rewarding her so much for a gold medal, more for two gold medals, Games records a little more again? The Commonwealth Games in Victoria, Canada were far away, not until next year. Nike could be confident of not having to pay Cathy too many bonuses. Even if Jamaica's world-class Merlene Ottey and Juliet Cuthbert didn't run in Canada, Gainsford and Poetschka both had superior times to Cathy over their sprints. Bideau backed Cathy to improve and if she did, it would cost Nike dearly, much more than if they had accepted Bideau's original contract. Further, the contracts expired the day the Games finished, 1 September 1994. By then, Bideau reckoned, they would be negotiating with a rising star of the athletics world. Cathy glanced at the contracts and, though interested, had no eye for the detail. Basically she said, 'Yes, OK, if you think it's good, that's

A SAD HOMECOMING

fine.' Negotiating coups like that, which gave Bideau such a buzz on Freeman's behalf, rarely impressed her. She was grateful, but it just wasn't her scene.

At the nationals in Brisbane, on 7 March, Gainsford fought back with a vengeance. Athletics Australia general manager Neil King talked Bideau into letting Cathy accompany world long jump champion, American Mike Powell, on a coaching clinic to Mackay, Cathy's home town. She relinquished her mental intensity, saw her relatives and friends, and more of the same back in Brisbane with her family. She wound down to a degree that escaped the eye of Bideau and Fortune. They kept her out of the 100m, following the same formula as in Melbourne, hoping to keep her fresh for the 200m. But instead of fresh she went flat.

'We made a mistake,' admits Bideau. 'Those days we were still learning about her. She hadn't done enough. I should have had her run the 100m. She would have been beaten and that would have sharpened her for the 200m.' Gainsford was unstoppable. She won the 100m and then, in the 200m, trounced Cathy by three metres, running 22.49s, her own PB and the fastest by either athlete all season. With 30m to go Cathy sensed she couldn't catch the fleeing Gainsford and, for once lacking her usual never-say-die grit, slowed to record 22.67s.

Cathy walked across to Bideau with a confused look in her eyes, spoke about the difficulty of hearing the starter over the PA speaker beside her blocks, and generally looked dazed. Bideau could have said it was he who had stuffed up, allowing her form to lapse. But the saying goes that more is learnt from one defeat than a thousand victories, and so it was a lesson to them both.

Subsequently it emerged that Gainsford had an extra incentive to defeat Cathy in that last 200m of the domestic grand prix circuit—a promise of a gold bracelet from the combative Jane Flemming. The reason: if Melinda beat Cathy, Flemming would edge out Freeman for the female

Athlete of the Year award. Gainsford didn't really need any extra incentive. These were the national titles and she had not once beaten Cathy over 200m that season.

Not content with the bracelet strategy, Flemming had also fired Gainsford up before the race by relaying criticism of Melinda that Jane had heard—she said—from several coaches. 'I've put up with criticism my whole career,' says Gainsford. 'I think I must be the most criticised athlete in track and field. They were apparently running me down in some way or other, and that upset me, really got me going.' And the bracelet? 'Yeah, I got it. I was a little bit embarrassed about it, but at the same time I was a little bit hypocritical because I did accept it.'

So Flemming won the award, and was presented with it by long jumper-cum-compere David Culbert at the athletes' gala ball. In her acceptance speech Flemming, resplendent under the spotlight in black gauze evening dress, her hair a halo of long blonde tresses, thanked Melinda for defeating Cathy and mentioned the gold bracelet pay-off. Flemming related all this with great humour, but not everyone saw the joke. Glynis Nunn turned to Cathy and said, 'That's a disgrace. That's very unfair.'

To top it off, the whole matter was captured by Peter Wilkinson for 'A Current Affair' and Channel Nine broadcast it on 8 March, the day after the 200m. It came with close-ups of Flemming in the grandstand screaming, 'C'mon, Mel! C'mon, Melinda!' during the race, and standing and applauding afterwards. Flemming reckoned without the underdog sympathy which accompanies Freeman's career, and Athletics Australia received telephone calls the next day complaining at the unsavoury nature of the matter. Says Nick Bideau, 'It was as if Nick Faldo, watching Greg Norman putt, had gone "Miss! Miss! Miss!"'

Flemming denies she exhibited bad sportsmanship. 'I think if you speak to anyone, when I compete I'm not a bad sportsperson,' she says. 'It was all fun and a bit of a joke

A SAD HOMECOMING

really, with Melinda and me. We are quite good friends and it was a bit of a laugh between us.' But could she see how Freeman might not share in the joke? 'Well yes, maybe, yeah.' Flemming says the award was important to her, having torn her hamstring on the eve of the Olympics the previous year, which subsequently felled her two hurdles into her Games heat. 'For me it was something I was aiming for, to win that particular prize,' she says. 'Not so much the money, it was more about the actual award.'

Glynis Nunn was disgusted with the whole affair. 'It just goes to show something's lacking in the feeling between athletes,' she says. 'It was a real bunfight, that Athlete of the Year, but I think it's childish to get up on stage and say publicly what Jane said. Say it to Mel, say it away from the crowd, but don't say it up front. It's just off.'

Renee Poetschka took advantage of Cathy's absence to notch the national 400m and 400m hurdles double. So Cathy won neither the 100m, 200m or 400m national titles, she lost out on the $10,000, put up with Flemming's comments at the awards and suffered her cheering for Melinda on 'A Current Affair'. Freeman and Flemming were conflicting personalities—Flemming, extroverted, candid and exploitative of every ounce of her talent; Freeman, introverted, sensitive and yet to fully realise her undoubted potential. 'I admire the fact that Jane persevered with her athletics,' says Cathy carefully. 'But Jane is very commercial, loves marketing herself and she's very much turned on by the money. It wasn't very admirable, what she did that year. Maybe it was supposed to be funny but from my point of view it was uncalled for, just unprofessional.'

A postscript to the Athlete of the Year award was that Freeman, and Gainsford, with times in the world top 20 over 200m on 1992 comparisons, were a class above Jane Flemming internationally that year, yet she won the award. The following season the rules were changed so that if athletes recorded world top 10 or 20 performances compared with the previous year's rankings, they received extra bonus points.

Bideau readily concedes he made errors with Cathy's career; that's how they learnt, gradually evolving into an experienced racing team. There is no school which teaches athletic management, no text book for Bideau to unerringly unlock Cathy's talent. What he brought to the nexus was enthusiasm, motivation and some 20 years of ardour for track and field. Bideau is a French name. Nick's father, a chef, came to Australia from Sardinia in 1954. The Bideaus lived at Box Hill, 16km out of Melbourne, where Nick ran as a Little Athlete. He remembers a collective concerned sigh sweeping across the Bennettswood State School assembly when the headmaster announced that Ron Clarke had collapsed after the 10,000m in Mexico City at the 1968 Olympics.

At Burwood High School, Nick teetered around four minutes for 1500m and 15 minutes for the 5000m and, aged 16, recalls being passed by a small-framed boy in a cross-country race at Sunbury. Ego pricked—'That little kid's not going to beat me'—he chased and passed him. Amused friends told him later, 'That kid is Steve Moneghetti, he's going to be a good runner.' 'Not bad for a 10-year-old,' puffed Nick. 'He's 14!' they all chorused, laughing.

Bideau was invited by the track and cross country coach, Ray Kring, to attend Allan Hancock College, a community college in California. He trained hard and discovered that, at anything over 1500m, where black athletes tail off, Americans don't rate. 'I won a few college races over there,' he says. 'It used to amuse me how the Americans are so insulated they lose touch with reality. They thought they were great and I'd tell them, "How can you guys be any good, you can't even beat me!"' After two years he returned home, completed a physical education degree, and then came a turning point when he struck up his friendship with the great New Zealand 1500m runner John Walker.

Indirectly, Walker had a substantial influence on Freeman

A SAD HOMECOMING

via Bideau. Walker ran his last race for New Zealand when he tripped and fell in the 1990 Commonwealth Games 1500m on the same day that Cathy won her relay gold medal. Walker, in his black Kiwi strip, long hair flying, had always been a hero of Bideau's. Nick met him while working at the 1985 Zatopek meeting in Melbourne at which Walker ran.

That year, aged 25, Bideau's interest took him to the World Cup in Canberra where he saw Marita Koch set her phenomenal 400m world record which, as I write, still stands. 'I thought there was something wrong that day,' says Nick. 'I thought she must be in the wrong lane. You know, started off the wrong line.' Raelene Boyle saw that run too but disregards it. 'I don't include that in performances I wish to remember,' she says. 'There's no doubt she was running like a man and it's particularly sad that those records still stand and that the IAAF won't do anything about it.' Boyle concedes there are drugs in sport today, but not quite as blatantly as there were then.

Maurie Plant was there too and couldn't believe it, but says, 'Despite all the special breakfasts she might have had, I still think we've got the potential to reach those levels again.' Bideau agrees. 'People talk about how she was cheating, OK, but my belief is that it is possible to run that fast. Just takes a while to catch up.'

The following year, 1986, Nick planned a tour of Europe until, riding his bike in Fitzroy one day, a truck turned unexpectedly in front of him and knocked him down. He was lucky to survive. 'I could see the back wheels coming towards my head and I thought my days were over,' he says. 'I rolled away and looking back saw the back wheels run straight over my legs.'

After he recovered, Nick attended the 1986 Commonwealth Games in Edinburgh, jogging regularly with Walker who then invited him to travel the Euro circuit with him. 'Being introduced to people by Walker made a big difference to how I was treated,' says Bideau. 'He was a legend, knew everyone, had their respect.' Nick loved the circuit and Walker encouraged him to get involved. But how? Well, to start with by learning, and Nick watched how Walker would train specifically for big races and use smaller races in between to improve his form. A star of the 1970s, Walker was also a pioneer of the circuit in being well paid, though he never asked to be treated like royalty and always made major races his priority ahead of money. All this would manifest itself in Bideau's management of Freeman years later.

That 1986 tour left Bideau with a reservoir of experience and enthusiasm which he would later devote to Cathy Freeman and which later propelled him into a career in track and field management. He was a physical education teacher but in 1985 had begun writing small pieces for *Australian Runner* magazine. That same year he got to know television sports identity Bruce McAvaney who recommended he write contributions for the *Herald Sun*. In 1988 when the *Herald Sun*'s long-time athletics writer, Judy-Joy Davies, resigned, Bideau became a full-time journalist.

To complete the cycle, on 16 September 1990, he ran, and reported upon, the Great North half-marathon in South Shields, northern England, in which Moneghetti, now a good friend, was entered. The race would finish close to midnight Australian time, so he told Moneghetti, 'Wayne Gardner's just won the Australian Grand Prix at Phillip Island, you'll have to do something pretty special here to make the Aussie papers.' Nick came in with a creditable 1hr 9min 34s to find Monners waiting, grinning and asking, 'What about a world record, is that special enough?' Nick laughed, disbelievingly. 'I did, I ran 1hr and 34s,' insisted Monners. Nick stirred his weary legs and ran another mile to the nearest pub phone to bring the glad news to the *Herald Sun* in Melbourne. Three months later he was sitting on the grass oval at Kooralbyn telling Cathy Freeman she should come to Melbourne.

A SAD HOMECOMING

Freeman was now in her second domestic season since moving to Melbourne and it ended with her and Bideau heading for the world indoor titles in Toronto, Canada. Cathy slept almost the entire flight. 'If I was a racehorse they'd say that I travel well,' she says, pleased at her unusual skill. It is no small attribute. Not all Australians run well overseas. 'They're fine at home,' says Maurie Plant. 'Then, as soon as they hit different tucker, get mucked around at airports, "Where's my bags? Where's the car?"—when things go wrong, it throws them. Cathy's an easy goer, a smooth traveller, those things aren't a problem to her.' Not when you have Bideau doing all the worrying.

Toronto, where it was snowing, became a great meet for the sun-fit Australians, fresh from their Down Under season. Gainsford ran second in the 200m behind Russia's Irina Privalova; Damien Marsh won a 200m silver; Darren Clark won a 400m bronze; Renee Poetschka was fifth in the 400m final and Kerry Saxby was second in the 3km walk. A happy meet for all except Cathy, who was disqualified for running out of her lane in her heat. Cathy had never run on a 200m indoor track in her life, nor a track with two sharply banked bends like a cycling track. Outdoor tracks are 400 metres per lap.

'I hate running indoors,' she says. 'I can't run my normal way, I can't spread out with my long strides. I can't do what comes naturally to me, and I feel claustrophobic. I was a long way in front so I eased up a bit around the second bend and whenever you slow down you fall inwards because of the track slant. I felt myself falling sideways a bit, but I didn't know I'd run out of my lane.'

Since the runner who came second to Cathy in her heat, Russian Natalya Voronova, ran third in the final behind Privalova and Gainsford, Cathy probably lost a medal through her inexperience. She consoled herself that the indoors were nowhere near the standard of the outdoor world titles, and probably not even as strong as some of the major Euro-circuit meets. 'This is a waste of time,' she told Nick. 'I'm not coming back here.' It was a rare prima donna outburst, prompted partially because she had been eager to make amends for her Brisbane defeat by Melinda. But, says Bideau, 'As it turns out Gainsford is an outstanding indoor runner because the two bends suit her, so Freeman might not have beaten her anyway.'

After big meets, Cathy likes to boogie and so she, Nick and Darren Clark headed for Toronto's nightlife where they found themselves queuing for a dim-lit, downtown club. The club's ambience made Nick feel distinctly uneasy. 'Let's go in here,' said Cathy. Nick was distinctly cool. 'What's the problem, what's the problem?' Cathy asked. Nick had spent a long time in Los Angeles as a student and saw racism from both sides. Once, while out for a run, he was chased by a gun-waving youth. 'Have a look around, we're the only white blokes here,' he said. 'It's a bit intimidating.' Cathy looked at him amusedly. 'Now you know how I feel.'

In fact Nick knew a little how Cathy felt because of his olive skin tone. At school, kids used to call him Coco, brown-bread or an Aborigine, though his features are sharply Mediterranean. His mother believes some far back Moorish ancestry of his father's has emerged in him. 'The only time it really bothered me was when I was in a science class once,' says Nick. 'We were experimenting with some eggs and one of them was really dark. This kid picks this brown egg out and says, "See this egg here, Nick, that's you," and puts that by itself, gets the rest and says, "This is all of us." It made me feel like I wasn't one of them.'

Cathy and Nick flew out to LA for a holiday, staying with black American friends, Denny and Beverly Scott, who Bideau knew from his college days. Nick hired a convertible and they cruised the Santa Barbara coast in great style, until one day they got lost and found themselves in central LA, not far from Watts, scene of destructive race riots in 1965. Nick immediately raised the convertible's roof and locked the doors. He knew it was dangerous. Denny had told him, 'Don't walk around here, don't run around here, don't leave your car. People will shoot you, laugh and walk away.'

Cathy urged Nick, 'Stop and I'll ask these kids which way,' pointing to a group of young black kids hanging out on a street corner. 'No way,' exclaimed Nick. 'This is the hood. They could be on smack, and might pull a gun and blow your head off!' Says Cathy, 'It was cool, I felt pretty relaxed there. I think because I'm black I just mix in.' Says Nick, 'Cathy's got this confidence in not knowing who she is, plus she's black, but over there it's not whether you're black or white, it's because they don't know you, you're not from the hood.' One evening they went to a black nightclub with world long jump champion Mike Powell. 'I could feel people looking at me dancing with Cathy, because I was white,' says Nick. Powell told him, 'No, no, they're OK, they're cool.' Nick told him, 'I'll take your word for it, Mike.'

Bideau now recognised how Cathy relaxed in predominantly black communities. 'She just loved it,' he says. 'Suddenly I was the minority, that's what she likes about America. When we go to places where there are few black people, like Ireland, she'll say, "There's no blacks here. Are these people racist?" I said I didn't know. I said, "They have enough problems with the British to be worried about an Australian Aborigine."'

After a short break back in Australia, the athletes headed for the world outdoor championships in Stuttgart, Germany, in August. Bruce McAvaney told Bideau, 'Cathy'll go all right in the 200m, but I don't think she'll make the final.' Bideau begged to differ and after she won the 200m at both the British AAAs and the Welsh Games in July, each time defeating Gainsford, it seemed McAvaney had underestimated her improvement.

Before the trip, Bideau had asked Davis Cup tennis player, Wally Masur, where all the players stayed during Wimbledon. They didn't stay in hotels, surely? Masur put

Nick on to a holiday renting company and he signed on for six weeks for a house in Balham, south London, complete with television, phone, video and home-cooking facilities. It became home for Cathy, Bideau, coach Fortune and Peter O'Donoghue, the Australian 5000m champion. It was also not far from Crystal Palace, where Cathy ran one of her few 400m races of the tour, a close second in 51.34s to American Natasha Kaiser-Brown. The arrangement suddenly threw them into close proximity, all day, with Peter Fortune who they normally only saw at training for two hours a day. Of different ages and interests, they gallantly talked endless athletics until Nick, who had hired a car for him and Cathy to go training, took off for drives, and Fortune went his own way, his own happy tourist.

Cathy was due to run the 300m at Gateshead, where she had run so well before Barcelona the previous year, but fell ill and withdrew. Nick sighed and handed back the handy appearance fee she had been paid. He asked Maurie Plant, 'Is there any warm place where Catherine can run a good time, in good conditions?' He wanted Cathy to gain confidence in herself with a good result. Plant set them up at a little meet in Massa Maritima in Italy where Cathy defeated Bahamian Pauline Davis and ran 22.72s, her third win in three starts.

As a bonus, their return flight was from Pisa and they spent the day wandering the ancient town, a leisure their busy schedule usually precluded. After all the tourist talk, Cathy was amazed at how small the leaning tower was. 'It was closed, so we couldn't climb it, but it was no higher than a two-storey house,' says Cathy. 'I love Italy, I could easily live there, especially the northern parts. But I didn't like the heaps of beggars, women and children dressed in black, hanging around.' Of course the athletes, in their tracksuits and shoes, and sharp wraparound shades, looked distinctly like wealthy Americans.

At the world titles in Stuttgart, Merlene Ottey asked Bideau, 'Why isn't Cathy running the 400m?' Bideau explained: 200m this year, get fast, then 400m next year. Even so he glanced enviously at the field for the 400m—no Pérec, who had also decided to run the 200m. American Jearl Miles won it in 49.82s, a time beyond Cathy at that stage, but she might have challenged Kaiser-Brown's 50.17 for second, or Sandie Richards's 50.44 for third. Perhaps she had missed an opportunity, perhaps not—she still had not broken 51s herself.

Cathy, the youngest in the 200m field, was now definitely faster than in Barcelona in 1992, but not as strong as the top-level runners. She won through to the semi-final, looked up her draw and, once more, there was Marie-José Pérec beside her. 'I knew the semi-final would be tough,' says Bideau. 'Often people run their best race in the semi, just to make the final.' Pérec got the staggers halfway down the straight but held on to run fourth, ahead of Cathy who was fifth in 22.58, just 4/100ths off her best. It was the old story: out of the final. If she'd been in the other semi she may have made the final. But she had better luck than Gainsford whose hamstring strain forced her out of the titles.

Merlene Ottey won the 200m final from America's Gwen Torrence, Russia's Irina Privalova, with Pérec fourth. In the grandstand sat Cathy and Nick, two very frustrated Aussies, Cathy declaring, 'That's the last time I don't make the final.' She kept her promise as she had with her others: to go beyond the mere relay after Tokyo in 1991, beyond the second round after Barcelona in 1992. Bideau had been waiting, and the promise came. Bruce McAvaney said, in the nicest possible way, 'Nick, I told you she wouldn't make the final.' 'Yeah, yeah,' said Nick. 'But she was stiff.'

Coach Fortune was more upbeat. 'She was ninth qualifier, but to my way of thinking she'd arrived as a world-class sprinter,' he says. 'Not quite in the upper echelons, but consistently there. And it's not always about conditioning, or physique, or technique or science. A lot of it comes from within her.'

After the titles, Flemming, Gainsford and long jumper

Nicole Boegman were off to a nightclub and invited Cathy to join them. Cathy, who unintentionally emanates a social separateness, was delighted to be asked along. As they piled into taxis, Cathy found herself stuck in the back with two male athletes unknown to them and Flemming called anxiously to Gainsford, 'Melinda, Melinda, look after Cathy!' Says Cathy, 'That was really nice, she did show me kindness. I remember those little things.' It was certainly a pleasant advance upon the 'golden bracelet' affair.

Most runners high-tailed it home after the worlds, but Cathy coped so well with travel that Maurie Plant urged her to stay on the circuit. So they flew back to the north of England for a 400m race in Sheffield, where Cathy ran second to world champion Jearl Miles, who said to Bideau good-naturedly, 'Got your girl this time!'—as though she sensed her victories over Cathy would eventually come to an end.

Arriving back in London on Sunday night, Cathy, Nick and Maurie drove to Plant's parents-in-law's house near Bromley. While in Sheffield, Plant had learnt his father had died in Melbourne after a long illness. Maurie could make it back to Melbourne, but he couldn't be guaranteed a flight back to London. Plant had just broken through to work for the International Amateur Athletics Federation at three upcoming grand prix. It was so important to his livelihood that he couldn't afford to reject the opportunity. Thus it was a sad return to London for the group, made sadder still when Plant's wife, Kate, put down the phone as he walked in. 'Where's Cathy?' she asked quietly. 'I've just had a message that her dad has died.'

Norman Freeman, 53, diabetic, had died of a stroke at Woorabinda. Maurie told Nick, who motioned Cathy, upstairs to break the news. She took it badly: angry, weeping, distraught. All the emotions pent up from her separation from him over the years came rushing out. Maurie climbed the stairs and he and Cathy shared their mutual sadnesses, just two days apart. 'I didn't know he was that sick,' she told

A SAD HOMECOMING

Maurie. 'You'd never know, because he never complained.' Since Anne-Marie's funeral in 1990 Cathy's running schedule had kept her busy and she would have loved to have spent more time with him.

Cathy said she wrote him letters, phoned, and set up meetings. She always warned him not to drink before their meetings, and once was devastated when he failed to show at a planned meeting in Rockhampton to meet Nick. So Nick never met him. Despite that disappointment, Nick never heard her speak ill of him. She loved her father's charisma and flamboyance. 'He was the funniest guy I think I've ever met,' she says. 'He just made me break up on the phone, with belly laughs. He was always larger than life. Once he started telling a story, everyone wanted to be around him.' This was Fringey Freeman, life of any bar, teller of yarns, footy star of yore. 'But he didn't take good care of himself,' says Cathy wistfully. Alcohol didn't kill Norman Freeman, diabetes did, as it did Cathy's maternal grandfather, George Sibley. It is estimated that 30 per cent of all Aboriginal adults suffer from diabetes, four times the rate for other Australians. Research is ongoing, but a poor diet, often combined with alcohol abuse and smoking, is said to contribute to the onset of the condition.

Bideau tried to book flights home in time for the funeral but to no avail. He called the airlines constantly, but Cathy didn't sense any desperation in his voice. He was not in touch with her spiritual side, with her need to get home, or the powerful need within Aboriginal culture for family to mourn together. 'Maybe it was my problem, that I didn't show enough panic or impress upon Nick the urgency,' she says. But Cathy was used to Nick organising her. 'I was used to being told what to do, that I was going to run here and run there,' she says. So she was not about to start ringing the airlines herself and hectoring them for a seat. Though she would today. 'We just had different views,' she says. 'Nick's attitude was, "It's sad, but he's gone, your Dad's gone," sort of thing,' says Cathy. 'It was a hard time for me. I don't want to bring the whole thing up again, but I still get very angry today. It's pretty serious, I missed an important moment in my life there.'

Nick defends himself by saying that in her grief, Cathy withdrew and he could not read her mood. He says he didn't want her to think he was pushing her in any particular direction. Bideau spent years second-guessing Freeman's true feelings, no matter what she actually said. It was integral to their communication but in this particular instance it failed. It was an unfortunate breakdown in understanding between them. As with divorce, unless you were there at the time, a satisfactory answer is not always available.

A solemn Team Freeman decided to press on with their short racing schedule, the first a 200m in Brussels, and then headed for a tiny little town, Rieti, 100km into the foothills above Rome. As they filed into the Maramonte Hotel, in Rieti, no English spoken, the management haphazardly allocated rooms, Nick and Cathy ending up in a magnificent double bedroom suite, with spa bath and massive lounge-room. But world champion Linford Christie and fellow British 200m champion John Regis, two huge men, were cooped up in a tiny dog box unit. Amid great indignation from the shrill Brits, and great hilarity for the Aussies, the rooms were sorted out. It brought a more cheerful note to the group and next day Cathy went out and ran 22.37s, a PB, topping Gainsford's best, an amazing run under the circumstances. 'Oh, I ran from my heart that day, for my father, that's why I ran so well,' says Cathy simply.

Exhausting days of air flights finally delivered them back to Australia and up to Rockhampton, where Cecelia, Cathy, Nick and Cathy's brothers, Gavin, Norman and Garth, drove in a station wagon to Norman Freeman's grave site at Woorabinda. Cathy stayed strong throughout, believing that after battling his debilitating alcoholism for so long, her father was now at peace.

A SAD HOMECOMING

It was reassuring, also, that when her father died, her uncle, John Talbot, had organised a bus to take mourners from Mackay to the funeral. 'I had no problem getting 45 people paying $20 a head for the five-hour trip,' says Talbot. 'They had that much respect for him.' Norman Freeman's brother, Norman Tolibah Fisher, had written a small obituary notice for the local paper: 'Rugby league was his forte, the saddle was his throne.'

During that visit up north, Cathy was taken aback when her cousins told her, 'Oh, you look like a white girl,' and 'Gees, you're talking like a white girl.' The more Cathy thought about it, the more she knew it was true. 'I had become confident, and I did dress, you know, like a white person,' she says. 'I felt comfortable among white people. And I accepted it, you just have to be like that, that's the way things are. You can't say "Shame" to me any more because I'm not ashamed or embarrassed at being black among white people. I'm out there every day.'

During the flight home from England, Cathy had thought some deep and meaningfuls about herself. 'I hadn't believed I could be as good an athlete as I was becoming,' she says. 'I didn't think I could turn this running gig into something so fulfilling. It was a big turnaround in my thinking. But I worried if I could keep it up. I thought, "Catherine, do you really want to go ahead with all this?" It was all getting so complicated. Sometimes before a race I'd think, "Oh shit, I wish I wasn't here." I thought about the pressure, the training, the Aboriginal thing. Then I remembered that everyone is human, and you're allowed to try and make something of your life, tackle it with your heart and soul and guts and nothing less. That way it was all up to me, wasn't it? But was I capable of doing it?'

On the flight, she retrieved a gift paper bag from her purse and wrote down the following:

'Some clear objectives and new aims involving my training preparation for the 1994 Commonwealths. Events at this

CATHY FREEMAN—A JOURNEY JUST BEGUN

stage—200 & 400. 200pb—22.37, 400pb—51.14. My 400pb has to improve—*has to*! Nick and I both agree that more 300, 400 & 500 sessions have to be done and they have to be of good quality. As a matter of fact I have to aim at making all my training sessions of higher and better quality: *much more solid*, good, decent, solid sessions.

As Laurie Lawrence says, '*Failing to prepare is preparing to fail*' and I certainly do not want that to happen! *I do not want to fail!*'

12

NO BIG CAT FIGHT.
PRE-COMMONWEALTH GAMES,
1993–94

Late in 1993, John Moriarty, of Balarinji designs, Cathy's first sponsor, arranged with mining giant CRA for a series of sport coaching clinics for Aborigines in the far north, including Doomadgee, a sparse community in the Gulf country. Cathy and Nick flew in with rugby league great Wally Lewis, and Aboriginal players, Ricky Walford of St George, and Larry Corowa who had coached with Lewis on the Gold Coast.

The footballers made for a humorous trip. At one landing strip, Lewis took one look at his tiny light aircraft and swapped planes with Cathy. He proved a good judge because soon after they took off, the door flew open in Cathy's plane. 'The poor guy near it was holding on for dear life,' says Cathy. 'It was really scary until we turned around and landed. Actually I was excited by it all, I got a buzz, but I wasn't next to the door!'

At Doomadgee, in steaming midday heat, as the Aboriginal children lined up, Corowa said softly to Wally, 'Gees, I don't know how these blackfellas put up with this heat.' Wally subdued a laugh with his friend. Then an Aborigine crept up close to Wally and whispered conspiratorially, 'Hey! How do you feel being a white fella out here?' Wally started giggling. The crowd of kids stood and stared at him in awe. They had all heard of King Wally. 'OK, play the ball,' said Wally, who has good rapport with children. 'Go on, play the ball.' An eight-year-old just gawked. 'C'mon, play the ball!' said Wally, wiping perspiration from his face. Larry Corowa came over. 'I think you better speak to them in our language, Wal.' 'What's that?' said Wally, puzzled. Corowa called out, 'Hey bro, play the ball now.'

While the footballers played games, Cathy was a star with a group of runners, wowing them with her 200m silver medal from the 1992 world juniors. She organised a race and found herself being chased home by a barefoot, 14-year-old girl in a red dress. Nick said to Cathy, 'That girl can run.' 'Yes, she can really go,' Cathy agreed. Bideau sought out the girl's father and spoke to him about his daughter's potential. 'Yeah, mate, she beats them all, boys too.' 'Ever take her to run in Townsville or Brisbane?' 'Ahh, no mate, too far to go down there. How we going to get there? Nah, too far. We're OK here, hey?'

Bideau was struck by the Aboriginal children's natural athleticism. 'That's what they do up there, they run,' he says. 'They play games, run around with a ball, chase each other, it's in their nature,' he says. 'They don't watch television, or play video games, or become computer nerds. They run and play.' While not exactly recommending the Aboriginal nation as Australia's equivalent of Kenya's Rift Valley—creche of the world's great male distance runners—Bideau laments the Aboriginal running talent lost through no development structure or path. Aborigines comprise two per cent of the Australian population, yet they constitute six per cent of the players in the AFL. The Norm Smith medal for the best player in the AFL grand final has been won four times (about 20 per cent) by players of Aboriginal descent. In the 1990s, indigenous players have comprised about half the backline in the Queensland State of Origin rugby league team. The paths for Aborigines to express themselves in AFL and rugby league are well trodden, but not in athletics. It gave Bideau fresh regard for the distance that Cathy Freeman's career had travelled in such a short time.

The trip made Cathy acutely aware of the black–white opportunity divide and, in early 1994, when the AFL began their 'I'd Like To See That' television advertisements, she asked Bideau, 'How come they have American blacks, Carl Lewis and Evander Holyfield, in these ads but no Australian Aborigines like Nicky Winmar and Michael Long? They're the most exciting in the game.' She wrote a letter to this effect to the *Herald Sun* newspaper in Melbourne, which published the letter large on 24 April 1994. 'We Australian blacks are the first and true Australians, and don't they call the AFL the Australian Football League?' she wrote in the letter. 'Could it be the AFL are not as proud of its Aboriginal players as are the fans that pay money to see the game?' The letter created quite a kerfuffle, and then AFL chief commissioner, Ross Oakley, published a response two days later, explaining that a new series of commercials did feature indigenous players, Nicky Winmar and Chris Lewis. After it all subsided, Cathy exclaimed to Bideau, 'Gees, I didn't know I had such a loud voice!'

Her Aboriginal voice was about to be heard louder than she could imagine in the most extraordinary manner, on the track and in the media at the 1994 Commonwealth Games in Victoria, Canada. Freeman, now ranked eighth in the world over 200m by *Track and Field News* magazine, began the season as usual with warm-up races in Devonport, this time a professional 400m handicap race in which she gave the field a huge start and won. A local journalist wrote the next day in wonderment, 'If she's ranked number eight in the world I'd like to see who's ranked number one!'

On the grand prix circuit she renewed her duel with Melinda Gainsford although, with the Games not until

CATHY FREEMAN—A JOURNEY JUST BEGUN

August, seven months off, domestic results were comparatively unimportant. Thus on 29 January, in Canberra, Cathy ran 51.68s for 400m, half a second outside her best, but that same night, after the 400m, she defeated Gainsford over 200m. A few days later she trained one evening and later casually strode through a club 100m race at Olympic Park, losing in a photo-finish to 15-year-old Lauren Hewitt in slow time. Debbie Flintoff-King, Hewitt's coach, leapt up and down and hugged her husband, Phil. Cathy and Nick looked at each other, like 'Huh?' Next day it made the radio news, 'Schoolgirl Downs Freeman.' Cathy was annoyed. She'd show them how significant it was.

Next meet in Brisbane, on 5 February, she strolled through 400m in 51.90s and then backed up in the 100m later in the night, scorching out in 11.24s. It bettered her previous best of 11.43s and was just 0.05s outside Kerry Johnson's national record. As I write, in 1998, it still stands as her PB for 100m. Gainsford was a close second in 11.45s. 'I don't know what came over me that night,' says Cathy. 'I think my mum and Bruce being in the crowd inspired me. I was just in the zone. After getting beaten by Lauren I thought I better get my 100m right.'

That run showed there could be no truce between Freeman and Gainsford. Once more both came under pressure from public interest. Later that month, in Melbourne, hometown crowd expectations high, Cathy moved on her blocks in the 100m, hesitated, blew the start and Gainsford blew her away. Even though she still had the 400m to run, Cathy stormed off the track and struggled with herself to actually remain at the stadium. She escaped to behind one of the grandstands. 'It wasn't the fact that I was beaten, Melinda's done that often enough, but that I missed the start,' says Cathy. 'I just got so angry with myself, I don't know what came over me but I nearly took off, I nearly left. I wasn't crying but I had tears of frustration. I had to go and spend some time on my own.'

NO BIG CAT FIGHT

She restored her spirits a few hours later by winning the 400m, defeating Poetschka in 51.15s, just outside her then best time, 51.14s set in 1992 at the English AAAs. But the relief was shortlived. In Hobart, on 26 February, the two premier sprinters met again over 200m in perfect conditions —a good tailwind around the bend, little headwind in the straight. Gainsford's bend was sensational, slinging her several metres ahead into the straight and, try as she might, Cathy couldn't make an impression. Gainsford in 22.32s, a new Australian record, breaking Denise Boyd's well-respected 22.35s which had stood since 1980. A great coup for Gainsford.

'Well done, Mel,' Cathy called out, but back in her hotel room it was a different tune. 'Do you think Gainsford's a better runner than me?' a depressed Cathy asked Nick, her voice small and full of doubts. 'Do people think she is? Why couldn't I run her down? What happened?' Nick reassured her as best he could, she was tired, she'd had a lot of races, Gainsford did run a super race.

This was galling for Cathy, to feel the pain that Melinda felt in losing, the price both paid for their head-to-head clashes. Coach Peter Fortune never considered Freeman to be egotistical, even though he knew that with athletes the problem was often to keep their mind on the job and the ego in check. 'She never bragged about herself,' he says. 'As a matter of fact she's almost the opposite, but she has a lot of inner ideas on who she is and how good she can be.'

Cathy flew home to Melbourne and that evening drove to Maurie and Kate Plant's house for some TLC for her bruised ego. Kate Plant is Anglo-Indian, and closer to Cathy's age than Maurie's. She and Cathy get on well, joke about their dark skins, and how their watches leave light, untanned outlines on their wrists. It is about as close to black companionship that Cathy gets in Melbourne. Eventually Cathy became godmother to one of their children.

'Catherine has a lot to give, up here,' says Maurie Plant,

tapping his temple. 'I told her she had the nationals to come in 10 days and the Games up ahead, why worry about a Hobart 200m? But she doesn't like getting done, and a kick in the pants goes a long way with her.'

Plant's psych-up therapy worked. One night at Olympic Park that week, ABC reporter Kathy Bowlen asked Freeman about her chances at the national titles in Sydney. 'Oh, I'll win the nationals,' she replied confidently, back to her usual blithe self. To celebrate the opening of the Betty Cuthbert stadium at Homebush—the warm-up track for the Sydney Olympics—the NSW government paid for US stars, Gwen Torrence and Michael Johnson, to come and compete. The 400m was the grand prix event in Europe that year. Cathy intended to run the 200–400m double at the Commonwealth Games, but Bideau always pushed Cathy to race the best sprinters, anywhere, any time, any distance. So it was the 100m and 200m and her ego on the line again.

The nationals, 12–13 March, were also the Games trials, and though narrowly beaten by Torrence, 11.46s to her own 11.52s, Cathy finished ahead of Gainsford. Next day she won the 200m (22.75s) outright from Melinda. So now it was Cathy's reversal of form which kick-started the media into duel mode again.

'Athletics Australia pumps it up because it brings crowds,' says Cathy. 'One-on-one rivalry makes for good headlines, but it wasn't just two athletes against each other, it was our differences as well, black against white, big girl against little girl.' Cathy was annoyed when many of her media interviews inevitably revolved around this rivalry when in reality she had higher priorities in mind, like the Games and the Euro circuit. 'That's what people didn't understand,' she says. 'I mean, there was no big cat fight between us. We're fine. Melinda is good to race because she is so competitive, she's never beaten. But we're different, we're not friends, so it gets a little awkward sometimes. It's all right, it's OK—though it's not great either, the way it's turned out.'

Gainsford agrees they are different personalities and might not be friends anyway, even without the rivalry. 'I respect Cathy, I think she's a lovely girl and she's a great athlete,' says Gainsford. 'But it's not nice, you hear different things second-hand, read things each other say in the media, even though half of them are probably not true anyway. It puts a bit of a strain on us and that's probably why we can never be best buddies.'

Renee Poetschka then opened another front in the war of words. Having won the 100 and 200m, Cathy did not run the 400m and in her absence Renee blazed around the track in 50.19s, an Australian record, nearly a second faster than Cathy had ever run. This was Cathy's first love, the 400m, and here she was watching Renee steal it from beneath her nose. 'I remember sitting with my mother on the hill and getting really angry that I wasn't in the race,' says Cathy. 'I was surprised by the time, it was a great run by Renee, but I wished I had been down there.'

Poetschka went into print saying that the media obsession with Freeman–Gainsford was detracting from the attention Renee deserved. 'It's getting to the stage where I'm getting annoyed they aren't putting enough emphasis on my performances,' she told Mike Hurst in the Sydney *Telegraph Mirror* on 4 June 1994. 'Stories are coming out saying Cathy is the better big-meet performer. Well, how can you really say that when at most world championships and world indoor champs and the Olympics, I've done a better performance than her?'

It was true too. She was Australian 400m champion in 1991, 1993 and 1994. As well she made the 400m semis in the 1991 worlds and 1992 Olympics, and was a finalist in the 1993 world indoors—each a superior result to Cathy's. On the other hand she had a 0–6 record against Freeman in the 1993–94 season over 400m. Renee honeyed her comments by adding that she got on famously with Freeman. 'You can't have a go at Cathy because she doesn't have a nasty word to say about anyone,' she said. 'But that all can change. You say something and the media takes it out of context and you've got this big horrible rivalry between you.' Just so, Renee.

Cathy's national victories galvanised the commercial world of sponsors who started piecing together her unique appeal and the approaching Commonwealth Games. Ford and Telstra came on board to join Nike, as Freeman began acquiring a portfolio of the biggest company names in Australia.

For the first time, Bideau and Plant decided Cathy should tackle America to prepare for Europe and Canada, but not without opposition from Fortune. The coach was worried about her strength training, which he would have to reduce if she was to race in the US. And he was worried about Poetschka at the Games. He was just ... worried. Bideau insisted Cathy simply train on, and race. This stemmed from one of Nick's insights into a great track self-delusion—athletes' belief that they are never ever quite ready to race, if only they had another month, another week, then they'd be ready. Maybe.

'The Americans, the Europeans are all starting to race by April,' Bideau told Fortune. 'The big meets are in July and August. Forget double peaks and returning to basics. Let's just go forward.' As for Poetschka, Nick was sizing up Pérec now, the A team, not Poetschka, the B team! This was what John Walker had taught Bideau, to think beyond Antipodean shores, think Europe and the US. Plant backed Bideau. He wanted Cathy to toughen up, learn to race 400m every which way, on different tracks against unknown opposition.

Cathy and Nick flew into New York on Saturday and had dinner that night with Plant, Tim Forsyth and ... Peter Jess who, on a whim and because he is an ardent fan and friend of Cathy's, had jetted in from London where he had been on business. Next day, up against Pérec, American champion Natasha Kaiser-Brown, and 1993 world champion Jearl

Miles, Cathy drew lane two, inside Pérec in three. Perfect, she had the look on Marie-José. What she saw was Pérec running very, very quickly and even though she drew level with the Olympic champion as they entered the straight, the effort took the sting out of Cathy. She faded to finish fourth, behind Pérec, Miles and Kaiser-Brown. Cathy immediately walked over and put her arm around Pérec's shoulders, who was quite spent.

'Our girl wasn't strong in the last 100m,' Jess told Bideau. 'No,' Nick agreed. 'But she just flew in from Australia. It's four in the morning for her.' Next day, tourism day, they spent boating around the Statue of Liberty and sightseeing New York. 'We always try and do some small thing, so we don't become couch potatoes,' says Plant. 'We don't chase around and get knackered, just turn off the mind.'

Then, across America to San Jose on the west coast for a five-day visit with Tim Forsyth and long jumper Nicole Boegman. They stayed in a small apartment next to a high school track in Los Garros, a small village near San Jose. Their tourist trek here took them up to San Francisco to ride the cable cars over the steep hills, scene of most memorable American film car chases. They cruised Fisherman's Wharf restaurant strip and strolled the shops in Ghirardelli Square. Kenyan 400m hurdler Erick Keter joined them and kept Cathy enthralled with stories of Kenyan culture, about their polygamy, and how Kenyan husbands only tell their wives they love them once, and never again. Cathy, doubting, looked at Maurie for confirmation. 'That often, eh?' cracked the irrepressible Plant.

In the serious business of the San Jose 400m, Cathy was given lane two, Pérec, as always was in lane four, with Sandie Richards in lane five. Richards's manager Cubie Seegobin objected to Sandie having to lead out Pérec. 'Man, I'm not happy. Don't give my girl that lane,' he complained, eventually laying down an ultimatum: 'OK, if she don't change, she's not running!'

Seegobin's argument was that the previous season, in 1993, Richards won the world indoors 400m in Toronto and then ran third in the world championships 400m in Stuttgart. She had status. With an inside lane draw she could chase Pérec, a better option than being outside the Olympic champion and becoming Pérec's hare. US track meets don't have a budget for appearance money, just prize money, so Nick and Cathy were astounded when Sandie, who could ill afford it, pulled out. 'That took guts,' says Cathy. 'She's a person of principle and she obviously thought she deserved better.' On the other hand, Pérec was the best, and lane five was one of the best and probably as good as Richards deserved.

Five minutes before the race, the IAAF official, former Jamaican Olympic sprinter Don Quarrie, told Bideau, 'Lane five's empty, Cathy can switch if she likes.' But this was another pet mindset of Bideau's which would pay its ultimate dividend in later years. Says Nick, 'We always used to say, "The 400m is round, everyone has to run one lap," so we never made an issue of the lanes.' Cathy had the final say, stuck with lane two, ran second to Pérec, and achieved a milestone: her first under 51s.

Nick congratulated her after the race. A PB he said, 50.82s. 'Is that faster than Renee's time?' asked Cathy. No, it wasn't. 'Then it's not so good, is it?' said Cathy. Well, yes, and therefore very revealing of Cathy herself. Though she aimed for international standards, she knew her first step was to become the best in Australia, and Renee's time remained an obstacle to that. As an adjunct, for her to not know automatically that Poetschka's Australian record was 50.19s showed how she delegated such responsibilities to her team.

Back home she trained for a month in Melbourne before flying out to London for a brief European tour before the Games. At Brisbane international airport Cathy paused at the walkway into the aircraft, held up two fingers and said to her parents, Cecelia and Bruce, 'Two golds. I'm going to win two golds.' It was a breathtaking prediction even for

NO BIG CAT FIGHT

someone as candid as Cathy. 'I don't know what came over me to say that,' she says. 'They were my last words to them as I walked away. Sometimes I just know.' At that stage Cathy knew from her recent American visit that Jamaica's Olympic medallists Merlene Ottey and Juliet Cuthbert wouldn't be at the Games. And she had convincing win–loss records over both Gainsford and Poetschka at home. Nevertheless, with the Games still two months off, it was a big call.

In London it was business as usual, renting the same house as the previous year, car hired, all ticking over like clockwork. Nick, Maurie Plant and Fortune set Cathy's race program—mostly Maurie, who had become an integral part of Team Freeman, not just as a circuit agent but because he admired what Freeman was achieving. Plant, a large man with a short haircut, is renowned in athletics for his brusque, blustering manner. Jokes and good-natured insults flow ceaselessly, the better to disguise the shrewd eye he casts upon athletic meets. He had been an athlete, but not of the calibre of his brother Vin Plant, who was a Commonwealth Games standard hurdler in the 1970s.

Plant met British big wheel Andy Norman in 1978 and two years later, when star Kenyan middle distance runner Henry Rono didn't turn up to tour Australia as scheduled, Norman sent Plant after him to Africa. Maurie brought him back alive and gained a reputation as a can-do man. 'I went overseas in 1982 with $200 in my pocket and began picking up work, listening, learning and working with the major meet directors,' says Plant. 'You gravitate towards certain people. I got along well with Svein-Arne Hansen, who runs the Bislett Games in Oslo, and Wilfried Meert, director of the Van Damme Memorial in Brussels, and I do some work for Zurich.' These three just happened to be three of the biggest meets of the season, with Berlin a close fourth. Plant argues that Stockholm, with its tradition and quality, is often a match for any, and down a notch are Lausanne, Monte

Carlo, Nice, Paris, Monaco and Rome. Behind them come the smaller British and Italian meets. Plant is often contracted by meet directors to shepherd groups of athletes, from young Kenyan distance champions to senior British Olympic sprint champions, from one city to the next so the circus can go on.

Says Bideau, 'Maurie learned from Andy Norman who spent years preparing champions like Steve Ovett and Seb Coe with races. Maurie knows that Stockholm and Oslo are often close together these days and all the Americans arrive to run in Stockholm on Wednesday and back up in Oslo on Friday. They arrive tired, run once, have a late night, can't sleep, then move to Oslo where we've been waiting to pounce on them. Maurie knows not to be on the road for more than two meets without returning to rest at home base, and not to race in places where you have to fly for three hours and then a long bus trip at the other end. He knows places where the hotel is bad, the food worse. You don't catch us running in Moscow, but you'll see us in Oslo every year.' Plant's expertise earned him work with the Ten Network at the 1987 world titles and 1988 Olympics, the BBC from 1990, and with Seven as well thereafter. Bideau began to get to know Plant in Europe in 1986 when Plant was guiding Darren Clark and Nick was travelling with Kiwi John Walker. Plant first saw Cathy at the 1989 trials for the Auckland Games where, he says, 'She had a certain lightness of step, a stride and rhythm that a lot of duffers couldn't obtain with a lifetime of training.'

First up, Cathy ran at Gateshead in England where, though sick with a cold, she ran third behind Jearl Miles and compatriot Natasha Kaiser-Brown over 400m. Then, in Lausanne, on 6 July, from lane seven, Cathy found how difficult it is to pace a class 400m. She ran so easily down the back straight that Kaiser-Brown, in lane five, caught her. Thus prompted, Cathy accelerated so that Kaiser-Brown never actually passed her, then showed great stamina to

NO BIG CAT FIGHT

outstay runners like Sandie Richards and Pauline Davis to finish third behind the talented, but mostly injured, American Maicel Malone, who held off Miles to win in 50.05s.

Cathy's time, 50.23s, was another PB, and ranked her fourth in the world that season. A more smoothly judged race would certainly have brought her home inside Poetschka's national record of 50.19s. Back across the Channel and up to Edinburgh for a dismal 200m race—'It was cold and yukky,' says Cathy—and then down to London and another 400m at Crystal Palace.

Bideau was urging her to learn the tactics of the 400m, to feel the pace, control it. 'Don't go too hard the first 200m, just keep up,' he said. 'Attack the third 100m, hold your form down the last 100m.' She ran precisely to instructions, from lovely lane four, easing up to a metre inside Jearl Miles in five at the bottom of the back straight. Then she kicked clear by several metres, held it coming into the straight and, too late, Miles closed to within a metre on the line. Puffed and excited, Cathy drank from a Lucozade bottle, and accepted a hug from Miles.

It was a big moment, defeating the feisty American, Jearl Miles, for the first time. Each race, it seemed, Cathy climbed another step up the ladder. Her 50.77s meant she was regularly breaking 51s now. The BBC TV commentator said of her win, 'The manner of that victory showed the strength of character of this young woman. When she gets some more hard training into those legs, she can go a great deal faster, way, way below 50s.' But in Nice a few days later she received a reality check, relegated to fourth behind Kaiser-Brown (50.92s), Malone (50.93s) and Miles (50.95s). Cathy ran 51s flat in a photo-finish in which only 8/100ths of a second separated the four runners.

The pace of travelling was frantic as they took off for Scandinavia, firstly Stockholm then Oslo. Melinda Gainsford had arrived to begin her European season but the Stockholm director, Raijne Soderberg, told Maurie Plant, who was representing Athletics Australia, that he could not run two Australians in the same race: choose between the 100m and 200m for Freeman and Gainsford. Gainsford was the national 200m record holder, Cathy the current national 200m champion. Plant sensibly put Melinda, the better short sprinter, in the 100m and Cathy in the 200m.

Gainsford's coach, Jackie Byrnes, was ropable. 'She's the national record holder in both, she should run in both,' she argued. Says Melinda, 'It was frustrating. Maurie was supposed to be looking after me. I was the 200m silver medallist at the world indoors the previous year. Yet Cathy got the 200m place ahead of me.' Plant was in an awkward spot. 'Mel wasn't running well at that stage and subsequently I think I more than made up for it with more races,' he says. 'Originally she didn't want many races and then she did. I've always been available to help with her race program but she regards me as being part of Cathy's camp and I don't blame her for that. But whenever people are disappointed, fingers get pointed at me, it's the normal syndrome when competition is involved.' The following year Gainsford changed to use Linford Christie's race agent.

The clash between the Big Two, Russian Irina Privalova and Olympic champion Gwen Torrence, had the Stockholm crowd so excited the officials had to abort the first start because of the noise. Privalova prevailed over Torrence with Cathy third in 22.54s. In truth, daylight was third, so superior were the first two, but Cathy never stopped trying. In lane eight, coming into the straight, she was half a metre behind Nigerian Mary Onyali in lane six, but battled on to outdip her. Onyali was one of Cathy's main 200m dangers for the Commonwealth Games. Maurie Plant raised his eyebrows at Cathy. 'That's a good one to take to Canada with you.'

And then in Oslo, on 22 July, a huge crowd turned out for the return bout between Privalova and Torrence. A rousing Mexican wave rippled around the packed stands before the start. With Oslo's six-lane track, the outside lane is so close to the fence that the first row of seated spectators can almost reach out and touch the lane six runner. Torrence obtained revenge on Privalova with Cathy an impressive third again, this time in 22.32s, equal to Gainsford's Australian record. Melinda ran in that race as well, from lane three, but finished six metres back, nowhere near as race fit as Cathy. Torrence received a hug from Cathy—the winners always do if Cathy's close enough to them.

Against policy, but on Plant's request as part of their Oslo deal, Cathy reluctantly agreed to race once more that trip, in Byrkjelo, Norway. So it was Stockholm Wednesday, Oslo Friday and now Byrkjelo, Sunday—heavy-duty 200m racing. 'Cathy didn't want to run,' says Bideau. 'I told her it was part of being a pro, sometimes you just have to do the job. This is how she became so hardened, why other athletes admire how she can back up.' Her edge held, 22.62s, with Gainsford second, slowly gathering form. Cathy's compensation was that they stayed in a picturesque hotel overlooking a scenic fiord. As well, an hour's drive away, they visited a mountain glacier, stream and lake. 'It was beautiful, really breathtaking,' says Cathy. 'The glacier was really blue, the air was crisp and clear, it was something special. And we had sheep and cows with bells clinking right beside us.'

After the meet, Andy Norman drove them at breakneck speed back to a ferry, en route to an airport for a connecting flight to Oslo and thence to London. Around winding mountainsides they sped, overtaking traffic with the mountain rock face one side, sheer drops the other. 'We were sliding and you looked down, and AHHH! it was a long, long way down,' says Cathy. All the time Andy Norman was telling them reassuringly, 'Don't worry, these other cars don't want to hit us any more than we want to hit them.' As she often does in such situations, Cathy took the slumber option in the back seat.

It was late July and Peter Fortune wanted Cathy to run at

Sestriere, in Italy, to record a confidence-boosting fast time for the approaching Commonwealth Games. Sestriere is a high-altitude meet where the thin air assists athletes to break world records, encouraged by rewards of Ferraris and Mercedes. Plant successfully argued that Cathy had raced enough and Nick could see the benefit of Cathy concentrating on two weeks solid training. But Plant also felt, after Stockholm, he owed Melinda Gainsford a free rein, without Freeman's shadow on her shoulder. Gainsford went to Italy and on 31 July, in perfect conditions, legal 1.9m wind assisting, ran 11.12s, an Australian 100m record, breaking Kerry Johnson's 11.19s set at the Commonwealth Games in Auckland. She now held the national 100m record and co-held the 200m record with Cathy.

Bideau and Fortune both wondered what time Cathy would have run had she gone. Long jumper, David Culbert, later said he thought that based on how easily Freeman had beaten Gainsford in their previous two races, that Cathy might have run 10.9s that day. But Bideau was adamant they weren't in Europe to chase Gainsford or gainsay her records. Cathy's rivalry with Gainsford was fierce. 'But if Cathy wasn't in the race, we always wanted Gainsford to do well,' says Bideau. 'We didn't want Melinda not to be a star. Sometimes she must have been sick of the sight of us, so good luck to her.' Bideau, in his journalist's role, often interviewed Gainsford on that trip. 'She was defensive, on guard,' he says. 'She never acted disappointed even if she was shattered. And if I said, "Well done, Mel," she'd say, "Thanks, but Cathy ran really well." She held it together, all the time.'

Fortune now concedes that the degree of difficulty of reaching Sestriere, a remote town requiring a long bus trip at the end of the flight, might have risked Freeman's energies. This was the second season that Fortune stayed with Cathy and Nick in London and, though they valued his presence, they were no more compatible 24 hours a day this trip than they were the previous year. Fortune's role, to work Cathy's training around the program Nick and Maurie set, was not a full-time task. He was travelling with the Australian junior squad in Europe that year. But Fortune's impression was that Bideau regarded coaches as a vaguely necessary evil, since at that stage Bideau had neither the expertise, nor the time, to coach Freeman himself. 'Occasionally I would be of some use but I didn't have that much pull with Cathy anyway,' says Fortune. When I repeated that to Cathy she said, 'Nice guy, Fort, I really like him, but sometimes too sensitive in training me. Later, I needed more than that.'

Cathy headed for another crack at Marie-José Pérec in Monte Carlo, one of Cathy's favourite European tracks. At the last minute Renee Poetschka's people asked Plant to help get Renee in the race. 'I knew she wouldn't get a start because the director had promised a lane to Maria Mutola,' says Plant. 'Now Mutola was out of shape and I genuinely argued for Renee to get a start, but Mutola's manager got up and said his runner was ready to break the 400m world record. I said, "Sit your silly arse down and shut up before someone hears you talking nonsense like that!" Anyway, Mutola ran.' France's darling, Pérec, who lives in the US to escape her fame in France, commands appearance money of $50,000 for the French meets in Monte Carlo, Paris and Nice, but less in Stockholm and Oslo. Since this was her first race of the season in Europe, television cameras draped cords along Cathy's lane preventing her from doing her usual starts and run-throughs to keep warm. Pérec, who has a love–hate relationship with the French media, has made being late an art and was true to form this meet. Some 10 minutes standing around flattened Cathy for the start. 'She was really confident, just the way she arrived and looked around,' says Cathy. La Formidable.

From lane two, it took Cathy 150m to find rhythm and another 150m to reel the field in. Pérec had Miles and Malone covered 20 seconds into the race, and running into the straight Cathy was a few metres back, a clear fourth. But halfway down the straight she found strength, passed Miles and then Malone, but Pérec had flown, first in 49.77s. Cathy rattled home second in 50.18s, beating Renee Poetschka's national record at last, by 1/100th of a second. Cathy saw it on the big replay screen at the track and smiled breathlessly. She says, 'Normally I'm not in a hurry to find out but I knew I felt good.'

This was the best 400m field assembled that year and Cathy had accounted for them all except Pérec. Her only Commonwealth opponent, Sandie Richards, was sixth in 51.23s. Mutola ran around 51.37s, not exactly the world record her manager predicted. Cathy gave Pérec her customary peck and then went looking for Nick. Renee was sitting in the stand, a double whammy for her, to miss the race and lose her record. Afterwards she congratulated Cathy and said, 'Only 1/100th!' It was more pointed than praise, yet it broke the yoke of complaint that Poetschka had about the Freeman publicity train.

'Nick Bideau managed Cathy so well, any athlete would be envious how well he did it,' says Renee. 'But before 1994, Cathy had won a gold medal in the relay in Auckland in 1990, and I used to say, "Can you please name for me the other three athletes who were in that team?" They couldn't. And why's that? Why did she get more publicity? I wasn't having a go at Cathy, I was saying that the other people should be getting equal respect and they weren't.' It was her Aboriginality, I ventured to Renee. 'Of course, and there's nothing wrong with that,' she says. 'But on the track we're all just athletes.'

To listen to Poetschka, it seemed almost a relief when Cathy's performances started to match her fame. 'Once she broke my record, Cathy shot to the front and I've been chasing her ever since,' says Renee. 'Realistically I was never a threat after that. In later years we occasionally went out socialising. The two of us both love having fun. She laughs at everything I say. She thinks I'm an absolute cack.'

NO BIG CAT FIGHT

More drama came when it became clear that Pérec had run out of her lane and should be disqualified. Said Nick, 'I'm not protesting, this is France, they'll hang us if they disqualify Mary-Jo. Anyway Pérec won easily, and they're not going to give her time to Cathy.' Plant tried to protest but the meet organiser, Jean Pierre Schobel, told him, 'Maurie, you're not going to win this one, are you!' Plant replied, 'No, but you know I'm right, and so does the technical director too.' At the end of the year Plant was vindicated when the IAAF disqualified Pérec's win in their records.

Back in London, as all the Australian athletes headed for Canada for the Games, Cathy watched the European championships on television. Maurie was keen for her to run in Zurich, for the experience of running in the biggest grand prix on the circuit, with stronger fields than anywhere except the world titles and the Olympics. Bideau deferred to Maurie's advice and, in bucketing rain and a cold wind, Cathy joined the best 200m field available, including a quartet of Olympic medallists—Torrence, Privalova, Pérec and Merlene Ottey. With 80m to go Ottey, Privalova and Torrence were a line across the track. Ottey faded, Privalova won the photo, Cathy finished ahead of Pérec, fourth in 22.59s and only a metre behind Ottey. This was world-class sprinting of the highest calibre.

If the loungerooms of Australia had been beamed that race, what ensued in Canada would have come as no surprise. Bideau had seen what he wanted to know. Torrence and Privalova weren't Commonwealth athletes and Ottey wasn't going to Canada, preferring to stay with the money meets in Europe. That left Cathy. By the time she flew into Victoria for the Games, the opening ceremony was over, but the real excitement for Australia was about to begin.

13.

BLACK IS FOR THE PEOPLE. COMMONWEALTH GAMES, 1994

When Peter Jess heard that Cathy Freeman had always dreamed of winning a gold medal and doing a victory lap draped in the Aboriginal flag, Jess was fired with enthusiasm. He told Nick Bideau, 'If she wins with the flag, she'll be on every front page around the world because it's a political statement. In fact if she wins with the flag, she'll be front, back and centre! If she wins without the flag she'll just be on the back page because then it's only a sporting achievement.' It mattered little to Bideau. He was only concerned with getting the job done on the track.

As one of the AFL's top agents, Jess had represented several footballers, including Greg Williams, Justin Madden and Aboriginal Nicky Winmar. As such, he had formed certain opinions about indigenous sportspeople, confirmed by his contact with Cathy Freeman as her financial adviser. He knew that Cathy would have liked an Aboriginal friend in Melbourne, a mate who knew her culture. 'Someone who understood her central being, who understood for instance the indigenous philosophy of not owning things but using them, that ownership is not necessary,' he says. Jess spoke with Cathy at length about herself, about her motives for

BLACK IS FOR THE PEOPLE

running and about how, unavoidably, she would be running for her people as much as for herself.

'She loves being an indigenous person of note,' he says. 'She wants to inspire, she has a mission to inspire black athletes. She asks us all the time, "When are we going to look for more black kids?" Before the Games she had this dream of going from being nobody in north Queensland to being a gold medallist. She told me how it would make a massive statement about who she is, and how she wouldn't be embarrassed. She was rapt in that idea. And she loves the flag.'

As does Jess. That's why he was determined to be the person who handed it to her if she won. 'I'd never have handed her the Australian flag, I think it's a flag of oppression to our indigenous people,' he says. 'What's it ever done for them? And the Union Jack?' Jess scowls. 'It really leaves a lot to be desired. I think it's a flag of killing, wherever it's gone around the world from Great Britain it's stuffed countries up.' For a non-indigenous, pony-tailed, in-your-face, sports agent-cum-accountant, Peter Jess would make a militant Aborigine.

So Cathy arrived in Victoria with her own flag folded in her backpack. 'I take it with me everywhere I go overseas,' she says. 'It's part of me. I take it out and look at it occasionally, I get quite emotional about it.' She had delayed her arrival in Victoria as a deliberate ploy to avoid the stress of the Games hype. She raced in Zurich on Wednesday, arrived in Canada on Friday, stayed with Nick in his hotel that night, and made her first appearance in the village on Saturday morning. Her first race, a 400m heat, was the next day, Sunday. The Australian team had arrived days before, so a buzz swept the village when Cathy was sighted: Freeman's here! The Australian media revved up.

Nick took Cathy shopping for clothes. His attitude to shopping reflects his attitude to food—occasionally necessary, but the less the better. But he knew Cathy enjoyed shopping and that it took her mind off running. Nick was working for the Ten Network, Maurie Plant for the BBC, and they teamed up with the BBC's Brendan Foster, a 10,000m champion of the 1970s, who was staying in a hotel nearby.

Foster, with his Geordie Englishman's wry humour, sought to ease the pressure on Cathy. 'See this little book here,' he said holding up a statistics book. 'This has the names of all the winners at the Commonwealth Games in it. So all that's going to happen if you win, is you'll get your name in this little book!' He tossed it casually on a lounge. 'So what's the big deal?' Cathy laughed and said he was crazy, which was the intended effect.

The big deal was that Bideau, Plant, Fortune and Foster had all studied the fields and knew Cathy was a chance for a unique Games double, the 200m and 400m golds. Nigerian Mary Onyali was favourite for the 100m, but Cathy had run her down over 200m in Stockholm. Nobody could get a bead on the defending 400m champion, Nigerian Fatima Yusuf, because she hadn't run the Euro circuit. That in itself gave them confidence because if she hadn't raced, she might not be race fit.

Cathy's first 400m heat was a jog, around 53s, as were the heats won by Poetschka, Richards and Yusuf. That's the problem with the Commonwealth Games compared with the European circuit: the lack of depth in so many events. 'Hey, that's not fair, that's cheating,' Foster called out to Cathy afterwards. What's not fair? 'That you're allowed to jog around to qualify for the semi and all the rest have to run,' said Foster.

That evening Bideau, Plant, Foster, Jess and Cathy went out for dinner to the Harvest Moon restaurant, and on the way home raced their cycle pedicabs through the streets, Cathy, Nick and Jess in one cab, Plant and Foster in the other. 'Good for her to stay relaxed,' says Plant. 'No sense in spending your emotional penny until you need to.'

For the semi-final, Nick emphasised to her: finish first or

second, that's always the rule, that gets you the lane draw of 3,4,5 or 6 in the final. Cathy and Sandie Richards went stride for stride down the straight, Cathy switching off in the final few metres. Richards first in 51.23s, Cathy second in 51.57s. Yusuf won the second semi-final easily in 52.03s, Poetschka third in 52.66s. Another Australian, Kylie Hanigan (52.87s) also made it through to the final as one of the fastest non-placegetters. That made their 4 x 400m relay look good for later in the Games.

Peter Jess had become Team Freeman's forward scout, strolling the city streets, sussing out places for breakfast, and he'd come up with a cafe overlooking picturesque Victoria Harbour. One morning in walked an imposing-looking native North American with two plaits down the side of his head. He surveyed the cafe, saw Cathy, and gave just the smallest nod. 'It was the most amazing moment,' says Jess. 'It was a knowing glance of comradeship—different nations, different languages, but same struggle.'

The night before the final, Nick and Cathy went for a walk in a park where an Aboriginal group was performing at the Victoria Harbour Festival. They were the Tjapukai dance theatre, of which the co-founder was Cathy's cousin David Hudson. Hudson wasn't there but she talked to the dancers and musicians for a few minutes, momentarily putting aside thoughts of tomorrow.

At breakfast, the morning of the final, Cathy said, 'Jess,'—she uses it like a christian name—'Jess, can you do something for me? Can you be near the finish line and wave this flag for me so I'll know where you are?' He would, he said. It was so extraordinarily premeditated it really does offer an insight into the Freeman mind, clear cut, confident and uncluttered by any fears or superstitions. Cathy didn't ask Jess if he had a ticket. 'She just trusted me to be at the right spot,' says Jess. It wasn't without its difficulties—the section in the stand opposite the start–finish line is not reserved for ex-St Kilda thirds footballers carrying Aboriginal flags. Jess's ticket was for a seat on the other side of the ground, but he prides himself on defeating bureaucracy. Only Cathy, Nick and Jess knew of the flag.

Peter Fortune took Cathy to the warm-up track and used Nick's accreditation card to let Tiffany Cherry, a former training friend from Melbourne who was on holidays in Canada, jog with Cathy to help her relax. Nick's race advice was the same as that which Cathy used to defeat Jearl Miles in London. 'Quick out, rotate your legs quickly down the back straight as though you're freewheeling on a bike, attack the third 100m,' said Nick. 'If you get in front, concentrate, make sure you run right through to the line.' Cathy had this tendency to slow once she had the field beaten. Says Nick, 'She runs just fast enough to win.'

In Centennial Stadium, under a beautiful blue-sky afternoon, Cathy was aware of the crowd only as a mass of colour and noise as she entered her own mental glass capsule. 'You can see and hear and feel, but at the same time it's all blocked out,' she says. 'Like it's soundproofed or something.' She adjusted her bodysuit, adjusted her hair held by a black, red and gold scrunchie, kicked the track with her toes and got set.

Then she stuck to orders. She was in lane three, Yusuf in four, Richards in five. Yusuf would go out hard and hope to hold Cathy off; Richards, lacking early speed, would come home strongly. Cathy must balance her race. They remained in their starting order to the first 200m although Cathy had made up all but a metre of the stagger on Yusuf, and Richards was only another metre ahead on the outside. Halfway around the second bend Cathy noticeably accelerated. Psyched-up energy unleashed, she skipped clear and ran into the straight three metres in front.

But she'd spent too heavily and with 30m to go started to tire. Yusuf began closing the gap alarmingly. Cathy was slowing measurably, Yusuf made up a metre, then another. 'I couldn't hear her footsteps, or her breathing, or even feel her presence behind me, I was concentrating so much on my own race,' says Cathy. Australia, rising at 8 a.m. that day, sat riveted as Channel 10's Peter Donegan called in a rising crescendo: 'Yusuf is making a late dive at her. *Keep going, Cathy!* She's Won! Gold for Australia!' Co-commentator Kerry Johnson yelled 'Yes!' and a few seconds later, 'Oh, I feel like crying. Good run, Cathy.' And then, a moment later she said, 'We should also congratulate her coach Peter Fortune, and Nick Bideau who helps her. They've done a great job with Cathy.'

Bideau had watched enough athletics to know Yusuf wouldn't catch Cathy, and so did Plant. 'Cathy was running within herself,' says Plant knowingly. 'In those days you couldn't get her to commit herself through the whole race. See, nobody has ever pipped her on the post.' Says Cathy, 'I always find something extra if I have to. You don't let them beat you.'

Cathy had run 50.38s, a new Games record, breaking the 51.02s set by Jamaican Marilyn Neufville way back in 1970, a world record at the time. Yusuf was second in 50.53s and Richards third in 50.69s. Renee, who finished fifth, came over to hug Cathy, who seemed strangely preoccupied, staring over Renee's shoulder. She was anxious rather than relieved, unsmiling, not the exhilarated face of a victor. She stopped for a half-retch from her race effort, and then walked over to scan the crowd. Sure enough, down the steps came Peter Jess, having hoaxed his way through a horde of guards, pushing, shoving, holding the Aboriginal flag aloft.

He handed it to her —'One of the proudest moments of my life,' he says—and off she trotted, draping it over her shoulders like a cape. She ran 50m holding that flag, defiance beaming from her eyes, living the fulfilment of her dream. This was the act of atonement for all the pent-up hurt within a shy Aboriginal girl who grew up with the word 'shame' attached to her embarrassment about being black in contemporary Australia. This was her amazing coming out and she saved it for when she knew the world would be watching. Indeed the dream of this sweetest of moments had driven her to these heights. Nothing less than this stage was worthy of her declaration of love of herself and her people. Ah, Cathy. Ah, sister! Only when she had savoured this joy did she survey the crowd for an Australian flag. She walked over and accepted it from a woman in a blue terry-towelling sun hat. By the time Freeman finished her victory lap, news of her demonstration of Aboriginal identity was being digested in the world's newsrooms. At home, in Brisbane, Cecelia Barber watched all this with growing pride in her daughter, who she had always considered to be politically unaware. 'It dawned on me that she really feels what I feel after all,' says Cecelia. 'She had feelings for what being Aboriginal meant. She knew that Aboriginal people needed someone to give them an incentive to do better. And she did it.' She did, and patiently explained the flag to the international media, 'Black is for the people ...'

Aboriginal tennis champion Evonne Goolagong-Cawley, a friend of Cathy's, wrote in her biography *Home!* that occasionally her own people attacked her for failing to be the kind of Aborigine they believed she should be. Cathy, similarly self-absorbed in her sport up to this moment, dispelled any likelihood of such criticism with her singular gesture. Cathy, aged 21, had publicly acknowledged her unequivocal identification with her inseparable Aboriginality.

Cathy dined and slept in the village that night, away from the publicity, sharing her victory with other team members, especially her buddy Tim Forsyth, who had been out in the centre at the high jump when Cathy won. 'It's uncanny how often I'm out there and they start her race near me,' he says. 'I'm always there to give her a wave but the Games was one time I came very close to running over and giving her a hug. I thought maybe I better not, better stay back here, no-one else seems to do it. I don't know why I don't. I guess I think, "Oh well, there'll be another time."'

BLACK IS FOR THE PEOPLE

In the peace of her room, Cathy wrote in a diary she had begun on the Games, 'I won the gold today and I did what I wanted to do. I carried both the Aboriginal flag and the Australian flag on the victory lap. I know a lot of people would be happy to see me win, black Australians and white Australians, and that way they could all share what was a great moment for me.'

Nick and Jess had a few drinks with legendary BBC commentator David Coleman and then Nick walked back to his hotel alone. Cathy had arrived in Melbourne three years ago, and now, after so many hours training and preparing, she'd won. When Cathy hit the line, Nick had punched the air, just as Cathy does sometimes. Now, as he walked through the night he thought, 'Yeah, we got one.'

Next morning he got more than he bargained for. At the media room the news was everywhere: the Australian *chef de mission*, venerable Arthur Tunstall, had put out a statement critical of Cathy's Aboriginal flag. It was the sombre duty of media chief Ian Hanson to read it out: 'While the Australian Commonwealth Games Association acknowledges Cathy Freeman's heritage and her world-class 400m win yesterday, the Australian team is competing at these 15th Commonwealth Games under the Australian flag. Management met and they informed sectional track and field manager Margaret Mahony that they did not want any athlete acknowledging flags other than the Australian flag.'

Tunstall had indeed ordered Mahony to inform Freeman of his directive, and had summoned Hanson as a witness. Nick rang Mahony, whom he trusted, and asked her not to let the media speak to Cathy. Mahony said she would look after Freeman whose 200m hopes were in danger of sinking under the flag controversy. Nick earned media animosity by declaring to them, 'Freeman is not doing any interviews until after the 200m because all you blokes want to ask her about is the flag. So she's not talking.'

Back in Australia it had become a huge cause célèbre.

Goolagong-Cawley, Tony Mundine and Pat O'Shane applauded her action. Dawn Fraser said Tunstall was a joke and called on him to quit. CATHY UNITES NATION, the *Telegraph Mirror* told its 1.3 million readers on 25 August. But Cathy also flushed out some surprising conservatives, including the above paper's columnist Mike Gibson who wrote the next day: 'You cannot serve two masters ... And the same as you can't serve two masters I don't believe you can run under two flags.' Perhaps if the Australian flag included some recognition of Aboriginal existence, Cathy wouldn't have needed to.

Newspapers reported later that an opinion poll found 73 per cent of Australians supported Cathy's actions. This seemed to accurately reflect the mood of the nation. Politicians were almost unanimously behind her. Victorian Labor MP Clyde Holding called Tunstall a 'bloody old fogey'. Victorian Premier Jeff Kennett said that with Tunstall it was a case of 'three strikes and you're out', referring to two previous Tunstall bloopers. Federal Sports Minister John Faulkner supported her, as did former Prime Minister Bob Hawke. The Brisbane and Ipswich city councils emulated Cathy's victory lap by flying both the Aboriginal flag and the Australian flag from their poles.

Faxes and letters poured in, 5000 of them. Cathy sifted through them and found only one supporting Tunstall. 'He said if I wasn't proud of the Australian flag I should emigrate,' she says. More pleasant was one from her three childhood helpers in Mackay, Sue Evetts, Penny Pollock and Janice Saunders. 'No work being done here, I have square eyes. I am sure you would have heard me in Canada this morning, I cheered, screamed and then cried,' faxed Saunders. The Leader of the Opposition, Alexander Downer, sent her a letter in which he said, 'You have worked extremely hard for victory and you have every reason to take great pride in celebrating your heritage.'

And then came the letter that sealed her satisfaction that

Australia was behind her, a letter of congratulations from Prime Minister Paul Keating, which said in part, 'This is not only a personal achievement for yourself, reflecting your dedication and commitment to athletics—but also a great credit for Australia. You can be justly proud of your outstanding win which I am sure will serve as an inspiration for all young Australians particularly Aboriginal and Torres Strait Islanders. In the circumstances your carrying of both flags was an important reminder of your pride in your heritage as an Aboriginal Australian.'

Not everyone saw it so clearly. A blinkered Australian Nike executive approached Nick Bideau and asked him, 'What was that all about, that flag business? Did Cathy do it to cover up the Adidas on the bodysuit and the Reebok on the race number?' The Nike man's reference point was the 1992 Olympics at which the US team was sponsored by Reebok. When the US basketball Dream Team, many on million dollar contracts with Nike, went to receive their gold medals they draped large American flags over their Reebok tracksuits to remain loyal to Nike and the Swoosh logo—the 'tick' emblem which is the mark of Nike on all their products. Nick laughed and told the Nike man, 'No, mate, it's a bit bigger than that with Freeman.' Cathy was amused by the Nike man's response, but it demonstrated to her the fervour of her sponsor's employees. True believers can catch Nike fever, where all roads lead to Nike HQ in Oregon, and staff and athletes are a worldwide fraternity marching successfully to the rhythm of Swoosh! Swoosh! Swoosh!

Next morning Cathy awoke and contemplated her first individual Games gold. 'It takes a long time for a success like that to sink in,' she says. 'To me it was a Commonwealth gold, which was great, but it was also another step forward, with still more to go.' That morning she ventured forth for the first round of the 200m and encountered a sea of media, awash with questions. She ploughed silently through them for 50 metres, white baseball cap pulled down hard on her head, trackbag on her shoulder, until at the warm-up track gate, when the media could follow no further, she answered two questions. No, no regrets about carrying the flag, she said, and if she won the 200m would she carry the flag again? 'Yeah, I suppose so.'

Bideau saw Cathy on the local television news. 'There must have been 50 media, television crews, photographers and reporters following her asking questions,' says Bideau. 'I'm a journalist myself but I was shocked. It was the first time I'd seen her pursued like that.' Sportscaster and friend Bruce McAvaney told Bideau that in that brief walk, he saw an innocence take flight from Cathy's life. He warned Nick that while the media might love her then, the love affair would not last. They would try to bring her down, or those around her, namely him. Be wary, advised McAvaney.

So the word about Cathy's intention to fly the flag was out, the battle lines set. Yet, before the final, Arthur Tunstall had an opportunity to confront Cathy over her recalcitrance. 'I passed him in the village,' says Cathy. 'There was just the two of us and I wasn't going to say anything. Then he said, "Good luck in the 200m, Cathy." I was surprised, not that I cared. At the end of the day he didn't bother me. People don't understand, it's the running that I love, not the politics.'

Tunstall says he can't remember the encounter. 'But if she says so, maybe I did,' he says. 'I don't hold a grudge against anybody, all I want to do is make sure the rules are carried out. That was my duty as *chef de mission*.' I then asked Tunstall whether, hypothetically, if he had run into Cathy before the 200m, would he have warned her not to carry the flag again. 'No, I don't deal with athletes,' he says. 'I deal with sectional managers, that's my job. Their duty is to follow the orders that I give.'

Unbeknownst to Tunstall, Margaret Mahony was exercising what the Nazis failed to appreciate at Nuremberg: that personal moral values may justly override a superior officer's orders. 'I like Arthur very much, he is really a nice man,' says Mahony. 'But if he had all these strong feelings he should have told Cathy himself, because I had strong feelings of my own. I have a huge admiration for the Aboriginal people. They are entitled to self-determination and to show the flag of their culture. I think it would be wonderful if the Aboriginal flag was the flag of this country. I think it is a fabulous flag.'

Even so, Mahony confided in Neil King, general manager of Athletics Australia, and Tunstall's order fell upon deaf ears there too. King and Tunstall had been at political loggerheads for years. But it was still Mahony's call, so she then approached Geoff Rowe, Athletics Australia's business manager, and told him, 'We've got a bit of a problem. It's been decided we're not going to stop Cathy from carrying the flag. We'll say team management said that she could, but make sure she carries both flags simultaneously.'

Says Rowe, 'There were to be two of us sitting together and both flags were to come from the same place, rather than as in the 400m when she grabbed the Aussie flag from anybody. Because the criticism was that she had collected the Aboriginal flag first.'

So, all settled, just the little matter of Cathy having to win. ABC commentator Tim Lane said to Bideau, 'She's going to have a hard time beating Onyali.' Nick replied, 'Just don't give up on her, Tim. It could take a long time, might look like she's not going to win, but she could just get there.'

While all the politicking had been going on, Cathy had been working her way through the heat and semi-final, each time slower than African champion Mary Onyali of Nigeria, who had already won the 100m. Onyali was a formidable opponent, later proving her undoubted class by running third in the 200m at the Atlanta Olympics. It was far more traditional then, and still is despite Michael Johnson and Marie-José Pérec's feats, for the sprint double to be won as 100 and 200m rather than 200 and 400m. Melinda Gainsford had also clawed her way into the final, though still not running at her best. Cathy had met Melinda's parents in the village, all grand prix rivalry ceasing under their national banner.

The eve of the final, Maurie Plant, whose BBC hotel was superior to Bideau's with Channel 10, swapped hotels so Cathy could get a quiet night without telephone calls. Bideau rarely gives Cathy advice on race day. 'His style is to do all his talking in training, with maybe a few words the day before,' says Cathy. His advice to Cathy was plain—don't give up. 'No matter if it looks like you're gone. Remember Onyali gets the staggers all the time at the end of her 200m races,' he said. 'Don't worry, she'll be a long way in front at some stage, but just hang in there.' And he had another visual idea, too. 'Run 210m not 200m, so you'll run full out, right through the finish.'

So the main chances were blonde, pony-tailed Gainsford in lane two, brown pony-tailed Cathy in three, slick black-bobbed Bahamian Pauline Davis in four and Onyali, her hair laid in tight curls on her scalp, in five. The starter called them forward onto their blocks, and 30 seconds later: 'Set.' Their bodies coiled, two seconds later, the crack of the gun. Cathy was so slow out that Melinda gained a metre on her in the first 20m. Onyali flew out and took a metre off everyone outside her. So as they entered the straight with 80m to run, Melinda was beside Cathy but Onyali was three metres ahead of them both and looking strong. Maurie Plant admits that at that stage he had the thought, 'Uh oh, she ain't gonna make it.'

The same thought was dawning on Cathy. 'Melinda always gets up with me into the straight and that's what woke me up,' she says. 'I thought "Whoops, I better get going."' Freeman then ran possibly the most storming last 80m of a 200m sprint seen in women's athletics for many years. The key to Cathy's speed is her lightness of tread, her ability to lift her feet off the track quickly to take the next stride. She doesn't possess great power in her legs because she doesn't need it. She has spring instead. And like animals on the veldt, to increase speed she doesn't take more steps, she increases the length of her stride. Thus Cathy, Gainsford and Onyali ran almost the entire last 80m in identical stride cadence, with almost military precision. In video slow-mo the three ran the last 35 strides in perfect step. But Cathy was taking longer strides.

She gradually edged away from Melinda and went after Onyali. The pair kept step for 30 strides but then, as Cathy crept alongside, Mary started overstriding. Her step rotation actually became slower thus, although her stride gained a little extra distance, she lost overall speed. It is not enough just to be a long strider, it has to be long AND quick. Like Cathy, who overtook Onyali with just three strides to go. 'I could feel myself getting closer and closer and swallowing her up,' says Cathy. 'I just kept trying and trying.'

It was in this race that Cathy experienced the sense of lifting over the ground as described in the opening chapter. Of coming out of herself, feeling like she was flying not running, feeling a sense of magic carrying her forward. She was in the zone where effort is effortless, where energy is endless, where feet take flight. It looked all of that in the running as she steamrolled Onyali with sheer will and self-belief. As Channel 10's Peter Donegan called it, 'Onyali's pretty strong with 50m to go ... Cathy's coming at her. *She's flying home Freeman!* ... And she gets up for gold for Australia!' In 22.25s, a new Games and Australian record, a time Cathy has never, as I write, surpassed. Gainsford had to wait agonising moments before her bronze medal placing was posted, by 1/100th of a second over England's Paula Thomas. It was a measure of how Freeman had improved that Gainsford, her great Aussie rival, was ecstatic to have taken bronze though all of five metres behind.

This truly was a magnificent race, one which Cathy rates among the top three of her career. Sebastian Coe, the great English miler of the 1980s, told Nick excitedly afterwards,

'That was one of the best performances I've ever seen in a championship, coming from behind like that.' Cathy was far more emotional about this than the 400m. She put her hands to her face in disbelief, laughed and grinned, accepted her congratulatory hugs from the other runners, commiserated with a disappointed Onyali before heading off to look for Geoff Rowe. He had the Australian flag and Tiffany Cherry had the Aboriginal. Cathy backed off and said, 'Geoff, make sure I've got them both together.' Rowe matched the flag ends and passed them over to Cathy, who only then accepted them and trotted off, quickly joined by a delighted Gainsford, now draped in her own Australian flag. After her victory lap Cathy walked to the crowd and gave Nick Bideau a huge hug. It was, quite possibly, the peak of their personal and professional relationship.

A large group of Australian swimmers were chanting in the stands while in the trackside media zone it was chaos as international media caught on to Cathy's news value. Cathy was still in demand when England's Sally Gunnell, Olympic, world and European 400m hurdle champion, and world record holder, came in after winning her final. Normally she was the big star, but now she was overwhelmed by Freeman's fame. 'My, my, my,' she said to Cathy, good-naturedly. 'Who's a clever girl. Trying for Athlete of the Year, are we?' Cathy just giggled, and was duly selected as Commonwealth Athlete of the Year.

On BBC TV David Coleman said, 'There has been some criticism of Freeman for carrying her flag, but I have here a letter to her from the Prime Minister of Australia which I will read to you.' And he did, in his stentorian broadcaster's voice, to tens of millions of British viewers. Maurie Plant, working for the BBC, heard it all, including the director's sharp comment, 'You didn't tell us you were going to read that?' And Coleman's reply, 'No, and I don't bloody well have to.' Afterwards Coleman told Bideau, 'I stuck it up that Tunstall.' Now Cathy's fame extended to the British Isles as

BLACK IS FOR THE PEOPLE

well. Coleman liked Cathy and the courage she showed in her running. She reminded him of the glory days of England when Coe, Cram and Ovett ran with an heroic grace, in the romantic tradition of *Chariots of Fire*.

'Her beauty rich and rare,' Cathy sang during the victory ceremony, but the aftermath of victory is never quite the triumphant party everyone imagines. 'You've got to take a drug test, then people tell you to go here, go there, autograph please. I felt smothered,' says Cathy. 'Everything revolves around you when all you want to do is get out and be with your people. I wanted to have a feed and put my feet up and watch telly and just soak it all in. It's a weird feeling when everyone watches every move you make. Like, it's nice being the centre of attention but I wanted to just get the hell out and get some space.' Then emerges Cathy's real sensitivity about it all. 'You feel like people are going to get sick of you really quickly,' she says. Her modesty and basic humility emerge; she hates that she might appear egotistical and turn people off.

Her media duties appeared interminable that day because Bideau insisted she keep hanging around the Channel 10 studios for over an hour, though he knew she was desperate to leave. Meanwhile Ten's commentator Neil Brooks had raced out to the airport and collected Cecelia and Bruce Barber, who had just flown in courtesy of the Ten Network. As the 200m was run, they were just about to land. Brooks had enough time to tell them, 'Oh yes, Cathy won her second gold medal,' before delivering them to a surprise reunion with Cathy in the studios. All on camera, of course. Bideau watched the flood of emotions and regretted that they had missed her triumph by only an hour or so. Nick never minded Cathy's parents being on hand for her races provided Cathy and Cecelia's powerful mother and daughter reunions didn't interfere with Cathy's race focus.

How to celebrate? Well, Peter Jess knew how. He and Cathy were walking in downtown Victoria next day when they passed a tattooist. Cathy already had one, a small rose on her right ankle, courtesy of an impulse with a friend in Mackay late in 1993. The friend was too scared to have one by herself so Cathy had one, too. She's like that sometimes, anything to please.

'Why don't you get one?' she urged Jess. 'Oh, maybe,' he said. Cathy went off to training and Jess went to the parlour. True to his description of Cathy as a killer cat, he had a large spotted leopard tattooed on his shoulder. When he showed Cathy she exclaimed, 'Oh no, you did it!' When he returned home to Melbourne he was in the shower when his wife Bernie enquired enigmatically, 'Is that going to come off?' To which Jess replied, 'I've been trying for the last hour and nothing's happening so I think it's there for the duration!'

Back in the village, Arthur Tunstall was on the warpath. Margaret Mahony's morning had already been traumatic, nursing marathoner Tani Ruckle who had run herself into dehydration. Ruckle was put on a saline drip and then taken by ambulance back to the village. 'In the ambulance she gripped my arm so rigidly I had to keep uncurling her fingers,' says Mahony. 'I was worried about her.' She was speaking with Steve Moneghetti about it soon after when Tunstall caught up with her.

'He came down the path waving his arms, yelling that this was insubordination, why hadn't I done as I was told, rah, rah, rah,' says Mahony. Moneghetti stepped back. 'Arthur was obviously angry and it was enough to blow me out of the conversation,' says Monners. Tunstall demanded to know whether Mahony had warned Freeman. 'I told him my conscience would not let me,' says Mahony. 'Why should I? If he was so put out about it, he was the *chef de mission*, tell Cathy himself. It was fortunate I didn't cry in front of him. I went up to my room and I thought, "Oh God, is it really worthwhile being involved in all this?" I was really upset.'

Tunstall tells a more sedate version of the same incident, except that he says that Mahony also told him, 'Neil King told me to ignore your orders.' But wasn't Mahony in a superior position to King in the Games hierarchy? 'Yes,' he said. 'But Neil King wields a big stick at the other end.' Tunstall's attitude is unchanged today but he remains largely isolated on the issue. He admits himself that he had no luck when he raised the subject at the first meeting of the Commonwealth Games Association executive back in Australia. 'OK, Arthur, you told Mahony and she didn't agree,' they said. 'End of story.'

14.
WINNING YET LOSING. POST-COMMONWEALTH GAMES, 1994

The *Sydney Morning Herald*'s headline on 30 August 1994, above a photograph of a disconsolate Cathy Freeman, read, FREEMAN'S DREAM RUN ENDS IN NIGHTMARE. The Games had ended the previous day, so how could her happiness be tarnished by one day's events? The answer was the relays. They proved such a frustration for Cathy that it bears some explanation. Australia, in general, is very good at team sports, witness our history in cricket, hockey and Davis Cup tennis. Frustratingly this does not always extend to the relays in athletics.

If Cathy could help win the two relay golds in Victoria, her 1990 Auckland relay gold plus her 200m and 400m golds would equal 1938 star Decima Norman's record of five Commonwealth track gold medals. In Victoria, Australia's 4 x 100m relay was much the same team as in Auckland in 1990—Freeman, Dunstan (now Miers) and Sambell—except that Melinda Gainsford had replaced Kerry Johnson. Relay coaches Keith Connor and Cliff Mallett devised a strategy to have Freeman run the second leg in the belief that the second and third legs, with two changeovers, are slightly longer, though this is a moot point.

WINNING YET LOSING

Bideau went in to bat for Cathy. 'The theory's fine, but Cathy's running fast,' he told them. 'Where does Carl Lewis run, where do Linford Christie, Merlene Ottey and Gwen Torrence run? They don't run the second leg, they run the last. Put her last and she's just as likely to give Mary Onyali three metres and run her down on the line. She's a competitor, she's a fighter, you've all just seen that!' Nancy Atterton, relay coach from the 1990 Games, agrees with Bideau's analysis. 'The experience was there,' she says. 'Dunstan and Sambell—first leg to second—had their changes down to a fine art, Gainsford is a superb bend runner, Freeman anchors. Obvious, really.' Not to the coaches apparently. 'I tell you, I was a very scared girl when I walked out,' says Kathy Sambell who had to run the last leg. 'I was up against basically the gold and bronze medallists from the women's 100m final. I know the arguments, but personally I would have preferred to run the second leg, because Monique had changed to me so often, and I had changed to Melinda so often, I felt like we could do it in our sleep. And Cathy would have brought it home for us so well.'

The Nigerians were natural favourites having won bronze in Barcelona, and Australia was ranked only fourth in the Commonwealth. In the event, Nigeria won gold in 42.99s, Australia silver in 43.43s, a faster time than when they won gold in Auckland so they weren't too disappointed. But good judges considered that an inspired Freeman running last would have made up that half-second. Who knows?

An hour later Cathy backed up for the 4 x 400m for which Australia were warm favourites, with Victorian Lee Naylor added to the three 400m finalists—Cathy, Poetschka and Hanigan. 'Unfortunately no-one explained all the rules to us,' says Cathy. 'They were still telling us out on the track before the race start.' Though what ensued was more rule confusion than ignorance.

In the 4 x 400m relay, after the first lap, lane positions no longer apply. The race becomes like an 800m field. The major rule is that whatever order the relay runners are at the 200m mark of each lap—halfway around—is the position that the subsequent runners waiting to receive the baton must adopt at the start line, starting from the inside and working out. Poetschka, who ran the third leg, takes up the commentary. 'When I took the baton we were running fourth and, as I usually do, I busted my gut,' she says. 'I got to the 200m mark just as I was passing everybody to take the lead. Now Cathy probably didn't see that in the sense that she didn't move into the inside lane.'

Videos show Poetschka, three wide, had indeed narrowly nosed ahead of the English and Nigerian runners at 200m. But it took her another three seconds to catch the Jamaican leader and a full eight seconds before she had enough clear space in the lead to cross into the inside lane. At very best Cathy could have legally moved into second from the inside. As it was she was third out, England's Sally Gunnell was second out and Jamaica's Sandie Richards was on the inside. So it was not just Cathy who thought Renee had not made the lead soon enough to claim the inside lane.

'When I came around into the straight the last thing you're thinking of is trying to find your person, because you think you know where they're going to be,' says Renee. 'I was in lane one running inside the English girl and we were neck and neck.' Renee runs in dark reflecting sunglasses and looking ahead she saw a black athlete in lane one with swept back, pony-tailed hair, like Cathy's. The Australian outfit was a gold top, green shorts with gold stripes, the Jamaican was gold top, green shorts, with a black centre panel. Nick, in the stands, and Cathy, on the line, each had the same horrified thought. Renee was going to hand over to Sandie Richards of Jamaica. 'Yeah, coming down the straight I thought that Sandie was Cathy,' confirms Renee ruefully. 'Then I saw Cathy and the only thing I could do was stop dead in my tracks, pull out behind the rest and get the baton to her.' By then Sally Gunnell was away into the lead.

WINNING YET LOSING

Now it was Cathy's turn to show she was a greenhorn at this caper. She actually raced from the melee a clear second and settled in behind Gunnell. Richards was third but, with Gunnell's slow pace, Sandie cleverly moved up on Cathy's outside. An alert athlete, wise in the ways of bunched running, would have immediately slipped up to Gunnell's right shoulder, cutting off Richards's move. Cathy had never run an all-in, close quarters race like this before in her life.

So far, so bad. She was inside Richards who further snookered her by easing ahead slightly, allowing Fatima Yusuf to move up sufficiently to cut off Cathy's exit. In horseracing vernacular, Cathy was now pocketed, boxed, a terrible position to be in. With 150m to go, almost jogging behind the leaders, Cathy suddenly decided it was time to break out of the box. She half-panicked, moved out and checked Yusuf, spiking Yusuf's knee. Yusuf immediately threw her arm up in protest, virtually giving up. 'It wasn't that bad,' says Cathy. 'It wasn't a bump, it was a touch, a contact.' But she concedes if she'd known better she wouldn't have tried to pass on the bend. 'It's racing, it's competition,' she says. 'In the 800s and 1500s they bump, and thump each other no dramas. In fact they spike each other all the time and get away with it.'

England thought they had the race won with their champion pin-up girl Sally Gunnell leading by three metres into the straight. But having extricated herself, Cathy ran brilliantly, passed Richards and then Gunnell to take gold by a metre, throwing her arms in the air in triumph. She ran 50.70s, a phenomenal effort considering the strife she got into. The girls began a delirious victory lap but Bideau had his fears. 'When it happened I thought, "Whooa! This will be tough,"' he says. Australia is perceived as somewhat of a wealthy, first world bully boy of the Commonwealth Games, sweeping the swimming pool, and often the cycle track, of gold and topping the overall medal tallies. Poor little Nigeria would demand justice. And so it proved; Australia disqualified on the referee's call for Cathy's nudge on Fatima Yusuf on the crown of the final bend.

Poetschka considered it a rough call. 'These things happen and we all know Fatima's people were out for what they could get,' she says. 'If this chick can see she may be able to get something out of it, well, of course she'll put her hand up to protest. It was just unfortunate.' The irony was that Nigeria were then disqualified on two counts: for running out of their lane at the first changeover and because Yusuf threw her baton to the ground in disgust just before she crossed the finish line. So it was England gold, Jamaica silver, Canada bronze.

Cathy felt distraught. She knew that she had her medals whereas the other team members might never get another chance. 'I felt I was the one who let the team down,' says Cathy. 'Yeah, because I was the one who made the mistake. But I gave myself peace of mind because I tried my hardest and we placed first and that was all there was to it.'

Lee Naylor, in tears, said on television, 'We were laughing and crying when we won and it's really sad that we can't feel that any more. Catherine said we're still the best, we just won't get a medal for it, which was nice. But I still want to have a medal.' Cathy, having missed the opening ceremony, changed and dressed for the closing ceremony.

Cathy's first success in Auckland four years earlier had been in a relay but ever since then relays had just given her grief. In the *Sydney Morning Herald*, Jacquelin Magnay reported that Bideau and relay coach Keith Connor had a bitter altercation after Bideau said that the team should have had a better understanding of the rules. Bideau regrets that now, but he had just witnessed the possibility of Cathy winning four Games gold medals go totally awry. Team Freeman prepared thoroughly, took advice, went over and over plans, and brought Freeman success, Bideau says. 'I'm not saying we don't make mistakes,' he says. 'But Keith didn't give our viewpoint due consideration. We were disregarded.'

WINNING YET LOSING

If that had been the end of Cathy Freeman's 1994 season it would have been mammoth by any standards, but Bideau's philosophy, that you run through the tape in the race, extended to racing beyond the big championships in a season. 'That way you'll be in full flight on the important day,' he says. 'Plays a trick on the mind.' Thus the day after the Games ended, when the village and the venue became an instant ghost town, a sole athlete jogged around the warm-up track—Cathy Freeman. She was returning to Europe to run two more races, one against Pérec in France, another a World Cup race in London.

Coach Peter Fortune marvels at her stamina. 'We were lucky that we had such an amazing talent to deal with,' he says. 'A lot of athletes wouldn't have coped with it. She does travel well, and wherever she is becomes home for that moment. Most athletes would eventually start getting homesick, start wanting their boyfriend back in Australia. Well, Cathy had her boyfriend with her.'

Renee Poetschka, who survived the Games via needles stuck in her back to ease injury pains, is also in awe of Cathy's ability to race year-round at world-class level. 'She just kept going and going,' she says. 'I'd love to know the secret because that's something I haven't been able to do. I keep thinking she's got to break down sooner or later. But she doesn't. I don't know what the secret is but it's a damn good one. They should bottle it and sell it.'

Perhaps it was instinctive in her laidback nature. 'She's not difficult to train,' says Peter Fortune. 'She's regular and reliable. The only difficulty is getting her to work hard enough. The quantity is fine, but sometimes the quality lacks a lot.' Just as when she was a teenager, Cathy did not need to hammer herself in training. That's the privilege of the talented. Good athletes don't get injured as much, because they don't need to work so hard to win.

Cathy and Nick flew from Vancouver to Gatwick, stayed in London overnight, and next day flew out to Paris. At

4 o'clock the next morning they were still awake, jet-lagged and totally out of synch. They finally fell asleep and awoke at 11 a.m., befuddled and weary. Cathy was to race Pérec that afternoon and Nick thought to himself, 'If she feels like me, lousy, she's got no chance in this race. She'll come last.' Cathy showed just how tough she could be.

This was the grand prix grand final, 20,000 Parisians cheering their idol Pérec, $37,500 prize money for the winner, $25,000 for second. Cathy felt at peace with herself. It had been a great year, the big meets were run, she'd proven herself to herself. 'I'd proved I could endure everything I had to and still perform well,' she says. 'It was really special knowing that.' So this race wasn't worrying her. All the usual suspects were there, Pérec, Miles, Davis and Malone. Cathy, in lane six, was unlucky to be drawn outside Pérec in five and Bideau soon saw why. Cathy was slow from the blocks, Pérec leapt like a gazelle. Their start reaction times, measured by sensors recording the pressure of their feet leaving the blocks, were a stark contrast: Freeman 0.289s, the slowest in the field, Pérec 0.184s, the fastest. Pérec gained 0.105s, nearly a full metre on her right there, at the gun.

Pérec then pursued Cathy with such purpose that 11 seconds into the race she had caught up Cathy's lane stagger. 'My plan was to not let Marie-José get past for as long as I could,' says Cathy, which in itself was reactive instead of pro-active. She was so surprised to find Pérec at her elbow that she accelerated a metre ahead, a poor tactical move since it takes so much energy to step up pace. Pérec, the hunter, watched from behind, and halfway down the back straight was level with Cathy again.

To Cathy's credit she clung to Pérec, even around the bottom bend, to enter the straight on equal terms. But that's an impossible ask, matching an inside runner of Pérec's calibre, and the effort told. Just like Onyali in Victoria, Cathy started to overstride towards the finish. Malone even drew level with her but Cathy's greater fitness served her

WINNING YET LOSING

well. Pérec home first in 49.77s, the fastest 400m of the year, Cathy second in 50.04s, the second fastest, an Australian record, slicing 0.14s off the record she set in Monte Carlo only a month earlier. 'I think her long, rangy strides started to distract me over the last 20m and I lost my rhythm a bit,' Cathy said later. 'That probably cost me a time under 50s which would have been something special.' The BBC TV commentator nailed it: 'I really feel Cathy Freeman didn't give herself a chance, losing three to four metres to Pérec in the first 100m.'

Cathy was thrilled anyway, running a PB, and Bideau was lost for superlatives. From February to the end of August—seven months—she had run 20 tough grand prix races in Australia and Europe, and then eight more races in Canada, and here she was, in her 29th race, breaking the national record. 'She was unbelievable,' says Bideau. 'With 50m to go, instead of falling in a heap as you'd expect, she's still going ding-dong with Pérec!' Afterwards, in the stands, Cathy asked Pérec to sign her T-shirt, just like any admiring fan. Nick watched and thought, 'This is the last time she'll be doing that.' Cathy was making her mark. Pérec would have heard of Cathy's Games runs and no-one had battled Pérec down the straight like that since Olga Bryzgina in Barcelona in 1992. Olympic queens jealously guard their crowns and from now on Pérec would be ever watchful of 'leetle Cathee'.

Back at their hotel in Paris, Bideau, flagging from this endless summer, sat down to write a newspaper report on the race and struggled to concentrate. Cathy wanted to go out, look at shops, walk by the Seine, ride up the Eiffel Tower. 'Nick always had to make a deadline after I ran, when I needed to go out and unwind,' she says. 'My season was nearly over. I wanted to take off without him but he made me feel bad if I did that. He should have just let me go. I would have met up with him wherever he said.' Nick says he would have been glad for Cathy to clear out so he could write his story in peace and catch up with her later. But that she would not go by herself. Bideau now knew that in 1996, during the Olympics, he would not be able to work as a journalist. 'She was getting too good,' he says. 'The pressures were mounting, and she needed too much of my time.'

But equally, Bideau's journalism made him an acute observer and processor of race data and that day he went to school on Pérec. He noted the way she flew out in the first 50m, immediately putting pressure on the runner outside her and deflating the runner left in her wake inside her. 'Made sense. You have to get going anyway, so why not do it fast?' says Bideau. 'She puts a metre on them straight away and they panic. They think, "Oh no, she's up here with me already!" She beats them right there.'

One last race, the World Cup 200m at Crystal Palace in London. On a wet and miserable night Cathy ran a creditable third behind Ottey and Privalova, clocking 22.72s. Significantly she defeated Onyali, who came fourth. Even so, she looked at last as though she was running out of spark. The placing meant Cathy was ranked fourth in the world over 200m, to go with her second-placed ranking in the 400m, ratings which only Pérec herself had bettered in recent times. In the grandstand afterwards, Maurie Plant approached and sat beside Cathy and Nick. All stared numbly at the track, until Maurie said quietly, 'I don't often say this to Australians, but you've had one hell of a season.'

Back home in Melbourne, Freeman's arrival at the airport prompted spontaneous applause in the arrival lounge, after which she held her first individual press conference, cramming room only, as she saw for the first time the dimensions of her achievements. For months afterwards, newspapers, magazines, and television and radio stations rang Cathy incessantly for interviews. Charity after charity rang; could she make just one appearance for them? In shops she was suddenly a 'celeb' and received appropriate service, which she enjoyed. She was even elected Moomba Monarch, and tried on the royal robes over her track shoes and tracksuit pants.

WINNING YET LOSING

She was a fresh and attractive, politically correct product waiting to be exploited—or so commerce thought. 'Anyone with a hare-brained idea for a promotion rang up. It was non-stop,' says Bideau.

She explained her flag motivation over and over: to give self-esteem to Aborigines, be a role model for kids, instil pride in indigenous people. She visited schools and heard little Aboriginal kids racing around saying, 'I'm Cathy Freeman,' as though it made them six feet tall and bullet-proof. She almost felt grateful to Arthur Tunstall for stirring such controversy. 'It gained us a lot of international coverage which was good because it educated people about us,' says Cathy.

She received letters from elderly Aborigines which brought tears to her eyes. 'I'm 94 years old and I live in Cape York,' one lady wrote. 'And I've seen all these things happen with Stolen Children, being moved from our homes, seen cruelty and sadness and when I saw you run around with that flag, for the first time in my life I felt it was worth it all to be an Aborigine.'

Cathy says she would definitely work for a new national flag, if asked. A buyer rang to offer Cathy $10,000 for her Aboriginal flag. Not for sale, she said. The offers increased. What to do? It was part of history and that's what it has become, mounted in the Gallery of Sport at the MCG museum.

Prime Minister Keating invited her and Nick to afternoon tea. Cathy was pleased to get his supportive letter in Canada, but no more thrilled than when she read a fax from an old school friend. She hasn't changed, Cathy, and maybe never will. She didn't know whether to call him Prime Minister, Mr Keating or Paul, so she called him all three in the 20 minutes they were there. 'I didn't mind him,' says Cathy. 'But it's hard to get on the same plane as politicians because they are politicians.' Keating regaled them with his own swimming deeds at school. As they were ushered out, Bideau queried the PM's staffer: was Keating much good? 'Nah,' said the staffer, smiling. 'He always tells that story to sports visitors!'

The pair deserved a holiday and took one—as Cathy puts it, 'We hung out in the bush for a while.' They flew via Mackay where Cathy made a nostalgic visit to knock on the door of 10 Burston Street, her childhood home. 'The black family there seemed quite excited to see me,' says Cathy ingenuously, as though having the famous flag-carrying dual gold medallist walk into your loungeroom wouldn't excite most families.

They flew to Broome and then to a small Aboriginal community at Cape Leveque, where they stayed in a little shack and went boating, fishing and crabbing. 'It was blue skies, green sea, white sand, red hills,' says Nick. 'A beautiful place. Over dinner we talked about the year gone and the Olympics to come.' Then they flew to the Kimberleys to a property, El Questro station, where Nick knew the manager. The home overlooks a gorge where a tossed loaf of bread attracts brazen barramundi. They flew in a helicopter through deep gorges and, when they saw crocodiles, landed because they reasoned that where there were crocs there were fish. Nick caught catfish, Cathy barras, but the crocs kept tangling the lines. It was a wonderful experience for two world-weary people who were only a month out of the smog, crowds and rush of Europe.

One evening their hosts set up dinner on a balcony overlooking the gorge under a vast sky of stars, candles flickering on the table. Nick thought comfortably, 'We're going to be OK, this is working out,' and meandered into a conversation line in which he hoped to discover how Catherine felt about the future, whether she envisaged them spending the rest of their lives together. He could sense their relationship changing, but not how it was changing. In the circumstances any such conversation was bound to lead in a certain romantic direction, until Cathy thought she twigged and hurriedly interceded. 'Don't you ask me, Nick, don't you dare ask me, don't even think about it,' she said urgently. Nick says marriage was not on his mind in the near future, just whether that was the road they were heading along as a couple. Clearly it wasn't.

Nick was her first serious boyfriend, says Cathy. But right from the beginning it had been all very rushed. 'He was the one who organised the packing for me to move to Melbourne,' she says. 'He'd already made his mind up I was moving down with him. And really we didn't talk about it like adults. Well, how could we? I wasn't an adult, I was 18. He was always a few steps ahead of me and so it all moved much faster than I thought, even though that's what I wanted to do. Oh yes, no question. But everything's a bit of a gamble in the end, isn't it?'

Says Nick, 'She wasn't ready for it. I don't know exactly why, but she hadn't done enough things in her life and it was a bit frightening for her, so I dropped it pretty quick. It was a situation I should have discussed with her first. I could sense then that, no, we couldn't get married. It just wasn't going anywhere, that idea.' It was a difficult moment for Bideau to be thus pre-empted, because reverse is not a gear he enjoys engaging. His whole philosophy is to find his way around obstacles, to glean the positives from setbacks. But can there be a man alive who is not discouraged when his partner demurs reassuring him of their future?

It was even more serious than he knew. 'Part of it was fear,' says Cathy. 'I'm very in touch with my feelings and something told me it just wasn't right. Even before the Commonwealths I was getting doubts and little feelings were creeping in, just little moments. I told myself then I was going to break up with Nick after the Commonwealths. It was complicated because I was so happy with our professional relationship. So that even though you decide that something's not going to work, part of me was wanting to keep trying. But after the Commonwealths I said to myself, "This has got to stop. Take a break, and just see what happens." As it turned out I was with him for another two years. But all the time, I knew I couldn't be with him for the rest of my life.'

And so a marvellous year in Cathy Freeman's life ended in a stiff silence which quashed any growth in their personal relationship. It meant that inevitably the seeds of friction were sown in their working partnership as well. What could they do? So deeply entwined were their lives that the simplest answer was to do nothing. Which is what they did. But even this was a decision of sorts, because the longer it lasted, the more their differences showed. The only good to come from it all was that they both sublimated their personal doubts into the campaign for the Atlanta Olympics in 1996. That became their holy grail. They would deal with her career first, their relationship later.

15.
MICKEY MOUSE MEETS.
PRE-WORLDS, 1995

Cathy's free fall from her triumphant heights of 1994 was predictable, profound and painful. Motorcades followed on business functions, on top of school visits and media demands until she was sick of the sound of her own voice. Still only 22, she gave a lot of herself that Commonwealth Games year and it took its toll. Nick Bideau was run ragged dealing with the business enquiries. He tried to interest her in the business projects. 'Oh, yeah,' Cathy would say, wearily. 'Well, I don't want to not let you know about things,' he'd say. Normally she could escape to the track and immerse herself in training, but even this held little joy.

In December 1994, coach Peter Fortune alerted Nick to her malaise. She had returned to training about 4kg over her usual weight of 51kg. To the untrained eye, Cathy would still look the picture of health but, as horseracing handicappers say, weight will stop a train. Athletes watch their weight and judge their fitness by far harsher terms than the ordinary public.

Nick had not been attending her training because he was busy with business negotiations in November and December; then a painful but humorous gym accident kept him away even longer. Cathy normally lifted weights at Richmond football club, but when it closed over the Christmas break, Nick took her to the Victorian Swim Centre, in Batman Avenue, in the city. At Richmond, the bench press supports were set so wide apart that if the weights were removed from one end, the bar still remained stable. At the swim centre it was different. Cathy took about 50kg of weights off one end, the bar upended and the equivalent weights at the other end slid off and dropped onto Nick's foot.

'I knew straight away I had broken my toe,' says Nick, screwing up his face at the memory. 'I started hopping around and hopped outside to scream out. It hurt so much I just lay on the ground holding my foot and Cathy ran out to see how I was.' Nick, lying on his back, eyes closed, told her he needed ice. After a long minute passed he opened his eyes to see that Cathy, ever polite, even though flustered, had stopped to sign her autograph for a gym visitor! Nick laughs about it now, as they both did then, but it meant he did not oversee her training for six weeks while his foot recovered.

Now, at Fortune's request, he drove to Olympic Park and watched Cathy jog listlessly around. 'Why don't you tell her?' he asked Fortune. 'I have, but she won't listen,' said Fortune. It is a strongly implied axiom in athletics, as in most sports, that if the athlete doesn't perform, first blame the coach, think rationally later. Nick tried his luck. 'Catherine, this is crap, you're wasting your time,' he said. 'If you don't want to do it, don't do it, but don't pretend. You train like this and Gainsford is going to spank your batty! She'll belt you.' This was a standard Nick rev-up, but it backfired. 'Oh, I may as well give up then, because you don't motivate me, you just tell me I'm no good,' flared Cathy, and stormed off home in tears. She wasn't motivated, her heart wasn't in it. 'I was flat, flat, flat,' she says expressively. Nick called Maurie Plant who dropped in and talked her around, as he can. 'It's another day in the office,' he told her, 'sometimes it's hard, but that's your job.' Cathy gradually applied herself and life in Miller Street, Richmond resumed its ritual: rise by 7 a.m., Cathy trains until 8.30 a.m.; Nick makes breakfast—porridge and toast—while Cathy does push-ups and sit-ups; Nick irons her Australia Post uniform while Cathy showers; Nick drives her to work by 10 a.m. Cleaners come in during the day, Nick goes to work at the *Herald Sun*.

Evenings, around 6 o'clock, Cathy trains again accompanied by her dog Frankie, a cuddly chihuahua cross who Cathy rescued from death row at the RSPCA in Burwood that year. He's named after that fine Namibian sprinter, Frankie Fredericks, Barcelona silver medallist in the 100m and 200m, and gold medallist over 200m at the worlds in Stuttgart in 1993. Cathy is home by 8.30 p.m., more push-ups and sit-ups while Nick prepares dinner—pasta or stir fry, vegetables, rice, fish or chicken. He's content. 'You couldn't very well whip her into the kitchen after a hard training session,' he says. Just as Nick is ready to serve dinner, regular as clockwork, Cathy jumps in the shower. Ca-the-rine! She watches television, American sitcoms usually, reads popular women's magazines, asleep at the latest by 11 p.m.

Nick looked after the house bills, her public relations, private appointments, discussed investments with Peter Jess, coaching with Fortune and race agendas with Maurie. He was a one-stop shop for Freeman enterprises. Cathy was still not mature and Nick sensed that the way he ran her career, and life, was not an ideal development for a young woman. 'I knew what I was doing and I knew in one way I was making a mistake,' he says. 'But at the same time she wasn't going to win if I let her go. I could sense the power of the whole thing, what she was achieving, how even then she meant so much to so many people. Whenever I had doubts I'd ask myself: "What's more important, to let her go out and have a good time at the expense of her running, or help her to keep winning and change the face of Australia?"'

They didn't live like monks. Cathy always rested Saturday, they'd see an occasional film, or go dancing, but the conversation they had under the stars in the Kimberleys, though tucked to the back of their minds, had dulled a spark.

On the track, Cathy was still recovering from the demanding success of the Commonwealth Games year. She had taken a longer end-of-season break than normal and coach Fortune saw that he couldn't get her into peak form for the domestic season. She should aim for Europe. She ran in a pro 400m in Devonport at Christmas 1994 and essentially was handicapped out of it, unable even to make the final. Nick complained, 'She'd have had to run 49s to win that, even Pérec at her top couldn't have won it.' The handicapper apologised profusely but it was evidence nevertheless of Cathy's slow return to form.

Sri Lankan sprinter Susanthika Jayasinghe came to train with Cathy and proved a worthy partner, confirmed two years later when she won a 200m silver medal in the 1997 world championships. She often amused Cathy with her exclamations, 'No 200s today, back sore, headache, no run, no run, too tired.' Exactly how Cathy felt this season. Cathy, Susan and another Sri Lankan runner Sriyani Kulawansa trained together and came back to eat with her, a change from her usual all-white company. Melbourne has the lowest percentage of Aborigines of any Australian city. 'I was in a coffee shop in Richmond one day,' says Cathy, 'and I got really excited because there were three other black people there. They weren't Aboriginal, I didn't know them, they were complete strangers to me, but it just made me feel less alone.'

At length, in February, Cathy won her fourth consecutive Victorian sprint treble, 100, 200 and 400m, with reasonable opposition from Jayasinghe. In April she entered in the women's 400m at Stawell, home of the famous professional sprint, the Stawell Gift. The Nigerian sprint twins, Davidson and Osmond Ezinwa, training in Australia, came to watch and were amazed as Cathy gave the front markers up to 80m start. Strangers to the handicap system, the twins started calling out from the stands to the officials leading out the runners, 'Hey, come back you girls, that's too far, come back, not fair, too far!' Several of the girls started walking back and an official rushed up to reassure them, frowning awhile at the hecklers in the stand.

The Ezinwas were not aware of the vast difference in abilities of runners in the field and were relieved when Cathy eventually gathered them in and won by several metres. On a muddy track, and running four or five wide to find firm grass, Cathy looked impressive against the amateurish pro field. Nick said to the Ezinwas, who train with Nigerian Fatima Yusuf, silver medallist behind Cathy in Canada, 'Tell your girl Yusuf, Cathy's in good shape.' Even though she wasn't.

Afterwards Cathy performed one of her marathon signing sessions which would tax all but the sainted. I've seen her in action. She issues orders to a security officer. She will be at a certain spot at a certain time, have a table and chair ready. 'And make sure they get in line,' she says. Families and children queue for a hundred metres. Bideau tried handing out pre-signed photographs but the kids queue anyway, to see her sign again. She sits for an hour, and more, head down, signing, chatting, looking up occasionally to see the length of the queue, ever pleasant. Dusk falls, but she does not budge until the last fan departs. That all? OK, let's go.

Wherever she went, airports, hotels, she had only to pause and her autograph would be sought. She began to forgo the city streets. 'I can remember walking along the street and she'd be bumping into me from behind, hiding,' says Bideau. 'If I stopped and started talking to someone in the street, people would soon notice her and she'd say, "Come on, let's go."' Once she went lunchtime shopping in David Jones with Mark Pickering, a public relations colleague from Australia Post. She was browsing for shoes when a well-dressed man suddenly called out her name. 'I thought he must be a friend of hers, and I waited for him to catch up,' says Pickering. 'But out of the corner of her mouth, without looking up, she hissed, "I don't know him at all!" and ploughed on. She was very much public property.'

It had started as soon as she returned from Canada after the Games. That November, the year Jeune won the Melbourne Cup, Cathy and Nick got dressed up to the nines for the day out at Flemington, Cathy resplendent in a Cup hat. They joined friends in a private marquee in the car park until it was time to watch the race. But the journey to the track became an embarrassing obstacle race of half-drunk racegoers badgering Freeman instead of anticipating the Cup. If she went to a football match, she pulled on an oversize cap, and once even bought a wig of long dark brown hair to wear shopping in town. But really, her features are unmistakable. Bideau felt sorry for her. 'Just little things she was starting to be denied in life,' he says. It wasn't all bad. After Cathy won a magazine award as sports personality of 1995, Kylie Minogue introduced herself during an inter-city flight and said, 'I'm really glad you won that award, I think what you've done is terrific.'

Ironically, Australia Post had moved her out of their busy headquarters into a smaller branch in Collins Street before the Commonwealth Games because, whereas once occasional customers refused to be served by her, now they refused to be served by anyone but her. 'Is that really Cathy Freeman?' they'd whisper, queuing for her. Fame protects people from prejudice. Cathy simply does not experience discrimination today. And has never felt it on the track. 'We don't attract yobbos, athletics is just brilliant like that,' she says. After the Games she was so popular she had to be withdrawn from public contact altogether and transferred into public relations.

Some media appearances were quite fun, such as 'Burke's Backyard', during which Cathy shocked Burke by suggesting she would cut down a palm tree in the Miller Street backyard because it stopped the sun in winter. Burke aghast: 'The fan palm? No, no, it's beautiful! It will grow taller each year and it doesn't get any thicker on top. So it will gradually let more light in. No, it's a good friend.' Cathy shrugged, 'OK, I'll leave it then.' And off they went to eat witchetty grubs, crocodile meat, and bunya and quandong nuts, none of which Cathy had ever tasted before, at a restaurant specialising in native Australian cuisine.

When the Rolling Stones played the MCG in March that year, Premier Jeff Kennett threw a party for them afterwards at the Regent Hotel in Collins Place. Mick Jagger ran his eye over a party checklist and, being a cricket devotee, ticked Dean Jones's name. Then Keith Richards recognised Freeman's name because the Stones were on tour in Canada during the 1994 Games and they'd seen her run on television.

When the Stones made their entrance at the party, Cathy was immediately struck by the small stature of these rock and roll giants. She soon found herself confronted by the ravaged face of guitarist Keith Richards. 'Catheee! I thought you'd be wearing your little bodysuit,' he said amusedly. 'I hardly recognise you without your little suit.' Freeman stared into those hollow eyes, laughed and moved off to wish Jagger a pleasant stay in Melbourne.

At formal dinners Cathy was always seated with notable business figures, high achievers or politicians, many of whom she was interested in meeting. But there was no peace. After the speeches, as soon as she settled into a decent conversation, came the tap on the shoulder from other guests, even fellow sportspeople, ''Scuse me, Cathy?' Could she sign this menu, this program, this napkin? Invariably she left early, such evenings no longer enoyable.

'That's when it changed, in 1995,' says Nick Bideau. 'You could go places in public with her until then, but after the Games it became too uncomfortable to go out.' In a Perth hotel lobby Linford Christie chiacked, 'Oh, Cathy Freeman! Cathy Freeman! You're so famous, can you sign my ...' Cathy retorted coolly, 'Get lost, Linford!' He was always fooling around. In every capital city, billboards and posters of Freeman were appearing, an irritating reminder for proud Melinda Gainsford. At the Games welcoming home motorcade in Sydney, Cathy caught a glance from Melinda which puzzled her. 'I don't know what it was, something assessing, sizing me up,' says Cathy. 'Whatever it was, it worked.' Because Gainsford emerged in 1995 in slashing form, undefeated in 12 races in Australia, including two decisive wins over Freeman, the sprint double at the nationals and finally female Athlete of the Year. Wherever they raced that year, over 100m or 200m, Gainsford belted Cathy, sometimes by embarrassing margins.

Cathy's sprinting slump was exacerbated by Peter Fortune's decision to angle her training more towards 400m for the world championships in Gothenburg, Sweden, in August. 'Up until then we'd pretty well dual tracked the 200 and 400m,' says Fortune. 'I was starting to think it was compromising the 400m a bit, because she was still having trouble finishing the one lap strongly.' Fortune knew she could run faster than the 50.04s which she ran against Pérec in Paris, the previous September. 'Training for 400m requires more lactate-tolerance workouts. It's harder and tougher training,' he says, 'and not calculated to give her much zip in the 200s. I think Cathy may have been mentally turning off the 200m, and I was encouraging that frame of mind with the sets I gave her.'

The upshot was that Melinda Gainsford put Freeman under the hammer all summer. Says Bideau, 'Everyone was saying, "What's wrong with Cathy Freeman?" I kept telling the press, "There's nothing wrong, it's early days. Last year was hard, she's not a machine, she'll be back."' Bideau hoped for better at the Melbourne NEC meet, usually Freeman's favourite grand prix, but she had definitely switched off. Before the 200m, Melinda walked around with headphones on, totally inwardly focused, while Cathy stood around casually talking with friends.

After she lost, by some five metres, Cathy faced the media's microphone battery. Peter Fortune waited to hear the inevitable excuse, that she was training through, was not fit, and was aiming for later in the season, which were all true. 'You could see her mind working through the words, but she stopped herself,' says Fortune. 'And what she said was, "No, Melinda was the best tonight, that's all." She refused to take credit away from Melinda. I thought, "Gee, that's bloody impressive!" because I knew she was hurting. Mind you, I don't think she released any of her resolve to knock Melinda off.'

But later in another exclusive interview, with the Nine Network's Tony Jones, Cathy let slip her guard. 'Oh, this is just Mickey Mouse for me,' she told Jones, guilelessly. 'It's not the big meets, they're in Europe in July and August. I'll be ready for the worlds. I know this sounds cocky and arrogant, but I'm ranked four in the world for the 200m, and two in the 400m. So unless you're in the absolute top five, or top eight, I don't get turned on racing you. Melinda is not racing against the complete Cathy Freeman. Maybe it's a bad thing, but I'm not afraid of getting beaten here, it's not a big issue.'

That made it a very big issue on television news—'Freeman Tips Bucket on Australian Athletics'. Australian Athletics general manager Neil King leapt to Cathy's defence. She had supported the Australian circuit for years, he said. Her contests with Gainsford had given the domestic grand prix viability. 'The media were rough on me that year,' says Cathy. 'I meant no disrespect to any of my competitors. I was annoyed that I wasn't doing any better, but deep down I knew what the real story was. Looking back I was kind of angry that I was forced to run as many domestic races as I was. Because if I'd made the decisions myself, I wouldn't have raced hardly ever that year at home. I mean you can't force yourself.'

Equally irritating was the public's reaction. Groundsmen in parks, people sitting on benches, joggers running by, complete strangers, all asked her what was wrong. 'Even my family were asking me,' she says. 'That upset me a bit.' Bideau and Peta Powell, Cathy's best friend, worked overtime turning negatives into positives for her, but they were running out of time with only six weeks to the nationals in Sydney. Freeman jettisoned the 200m and opted for the 400m for the titles, no shoo-in itself with Poetschka once more back in form. Bideau was confident. 'Poetschka might be in good form, but Cathy's a good runner,' he said. So it proved at Homebush. Renee stole a two-metre lead in the first 100m and still led into the final straight, but Cathy's innate speed told and she surged to the line ahead, in 50.94s to Renee's 51.27s. 'Technically it wasn't a good run,' Cathy said afterwards. But who cares? A win was a win, her first of the season. And curiously it was her first national 400m title, four years after she first moved to Melbourne.

Cathy breathed more easily as the media phalanx retreated, but it was shortlived. A week later Gainsford won the world indoors 200m in Barcelona. Melinda was quick to concede that the field did not include Privalova, Torrence or Ottey. 'They're my idols and they're quicker than me,' she said. Gracious she was, but those runners weren't at the Commonwealth Games either and that didn't detract from Cathy's medals. Gainsford had beaten Freeman to a world title and Cathy didn't like it. It also meant the media would be back in the saddle again. Sure enough, next day Cathy heard Neil Mitchell on Melbourne's 3AW, 'Melinda Gainsford's gone right past Cathy Freeman to take over as Australia's speed queen.' Cathy's explanation for playing second fiddle? It was all ordained. 'Melinda's mother was really sick that year and it helped her mother pull through,' says Cathy, 'because she was so proud of her daughter.'

The best place for Freeman was out of the country and that's where Bideau took her, to the University of California in Los Angeles, to train on the same track as the mighty Marie-José Pérec. They would beard the lioness in her den.

Pérec's coach, John Smith, also trained extrovert American sprinter Jon Drummond and British sprint pair John Regis and Tony Jarrett. Cathy and Nick stayed in an apartment, owned by amino acids company Musashi, 10 minutes drive from the track. This trip Bideau took a training partner for Cathy, Mark Holcombe, a finalist in the world juniors over 800m in Bulgaria in 1990. Holcombe, a laconic Aussie, with a 400m PB of sub-48s, was faster than Cathy, the perfect training partner. 'He was a bit of a character, too, a bit of a ratbag,' says Cathy with a friendly smile. Holcombe, a self-confessed clown, also proved a handy buffer between Cathy and Nick, even though, as Cathy says, 'I was spending my life around men again!'

Cathy had returned from the end-of-season break above weight for an aspiring world 400m champion, so Nick became the food police, eliminating fat products like milk and cheese from her diet, and definitely no Big Macs. Cathy would have a bowl of cereal before training and then another afterwards. No good, said Nick. It's just sugar and fat. He sensed the temperature rising between them, but she was either a champion athlete or she wasn't, whatever their personal situation.

Good ol' Arthur Tunstall managed to intrude from afar in Australia when he told a private joke to an athletics official after a meeting, the punchline of which was that Cathy Freeman and Lionel Rose would probably pinch the pearly gates from Heaven given half a chance. The official was Athletics Australia business manager Geoff Rowe, who had handed Cathy her 200m flags in Canada. He was stunned at Tunstall's insensitivity, in telling the joke in the first place, and in telling Rowe, a Freeman supporter. 'Listen to this incredible joke Arthur told me,' he said to a staffer after the meeting. Athletics Australia secretary Neil King—who also opposed Tunstall over the flag incident in Canada—overheard it and next thing the media had it. On 9 May, Cathy's LA apartment phone began ringing non-stop.

At the track, Australian television crews screeched up to interview her, much to the amazement of the American athletes who were much bigger track stars. She gave a brief comment: she had no respect for Tunstall. 'It's sad when I'm spending so much energy proving to people that Aborigines can achieve to a high standard.' Says Cathy now, 'I was hurt and angry at first, but the more I settled down the more I saw that it made him look stupid and childish. I was determined not to let it get to me.'

Two weeks later, on 22 May, Tunstall released an apology, admitting he had told a joke, 'that probably should not have been told and I'm sorry for any hurt that it may have caused'. Cathy responded that she couldn't understand why Tunstall didn't denounce the sentiments in the joke: that Aborigines were renowned as petty thieves. This was untrue and has been identified by researchers as classic racist stereotyping. 'Whatever he says, I still find it disappointing,' she said.

Extraordinarily, Tunstall today has no regrets about telling the joke. 'Not at all, I've been telling jokes all my life,' he says. 'Everybody tells jokes about someone, they tell them about me.' Nor is he racist, he says. 'For God's sake, through boxing I've had more to do with Aboriginal athletes than all the other sports in Australia put together.' Well, I said, Aborigines are sensitive about issues such as the Wik debate … 'Which I don't believe in,' interrupted Arthur. 'I don't believe the generation of today should have to pay for what happened 200 bloody years ago. It's not my fault, none of my people came out as convicts and shot them. And what about the number of Aborigines who speared white people? You know, 80 per cent of people in this country don't believe in giving them land rights, and as a friend said to me, "They had the place for 40,000 bloody years, they never grew anything, they never built anything."' I couldn't believe my ears, one moment Tunstall talks rationally, the next he sounds like an 18th-century bigot.

Bideau watched Pérec train, Pérec watched Bideau watching, and Mark Holcombe watched them both. 'She knew Nick was watching,' says Mark. 'So she just jogged, pranced around a little bit, as Olympic champions are entitled to.' In that case, at the very least Bideau retarded her training for the world titles in Gothenburg. 'I never saw her do a decent workout the whole time,' says Nick. 'She seemed to be flustered that Cathy was there and I heard later that she was not pleased.' Cathy concedes she and Pérec are acquaintances rather than friends, 'We talk, and we're fine together,' she says. 'I find it quite easy to talk to the girls I race against. But I heard her coach, John Smith, tell Mary-Jo, "Don't speak to the enemy," which was just a load of bull.' Since Cathy and Nick were part of the track social group, Pérec invited them to her poolside 27th birthday in her ritzy Malibu mansion, the price of which gave them an insight into part of her motivation for being a great runner.

Before flying to the New York Games grand prix, Freeman diverted to Nike headquarters in Eugene, Oregon, and was amazed to arrive and find a huge flag flying outside: 'Nike Welcomes Commonwealth Champion, Cathy Freeman.' As Peter Jess had predicted, Cathy's Aboriginal flag had made headlines everywhere, and Nike made it known she was a Nike girl. From the moment she signed with Nike in 1993, Freeman moved beyond the realms of having to do television commercials for tummy-trimming inventions or pseudo health drinks. She was no longer merely a Nike image for 18 million Australians, her name was going worldwide. She enjoyed lunch with other visitors to Nike until one crass American executive began joking with a Kenyan Olympic official, 'So what will it be, Sammy? Chicken salad, elephant, giraffe, hippo, hahaha!' Cathy took exception. 'He annoyed me, showed such disrespect,' she says. So she befriended the Kenyan instead of the Nike bigwig. Freeman has never lost contact with the common man, forever identifies with the underdog no matter what heights she scales.

At the New York grand prix she ran fourth in 22.85s over 200m to Gwen Torrence, and the same afternoon outgunned world champion Jearl Miles and Jamaican Juliet Campbell over 400m in a slowish 51.52s. So there she was, in May 1995, two months after being deposed as Speed Queen of Australia, knocking off the world 400m champ, Jearl Miles. Fellow Aussie, Damien Marsh, ran in the 200m and talked enthusiastically about Atlanta where he was coached by Manly Waller, Gwen Torrence's husband and coach.

UCLA's smog was inducing Cathy's asthma, so Nick decided they should scout Atlanta for a training site for 1996. The first thing they noticed about Atlanta, the Olympic city, was the abundance of trees, which suggested clean air. The Olympic site didn't interest them. 'It'll be the same, 400m around, no hills,' Bideau was quick to quip. They watched Gwen Torrence train and were impressed. 'She was like a demon, one of the hardest working people I've ever seen train,' says Nick. Here was the role model he wanted for Cathy; not Pérec, whose slack routines made it seem you could succeed without effort. Cathy warmed up with Torrence, stretched, and listened. When observers said admiringly, 'Gee, Torrence is flying,' Cathy would go out and emulate her.

In late May, Cathy ran in the Bruce Jenner Classic meet in San Jose and scored a surprise win over 200m, relegating American Carlette Guidry-White and Pauline Davis to minor places, and poor Mary Onyali out of a place. Since the Commonwealths, Onyali hadn't been able to take a trick against Freeman. Cathy's time of 22.50s was, at that stage, the third best of her career. She was back on track for Europe. And Team Freeman got the message. 'It was an attitude thing. She regarded the US as stepping up, so she stepped up, and that taught a lot of people a lesson, including me,' says Maurie Plant.

Cathy came home briefly for brother Norman's 21st birthday, a happy evening with the Freeman family and friends in a function room at an Acacia Ridge hotel in Brisbane. At midnight Norman wanted Cathy to kick on, but Nick objected, it was late by a world championship athlete's standards. 'So I didn't go out,' says Cathy. 'Nick's a very dominant person. He was obsessed with my athletics, which was good for me, but my family is the most important thing in my life. There's lots I'm still angry with Nick about and that's one. I just wasn't allowed to be myself a lot of the time.' With hindsight Bideau concedes he was wrong. 'It had been really stressful getting her back into form,' he says. 'But, yeah, she's right, it was a total mistake. One night out, it wasn't going to kill her.'

Having recaptured her speed again, Cathy maintained training intensity but, only four days before she was due to fly out to Europe, disaster struck. Midway through a quick 150m at Olympic Park she pulled up suddenly, her leg cramping. She told Nick worriedly, 'My calf is sore.' Cathy wore tights that night but it was an icy five degrees, too cold for sprinting. That's the reason Cathy always goes overseas to train, away from Melbourne's winter. It was only a mild muscle tear, but it was her first injury. On another athlete, used to injury and normal recovery, it would have been nothing. But now Cathy's injury-free career rebounded on her. The psychological impact, her fear of re-injury, was crippling. She wouldn't stretch out in training. 'She wouldn't give it everything, she wasn't prepared to go 100 per cent because of the calf,' says Bideau. 'So she didn't progress to the next level of fitness as she should have after the US.' It did not bode well for the world championships. 'I feel a world title is in me,' Cathy told an interviewer before she left Australia. 'Given a bit of time and a little patience.' A little patience—such prophetic words.

16.
A TIN MEDAL.
WORLDS, GOTHENBURG, 1995

The Dancing Dingo, such an evocative, lyrical name for a dance club, especially for homesick Aussies in the far northern climes of Gothenburg, Sweden. Nick Bideau, renowned for his careful organisation, reconnoitred Gothenburg weeks before the world championships and rented an apartment in the centre of the city, a convenient walk from the Ullevi stadium, venue for the titles. Cathy inspected the apartment, looked out the window and gave it the thumbs up—'Oh, this is great,' she said.

They settled in for their first night before the titles started. Thump, thump, thump, the hammer of a bass guitar and the shrill sounds of rock music pierced the night. Bideau had not noticed the disco bar opposite the apartment, the Dancing Dingo, run by an Australian, which played loud music until 4 a.m. It was a mecca for Aussie tourists who emerged to shout, well taken with drink, in the street, fall over rubbish tins and create general mayhem. Peter Fortune spent a few nights there and says it was shocking. 'Not only the Dingo, but street-sweeping trucks were apparently housed down below as well. It was astounding the noise, all night long!'

Peter Jess had joined them and he went and bought an eye

mask, ear plugs and a beanie to try to cut out the Dingo dancing, but no hope. They closed the windows but with no air it became too stuffy. Jess tried a few pre-sleep drinks. He says, 'But I forgot we were in the land of the midnight sun and the longer I drank, the lighter it got. Weird!' Cathy opted to spend most nights in the athletes' village or with marathon runner Steve Moneghetti, his wife Tania and daughter Emma in their unit up the road.

Cathy's preparation for the titles had been mixed fare. That northern summer, Cathy put her increased sponsorship earnings to good use when she, Bideau and Peter Jess bought a new three-storey, three-bedroom, three-bathroom house in Hampton Hill, near Hampton Court palace, home of King Henry VIII. The house backed on to a bushy park, seven miles around, with deer roaming free. Cathy could choose from four nearby tracks, one of which, Kingsmeadow, in Kingston, hosted gaggles of great Kenyan distance runners, all managed by Yorkshireman Kim McDonald.

In Cathy's first race in England, at Gateshead over 200m, Nick wanted to see Cathy stretch out to gain confidence in her injured calf. She duly won in 23.10s, but when she still had sufficient breath left to smell the traditional bouquet of flowers given to her immediately after the finish, Nick knew she hadn't run that hard. On to Lausanne where the blessed Gainsford rivalry raised its nuisance head again. Against Torrence, Ottey et al, Cathy, smarting from her disastrous domestic season, ran hard with no thoughts of her injured calf, until she passed Melinda into fourth place and then switched off. Next big race was in Nice, a 400m against Pérec. As usual, Pérec caught her in the first 50m and that was that, except that Sandie Richards also passed Cathy, the only time she has ever beaten Freeman. Cathy was cranky and when Bideau approached her after the race, she waved him away saying, 'Don't talk to me. Get me a drink!' Says Cathy, 'I wasn't angry with Nick. I was getting asthma that night, and the air was humid and heavy by the sea. At the finish I couldn't breathe. Nick, good God, you know, he just wants to help, he can't help enough, but I needed space.'

Off to Oslo for a 200m and Cathy really wanted to beat Gainsford again, wanted it too much, tightened up on the bend and couldn't catch Melinda whose form in Europe started to match her magnificent home season.

'We couldn't get Catherine to run fast,' says Bideau. 'Whenever she went to sprint really fast, the speed wasn't there. It had become too important for her to beat Mel, and because she was not relaxed, she wasn't her usual flowing self.' Team Freeman tend to lay this blame on the Australian media's obsession with the Freeman–Gainsford rivalry, but as we have seen, there was no lack of personal intensity between them. Peter Fortune arrived, which pleased Cathy, but a worried Team Freeman headed for Monte Carlo and another 400m contest with Pérec in the last race before the world titles. By the pool in Monte Carlo's refined Loewes Hotel, Nick confided to Maurie Plant, 'We're in trouble. If Catherine doesn't run well tonight it will be hard work in the worlds.' Maurie's answer was to march everyone out for Norgen-Vaaz ice-cream. Nick looked at Maurie as if he was crazy. 'She's not carbo loading for a bloody marathon you know, it's only 400m!' he said. Plant knew ice-cream wasn't on Cathy's recommended diet, but if the choice was between an ice-cream cone and becoming emotionally drained sitting in a hotel room, he was for the Norgen-Vaaz. It worked. Cathy's mood lifted, followed closely by Nick's.

Pérec had not exerted herself at UCLA and was now trying to get fit quick. She had asked to run the 400m and 400m hurdles at the worlds, and the race program had been altered so she could enter both. But before Monte Carlo she had run on three of the previous five days. She had to be tired. Cathy, in lane three, had the look on Marie-José in four and stuck determinedly to her. The Frenchwoman couldn't gap her as she usually did. With 150m to go, sensing her chance, Cathy

A TIN MEDAL

surged past. Pérec, who had not lost a 400m race for five years, threw in the towel. She slowed so much that she allowed four more runners to pass her, Poetschka, Richards, Miles and Malone. It detracted somewhat from a victory singularly wrought by Freeman, but what matter. Australia first and second, Cathy in 50.34s, a good time, everyone ecstatic except the French meet director. Cathy had just blown away his French drawcard, the undefeated monarch of Monte Carlo, whom the crowds flocked to see. Cathy was never offered any real incentive to race in that city again.

Cathy had been vindicated in her comments about the Australian season not rating with the European season. She would never worry about her Australian form again. She had graduated to the world stage. Her aim would always be the next big European grand prix. 'It's nice to be able to say I've beaten Pérec at last, but she was tired, she wasn't in great shape that night,' Cathy told reporters back in London. But secretly it did give her confidence. 'Too much confidence,' says Cathy. Maurie Plant told Nick, 'She won, yes. When all around were losing theirs, she kept her head, but it was actually a bad race.' Bideau agreed. 'Yeah, she ran 50.34s, not 49.34s. She got away with that one, pat on the back, but I'm not convinced either.'

Before the championships, Nike called a press conference for their superstars. Up on a stage in the spotlight were Carl Lewis, Michael Johnson, Jackie Joyner-Kersee, Gail Devers, Dan O'Brien, Sergey Bubka, Irina Privalova and ... Cathy. The absurdity of it struck Bideau. Cathy didn't have their status, and he pleaded with Nike to let her off. 'We're paying her big money,' they said. She was the Australian Pacific region's best athlete. Finis.

'It's a big staged production with bright lights,' says Cathy. 'They treat you like a star and they have this big build-up. It was my first time and it was quite unnerving.' This would be her first worlds final, her first Nike all-star parade, it was pressure piled on pressure.

During 10 days in August 1995, over half a million fans packed Ullevi stadium to watch the world titles, and on the very first morning they saw Pérec win her heat of the 400m. What few noticed was Pérec running out of her lane for a full 15m. It was captured by an isolated BBC camera, not connected to the IAAF video circuit, and thus Pérec was not automatically disqualified. She was disqualified as a schoolgirl for the same offence, again in the 1989 World Cup and, of course, she ran out of her lane against Cathy in Monte Carlo in 1994.

'She should have been wiped off the map,' says Maurie Plant. 'They didn't have track referees out at the time. She's such a boofhead, Mary-Jo, she gets waited on hand and foot, and in France they never disqualify her so she never learns to run within the rules.' Boofhead, perhaps, but not stupid. The 400m lanes are 1.2m wide and the difference between running on the inside of the lane and running in the centre over a lap is about three metres, or 0.3s running at Pérec's speed. Bideau rejects the theory that Pérec races this way deliberately, arguing that it would not be worth the risk of being constantly disqualified. Yet she transgresses regularly and races are won by much lesser margins than 0.3s.

Bideau's BBC friends offered him their tape, but he went empty-handed to see Australian team managers Phil King and Bill Bailey. 'Did you see what happened? She ran out of her lane,' said Nick. Yes, they knew, but they weren't protesting, they said. 'We don't want to make Pérec angry, give her ammunition for the Olympics next year,' said King. 'Besides, I think Cathy can beat her anyway.' Bailey says that he could not protest because Australia did not have an athlete in Pérec's heat. He went to the US management, who did have a runner, put the case to them and asked them to enter a protest against Pérec. They declined. Embarrassed Swedish officials cast such an eagle eye over subsequent races that champions Gwen Torrence and Maria Mutola and the Jamaican 4 x 400m relay team were all disqualified in their

A TIN MEDAL

various events for lane violations far more mild than Pérec's.

People kept telling Bideau that Cathy could win, but Nick knew better. 'They'd all been fooled by Pérec. She's the master at it,' he says. But the more he was told, the more he started to believe it. Why be negative? Maybe I'm wrong, it could happen, yeah, she could win. Cathy struggled through her semi-final and Maurie Plant thought she looked caned. 'But we had to stay positive,' he says.

Before the titles began, Brendan Foster in an interview had asked her whether she had thought about being world champion. 'Of course. I've been thinking of the possibility ever since I won that race in Monte Carlo,' she said. Thought about little else actually. 'I was having sleepless nights, tossing and turning and thinking about the race all the time,' says Cathy. 'Every single minute it filled my head. Whenever I was alone my mind filled with the idea of being the world champion. I was even thinking about it when I went to the bathroom. Honestly, I was going crazy with it.'

Two days before the final, friends Mats Erixon and his wife Eva Svensson, both former international athletes, invited Cathy and Nick to stay overnight at their house 20 minutes out of Gothenburg. Cathy talked to Eva, and played with their child, listened to ABBA records and walked by the sea. Then it was back into inevitable Gothenburg where they dined that night with Jess, Plant and Fortune and distance coach Chris Wardlaw.

Race day, Cathy rose at 9.30 a.m., not feeling her normal self. She watched MTV, light lunched and dozed fitfully for an hour. Says Bideau, 'The race was not until 7 p.m. It grew into one of those endless days, tick, tick, tick, tick, hard to fill.' At one stage Cathy sighed and exclaimed, 'Gees, I can't wait for this race to be over with.' Nick nodded, yeah, I know Catherine, I know. Cathy burst out, 'No, you don't! How can you! You don't know what it's like, nobody does!' Nick didn't blink or speak. Peter Jess, who'd become their resident chef, says the stress in the room was palpable. Chris

Wardlaw had often remarked to Bideau that Cathy reminded him of Rob de Castella in their unbelievable capacity to relax under pressure. 'To be able to focus while the rest of us go crazy,' he said. Not today.

She rang her mother in Brisbane, where it was early morning, and then once more at 4 p.m. Swedish time, just as they left to walk to the stadium. 'When I hear her voice, it's nice,' says Cathy. 'It's like I'm at home again. It makes me feel better. But it doesn't make any difference to how I run, because business is business when I'm racing.' So what was she ringing her mother for? Cathy grins sheepishly. 'I thought I'd like to talk to my mother before I became world champion,' she says. 'It was part of me being really melodramatic. See, that's the thing, I'd let everything get out of hand.' Fortune walked to the stadium with them, biting his fingernails as he was wont. Cathy and Nick had been short with him, as well as with each other. Cathy laughed abruptly and said, 'Gees, it's like we're going to a funeral!' Nick had no accreditation to go into the warm-up area, but team head coach, Phil King, later told him that Cathy was absolutely whizzing around the track. 'I didn't think she was going to go mad,' says Bideau. 'I didn't think it was like Adelaide, not as bad. In some way I thought she needed to be in that state to produce something special, that sort of pumped-up state.'

But Peter Fortune was similarly worried, recalling Adelaide. But that was three years before, when she was only 19, now she was an experienced, dual Commonwealth gold medallist. 'I thought maybe she was just keyed up, was about to run the race of her life and this was her way of focusing,' he says.

Two factors mitigated against Fortune successfully interceding and they stemmed back to the original reason Bideau chose Fortune as coach. 'One was my relationship with Cathy, in which it was made pretty clear it was master–servant and I could only get away with saying so much to her,' he says. 'The second was that my personality is passive anyway, so I couldn't suddenly start acting out of character, you know, tell her to pull herself together, or whatever.' Another problem was that divining the psychological state of athletes is an imprecise science. Fortune tried to settle Cathy, to talk to her about a race plan. 'I got nowhere with it,' he says. 'She listened but she just wasn't hearing.' But Cathy did want to hear, it's just that Fortune couldn't break through. Cathy believes Fortune exaggerates his powerlessness in regard to her. 'He didn't have the strength to tell me what to do, but that was his nature, it wasn't something I imposed on our relationship,' she says.

As they walked from the warm-up track, Cathy noticed Tim Forsyth sitting with his head in his hands, having just been eliminated from the high jump. The bar had fallen off tantalising seconds after he had cleared it. He'd railed, remonstrated, to no avail. 'I was going through an awful time, I didn't want to see anyone,' says Tim. 'I was sitting over in a corner having a quiet cry, with photographers hanging over the fence. It was shocking, like something out of a movie. I saw Cathy talking to Fort, then she looked over at me and said to Fort, "Hang on," and she ran over to me and gave me a hug and said, "Don't worry, Tim, it's only a high jump."' It was just perfect, someone I knew to put it back in perspective again. That really stuck with me.'

It gave Fortune pause, too. 'I thought that maybe she was in control after all,' he says. 'I mean you wouldn't do that if you were totally out of your tree.' But Cathy's magnanimity of perspective did not extend to herself. 'I was aggressive, but my aggression wasn't at all controlled, it was out of control,' she says. 'I meant what I said to Tim, but it was because I was feeling so cocky. I was over the top.'

Psychological over-arousal feeds adrenalin into the body prematurely, and the effect on Cathy was to produce a state of euphoric calm and mild buoyancy. She saw Peter Jess waving her Aboriginal flag near the start, but it was all surreal until the reality of the race crashed into her consciousness. 'I settled into my blocks and suddenly just lost it,' she says. 'As I was getting down for "On your marks", I thought these exact words, "I'm f—ing shitting myself!" Those very words. I was terrified. I wasn't focusing on the start, the race, nothing, and then I just did a bolt.'

Cathy charged out, no rhythm, no relaxation, just speed. She was running Pérec's race, not her own. Fortune, in the stands, said out loud, 'Oh God, no!' And then to himself, 'This ain't gonna work.' He waited for her to blow. Cathy had no idea she was going too fast. She was exhilarated. 'Running down the back straight I was saying to myself, "I'm going to win this bloody thing. I'm going to win it!"' she says. She shakes her head in wonder. 'You just should not be thinking like that. When you're focused something overtakes you, so you do it, but you don't think about it.'

At 300m she was level with Pérec in 35.7s, her fastest ever, but whereas Pérec had run with flawless judgement, Cathy was a spent force. Bideau, too, had been living on hope. Down the back straight, he could see that Cathy was running with winning in her mind but he knew also that she could not just will it to happen. He wanted her to win but another thought had strayed forward—I hope she gets a medal. By the top of the straight he knew it was over.

'I started losing it about 80m to go,' says Cathy. 'It was a terrible feeling. I could feel first place slip away from me. That happened, and then I saw silver and bronze just dissolve before my eyes.' Dissolve as, with 30m to go, first Pauline Davis and then Jearl Miles ran past her. 'I won't easily forget the last 50m,' says Cathy. She ran out of everything with 20m to go, the lactic acid in her muscles rendering her legs so unresponsive she almost stumbled. 'I crossed the line and the first feeling I had was relief that it was over,' says Cathy. 'And then it hit me, it hit me that, oh no, I got fourth and I'd stuffed up. And then that was Ohhh, nooo!' To athletes, fourth is the most cruel of places, no medal, so near, so far. There should be a tin medal for fourth, then only half the field would feel heartache.

A TIN MEDAL

When Nick reached Cathy she immediately projected her own gloom. 'You're really disappointed in me, aren't you,' she said, downcast. Nick protested, 'No, no, no! You ran a great race, it doesn't kill us, we still love you.' He was hurting for her as she couldn't know. 'I'll tell you what I think,' he said. 'I think you showed today you'll be a champion one day because you took it on. You didn't have the strength or condition to do it, but you had the heart to do it. You ran to try to win.' Nick could see she was shattered and that it wasn't sinking in. Assistant team manager, and friend, Margaret Mahony, stood helpless. Console or congratulate was her motto, but this was terrible, beyond artificial sympathy. Cathy saw Len Johnson, athletics writer on the *Age* newspaper, in the mixed zone. 'I know Len well, he's one of those journalists it's a pleasure to work with,' says Cathy. 'Even he couldn't look at me in the eye. It was overwhelming for everybody.' Peter Jess held the black, red and yellow flag, still furled.

Cathy walked back to the athletes' village, her ears ringing with reassurances that people were proud of her, what a great fight she had put up. Ah, all except for Peter Jess, who gave it to her straight, as she expects him to. 'Well, you screwed up,' he said. Which she had. Pérec confirmed it. She told journalists, 'Cathee want to copy my race. This is something not good to do against me, because I am crazee!' Like a fox. Pérec, tall and powerful, set such a burning pace in the first 300m that she sapped Cathy's stamina. Then it became a race of Pérec's mature endurance against Cathy's young courage. Neither was going fast, but Cathy's last 100m took her 14.90s to Pérec's 13.58s.

In her heart, Cathy knew she could have medalled. Going into the race she had a 2–1 advantage over Davis (silver, 49.96s) and a 4–1 advantage over Miles (bronze, 50s flat). 'She would have had to run a PB to medal,' says Fortune. 'But she could have done that with a better race plan. Not winnable, but placeable.' Cathy had pushed Pérec to 49.28s, the world's fastest for three years. Cathy had run 50.60s herself, hung on to beat Yusuf, Ogunkoya, Malone and Richards, but had nothing to show for it. When she saw Tim Forsyth his two soft words conveyed all that was needed. 'Gee, Freeman,' he said, looking down from his 199cm at his 164cm friend. A little later he gave her his fuller race appreciation. 'The other girls ran to get medals in that race, but you ran to win,' he said. 'That's very, very honourable. Whenever I speak to anyone about it I'll say that was one of the most fantastic things I've ever seen. At least you had a go. That's all you can ask of someone.' Experienced distance runner, Carolyn Schuwalow, told Cathy she was an inspiration.

It meant a lot to her, getting respect from her peers. 'I wasn't destroyed, I was disillusioned I guess, with myself,' she says. 'I'd never been in a better position before, going in having beaten the world's best.' She told Peter Jess, 'Jess, I'm going to put some make-up on, I need to feel better about myself.' Oh yes, and Cathy made another of her resolutions: that was the last time she ran in a big race and didn't get a medal. That evening she was watching television when scenes of atrocities committed on women and children in the terrible war in Yugoslavia flashed on the screen. Suddenly Gothenburg shrivelled in importance, proportion was restored. It was good enough simply to not be in Bosnia.

But she didn't leave Gothenburg empty-handed. Freeman, Poetschka, Naylor and Gainsford ran fourth in the 4 x 400m relay, thanks to a sensational sub-50s last leg by Cathy. The Jamaicans were then disqualified for a lane infringement and Australia got the bronze. Notable in that relay was a powerful 400m leg by Gainsford who had previously made the semi-finals of the 100m and 200m.

Bideau felt compelled to say to Melinda after the relay, 'What you did out there today was good.' Not that he thought she could ever be good at 400m, but that he respected her effort. Bideau believes Gainsford could medal at the highest level over 200m. 'She's got the physical equipment, I'm just not sure if she is convinced of it herself,' he says. The Gainsford and Freeman camps would always be wary of each other. Just the way it was. I asked Gainsford, for this book, had she ever thought of running the 400m? 'Well, I wouldn't have minded starting 400s earlier in my career,' she said. 'A bit late now.'

Back in London, Cathy moped, convinced that Nick was disappointed in her. Says Nick, 'There was nothing that I could do to bring her around.' Says Cathy, 'We were having our problems, but I felt he distanced himself because I lost. Maybe it was just me, but I felt we'd drifted apart and I felt alone.'

Just as her season didn't finish with the peak of the Commonwealth Games in 1994, nor would it end in the trough of the worlds in 1995. Cathy was determined to redeem herself. 'You know I'm really looking forward to the last few races,' she told Nick. 'I want to run a PB.' Maurie Plant encouraged her. 'You don't become a bad runner overnight, you have one bad run,' he told her. 'It takes years to become a good runner, and it takes a few years to become a bad one, too.'

Pérec didn't run another 400m that year. Why would she? Team Freeman could learn from her clever, arrogant ways. In Brussels, on a cold Friday night, not conducive to quick times, up against Miles and Davis, Cathy did everything right and won in 50.21s. 'Ah, not a PB, though,' she said at the finish. Sunday, at Crystal Palace, she raced Miles again and won in 50.4s. The following Friday, in Berlin, the courtesy bus driver ferrying the circuit athletes to the stadium from their hotel was uncertain of the route. Maurie jumped up and told the driver, 'Listen, the stadium's over there.' 'Are you sure?' said the driver. 'Bloody hell, it's been there since 1936, unless it's moved in the last 59 years!' said Maurie. Safely delivered, Cathy ran 50.96s to hammer East German Grit Breuer, who was returning from a three-year drug suspension.

The powerful, stocky Breuer was Cathy's first race against a convicted drug cheat and although willing to concede Breuer had paid her penalty, Cathy still was not impressed. She finds the whole drugs in sport issue disturbing. 'It's dishonest, it's morally and ethically wrong,' she says. 'But who do you blame, the athletes or the system? In a way I feel sorry for athletes from communist regimes. I don't know their political systems, but it seems that in those countries winning was the only chance they had to improve their life.' What if, one day, they discovered that Marita Koch, the East German who holds the world record in Cathy's own event, the 400m, had been assisted by drugs, as everyone suspects? 'Well, I have a lot of respect for anyone who holds a world record,' she says. 'But sure, that was set more than 10 years ago. Now, it's not as if there's not enough talent in the world in track and field. It's easy to do, running, just need a dirt road, and everyone is trying their best. So how come someone hasn't come close to that world record? It says something about the record, doesn't it? It just doesn't make sense.'

Cathy's win in Berlin was her third in a row in eight days. She had gone through immense moments of self-doubt after the worlds. 'You ask yourself, "Should I be doing this?"' she says. 'You have to draw on this huge inner strength to get through it. Because it's more than racing, more than a physical thing, it's emotional. But even though I had my moments, I knew I was going to be all right.' After Berlin she'd had enough. She had won five international grand prix races that season, proved she could have won a medal in Gothenburg, was still ranked No 2 in the world over 400m. 'I'm so tired, Nick, I really don't want to run any more,' she said. But business is business and two more 200m runs, in Rieti and Monaco, saw her out.

Her thrill in Monaco was to watch comrade Damien Marsh run in the IAAF grand prix 100m final against the world's best including Donovan Bailey, Linford Christie, Mike Marsh, Jon Drummond, Bruny Surin and Dennis

A TIN MEDAL

Mitchell. In a tight finish, Drummond's coach John Smith turned to Bideau and asked, 'Who's got it? Who's won?' Said Nick, 'Marsh, I think.' Marsh? 'No, no, he came last,' said Smith. 'Not Mike Marsh, Damien Marsh!' said Nick. And Damien had, in 10.13s, an Australian record. Cathy was delighted since Marsh had been staying with them in their London house. Bideau had the final word, 'It's what I always say, you don't have to be better than them, but if you're ready on the day and they're not, you can beat them.'

Back in London they regathered their spirits, Cathy even venturing for a run with Bideau around the seven-mile circuit of the park behind the house, just so she could say she'd done it. 'It was sort of like making the place home for me, I think,' she says. She finished, leaden-legged in 56 minutes, not bad for a sprinter, maintaining 8-minute mile pace. Then they took off for a holiday in Ireland, spending time with Frank O'Mara, an Irish 5000m record holder and contemporary of Bideau's Kiwi friend, John Walker. O'Mara was astonished when, in a Limerick pub, people asked for Cathy's autograph. But no more impressed than when she stood at the bar throwing down pints of Guinness. 'It's good for you,' she said laughing, happy the season was over.

On the way home Cathy flew into Nike headquarters in Portland, Oregon, for an Olympic summit with all Nike's major stars. Nike is the world's leading sports fitness company, followed by Adidas, then Reebok. The chairman Phil Knight, still a majority shareholder, was a miler at the University of Oregon, where he was coached by Bill Bowerman, head of the 1972 US Olympic track team. Bowerman's hobby was crafting custom-made shoes for his athletes. When Knight graduated, he built Bowerman's idea into the massive multinational Nike shoes company of today. Cathy and Nick were picked up at the airport by a Nike stretch limousine, driven by a chauffeur in cap and uniform. 'Driven any interesting people lately?' asked Bideau. 'Yeah, Carl Lewis, Michael Jordan and Phil Knight himself, just the other day,' said the driver proudly. Just three of the biggest names in US sport. Cathy chatted away to him, thoroughly charming him, as she often does to people she meets as she travels. In their Oregon hotel room they were greeted by Nike's usual corporate generosity—jacket, T-shirts and track gear, as well as chocolates, champagne and flowers in a personalised basket. Nike knew the way to an athlete's heart.

The summit was to talk about how to best promote Nike during the Atlanta Olympics. All of the Nike stars there were either Olympic or world champions or world record holders, except Cathy. 'It was nice being close to the stars but I wondered what the hell I was doing there,' says Cathy. 'I was intimidated but I thought, "Well, they asked me."' They did one-on-one camera work as media training, at which Michael Johnson and Carl Lewis demonstrated their usual in-your-face, American trash talk for their mock interviews: 'I'm ready, I'm focused, I've done this and that, I'm prepared, so I'm gonna rock 'n roll ... rah rah rah.'

Cathy came on as her usual nervous, humble, hesitant, giggling self and feared the worst from the training officer. Instead the officer sat fascinated and finally said, 'That's fantastic. You move in the right way, you bring the viewer in, you show you're vulnerable. You have this childlike quality, you give a little of yourself but not too much and people want to hear the next thing you're going to say. It's perfect, don't change a thing.'

One evening, when Nick was out on business, Cathy was lying on her bed, ready for sleep, when two Nike girls rang from the lobby, 'Come on down, Cathy. It's end of season, come out and have a drink.' The Americans liked her different style, and found her refreshing to talk to. Then they put American sprinter Michael Johnson himself on the phone and all three hassled her to come out. 'I was quite excited that Michael asked, so we walked down the street to a bar and suddenly there's this tequila in front of me,' says Cathy. 'I'd never had one before so I said, "How do you drink it?"

A TIN MEDAL

And this guy, Alexander Bodecker, who's worked for Nike for about 15 years, said, "I'll show you" and he drank half and I drank half. Michael had about seven!' In years to come Bodecker was to play a large part in Cathy's personal life.

Back home in Melbourne, relations between Cathy and Nick were strained, without much to talk about, because they'd talked about everything. As a couple they experienced everything together, lived each other's lives. It wasn't as though each came home from work with a day's news to share. Cathy complained that Nick watched and read sport all the time, or was out running by himself. 'That was great for him, because he loves all that, but it means he takes his job with him wherever he goes,' says Cathy. 'Whereas I love culture, I love art, I love music, and I love talking about those sort of things. We didn't share a lot of interests.'

From Nick's side, the demands of their combined personal and business relationship had cut him off from old friends and lifestyles. It seemed, literally, that the only time they were out of each other's company was when one went to the bathroom or Nick went for a long run. One Saturday, her rest day, Cathy casually asked Nick what they were doing that day. 'Hang on, I organise your every hour during the week, now I've got to be a recreation officer on Saturday as well,' Nick responded. It was pressure-cooker living and it couldn't last.

In November 1995, Cathy announced she wanted to move out, she needed some space in her life. It is a common plea of people involved with dominant partners, and Cathy felt Nick was all that. 'I know I tried several times to leave, but nuh, he wouldn't let me go,' says Cathy. 'This time I did.' By now Nick was glad of the space too. But even though he believed a split was inevitable, he also knew how much trouble Cathy would have coping on her own. Cathy moved, but not far— into a house they had previously bought in Richmond Terrace, only a block up from Miller Street. Cathy shared there with a friend, Tiffany Cherry. But Cathy was used to Nick problem-solving for her, so she called him up, they ate most meals together, and Nick occasionally stayed the night.

Bideau could never see the logic in the way that Cathy gave her family gifts which never significantly improved their quality of life. 'I don't have any qualms about giving stuff away,' says Cathy. 'If I could, I'd give everything away.' Nick had an idea. Rather than constant gifts, why not reduce her parents' financial burdens and give Cathy enormous pleasure as well. Buy them a house. Soon after Christmas 1995, Nick flew to Brisbane and sealed a deal for a two-storey home in Sunnybank Hills, a short drive from QEII athletic stadium. Cathy called her mother excitedly. 'Mum wanted to go around right then and look at it,' says Cathy. That evening when Bruce Barber returned to their cramped Black Community Housing home in Acacia Ridge, Cecelia chided him—again—about when were they moving to a larger house? Just as he was about to bite, Cecelia sprang. 'What would you say if I told you Catherine's bought us a house!' Says Bruce, 'Cecelia was ecstatic, she wanted to move in straight away.' Cecelia, of course, would have gladly swapped the house to have Cathy living closer to her. 'I think about all the time she's been away, first at boarding school, then for athletics, and then in Melbourne,' says Cecelia. 'I realise I have to share Cathy with the rest of Australia. But when I see mothers and daughters going shopping, I envy them. I'm really sad about all the years we've missed being mother and daughter.'

By January 1996, Cathy and Nick were spending so much time with each other again that they bought a new house, in Stanley Street, Richmond, and Cathy moved back in. Cathy's move from Miller Street to Richmond Terrace to Stanley Street had taken only two months, so brief that she fobbed off suggestions of a split, even to close friends.

The Atlanta Olympics were just seven months off. Bideau contemplated his knife-edge task. To stumble at home or push too hard on the track could cause Cathy to blow up. Maybe he could lose her for all time. The balance for Cathy was crucial. She couldn't push herself to her utmost by herself. To run fast she needed Nick, she believed in him. If Nick said, 'You've got to do it, it's the right thing to do,' she did it. They had an understanding: each would give selflessly to the goal of gold in Atlanta.

English athletics agent Kim McDonald arrived in Australia for the 1996 domestic season and announced cheerfully, 'Good reports about Cathy.' Nick looked puzzled. McDonald had called in at Nike en route. He told Nick, 'I asked the limo driver if he'd driven any interesting people lately, and he says, "Yeah, I drove a really lovely girl recently, Cathy Freeman."' She'd superseded the superstars.

17.
A WOMAN AND THREE MEN. ATLANTA, 1996

Late in 1995 Nick Bideau called a council of war with Peter Fortune and Cathy to reveal his master plan for the Atlanta Olympics. The typed plan concluded: 'I strongly believe a gold medal can be won but it will require an increase in effort from everyone involved.' As he began his outline in their Miller Street home, Cathy listened but kept one eye on the television. Nick posed her a question. 'What?' said Cathy. Nick said, 'Catherine, we're trying to work out how to make sure you run as fast as you possibly can in 1996, so you're not disappointed like you were in 1995.' Cathy, without taking her eyes off the screen: 'Listen, can't we talk about this later, I'm trying to watch "Roseanne".' Nick tried again. 'Ah, this is very important, we're trying to get you to another level.' Cathy turned to face him and said, 'Look, I know how to run faster, I'll just train harder. That's all there is to it!' And went back to 'Roseanne'. Bideau and Fortune looked at each other blankly. 'Guess there's no need for this meeting, Fort,' said Nick gathering up his papers. 'She'll just train harder. That's it!'

And she did. 'I don't like it when things are made unnecessarily complicated,' says Cathy crossly. She already knew the path to improving, anyway. In Oregon, apart from drinking tequilas with Michael Johnson, she'd asked him how come he never seemed to be hurting at the end of his 400m races. 'Oh man, compared to how I feel in trainin', it's nothin',' he said. So Cathy began to get up earlier, run with purpose, and train until it hurt. 'I trained like a demon, I was possessed. I was a different athlete to 1995,' she says.

Bideau's master plan also revealed how he wanted to diminish his all-pervading control of Freeman's life. The plan addressed Fortune: 'I know it has been difficult for you to get her to carry out instructions but you must get through to her that you are the coach and she must do as you ask.' Bideau wrote that he wanted to have much less to do with the hands-on operation of Cathy's training this Olympic year. 'I want you to be tougher and take more charge. That way your message, which has always been sound, will be a hell of a lot clearer.' But it was probably already too late by then to ask Fortune to alter his coaching style. Fortune had always played soft cop to Nick's hard cop if Cathy stuffed up training. Fortune would say, 'Never mind,' whereas Bideau would say, 'Catherine, that was crap!'

Bideau also tried to get Cathy to be more independent, run her own life, do normal things like pay her own bills, catch the train to work at Australia Post. 'It was only a 10-minute train ride, the trains were empty at 10 a.m., so no hassle,' says Bideau. But if Cathy was late, she'd drive in and Nick would discover $25 all-day parking receipts in the car. 'She could afford it, but athletes lose a sense of reality if they don't live in the normal world,' says Bideau. 'They think everything comes easy, training is easy, then winning is easy. Except it's not.' This was in early 1996. Two years later Bideau was vindicated when Olympic legend Herb Elliott urged Australian Olympic hopefuls to get real jobs, to learn how to do it tough, on and off the track.

Nick's protective instincts and Cathy's lack of interest conspired to keep Cathy from running the minutiae of her life. 'I've always been scared of her getting into trouble, or getting hurt, I was very protective of her,' says Nick. 'I know I should have let her do more things on her own, even little things. I tried, and I know my intentions were right but it's very hard, when you really care about someone, to stand by and see them make mistakes.' In their new house in Stanley Street it was make or break. The first occasion that Nick began to correct Cathy, she said, 'This is not going to work if you don't let me be who I want to be. It's my house too, I'll do whatever I like.'

It was not all one way. Cathy is a tenacious debater for her point of view, which often tends towards being lateral rather than literal thinking. 'She has her own structure,' says Bideau. 'She can really convince you because she's totally convinced herself, and only afterwards does it sound illogical. But once she's got her mind made up, that's it.' One day Cathy asked, 'How much do I earn? Am I a millionaire?' It was very complicated, Nick replied. It's all done differently for tax reasons. Go and talk to Jess, he advised. Instead, Cathy asked Nick to write it down for her. Nick asked Jess, who gave him flow charts and lists, which Cathy examined for five minutes and did not look at again. He didn't blame her, it didn't stick in his head either. He trusted Jess. Cathy appreciated that Nick tried to shield her from the avalanche of paper-work and finance details so that she could concentrate on running. 'But in retrospect, even though I would have been a reluctant student, it would have been good if Nick had applied the same discipline to making me learn about finance as he did to turning me into a good athlete,' says Cathy. 'It would have helped make me a more well-rounded person today.'

At Australia Post she was assigned to assist journalist Mark Pickering in media and communications and he remembers her first day. 'She was like a little flower, very gentle and very private,' he says. Cathy told him, 'I've never written anything before, I'm raw at this game.' And she was.

The first few items she wrote, they went over and over, 20 times, each time picking up her previous errors. They worked side by side for 18 months, Cathy working 10 a.m.–4 p.m., before she left for Atlanta. 'When she concentrated she worked hard and learnt quickly,' says Mark. 'She reached a peak where you could give her a story or a briefing and she'd produce something excellent. Another year or so and she could have walked into any newspaper and held down a job as a cadet reporter.' Pickering became so confident in her that after she left for Atlanta, he once called out, 'Cathy, could you do a story ...' forgetting she had left.

On her own initiative, Cathy dealt with Gothenburg through sessions with Victoria University sports psychologist, Jeff Simons, a former distance runner who'd worked with the US Olympic track and field team in 1992. Cathy confided to him, 'I'm so scared of freaking out again.' Simons drew the perspective for her: it was abnormal to have a job where, at the word 'Go', she had 50 seconds to perform, to perfection, competing against others, in front of a crowd of thousands, and an audience of millions. 'Cathy is very strong in her focus, so she took all her uncertainties and worries in Gothenburg and just said *run*!' says Simons. 'Unfortunately that puts the body out there at the limits of physiology.' Nor was the answer to seek to blot out the uncertainties. 'That reduces the athlete's awareness of, and sensitivity to, the race,' says Simons. 'Besides, worries have a habit of sneaking back in and leaping out at the worst moment.' As with Cathy on her blocks at Gothenburg.

Says Cathy, 'He made it clear to me that I shouldn't worry about the things that are out of my control and concentrate on the things I can control. Even though it sounds basic, I needed to hear it from a professional to give it weight.' Simons also had Cathy practise deliberate relaxation 20 minutes before training or racing, to combat her tendency to over-arouse.

To avoid the fiasco of the previous domestic season, Nick

booked no 200s against Melinda Gainsford and, as well, entered Cathy in several early season November and December races. 'Just to win a few, get people off her back,' says Bideau. 'It didn't matter what race, people didn't care, they saw her win, Freeman first, that's it.' In Melbourne, Canberra and Perth, during November and December, she won over such unusual distances as 150m and 300m. The best way to check her fitness was in the Devonport pro 400m where, on 29 December 1995, she ran 50.93s in a heat, the fastest ever on grass. It was clear Freeman was fit, very fit. Another tactic, to avoid media attention, was to have Athletics Australia competitions manager, Brian Roe, enter her in a race under the name of some little known athlete, and substitute Freeman's name the morning of the race. On 28 January 1996, Cathy trained in the morning, ran hills on the grass near the Melbourne Hilton and then flew to Adelaide for a 400m. She won in 50.96s, went straight back to the airport, warmed down on the grass there, and was home for supper. Same in Hobart, 25 February: arrived two hours before the race, ran a superb 50.40s. She was in great shape, ready to run under 50s but how to get her to stretch herself? Nick and Maurie came up with the solution: create a big occasion, import Sandie Richards of Jamaica.

Richards, then 27, won a track scholarship to the US as a 17-year-old, and over the decade had won stacks of 400m medals, including gold in the world indoors and bronze in the world outdoors in 1993. She also won bronze behind Cathy at the Commonwealths in 1994. She had never been out of the world top 10 since 1992, but in seven years her 400m PB had scarcely fallen, from 50.92s to 50.19s. 'I count myself a very friendly person, I talk to everybody,' she says in her rich Jamaican-American drawl. 'At the Commonwealth Games, Cathy looked like somebody who would talk to me and so I said hello.' Talked to Bideau too and, being in decent shape, accepted his offer to be flown out from wintry

California for a few weeks in sunny Down Under, staying with Cathy and Nick.

On 29 February 1996, 13 days after Cathy turned 23, the Melbourne NEC classic offered the perfect opportunity to test Freeman's mettle. Bideau urged Richards to go hard for the first 250m. 'Then we'll know what shape you're in,' he told her. And Freeman too. It was Poetschka in lane three, Cathy in four and Richards in five—three of the world's fastest women over 400m, all ranked in the top 10. Sandie, in her blue two-piece outfit, went quickly, but in her yellow one-piece, Cathy could be seen collaring her at the bottom of the back straight and then striding away to the tape with unprecedented strength. She flicked a glance up to the electronic scoreboard at the finish and saw it: 49.85s! The first Australian woman to break the 50s barrier. Her nose screwed up with pleasure as she slowed, punching the air with both hands, shouting 'Yes!', leaping about, laughing and smiling, and carrying on just like, well, just like her father Norman Freeman used to when he scored a try.

'Oh, that was one of the best nights, a magical night,' says Cathy. 'There's racing and there's real racing where you move on to another plane. I didn't think in terms of times, you don't, you just do them. I was in another place. The crowd was on fire. Sandie took it out so hard but I've raced against her often enough to know her, and I went with her. When I saw the time and I was so happy. I was pumped.' For Freeman it was a major breakthrough, she'd been wanting to break 50s for so long. 'I should have done it ages before,' she says. 'People don't take you seriously until you've broken 50s. That's why I was so relieved when I did.' As she did a victory lap, ardent fans waved a large Aboriginal flag over the fence at her. She had made the flag universally accepted.

In following seasons, Cathy and Sandie Richards became firm friends. 'I came to think of her as a big sister,' says Cathy. 'I haven't had very close friendships with the girls I race against, but Sandie's different because she leaves it all on the track. It's wonderful, wonderful. I can't be bothered taking the competitiveness and rivalry thing with you everywhere you go. So she became a good friend.' But not quite on that night. Richards tired after going so fast early and finished third as Renee Poetschka passed her down the straight. 'Before they knew me and were looking after my best interests, they used me,' says Richards, carefully. She was understandably miffed at having been employed as a hare. For Cathy to break 50s, which Richards had never achieved in a decade of trying, heaped frustration upon defeat. But Bideau denies this. He says they invited Richards out so home crowds could see Cathy race an athlete of international class. As well, they liked Richards, paid her to run, Nick took her to training, gave her advice, and generally looked after her. As for the 50s, after Freeman's 50.40s in Hobart, Nick says he knew that the big atmopshere of the NEC meet would be worth half a second to Cathy with or without Richards.

That evening Cathy's usual doubts surfaced. 'Do you think I've peaked too soon?' she asked Nick. Said he, 'Hey, running 49.85s isn't the end, it's the start. It was good to do it, but you can run a lot faster than that.' 'You think so?' said Cathy. 'Yeah, yeah, of course you can,' said Nick. 'Oh, OK,' said Cathy, happily. A perfectionist, she always winkled out the suspect side to any performance until reassured otherwise.

The Australian titles in Sydney in March lost Gainsford with injury, leaving the 100 and 200m double to Freeman. Cathy didn't miss the aggro with Gainsford, but she missed Melinda's fire which gave title wins credibility. The domestic grand prix final in Brisbane was a formality in 50.21s, crowning Cathy, finally, as female Athlete of the Year, thus acquiring the honour, the cash, and the accolade that Flemming and Gainsford had won the previous two years. That left one more race before departing for overseas: the Stawell Gift pro 400m in April. Peter Jess, then 45, decided to make it fun for everyone by entering the veteran's 1500m. Jess lost an eye as a young man when, driving a car, he impetuously turned around and punched his brother who had pulled his hair. Unfortunately Jess drove straight into a tree and crashed through the windscreen. Perhaps that's why Cathy, fondly, calls him mad. A self-confessed sports nut, boxer, golfer, martial artist, tennis player, swimmer and occasional jogger, he asked Bideau for Stawell race tactics. Said Nick, 'All I want is to hear your name being called by the commentator in the running so, on your training form, I think you better get to the lead early!' That weekend Cathy and Nick stayed at Jess's holiday house in Avoca, surrounded by the Pyrenees Ranges foothills, about 80km from Stawell. When they arrived, Nick asked Jess how his training was going. 'Good,' said Jess. 'Six stubbies of beer yesterday and a bottle of wine with dinner!' Cathy laughs at the memory. 'He's such a dag, Jess,' she says. 'I admire him, because he always has a go.' On 7 April 1996 they drove down for Cathy's heat, and Jess's race—in which he did lead, briefly, before finishing last—and back to Avoca that evening, pausing en route for a few glasses of red, Cathy too, at the Summerfields winery. 'We had a ball, it's such fun that Stawell weekend,' says Cathy. Such a welcome change from her normally austere routine.

Next day, off scratch, with the traditional red backmarker's blouse tied in a knot at her back, Cathy surveyed the field ahead, or around the bend since the front markers were 40m ahead of her. No lanes, so there was no stagger to help Cathy catch the leaders as in the grand prix races. On grass, no starting blocks, just hands resting on her knees and off. For the first half of the race there was the field and there was Cathy, very chic in wraparound shades, but trailing way back. 'You can't panic,' says Cathy. 'It feels like they're miles away, but you can't go too hard, it's such good practice at control.' At 200m a collective sigh ran around the huge crowd of 20,000, Freeman couldn't do it. Too bad. Then their murmur changed to mild applause as, after an eternity, at about the 300m mark, she passed her first front runner, then another and another. Cathy enjoys that, reeling them in, leaving them behind, casting ahead for the next.

Now the crowd roared as she entered the straight full of fight, still 15m behind the leader, Shanie Coutts, to whom Cathy had given 30m start. 'Ah, I love it, I went Bang! in the home straight,' says Cathy. Another runner, Jackie Lewis, overtaking three wide, collided with Cathy, four wide, as they raced side by side. Cathy steadied, balanced and drove once more after Coutts and ... got her! Right on the line. 'I felt I was flying across the ground on air, that's what it felt like,' says Cathy. 'And the crowd, they lifted me, I just floated. Ah, it's a wonderful, wonderful feeling that only being fit can bring you.'

Steve Robilliard of ABC television said excitedly, 'We've just witnessed one of the great runs at Stawell.' Australia Post sponsored the meet and Cathy's colleague Mark Pickering was in tears as his wife, Pam, jumped up and down precariously on a chair. Karen Tighe of ABC TV captured Cathy for a few puffed words.

Tighe: Congratulations, Cathy, on a time of fifty-four-eight.

Freeman (disappointed):Oh ... I'm a little bit tired today, a little bit flat.

Tighe (surprised):You must be thrilled with the time if you were feeling tired.

Freeman: What was the time?

Tighe: Fifty-four-eight.

Freeman: 54.8s?

Tighe: No, 50.48s!

Freeman: Oh sheesh, Oh God! 50.48. I can't believe it, Omigod! I'm stoked then. I had three or four glasses of wine last night, maybe I should do that more often.

Faster even than her Devonport run, said Robilliard and then noticed what Team Freeman well knew. 'Gee,' he exclaimed, as Cathy did a victory lap to a standing ovation. 'Look at that muscle definition.' Compared to Pérec or Richards, Cathy looks small, but against non-elite athletes she looks powerful, her gluteals behind each hip far more pronounced than in other runners. Later that evening, Cathy said to Nick, 'Do you think I said the right thing about the wine?' Said Nick, 'Yeah, didn't hurt. Shows people you're normal, don't have to live like a monk to be a great athlete. It's not like you got pole-axed last night!' Bideau was so chuffed he didn't need alcohol. He confided to Plant, 'On grass, no blocks, got a bump, still runs 50-plus. She'll run 48s, this girl.'

That win by Freeman has gone into Stawell folklore and will be told 100 years from now with no need for embellishment of its wonder. At a Prahran professional running dinner in honour of Cathy two years later, club member John Tannock told me he had never before seen Stawell erupt like it did that day. 'They were still talking about it hours later, days later, still talking about it today,' says Tannock. 'Just one of those moving moments. She makes you feel good to be an Australian.'

Before the general media awoke to her feat, Freeman was gone, off to Atlanta where she set up base to train for six weeks in the Olympic city, familiarising herself, even though the Games were still three months off. After settling in, the team flew out to watch Steve Moneghetti run the centenary of the Boston marathon. 'The place was a total buzz, it was like a celebration,' says Monners' coach Chris Wardlaw. 'Everybody was there, and we've gone up to Monners' room, a really beautiful apartment in one of the best hotels in Boston, and in a corner asleep is Cathy, all curled up. We couldn't believe it, we're all hyped up and she's asleep.'

Six Weeks in Atlanta—it should be the name of a film shown to psychology classes for analysis of its bizarre group dynamics. The participants were: Cathy Freeman, 23, a highly strung female athlete preparing for an immense Olympic challenge carrying the hopes of all Australia; in a complex relationship with Nick Bideau, 35, an athletic ascetic, devoted to Freeman and obsessive in his quest for her success; Peter Fortune, 48, now a full-time Athletics Australia coach, whose original passive approach to training was waning with an increasingly assertive Freeman; and Mark Holcombe, 23, a laconic, ex-junior star, Cathy's training partner and amused witness to the whole proceedings. Three men and a woman for six weeks, and then Maurie Plant turned up as well. For a 23-year-old who had never enjoyed the freedoms of her age in any conventional sense, it was a formula for acute frustration.

Few athletes could afford such a retinue. Meet directors in Europe pay Cathy's fare and accommodation, but not Bideau's. In the US, air fares, accommodation, car and food for the four principals, all came out of Freeman's sponsorship budget. 'We don't look at how much it will cost, because it is expensive,' says Bideau. 'We just work out what we need to get the best result and find the money from somewhere.'

Their apartment had two bedrooms, Cathy and Nick upstairs, Holcombe had a sofa bed in the second bedroom, although it was only separated from the lounge by a divider, and Fortune slept in the lounge. 'It was a nice place, but we were pretty much sleeping within five metres of each other,' says Fortune. 'So we were all virtually living in this downstairs lounge.' For some meagre privacy, Cathy ate breakfast upstairs.

Bideau established a spartan routine, with brutal diets and a training routine to top even Gwen Torrence's, who was one of several US stars training at the same track. 'The regime permeates everyone, even Fort loses weight,' says Bideau. When he saw Cathy putting on a little weight, he confronted her. She would then ask Holcombe, 'You think I need to lose weight?' Holcombe knew his cue. 'I'd be perfectly blunt and say she wasn't looking like an Olympian,' he says. 'It was necessary to say it, yeah definitely. But I only had to do that once or twice, otherwise I supported her unconditionally.'

Cathy confesses, 'I was sneaking out every now and then and eating chocolate donuts.' Why did you sneak out? 'Because I'd be shot if they saw me!' Yes, but why did you need donuts? 'I had a craving for junk food, anything sweet, to make me feel normal.' I told Holcombe of Cathy's secret treats. 'Yeah, I even had to do that as well,' he admits, laughing. 'Because, hey, Nick is pretty influential, you know he gets in your head. I used to sneak out for Snickers bars. That helped.'

Cathy wasn't happy—with Nick's intensity, with being surrounded by men, with the claustrophobic living, with the rigid control of her life, with the lack of normal diversions, with her ... powerlessness. They rarely went out, although they did see Bob Dylan at a music festival in downtown Atlanta once. Cathy began to challenge Bideau at the track. 'She'd play games,' says Holcombe. 'Nick would say OK start, and she'd say she wasn't ready. He'd give us the routine and she'd question it. He'd say go, and she'd say there was a runner in her lane, even if they were 200 metres away. She could be stubborn.' So Nick would back off. Cathy hated being asked to run further than 400m, and after finishing one reluctant 500m, she said she had a stitch for the last 100m. Bideau wouldn't let her finish on a down note. OK, do a final 150m, he'd say. US champ Gwen Torrence interceded, 'Nick, you understand with women, we got things going on in our insides?' Yeah, Nick would say, but this girl is tough. After which Cathy would accomplish the 150m, stitch or no. In retrospect she suspects she had a mild oblique muscle strain in the side of her stomach, and should have stretched it out, as Torrence urged. Nonsense, says Nick. Muscle strains don't disappear overnight.

Next it would be Fortune's turn to complain, that Cathy didn't appreciate him, that he was sick of being pushed around. 'Every now and then I'd have a little whinge,' he says. 'Philosophically I'm different. I annoy them like hell, because I'm such a passive character whereas they're all tough and hard.' But he felt if he'd objected too strenuously they'd have dispensed with him, and he wanted to see the Olympics through. Fortune liked to be holistic in his training, but found it difficult to get close to Cathy. 'At times I could but she was hard to read in that regard and when the crunch came there would be a rejection. But, in a way, it didn't matter if we had blues, because she was getting terrifically fit.'

In their close-quarters living, with the Olympic pressure building, and razor-edge nerves, a blow-up was inevitable. Nobody can even remember what brought it on, but Bideau announced to Cathy, 'Right, that's it! I'm going home, obviously it's better if I'm not here!' and bounded downstairs to pay the apartment bill. Like some classic tale told in separate parts, each of the other three characters had distinct reactions.

Cathy says she was not scared at the prospect of Nick leaving, but preferred he didn't. It was just symptomatic of how their relationship had changed. Fortune, she says, was definitely nervous and worried. But Fortune says he thought it was all ridiculous. He said to Cathy, 'Well, do you want to stay here or go home?' Cathy said she wanted to keep training. Then, when Nick returned, Holcombe piped up confidently, 'OK, Nick, just leave the car keys and the plane tickets and I'll take care of this. We'll ring you in a month and tell you how we're going.' Holcombe says now, laughing at his naivety, 'I'd done three years of a sports management course at Deakin University in Melbourne, and I thought, "Yeah, I'll handle this. I'll succeed where Nick can't!"'

Sanity prevailed. Fortune invited Bideau down to the local Irish pub, the Fado Fado, where Nick explained that he would stay to the Olympics, he was committed, but everything would change after that. 'I'm not stupid,' Bideau told Fort. 'I'm not going anywhere, but I need to get her to be frightened of me leaving.' Bideau also revealed that in order to get Cathy to comply with his strict management, he

1993. Stuttgart. The opening ceremony for the world championships included Cathy's favourite band, Yothu Yindi. Lead singer Mandawuy Yunupingu is wearing the garland, Aboriginal hurdler, Kyle Vander-Kuyp the cap.

1994. Sydney. One of the fiercest rivalries in Australian athletic history. Cathy snatches the national 200m title from Melinda Gainsford. Note Gainsford's daunting musculature, Freeman's sheer determination.

1994. Melbourne. Cathy began weights the previous year. She can lift well over her body weight, but most sessions are designed to increase her leg spring and body torque. (*Photo:* courtesy of Department of Sport)

1994. St George's Road, Thornbury, Melbourne. Given her antecedents, an appropriate shot of Cathy training in the shadow of a poster depicting Australia's historic shame. (*Photo:* courtesy of the *Herald & Weekly Times*)

1994. Commonwealth Games, Victoria, Canada. The 200m final, with Melinda Gainsford inside her and Pauline Davis, Bahamas, on her outside. When she glimpsed Gainsford she thought 'Whoops! I better get going.'
(*Photo:* courtesy of Sporting Pix)

1994. Victoria. Eyes shut, mouth open, Cathy in typical triumphant mode crossing the line for gold in the 200m. She ranks this in her top five best runs of her career.
(*Photo:* courtesy of Sporting Pix)

1994. Victoria. One nation, but two flags. As Peter Jess, Cathy's long-time accountant, predicted this image sped around the world and landed on front pages everywhere.

1994. Victoria. Cathy's pride in her Aboriginality sparked a huge controversy. Cathy had been toting that flag around for several years awaiting her opportunity to fly it.

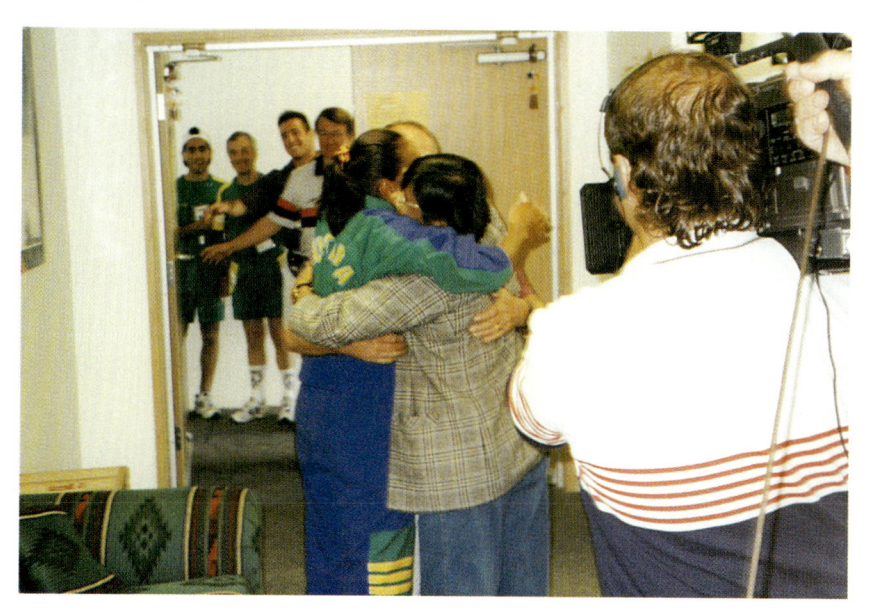

1994. Victoria. Surprise, surprise! Cathy's day is complete with the arrival of her mother, Cecelia, and stepfather, Bruce Barber, in the Channel 7 studios after her dramatic 200m victory.

1993. Prime Minister Paul Keating told Cathy he was no slouch as a schoolboy swimmer. At the PM's Women in Sport awards, Cathy has Sports Minister Ros Kelly on her left and in the foreground, Annita Keating.

1993. Melbourne. At home, by the pool, among the jasmine in Miller Street, Richmond. Saturday was rest day, no weights, no track work, sleep in, enjoy life.

1996. Melbourne. At Black Rock, a bayside suburb. She and Nick Bideau often drove to quiet locations to jog and escape the stress of her frenetic pace of life.

1995. Australia's two premier Aboriginal sportswomen. Evonne Goolagong-Cawley's tennis career, guided by white advisers, closely resembles that of Cathy's own career.
(*Photo:* courtesy of the *Herald & Weekly Times*)

1995. Gothenburg. The world championships and a bronze medal for the 4 x 400m relay. Left to right: Renee Poetschka, Lee Naylor, Melinda Gainsford and Cathy, who ran a sensational relay leg after blowing up in the individual 400m final.

1996. Atlanta. Sinew, muscle, even arteries are outlined in Cathy's body, so fit was she approaching the Olympics. Australia Post used this image as a corporate postcard. (*Photo:* courtesy of the *Herald & Weekly Times* and Australia Post)

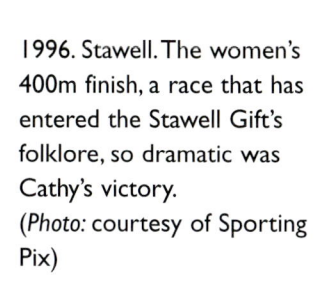

1996. Stawell. The women's 400m finish, a race that has entered the Stawell Gift's folklore, so dramatic was Cathy's victory.
(*Photo:* courtesy of Sporting Pix)

1996. Atlanta. Olympic Games, 400m final. On their marks. All quiet. Marie-José Pérec is in lane three. After a nerve-racking build-up, Cathy is calm, about to run the race of her life. (*Photo:* courtesy of Sporting Pix)

1996. Atlanta. 400m final. At 300m Cathy passed Nigerian Falilat Ogunkoya, in the lane outside her, and thought 'I've got silver.' Looming inside is the giant figure of Pérec. (*Photo:* courtesy of Sporting Pix)

1996. Atlanta, 400m final. One gold, but two winners. Cathy, gracious in defeat as ever, about to congratulate Pérec.
(*Photo:* courtesy of Sporting Pix)

1996. Atlanta. Cathy embraces Nick Bideau after the race. A tender moment for these two, who did great things together. She's high on endorphins, he's just plain proud.
(*Photo:* courtesy of Sporting Pix)

1996. Atlanta. The victory ceremony. Cathy on the podium with her silver medal and bouquet of flowers. Pérec and Ogunkoya primped and powdered her in the change rooms.
(*Photo:* courtesy of Sporting Pix)

1996. Atlanta. The main stadium. Against the night sky for 85,000 to see: *Medaille d'argent* for Cathy Freeman AUS. In Sydney she hopes for *Medaille d'or*.

1996. Atlanta. The day after. With Cecelia and Bruce Barber and the great Carl Lewis, who was in the long jump sand when he saw Cathy streak by in the 400m.

1997. Melbourne. Distressed by personal troubles, Cathy overcomes Lauren Hewitt (289), but can't catch Melinda Gainsford-Taylor in the 200m at the national titles at Olympic Park. (*Photo:* courtesy of *The Age*)

1996. The clan gather for Christmas. Left to right: brother Norman, Cathy, Cecelia, brother Garth, and forefront, Gavin jnr and his father—Cathy's brother—Gavin snr.

1996. Brisbane. Cathy's trophies, medals and prizes adorn many houses but Cecelia and stepdad Bruce Barber possess the largest collection. (*Photo:* courtesy of the *Courier Mail*)

1997. Melbourne. Reclaiming her social life. In South Yarra, left to right: best friend Peta Powell, Cathy, Amanda Toombs, Nova Peris-Kneebone and Tiffany Cherry.

1997. Talking not training, with Jason Richardson, who became a good friend during the troubles in El Paso. Richardson, among others, talked her out of withdrawing from the worlds in Athens. (*Photo*: courtesy of Cameron McKenzie)

1997. Eugene, Oregon. Cathy (110) looks composed in the Prefontaine 200m, but she finished third in the slowest time she has ever run outside Australia.

1997. London. The number-one-blade mob, left to right: Jason Richardson, Kyle Vander-Kuyp, Cameron McKenzie, and Richie Robinson, holding Conchita Freeman. Friends in need were friends indeed. (*Photos left and above*: courtesy of Cameron McKenzie)

had made Fortune the victim. 'There has to be one and you're it,' said Nick. 'I know it's not comfortable for you, but that's how it works. Better you than me, because we're stuffed if it's me.'

When I repeated that to Fortune he said, 'At least he's been pretty honest with you.' So Fortune drew the short straw. It explained partly why he and Cathy couldn't quite gel. 'It's an absolutely deplorable way to behave,' says Fortune. 'It's morally bereft and you can see why I'm no longer involved with Freeman. That's Nick's bloody style. He's a Svengali. I thought I was doing some good, but maybe it was all a part of his scheme and I wasted my time going to the pub.'

To the lay observer, Bideau looked the puppeteer, but he knew one thing better than anyone else—he knew Freeman. He knew the pressure she was under, knew how her ego needed nurturing, her confidence stroked. His motto was: whatever it takes. The drama was breathtaking in its absurdity. I asked Fortune: surely it could have been managed in a less dramatic way? Fortune thought a moment, and replied, 'Maybe it couldn't have, and maybe that tells you a lot about Cathy.' Cathy feels guilt-free about it all. 'I certainly didn't do anything, but a few times Nick could have caused everything to collapse,' she says. 'I eventually told him I didn't want him to go. It was such a big change so close to the Olympics.'

I asked Cathy if she was aware of the games Bideau played to motivate her. 'I'm very self-motivated,' she says defensively. But what about when Bideau came to training and said that he'd heard rumours Pérec was training the house down? 'Oh yeah, he does it all the time,' she says. So she did pick up on his games after all? Surprisingly Cathy replies, 'It works, because he knows it will, otherwise he wouldn't say it. He knows it's going to affect me because I'm competitive and it does actually snap me into gear. I don't mind because it gets my mind thinking. I think Nick likes to take pride in those funny little games. I don't pick up on all of them, but at the end of the day, I'm always going to be motivated.'

Holcombe told me earnestly: 'Document this—people bag Nick, man, saying he's in it for what he can get out of Cath, but he went through hell at times, and he did it basically for her.' This was a remarkably forthright statement by Holcombe. Specifically, what hell was this? 'Oh, typical female stuff,' says Mark. 'I mean, she's no different to any other girl in a relationship. You get sick of the games they play.' Uh huh.

The blow-up cleared the air spectacularly and Cathy's training went up another notch. Bideau's own training, and minimalist eating, made him so lean and fit he began running in local Atlanta all-comers races. He challenged the others that he could run 1500m under 4min 10s. No way, they'd say, you're too old, too slow. They all came to watch, including Damien Marsh, who, on crutches having tragically torn his Achilles tendon, was out of the Olympics.

Cathy enjoyed the focus switching from her briefly. She cheered Nick on, organised a drink afterwards, anything else you want? Just as he did for her. Nick borrowed Holcombe's spikes, two sizes too small, and surprised everyone by running 4min 07s. 'I'm like Cathy. However well I train, I do better racing,' says Bideau. Cathy got a kick out of watching. 'He tried his absolute hardest, ran his guts out,' she says. 'He actually did a little better than he should have.' Bideau's subliminal message to Freeman: I'm a no-talent, so you can't prepare for the Olympics and not look fitter than me.

Towards the end of the camp they picked up Maurie Plant from the airport. How's it going? he asked warily, having heard of the early dramas. 'Oh great, Nick's been going really good. Been running in races himself,' said Cathy delightedly. But it was Cathy who was going well. 'When I knew it was going to hurt, I'd swear like a trooper in anticipation, abuse Mark, Nick, anyone,' she says. 'But once I set my heart on it, I did it, and I wouldn't let it hurt until it was all over.'

Nick noticed and towards the end of the camp, after one super session, cautioned her, 'Don't dig in today, don't go over the top, you're in great shape,' he said. 'Whatever Fort gives you from now on, only run at 90 per cent.' Athletes in training don't continue to get fitter and fitter. Eventually they train past their peak and get tired, injured, and go backwards. Nick wanted Cathy to back off and just tick over.

Her first race in the US, on 18 May 1996, supposedly a preview of the Olympics in Atlanta, was against Pérec. The protagonists knew their roles—Pérec was to retain her dominance, Cathy was not to show too much of her true form. And so it went; Pérec first in 50.17s, Freeman second in 50.39s. But the Gothenburg experience was still hovering in that Cathy made no attempt to take on Pérec in the early stages, then rattled home with some in reserve. Fortune didn't want Cathy to take on Pérec, but he expected her to run a more even-paced race. Says Fortune, 'She probably didn't have enough faith in what I said. Maybe if Nick told her she'd have respected the advice. But I was always given the job.' In theory Cathy should have profited from realising that by not following Fortune's instructions, she had not run well. But this was their problem area. Fortune's advice was sound—Cathy didn't always hear it.

Ros Moriarty of Balarinji arrived in town and briefly released Cathy from her all-male prison. 'I was so excited,' says Cathy. 'Oh, it was lovely! So refreshing. It was like seeing my mother, just to have a woman around.' For four years, Cathy had been flying around the world, staying in hotel rooms—until she bought the London house—and her constant companions were Bideau, 13 years her senior, and three others who were all nearly twice her age—coach Fortune, agent Plant, and occasionally her accountant Jess.

Her training partner had to be male because no female could keep up with her. Although they were there to help her, these men related to her principally as a runner, except for

Bideau, who was even more obsessed with athletics than the others. She didn't have good friends among the athletes because most, like Gwen Torrence and Pauline Davis who were at the track every day too, were also her competitors. And Cathy was an introspective young woman anyway. Films, television and books were her diversions, but rarely female companionship. If she argued with Nick, and needed a sympathetic ear, it was usually her mother she rang, rarely women of her own age from whom she could glean contemporary opinions from their own experiences. As for Aboriginal company, once overseas she could go months without seeing another indigenous Australian. I thought of a passage in *Home*, Evonne Goolagong-Cawley's biography, where she said, 'I answered my Aboriginal critics repeatedly with the explanation that I had served my people best by becoming a great tennis player, a symbol of achievement.' Only to find that her sport had put such a distance between her and her people, that she had to deliberately return to her roots when her career was over.

The caravan moved to Eugene, Oregon for another 400m, still searching for Cathy's best race model. On a gusty, windy morning, at the ungodly hour, for racing, of 10 o'clock, Cathy won in 50.40s. She still didn't run the race right and back in their motel Cathy sat disappointed until Bideau exclaimed, 'Hang on! This is how far we've come. In London in 1994 you ran 50.77s and we were thrilled. Here we are now, you win in 50.40s and it's "Oh yeah, should have run better!" We've just got greedy.' Plant puts it in perspective: 'I went to Europe for four years before I saw a single Australian win on the international circuit, and now I reckon I've forgotten the number of times Freeman has won.' And now she was off to Europe to put a hard racing edge on top of her hard training. The Olympics were just six weeks off.

18.
LA GAZELLE.
PRE-OLYMPICS, 1996

Australia Post put out a postcard of Cathy Freeman, a photograph of her in full stride in training before Atlanta. Her ribs are evident, her stomach a tight washboard, her quadriceps and biceps ripple; sinews, muscle, even arteries are outlined on her lean body. 'Cut' is the word athletes use to describe such super fitness, and Cathy was. Only bodybuilders, the day of a contest, would score a lower skinfold test. Distance coach Chris Wardlaw forever told Nick Bideau afterwards, 'If you want to get Cathy to run fast, make her look like the postcard again.' The picture also shows how Cathy keeps her torso firm as her arms drive and her legs propel her. Her sports physician, Dr Peter Fuller, says that when people remark that he looks after Cathy Freeman, he says, 'Well she doesn't take much looking after, because she doesn't get many injuries. I think it has a bit to do with her attitude, she's determined but happy-go-lucky, follows good advice and doesn't get carried away with overtraining.'

Fuller loves to watch her stretch out down the back straight of a 400m race, with her classic straight leg, and beautiful leg length to upper body ratio. 'She has a superb-looking action, fairly upright, but not leaning back,' he says.

'Her shoulders are relaxed, and her pumping arm action has improved with her weight training. She has good knee lift and a very high back-kick, which is good for a runner. If your heel is close to your bum on the back swing, when you bring your leg through it has a shorter lever, more efficient. It's just a beautiful running style.'

As Cathy and Nick settled into their London house in Hampton Hill, Freeman's bank of fitness, built in Atlanta, imbued their household with a sense of wellbeing. Over the next six weeks, Cathy won a series of 400m to set the scene for the Olympics. She trained with a troupe of Kenyans, including middle distance stars, Sammy Langat and Robert Kibet. One day the Kenyans were running 400m intervals and Cathy tacked on the back, maintaining touch for 350m before easing back. Bideau checked his watch for the Kenyans—49.1s. So she was close to that.

She eased training because of a sore foot—the nearer Atlanta drew, the more jumpy Team Freeman became about injury—before racing at Gateshead on 30 June: exactly one month to the Olympic final. Gateshead was a meet at Newcastle-on-Tyne on England's north-east coast, Brendan Foster's home town. Foster, a champion 5000m runner in his day, had run a 50s-plus lap at the track and challenged Cathy, 'I bet you can't beat my best time here.' That's all Cathy needed. She beat Sally Gunnell by some 15 metres in 49.96s, prompting Gunnell to tell Plant, 'Your girl's ready. She's in good shape.' Plant rates that among Freeman's top five 400m runs. 'It was windy, a cow of a day, people were running slow times, and she runs a sub-50s,' says Plant. 'Discerning eyebrows were raised, I know.' An English journalist approached Bideau and said, 'Freeman can run 48s, you know.' 'Do you think so?' Bideau replied disingenuously.

More to the point, Cathy got the tactics right, running the first 200m at a fast clip, attacking the third 100m and finishing on. 'Until then I'd always run too much within myself for the first 200m,' says Cathy. 'For the first time I ran out hard and I wasn't scared, and I just kept going. I ran my own race and I was so happy, not because of the time, but the way I did it.' She had slain the ghost of Gothenburg at last.

Another scare. Cathy came down with mild food poisoning, spent Monday in bed, nil by mouth except for soda water, up on Tuesday but weak, light training Wednesday and flew to Oslo for the Friday night grand prix 400m. She had lost a little strength, slowed after running the first 150m well and then had to fight off Jamaican Juliet Campbell in the last 60m. Still she ran 49.81s, faster than her Melbourne sub-50s, a new Australian record.

At Crystal Palace on 12 July, back in London for her last race before Atlanta, she rehearsed her Olympic plan. She and Bideau spent a day watching videos of Pérec's races, and her own, until she had her own plan imprinted on her mind. Then one day, washing the dishes and listening to the BBC radio commentary of a 400m race in Europe, Cathy heard the race caller say that Pérec had won in 48.48s—'*NIIIICK!*' Nick, watching the European soccer championships upstairs, came slowly down, puzzled by the distress in her voice. 'What's up? No, that's a mistake,' he said. 'You sure?' 'Sure I'm sure,' he said. 'No way she can run 48.48s.' Fortunately, about five minutes later, the BBC announced, 'Oh, sorry we were wrong there, that should be 49.48s.' Says Nick, 'Catherine panicked, because she had in her head 48.60s, the time she had on the mirror. And I had in my mind 48.83s, the time Pérec ran in Barcelona. Neither of us wanted to believe she was already running 48.48s.'

At Crystal Palace, like an actor hitting the mark, Cathy ran her ideal race. Started as though it was a 200m, good speed by the end of the first bend—that's how she intended to ward off Pérec. Bicycled down the back straight, squeezed the throttle on the second bend and had it won by the 300m. Jearl Miles was a distant second. On film, face on, Cathy is totally relaxed, looking around, under no pressure, just doing a stride-through. Her time: 49.59s, another Australian record and now everybody, including Marie-José Pérec, knew who the threat would be in Atlanta.

Two days before Cathy's London run, Pérec hit the news with comments that the other 400m runners were scared of her. 'When I run the other girls freeze,' she said. 'They run slower when I am there. It's a pity. Cathy could use my presence to produce a top performance. If the others don't push me, there can't be a top time.' Pérec had a hide naming Cathy, considering how Freeman burnt herself out pushing Pérec to a season's best time at the world titles the previous year. But this was all pre-Olympic psych by the Frenchwoman. It was wasted on Cathy because she rarely read newspapers, except perhaps to glance at the headlines. Bideau knew about Pérec's comments when Cathy went to a media conference after her London run, but Cathy didn't. Bideau enjoyed watching Cathy handle curly questions, she did it so well. She didn't disappoint him.

The question was put: was she scared? Cathy crinkled her nose. 'Scared? I'm trying to think of the last person I was scared of,' she said. 'It was probably my mother. Yes, having to run against my mother would be scary. Competition actually excites me.' Afterwards, Cathy asked Nick why he hadn't told her about Pérec's comments. Nick replied, 'Why would I? She's just trying to psych you out.' Privately Bideau was pleased. Freeman, undefeated in her four-race European campaign, three times under 50s in two weeks, had the grande dame's attention.

France is famous for haute couture, haute cuisine and haughty Marie-José Pérec. When Cathy became a 400m runner she slammed head-on into the most formidable female athlete of the modern era. Defeated just once—by Cathy—in six years over 400m, Pérec, 28, was defending Olympic champion from Barcelona in 1992, and had twice won the world title, in 1991 and 1995. When Reebok used her in an advertising campaign with the slogan, 'This is my planet!'

they meant it. At 180cm (6 feet) and 60kg, she was one of the most imposing athletes on the international circuit.

Added to her glamour was her career as a fashion photography model, a combination of talents which saw her on the front cover and as editorial theme of an edition of *Elle* magazine. Media harassment in France had eventually driven her to California to live. She complained to the French media that they were obsessed with pictures of her bottom. This was a reference to how her running tights rode up her buttocks at the end of races, as television audiences worldwide would soon observe in Atlanta.

Pérec is from the island of Guadeloupe, a French-speaking territory in the same chain of islands as Trinidad and Tobago in the Caribbean. She grew up in the capital Basse Terre, which is located near an active volcano, La Soufriere, which last blew in 1976. Her parents divorced very early and she lived with her mother who ran a busy bar and restaurant in Basse Terre, leaving Marie-José to grow very close to her grandmother. She has an elder sister called Catherine. They were fond of camping and on weekends the family swam in the myriad rivers which flow from the volcanic hills around Basse Terre.

As a little girl she dreamed of visiting Australia. 'I will save my money to go to see the koala and the kangaroo,' she told her mother. At school Marie-José played the European game of handball, but was very awkward because of her height. Aged 13, she was already 175cm (5 feet 10 inches)—Freeman is only 164 centimetres (5 foot 5 inches)—and was nicknamed 'Sugarcane' by her schoolmates. At 15 her sports teacher took Marie-José's class for athletics and asked them to all run 60m. When she checked her stopwatch for Pérec it showed eight seconds, a fast time by any standards. Believing she had made a mistake with the timing, she asked Marie-José to run again: same result.

Pérec was encouraged to join the local athletic club, Cygne Noir (Black Swan), and began training at the Felix Eboue stadium—four lanes, packed red sand, only 354 metres around. But training did not appeal to her and when first asked to warm up for four laps by the coach, she ran three and then hid behind a mango tree.

Aged 16, she was flown 7000km to Paris for the French school championships, together with other athletes from French-speaking territories around the world, such as New Caledonia. When she saw all her opponents jogging and stretching she was astonished and believed they would tire themselves. They may have too, because she won the 200m though she was then disqualified for putting her foot outside the lane. Shades of habits to come. She moved to France shortly afterwards—part of a black minority in a white society, as is Freeman—and was resident there for the next decade as her career soared to its current heights.

She became among the highest-paid sportswomen in the world, with sponsorship deals in Europe and the US with Reebok and Pepsi worth $1 million a year. Added to that are her earnings from the track circuit. Her official appearances at Paris are carried off with stunning entrances, all eyes upon her regal carriage as she arrives, always fashionably late. The media christened her La Gazelle.

Pérec is not always popular with her fellow athletes because at French meets she not only demands the best lane draw as part of her appearance deal—which can probably be excused given her status—but she also wants to dictate what lanes her main rivals should have, usually outside her so she can run them down. Nor does she take defeat with humility. She and Sandie Richards were great friends, on the phone to each other every day, but when Sandie—trailing in third behind Cathy at Monaco in 1995—finished ahead of Pérec, who came sixth in that race, Pérec refused to talk to Sandie afterwards. At the next meet, Sandie was on the ground in the warm-up field and Pérec walked straight past her to the other side of the oval.

It is easy to become obsessed with Marie-José. In her

career, Cathy seemed sometimes to be on a neverending quest in which her failure to overcome Pérec threatened to overshadow the successes of Freeman's own career. Maurie Plant concedes this danger but emphasises that an athlete of Pérec's calibre had to be respected. 'Physically she's so imposing,' says Plant. 'She's nearly six foot and has very big legs. Don't ever think she doesn't have big muscles. She looks tall and stately, but if those legs were on a woman 5 foot 7 inches, they'd look bloody gigantic. Because they're so long you don't notice, but they still have size and strength in them.' Peter Fortune found no harm in it. 'Maybe Cathy's preoccupied with Pérec a bit,' he says. 'But Cathy is also preoccupied with winning and the one thing that drives her is putting up someone's name to race, because she doesn't take much notice of times.'

Pérec's advantage was that she had run 10.96s for 100m and 21.99s for 200m. No other 400m runner in the modern drug-tested era had broken 11s and 22s for those distances, including Cathy whose best were 11.24s and 22.25s. Cathy does not have Pérec's power, but nor is she Pérec's size. Cathy's trick is how she combines speed with endurance. Indeed several commentators have wondered out loud how Cathy would go over 800m. Says Sandie Richards, 'Marie-José is fast. Nowadays the quarter is 60 per cent sprint and 40 per cent strength and she uses her speed to kill us. She starts so hot that she's in front of us in the first 100m. She's rarely behind so we have to catch up.'

Her winning time in Barcelona, 48.83s, made her the fifth fastest of all time, even compared with the athletes from the eastern European drug culture. Pérec says she was nervous before Barcelona, afraid she would lose. But since moving to the US, and dominating the world scene, she had grown in confidence. So confident she welcomed the challenge of Freeman to give her competition to run even faster than Barcelona.

The 100m is normally the glamour event of the Olympics

—determining the world's fastest human—but Michael Johnson's, and Pérec's, attempts to win the 200 and 400m doubles in Atlanta had galvanised American interest in the longer sprints. The 400m echoes down through the millennium as the athletes' race. It is neither sprint nor distance race. In the ancient Olympics, which began in 776 BC and were contested for a thousand years, the length of the running track—at Olympia in southern Greece—was a 'stade', 193.27 metres. Originally there was but one race, a straight stade sprint. After 52 years—a blink in the overall timespan of the Games—another race was added, the double stade—up and back the narrow stadium track, a distance of 386.54 metres, the beginning of the modern 400m. When Baron de Coubertin revived the Games in Athens in 1896, the stadium was constructed as closely as possible to the ancient stade except that the track consisted of two full straights of 206m, joined before each end by sharp curves. The 400m was one of only four track events listed. It was not introduced as a women's Olympic event for another 68 years, until Tokyo in 1964 when it was won by Australia's own flying Betty Cuthbert in 52s flat.

Olympic 100m and 200m medallist Raelene Boyle calls the 400m the Sprinter's Torture, and hated moving up from her shorter sprints, even though she won the 400m Commonwealth Games gold in Brisbane in 1982. Boyle, whose PB was 51.26s, says the 400m requires intelligence and discipline. 'It's not a matter of putting your head down and bum in the air and going like hell, as you can in shorter sprints,' she says. 'It's knowing how to run fast but with reserve.' Others call the 400m the Sprinter's Marathon or the Unforgiving Sprint. Says dual Olympic finalist, Darren Clark, 'I can tell you now and it's the same with Cathy, we run 400s because that's what we do best, and because most other athletes are scared of it. But if Cathy could run the 100m in 10.7s, she wouldn't run the 400m.' Clark says that running a 400m properly is an art, a finesse thing. 'Quite honestly, I don't think many people have perfected it,' he says. So Freeman's search was for her own ideal 400m.

In their last days in London, nearly every other athlete departed for Atlanta. Cathy asked Nick, 'Do you think I can do it? I'm starting to get nervous, starting to worry about it.' Nick assured her she was in fine shape. 'All you can do now is run what you can run,' he said. 'I've seen what you can do.' As Jeff Simons had told her, all else was beyond her control. Back home in Melbourne, Mark Holcombe didn't think twice about how Cathy would go. He told friends, 'I trained with her, I know how fit I am. Man, she's going to kick arse.'

19.
F-L-A-G.
Atlanta Olympics, 1996

In the film *Kiss of Death*, a violent crime drama, Nicolas Cage tells David Caruso what an acronym is. 'It's letters that stand for things, like FBI and TGIF, you understand?' says Cage. 'I've got an acronym for myself, you know what it is? BAD— Balls, Attitude, Direction.' Cage urges Caruso, 'You should get yourself an acronym. It helps you visualise your goals.'

Cathy and Nick saw the film with Mark Holcombe in LA in 1995, and they often joked about acronyms for each other. Nick hired it on video in London in 1996 and it struck a chord with them anew. Cathy wondered whether she should have an acronym to visualise her race plan for the 400m final. In Atlanta, the Niketown shop was in Phipps Plaza, Buckhead, an expensive shopping precinct, and the outside of the shop was covered with huge posters of Nike's stars, including Cathy. She and Nick often visited the precinct and next door to Niketown was a coffee shop where Cathy liked to sit and enjoy a hot chocolate. Nick remembered Brendan Foster's advice to Cathy after Gothenburg, 'You can't be getting to run this race too many times in your head.' Nick wanted to give her an alternative.

He had written out her six-point race plan, devised

F-L-A-G

basically by tape-recording Michael Johnson's answers to questions Nick asked him about how he ran his races. Cathy had grown too used to that instruction sheet, and so she suggested they rekindle the acronym idea. In the coffee shop they followed Nicolas Cage's advice and composed an acronym for Cathy. Nick came up with FLAG, a powerful word guaranteed to survive the week leading to the race as well as the Olympic stadium's inrush of colour, noise and emotional static.

The waitress brought them their bill, Nick paid for it with his Visa card and on the credit slip, which is in duplicate, he wrote: '1st 100m: F-ly away from your blocks; 2nd 100m: L-eg Speed, quick, quick, quick; 3rd 100m: A-ttack; home straight: G-rind every last ounce of energy out of you all the way thru the line.' F-L-A-G. For good measure he wrote three more phrases: 'Run your own race, stay calm, no mistakes.' He gave Cathy the top copy and kept the duplicate himself. I have the duplicate in my hand and the acronym is very clear because he has written the F-L-A-G letters down the page in very large capitals. So much of what transpires between Cathy and Nick is verbal, mental or intangible that it was reassuring to have this written evidence to hand. In the forests of their lives it was a small clue along an obscure track. They did indeed pass this way.

Cathy liked all of FLAG except G-rind. 'Grind feels like slow and under pressure,' she told Nick. 'You're trying hard but not getting anywhere, that's what grind means to me.' She thought about G for Go! But she would have to be careful that she didn't run slowly, waiting for Go before she began to run fast. Nick liked G-rind because it meant she would be fighting off the lactic acid and would have to force herself over the line. So G-rind it was.

Brendan Foster also passed on to Bideau a stratagem he employed with Steve Cram, the champion English 1500m runner of the 1980s. It involved Bideau asking Cathy if there was any reason she thought she couldn't defeat Pérec. Bideau would then have to anticipate every reply she could make and have a rebuttal ready. Every day during his morning runs in Atlanta, Bideau spent hours scrolling through her possible doubts and thinking up an answer. He thought, 'If Catherine says Pérec's got a huge stride, I'll say yeah, that's why she runs out of her lane, she might end up being disqualified. If Catherine says that Pérec's the defending champion, she's more experienced, I'll say that she can't be as hungry as you, she won't have the same desire. If Catherine says Pérec's big and strong, I'll say that your heart is twice as big as hers.' So he sat her down, confident he had all bases covered, and asked her: Was there any reason she thought she couldn't beat Pérec. Cathy thought a moment and said, 'Nope, no reason.' Nick suppressed an urge to burst out laughing with admiration and relief. You could never pick what she would say, this girl. Just when you thought you knew her, she could be unfathomable. Foster was highly amused, and impressed, when Bideau related Cathy's response to him. Until then Foster considered that Cathy was dead stiff to have prepared so thoroughly, only to face possibly the greatest of all time. He didn't give Cathy much hope. But he also knew that, as well as fitness and ability, athletes needed attitude to win and plainly Cathy had that.

Cathy started a Games diary for her eight days in Atlanta and it rings with one desire: to avoid media, crowds and stress, but even more, to avoid a repetition of Gothenburg. Her determination to avoid the media had been reinforced by a newspaper article she had read in London before leaving for Atlanta. Nick had been sent a newspaper feature from Australia written by Mike Hurst for News Ltd papers. It was about Cathy, mostly positive except for two stings. The first was to question Freeman's strength over four rounds of races in Atlanta, based upon her Gothenburg burnout over three rounds. The second was to suggest that Freeman had succeeded in an era when the women's 400m was at its weakest since the mid-1970s.

Neither comment was legitimate to anyone who knew athletics, and Hurst does. Cathy blew Gothenburg with boom-or-bust tactics, not lack of genuine stamina. And nobody seriously accepts the drug-fuelled 400m times run by eastern Europeans in the 1970–80s. It was puzzling that Hurst, who once coached 400m champion Darren Clark, wrote otherwise. Nick hesitated before showing the feature to Cathy, but there was much of interest in it as well. But Cathy, tension-sensitive, was irritated by Hurst's comments. Nick, who had been carefully nursing Cathy's confidence, cursed himself for allowing the Trojan horse into the house. He patiently set about repairing the damage and by the time she flew in to Atlanta on 18 July, Hurst's comments were forgotten. They slipped quietly through the media barrage that awaited Perth sprinter Dean Capobianco, who was fighting drug charges. Cathy and Nick settled into a condominium in Marietta, about 15 minutes drive north of Atlanta. That evening they met her parents, Cecelia and Bruce, who were staying with an African-American Baha'i family, arranged through the faith's worldwide spiritual assembly. High-profile Aboriginal figure Charlie Perkins had organised Cecelia's flight through the Aboriginal and Torres Strait Islander Commission, while Bruce got a loan from his credit union. Cathy's six weeks training camp in Atlanta, for all its dramas, now proved a boon. She felt at home, fearlessly drove a left-hand drive hire car and knew her way about.

On 19 July, Cathy trained at nearby Oglethorpe University, not a designated Olympic track and thus mercifully free of crowds. Loose lips sink ships, so Nick had taken secrecy to a battleground level—even Peter Fortune didn't have Cathy's phone number or address. That evening Cathy and Cecelia watched the opening ceremony at the stadium, but as the night dragged on they left and, by midnight, as Mohammed Ali shakily lit the flame, Cathy was climbing into bed.

CATHY FREEMAN—A JOURNEY JUST BEGUN

Saturday, 20 July, she trained lightly and saw on television her Melbourne friend, Daniel Kowalski, storm home for an unexpected bronze in the 200m freestyle. On Sunday, Peter Fortune organised Cathy's last decent workout, watched by Maurie Plant and Brendan Foster. Catherine liked the lads turning up, exhorting her, calling out insults and wisecracks, and always thanked them for coming along. Behind their jokes was an admiration for her superb fitness. Athletes can only hold that ultra-condition for about a month every season. The sacrifices demanded of diet, lifestyle and physical wear are simply not sustainable for longer than that. Indeed, many athletes consider the peak so difficult to ascend, they attempt it only once every four years for the Olympics or, as does Pérec, every other year, for the Olympics and worlds. Thus, in a career lasting 12 years, training nine months of the year, an athlete will spend the equivalent of nine years training, but may experience the elan of peak form for the equivalent of just a precious six months.

Cathy checked in at the Games village and saw good friend and masseur Garry Miritis. Outgoing Miritis, who exudes confidence and projects it on to his patients, had been treating Cathy since 1991. Bideau had quietly lobbied for Miritis to be on the Olympic team, to be in the warm-up area with Cathy before the final. After a massage, Cathy invited home Peta Powell and they sunbaked by the apartment pool while Nick prepared an evening meal. Powell felt honoured. Bideau always suspected Cathy's female friends of wanting to take her out dancing and drinking during the athletics season. In Bideau's view, while these might be natural activities in any young woman's life, they weren't for an athlete aspiring to win an Olympic medal. He felt Cathy's friends never fully appreciated the sacrifices required or the magnitude of Cathy's task. Team manager and great supporter, Margaret Mahony, who watched Cathy's growth from the age of 18 to her Atlanta age, 23, gives full credit to Bideau for his role, but saw the price being paid. 'Girls like to do silly things with girlfriends during those years,' says Mahony. 'I think Cathy missed that opportunity, she missed that phase in her life.' Anyway, Cathy was delighted for Peta, especially, to be there. They ate pizza together, went grocery shopping, and yarned about films, books, shopping, relationships—anything, as long as it wasn't the race. 'Petie helped me feel normal,' says Cathy. 'She makes me laugh heaps and that helped relax me.'

So far all quiet. Monday at the supermarket a Norwegian man gallantly insisted on paying for Cathy's groceries, adding, 'You are my favourite for the gold medal and you must not disappoint me.' Though flattered by his generosity, Cathy was irritated by his comment. It just built pressure. Tuesday, 23 July, Cathy and Nick drove to Phipps Plaza and, in the coffee shop, devised her FLAG acronym. Nick also gave Cathy a pair of race shoes in the colours of the Aboriginal flag. Cathy had brought a flag with her, Aboriginal one side and Australian the other. 'I had no intention of doing a lap with it,' says Cathy. 'I didn't want to risk being disqualified.' On the back of Olympic tickets it says that even spectators can be thrown out for waving flags other than those of the competing countries. 'Anyway, everyone knew how I felt about that issue,' says Cathy. 'I wasn't going to ram it down people's throats all over again.'

Australian *chef de mission*, John Coates, warned Bideau before they left Australia, 'You'll have to be a bit more imaginative, Nick. We're all for Cathy, the flag and stuff, but think of something else.' Bideau asked Nike and they made her a pair of running shoes with the Aboriginal flag and Cathy's name written on the heel. Unfortunately, being handmade, an errant stitch hurt Cathy's toe and she wore them only once, in her semi-final.

Wednesday, 24 July, Cathy checked into the village accommodation, a university campus, where she was rooming with Lauren Hewitt. She slept there from then on to be close to massage and transport. That night she strolled over to the pool and saw butterfly swimmer Scott Miller win his silver medal. 'Well, you couldn't see much, just a lot of splashing,' she says. At the entrance she ran into Samantha Riley and Susie O'Neill, both of whom she knows and likes. Afterwards she got her legs waxed. Why did she get them waxed? 'Because I don't like shaving.' Yes, but why wax them? 'Because they're hairy.' Sorry, start again. Do you wax them for speed, like swimmers? 'No,' she says, amused at my confusion. Thursday she tapered and rested, and on Friday, 26 July, began her Olympics—two heats, a semi-final and a final, in four days.

At 9 a.m., she and team mates Renee Poetschka and Lee Naylor warmed up together. Later in the main stadium, for her heat, Cathy was sufficiently relaxed to spot her parents sitting near the 100m start. She ran a comfortable second to Nigerian Olabisi Afolabi in 51.99s, returned to the village for a massage and met Nick and Peter Jess for dinner. After another massage later for a sore gluteal muscle, she saw Susie O'Neill win her 200m butterfly gold on television but was disappointed that American television didn't broadcast Kieren Perkins's golden swim in the 1500m. 'Gees, I was bloody annoyed,' she says, and she was, in a way that she rarely is. 'I've only seen a little bit of it since. I like the part where he gets out of the pool and is absolutely exuberant.'

Next morning, Saturday, 27 July, a bomb exploded in the Centennial Olympic park, killing two people. Cathy's first concern was for her parents, and Bideau, who could all have been out and about that day. 'It was terrible news, very upsetting,' she wrote in her diary. 'But eventually I was able to get my mind back on my race.' She won her second-round race in 50.43s and was surprised at the time, quick, considering how easy it felt. She immediately went for an ice bath. She often has these, fills a bath with cold water and empties a couple of bags of ice from the medical tents into it. The ice restricts blood flow, reduces any swelling or tissue inflammation, helps overall recovery. She asked Nick whether she'd gone too fast. She'd heard people say that. 'No, no, they think you can only run 49.50s,' said Nick. 'I know you can run much better.'

Afterwards she returned to the condo to watch Linford Christie's antics after being disqualified for breaking twice in the 100m. Her sympathies, oddly enough, were with the other athletes, as well as Christie. 'I was feeling for them because it is so hard,' she says. 'All your preparation comes down to this one moment, and someone stuffs it and breaks and all that nervous energy is just wasted. And to break twice! Linford should have known better.'

Around 10 p.m. Nick prepared to drop Cathy back at the village as he did each evening, so she would be in bed by 10.30 p.m. It was their established routine, essential to Cathy's sense of being settled. This evening Nick had lent his car to 5000m runner Julian Paynter to pick his girlfriend up from the airport. As long as you're back by 9.30 p.m. warned Nick, but as 10 p.m. approached Cathy started to get edgy. On the eve of her semi-final, the last thing Nick wanted was her routine broken. He knew some Australian coaches had an apartment in the same block, ran around, tapped on the door and opened it. He saw a woman asleep on a couch and two sets of car keys on a table, with tags marked red and grey. He looked outside and saw a red and a grey car, grabbed the red set for a four-wheel drive mini-van and drove around to collect Cathy. 'Whose car is this?' she asked, curious. 'Oh, just a car I've borrowed,' said Nick. He dropped her at the village at 10.15 p.m., spot on schedule. En route back to the apartment he picked up Jess who asked, 'Whose car is this?' I don't know, said Nick, laughing at his own audacity—I stole it! He returned the van and walked into the apartment to discover the woman now awake. As she looked on, astonished, Nick put the keys on the table, said, 'Thanks for the car,' and left. When it came to maintaining Freeman's peace of mind, Bideau was a desperado.

Sunday, semi-final day, they went to the zoo. 'When we were in Atlanta training I often thought of going to the zoo,' says Bideau. 'But I didn't because I wanted to save it up as a distraction during the Olympics.' Cathy was fascinated by the power of the big cats. The visit preoccupied her until they returned to prepare for her 8 p.m. race against a star-studded field, including Grit Breuer, Fatima Yusuf, Sandie Richards and Maicel Malone. This was the one time she wore her Aboriginal flag shoes.

Chris Wardlaw claims he got Cathy to her semi. 'The bloody queues to get into the village were getting ridiculously long and we'd just been out for a cup of tea,' says Wardlaw. 'The baggage X-ray machine was broken, and the security guard had one long queue,' says Wardlaw. He told the guard, 'Listen, mate, we've got to get this girl to a race otherwise she's not going to have a chance to win.' Wardlaw suggested they create two queues, one for people with bags and one for people without. Wardlaw imitates a slow-dawning, slow-drawling American. 'Oh, hey, that's a good idea!'

The semi-final is the final before the final. Some lesser athletes actually run better in the semi than in the final, give their all, so desperate are they to gain the prestige of making the final. Cathy won her semi in 50.32s, but found it harder to recover than after the previous two rounds. Like the 400m itself, the Olympics is a test of stamina as well as speed. Pérec won the second semi in a phenomenal 49.19s, the fastest time since her own run in Barcelona four years before. Cathy said to Nick later that evening, 'Gee, Pérec was impressive.' Nick did not attempt to deny its merit. 'That's how champions run,' he said. 'They're the boss, until they're beaten.'

Parking space near the athletes' village was at a premium so each day Bideau drove into a service station near the village entrance and bought five dollars worth of petrol, which in effect bought him brief parking time. Cathy walked to the village gate and waited to meet him. Her semi-final that day was at 8 p.m. so it was 11 p.m. before they met to sit and talk on the footpath beside the service station. Nick congratulated her on making her first Olympic final and assured her she would enjoy running the next day. It was a strange ritual, but great drama transforms the ordinary into the sacred. They had been through much together and they enjoyed this quiet moment, the eve of the realisation of their plans, the enormity of it sweeping aside many recent pains.

Next morning, Monday, 29 July, the day of the final, Nick took Cathy shopping—he would submit to anything to kill time—and sat on a stool while Cathy tried on denim shorts. Yeah, they look good, he said, knowing full well the question was coming, just a matter of when. 'How do you think I'll go?' she finally asked. Well, she had prepared well, he said, she would run well. 'No, be more specific,' Cathy insisted, turning this way and that in front of a store mirror. 'Where do you think I'll come?' If she ran as she could, she would either be first or second, he said. 'Mmm, I think I'll be second,' she said. Bideau had deliberately remained blasé, but now he eased into positive mode. 'I don't know about that,' he said. 'The other girl's never really been tested, under pressure, in the straight. She's always had it her way, so we'll find out tonight.'

In fact, Cathy had been practising her own artifice, because she secretly thought she would win. As she told Nick later, 'I didn't want anyone to think I was going to win because I didn't want them to be disappointed if I didn't. Even you. I wanted it just to be me expecting to win.' That way, no pressure. That way, taking responsibility for herself.

While she rested, her cohorts were dealing with the wait in their own way. One day it rained heavily and Peter Jess, scouting the Chinese markets, bought a box of 20 plastic ponchos at $1.70 each, and hawked them outside the stadium for $5 each, aided by the novelty of his broad Australian accent. He was also enjoying conning his way into the night session of the athletics even though he only had a morning pass. He ended up sitting in the media section through an adroit exchange of Olympic pins with media officials. 'He just enjoyed winding these Americans up,' says Bideau, who was having his own fun with an Australian million dollar note snaffled from Jess. It has a Victa motor-mower, a Hills hoist, a blue cattle dog and an old Holden on one side, and Dame Edna Everage and Dawn Fraser on the reverse. That finals day, after being asked for the umpteenth time how Cathy would go, Nick pulled the note from his pocket, brandished it and said, 'I'll tell you how she'll go. I'm feeling that confident I've brought this along to buy drinks to celebrate tonight!'

Cathy had toast and honey for lunch, and Bideau drove her to the village at 4 p.m. to prepare for the race start at 7.35 p.m. No big emotional farewells, just business as usual. Cathy was surprised at how calm the pair of them were. 'This was IT,' says Cathy. 'Our last contact before the big race. It's funny. Even then, you're there but you're not there. You've run the race before you've even run it in the sense that there was nothing more at that stage that anyone could do to change the result.' It was writ. She caught a bus to the warm-up track with Fortune and Lauren Hewitt and she overheard Fortune talking to Dean Capobianco about scary amusement park rides. This too was a scary ride, Cathy thought, with the proviso that she was firmly in control. She'd replaced the special Aboriginal-flag shoes with a brand new pair of Nikes the same colour as Carl Lewis's. Tried them on once, yep they'll do.

She says, 'As the time draws near you get this sense of the final countdown, and it's a terrible feeling because the time goes so quickly and there's nothing you can friggin' do about it. Just keep living. There's a part of you that's scared, and a part of you that wants to get it over and done with. I was nervous, but I was relaxed too, because I just wanted it to be different to 1995.' Gothenburg again. That scar ran deep.

Hewitt chatted excitedly to Cathy during the warm-up,

which enabled Cathy to play straight guy—ideal. Cathy told Miritis she could feel her hamstring. Ah yes, why was Miritis not surprised! 'Virtually before every major event, Catherine comes over with something,' he says. 'I got her over the hamstring, and five minutes later she called me over and said it was her back. So we got that one over with, too.' This was routine, but attention had to be paid. 'You are put in a very serious position,' says Miritis. 'You can't just say "Oh, there's nothing wrong with you," because there could be.' So he spent five minutes treating her muscles with massage and 20 minutes treating her doubts with TLC. She unwound a little.

Apart from Fortune, Miritis is usually the last person to speak to Freeman before she leaves for the main track. Psychologist Jeff Simons knew this and had told Miritis that the final thing Miritis should say to her was to remind her to control what she could control. Says Miritis, 'Before I let her go, I said, "Now go for a run-through and test it out for me," and she came back and said, "That feels great now."' Miritis told her that he'd be by the track if she wanted him. It was all balm for the soul of the athlete as Cathy slowly peeled back the protective layers of hope and confidence to expose her natural fears and doubts.

Over the public address speakers around the warm-up track came the electrifying announcement, 'First call, women's 400m final.' It resounded around the track like a shattering brass gong, galvanising the eight finalists. They were now on notice, 10 minutes before the next call, eight athletes stretching, jogging, but gradually withdrawing into their own thought zones. At 7 p.m., the electronic screen, fluorescent yellow on a green background, flashed the next message: second call for the women's 400m final. Just 35 minutes to take-off. Cathy walked over to the call area, an open marquee where they checked her spikes, numbers, correct national uniform, no mobile phones, and what's in your bag? Cathy had a towel, water bottle, yoghurt, spare pair of spikes and spike key, accreditation and tape measure to adjust her blocks out on the track. And a small slip of paper she had brought with her ... FLAG.

In that confined area, talking to their coaches, the athletes were skittish. 'We were like caged animals, so toey,' says Cathy. 'It's terrible to have to stay still.' She listened attentively to Fortune as he went through her race plan, again. Then came the order, all stand please, in your lane order, with your bags. 'They marched us off to the bus like a bloody boarding school,' says Cathy, who knew all about those. Just as she reached the bus she turned to Peter Fortune and said, feelingly, 'Hug me, Fort, hug me. Just keep hugging me.' Cathy wasn't scared but, she says, there's a vulnerable side to everyone, and this was hers. It surprised Fortune; he was not usually asked for such emotional support, but he willingly obliged. 'I felt pretty good about the situation compared with 1995,' says Fortune. He sent her off with a warm embrace.

For the three-minute ride from the warm-up track to the main stadium, Pérec sat at the front of the bus, Cathy down the centre, opposite Sandie Richards. 'I had very, very brief eye contact with Sandie, but we could not talk, could *not* talk,' says Cathy. 'We all had bottles of water but our mouths were still dry. Whoo! I wanted to say something but it didn't seem right. Olympics does something to you that nothing else, nobody, can do to you. You feel almost sick with nerves, not to the point of ... you can't fight how you're feeling, you're just, ooohh! Your body's moving, you're psyched and so wanting to go and there's nothing you can do. It's getting closer and closer and you've just got to get through it.'

The second call room, under the stands, was a small carpeted area where the competitors sat and fidgeted or stood and paced, until they were moved into a larger room where they could do run-throughs to keep warm. Or go to the toilet, which Cathy did. Some of the women sat quietly, watched the Games on television, others talked to themselves, even their legs—'Now come on, boys!' To Cathy the tension is what teaches her to deal with life. To accept how she's feeling, and not fight it, but to control it.

Finally the last call. Their bags were carried by the basket assistants and they filed out into the open stadium to be hit by a momentous wall of noise, lights, sights and sounds which resonated against the senses. As Cathy walked down the straight, behind Pérec, she passed within 10 metres of Peta and Tiffany, both shouting to her at the top of their lungs. She didn't hear a thing. 'I knew she wouldn't,' says Powell. 'I've seen her run a few times and when I saw her I thought, "This girl is ready for something special." I could see the concentration in her face, and she seemed to be walking light. I'd never seen her do that before. It gave me goose bumps just looking at her.'

Says Cathy, 'It's really scary. I was so focused anything could have been going wrong around me, and it wouldn't have sunk in. It's like I'm hypnotised.' Back home in Mackay, her childhood athletics organiser and fond fan, Janice Saunders, who'd dragged her television set into her bedroom for all-night Olympic viewing, sat watching, equally hypnotised.

Cathy set up her blocks with her tape measure, very precise, 57.5cm from the front block to the white start line. She did a few starts, a few run-throughs to the bend, got her arms pumping, lifted on her toes. Peeled off her T-shirt and long tights to stand in her two-piece Aussie race gear. The basket people departed with her discarded clothes. 'I knew exactly what I was doing,' says Cathy. 'I felt comfortable, confident and cool. I felt good.'

Up in the stands Bideau had placed himself beside a BBC camera half an hour before the race. With 10 minutes to go he got super nervous but when he saw Cathy he was reassured. She was doing her usual, kicking the track, pulling at her pants, touching her number, but he also noticed, 'Gee, she looks on top of it. She looks calm.' She did too, serene almost. What a field. Breuer 1, Davis 2, Pérec 3, Freeman 4,

CATHY FREEMAN—A JOURNEY JUST BEGUN

Ogunkoya 5, Yusuf 6, Richards 7 and Miles 8. Pérec looked imperious, her trademark frown wrinkling her brow. Her coach John Smith had told her she had a 48s run in her and, after her superlative heat win, she was beginning to believe him. Bideau had been telling Maurie Plant all season that Cathy could run 48s. In women's sprinting, where testosterone triumphed for too many years, the two women looked lean and feminine, adorning the tartan track rather than subduing it. The stage was set, before 85,000 people, for the greatest women's 400m race of the modern era.

20.
Roll the Dice.
Atlanta Olympics, 1996

At the gun, Cathy took off urgently but was overshadowed by Pérec who accelerated with a grace which belied her long limbs. She didn't flail or tangle, she ran with power and precision. Cathy's reaction time from the blocks was 0.32s, Pérec's a lightning 0.20s. Pérec had picked up a metre even before Cathy had left the blocks. Who could withstand this woman's attack? Hem her in and she would run over the top of you. She had made up at least half the seven-metre lane stagger on Cathy by the end of the first bend. Cathy's stride pattern was faster but she took longer to reach cruising speed. Once both runners settled, it looked to be Cathy's two-stroke motor against Pérec's larger four-stroke beat. Crucially, Pérec made no more impression on Freeman all the way down the back straight, but by then the powerful Frenchwoman was only about two metres behind Freeman. In her subconscious—she didn't think it then but remembered it afterwards—Cathy knew that, for the first time in a dozen races, Pérec had not passed her. She felt competitive, felt buoyed. At 200m Nick glanced at his stopwatch: 23.4s, perfect, not too fast, matching Pérec.

It was there that Marie-José launched her second attack,

running to within half a metre of Cathy, trying to pass but, once more, could not. 'Now Pérec will go up alongside of her,' called Bruce McAvaney for Channel Seven. 'No! Freeman kicks, holds her for the moment!' At the long jump pit, by the back straight, Carl Lewis, climbing from the sand, looked up and saw Cathy flash by, keeping Pérec at bay.

In Australia, where it was 9.35 a.m., nearly two million viewers sat riveted by this unfolding duel. Cathy did not know Pérec was so close, she knew only her own plan and that it was time to gently squeeze the throttle. She widened the gap over Pérec to a metre. 'Here goes the attack,' thought Nick. 'She's having a go at Mary-Jo, she's putting it to the champion.' After 32 seconds, another 120m still to run, Cathy had gathered in Ogunkoya in lane five, and Pérec still had not caught Freeman. As she passed Ogunkoya, Cathy rejoiced in a fleeting thought, 'I've got the silver!'

But now the second bend lane stagger came into play and Pérec powered into the straight half a metre in front. The crowd roared, for this was pure Olympics. With 80m to go Cathy went for glory. McAvaney picked it up instantly: 'Can Freeman lift? ... *She is lifting! She goes up to Perec!*' Pérec's nerves clamoured and rang, teetering on panic. 'I kick, she kick, I push, she push, I did not think she was ever going to give up,' she says. At the high jump, Tim Forsyth paused, as he always does, and saw in Cathy's face, as she battled down the straight, that she was digging deeper and deeper.

Pérec had fought and clawed her way into the lead and yet here was Cathy at her elbow, duelling with her still. As Cathy challenged, Nick exclaimed involuntarily, 'Give it up!', willing Pérec to say 'No more, too hard!' and to squib it, as she had when Cathy beat her in Monte Carlo in 1995. But proud Pérec wouldn't and rolled the dice one more time. 'This is my turn. Next time is hers, she is still young,' Pérec said to herself and it was Cathy who reached the end of her range. 'It was because of that spurt,' says Cathy. 'You spend it, you pay for it. It catches up with you. I fired up, a mistake.

I wasn't strong enough, she was stronger.' With 10 metres to go Cathy lost a fraction of her form and slowed. 'I knew it was over and I was second.'

Pérec won by about three metres in 48.25s, the world's fastest for 11 years, or as McAvaney diplomatically put it, 'No legitimate athlete has ever run that fast.' Two magnificent drug-free athletes had pushed each other close to a world record that is suspected of being a drug-assisted fiction. Cathy's time, 48.63s, made her the sixth fastest 400m runner of all time. And she, too, went under Russian Olga Bryzgina's Olympic record of 48.65s. Ogunkoya ran third in 49.10s and, for the first time ever, six runners went under 50s. It was unsurpassed in women's 400m history.

Cathy clapped her hands past the line, applauding herself, and that it was all over. She kissed Pérec on each cheek, Euro-style, Miles patted Cathy's shoulder, Cathy unlaced her shoes and fetched an Aussie flag from Peter Jess in the crowd. He mischievously flashed the Aboriginal flag at her. 'No, gees, you bloody idiot,' she said, laughing and dancing away to embrace Bideau. She says he had tears in his eyes. 'You ran 48.6, the time on the mirror,' he said.

She nodded and smiled. She was dazed and elated, so high on endorphins she was in another world. The natural narcotic produced by the body results in a feel-good high that lasts for hours. 'You're still puffed, and your tongue's sticking to the top of your mouth, and there's interviews and photographs and cameras, people are shaking your hand, patting your back, crying, telling you how sensational you are, yet you just ignore it,' says Cathy. 'If you could draw a picture of how you feel your whole body would be full of air and you'd be walking around with your arms raised.'

Natural opiates. It sounded heavenly, sounded euphoric, I said. Cathy nodded. 'Well, you're in, sort of, shock, it's a place where you've never been before, and you only dream of being there, but you can't exactly pinpoint where, all you know is that you want more in the future. I don't know, I can't compare it to having a child, but it's elation, it's a great place to be. It makes your head spin, the whole thing.'

Nick urged her, 'Stay out there, don't rush, soak it in. You worked hard for this moment.' Cathy gave Maurie a huge hug, and eventually saw Fortune and Lauren Hewitt, Phil King and Debbie Flintoff-King—still Australia's last track gold medallist, in Seoul in 1988. Nick watched, proud, pleased, involved yet content to remain in the background. The next race was the men's 400m final for The Man, Michael Johnson. The American crowd had already forgotten the Frenchie and the Aussie. As usual they were in hot-dog queues, waiting for Johnson and their favourite event—standing and clapping their hand over their heart to their anthem, 'The Star-Spangled Banner'.

Back in the real world, Moscow 800m gold medallist, Steve Ovett, told McAvaney, 'She challenged as much as she could. She pushed her as hard as she could, tried to crack her. The other girl didn't, so can't do more than that, can you?' Seven's Pat Welsh grabbed Cathy in the mixed zone. 'I'm just so happy I got a silver and ran a PB,' she gasped. A PB by a whopping 0.96s—nearly a second faster than she had run in London, just two weeks earlier. In the background a crowd of Australian swimmers, their events over, could be heard with their unmistakable chant, 'Aussie-Aussie-Aussie! Oy-Oy-Oy!' When Pat Welsh brought it to Cathy's attention, she delivered her memorable quote, 'Yeah, anyone would think I'd won the bloody thing! No, it's great, thanks Australia.'

David Culbert, working as a liaison officer with the Australian Olympic Committee, had been scanning the stands in vain with his binoculars, searching for Cecelia and Bruce. On a whim, Cecelia suddenly waved her small Aboriginal flag and, even in that vast crowd, Culbert spotted it, raced around to take them to the television studios for interviews with Cathy. Charlie Perkins went public that Cathy should have paraded that black, red and yellow flag as well as the Australian flag. A hard man, Charlie, generous, but a hardliner.

At one point the cameras settled on Daniel Kowalski, sitting pensively in the stand with an Aussie flag around his shoulders. Of all people, having won a silver in the pool behind Kieren Perkins in the 1500m three days earlier, he knew what it was like to go under to a super champion. In Melbourne, training partner Mark Holcombe sat back from his television set with tension unwound, all overcome with emotion. 'I got a tingle in my stomach, yeah, I did,' he says.

A great race can be likened to a major trauma, in an accident or war, such is the camaraderie engendered among the participants. Cathy, Marie-José and Falilat Ogunkoya prepared for their medal ceremony like schoolgirls for their first dance. Marie-José lent Cathy her lipstick, eyeshadow, mascara and eyeliner and helped apply them. 'We were all happy little Vegemites,' says Cathy. 'It's uncanny, you sort of become sisters. You only go through these moments with certain people and only they understand what it's like. And it brings us closer together, it's almost like we're in our own exclusive club.'

Having forgotten to bring her team tracksuit, Cathy borrowed Flintoff-King's bottoms and distance runner Carolyn Schuwalow's top for the medal ceremony. Shining with happiness she walked to the trackside and threw her flowers to, who else, Jess, who'd bluffed his way past the gate coppers into prime position.

From the moment the race finished Cathy was assigned a drug medico who watched her every move until she was led into the drug testing room. There she sat with other testing athletes, drinking water or soft drink from sealed bottles, never their own drink bottles. It's often hard to provide a sample because athletes dehydrate during their event, but when Cathy felt able they gave her a special plastic beaker from a sterile packet. She went into a small toilet cubicle, door wide open, rolled up her top and pulled down her pants, stood astride the bowl facing the open doorway and urinated into the beaker, under the direct gaze of a drug offical standing a few metres away.

'It's bizarre, I know,' says Cathy. 'But luckily, if you've medalled, it's one of the few times you're glad to do anything, you're so happy.' Not self-conscious? I enquired, amazed. 'The first time you're tested, yeah, but I've done so many, you get used to it.' Only convicted criminals entering prison are subjected to such an undignified visual assault on their person from their guardians. The sooner a thumb-prick blood test for drugs is legalised, the better for athletes' dignity. To the chief medical officer she declared she'd been taking standard iron tablets, amino acids and the contraceptive pill.

An hour and a half after the race she delivered her second famous quote, to McAvaney, on whether she knew Pérec had challenged at 200m. 'I didn't know she was there,' said Cathy. 'I just ran my little black butt off!' And she revealed once more her childlike sense of humility, saying, 'To push a girl of her ability to do her very best, that was me, little ol' me.' Then she said a heartfelt thanks to Nick Bideau, 'My darling boyfriend, he's been fantastic, he's been wonderful.' It is important to remember that despite their blow-ups, anger and frustration, Cathy and Nick operated like a well-oiled team, at one in their aims, close and supportive.

Nobody could fathom their relationship but they were unfailingly loyal, quick to snuff criticism of each other from outsiders. 'Are you disappointed?' she asked Nick, several times during the night. 'Did you think I was only running for second?' Nick could not have been more genuine in his reply. 'No, no, look at your time,' he said. 'You ran great, anyone who puts their head down and has a whack like you did, isn't running for second. I'm proud of what you did.'

Maurie Plant and David Culbert shepherded her through hours of interviews until she arrived at Nike at about 2 a.m. for a small party. They were still being pursued by television crews Nike had a fistful of phoned media requests as well.

ROLL THE DICE

Waiting for them were about 20 people including Cecelia and Bruce, Peter Jess, Maurie Plant, Peter Fortune, Nike and Oakley friends and, a pleasant surprise for Cathy, Raelene Boyle. Still recovering from treatment for breast cancer, Boyle watched the race, went back to her hotel, rested for several hours and then joined the party. Cathy had rung her every few weeks during Raelene's illness. Boyle counts the Pérec–Freeman contest as one of the all-time great women's 400m races. She says, 'I've seen many and it was up there with watching Irena Szewinska of Poland become the first woman to break 50s in Montreal in 1976.' Cathy rang competitions chief Brian Roe in Australia to thank him for all his help, to which Roe replied, 'I'm just glad I'm your friend, Cathy, that's all.'

At 4 a.m. Nick went and collected his car from an old lady's front lawn near the stadium where he parked each day. She was still up, vigilant as ever. He usually paid her $10 but this time he tipped her $100 and, as happy as that made her, she was not as happy as Bideau as he drove slowly home. At the same time in the village, still dark outside, Louise McPaul, silver medallist in the javelin three days earlier, sat in the team common room in her pyjamas, watching television, still unable to sleep from the excitement of her medal. In walked Cathy. 'Oh, hello. I can't sleep, I'm still on a high,' said McPaul. 'Neither can I,' said Cathy, slumping down. Endorphins have a half-life of about two hours, so Cathy had come down from her euphoria. She had tried sleeping but her senses were still buzzing. With nothing on telly they compared experiences for half an hour. 'I was definitely on cloud nine and she was up there with me,' says McPaul. 'It was strange because Cathy was by far the athlete most expected to get a medal, but here she was just as rapt as I was at getting my silver.' Even to other silver medallists Cathy was a star.

Back in bed, in the early morning dawn, Cathy reviewed the race in her mind. There were lessons to be learnt. She knew that momentary thought, 'I've got silver,' was not smart. 'I reckon I lost concentration because part of me was scared of not medalling again and I was a little bit too happy to accept the silver,' she says. 'I lost it for a split second, meanwhile Pérec was full-on focus.' Then she had foolishly tried to compete with Pérec in the straight. 'It's actually much harder to suddenly go faster, it takes the energy out of you,' she says. 'I should have just eased up alongside her, not got so excited.'

Back in Miller Street, Richmond, it's 1998, and stillness descends as Cathy and I both go a little flat from having so vividly relived that dramatic day in Atlanta. Cathy fetches a glass of water and returns to the lounge. Then she leans forward. 'Sitting here thinking about it gets me really pissed off, actually,' she says. 'I became weak for that moment, even though it was probably only for a millionth of a second.' Then she relents. 'But, it's all right. It will be all right from now on. Each year I pick things up, I detect these weaknesses and I always make sure I don't let it ever, ever happen again.'

To put her mind at rest, Plant acknowledges Cathy's error. 'When they straightened up, she gritted her teeth instead of relaxing,' says Maurie. 'But, on the day she wasn't going to beat Pérec. If she'd relaxed she might have found a tenth or two of a second, but she needed to find three or four.' Fortune agrees. 'When Cathy realised she'd lost the race, she just dropped off a bit, like "Oh, bugger it! I haven't won." She could have run 48.50s, but Pérec still wins the race.'

There is another explanation of how Cathy lost. The 400m stagger is seven metres per lane which, travelling at Cathy's average speed—8.2m per second—equates to 0.85s. If Pérec ran at exactly the same speed as Freeman over 400m, that's how much her inside lane would naturally make up. In the race, Pérec actually gained 0.12s of that 0.85s straight out of the blocks. Then, on the video race clock—perhaps a crude measure—I appointed a set marker on the track early in the race and saw Cathy pass it in 9.2s and Pérec the same point in 9.5s—only 0.3s behind after less than 100m. Pérec had already made up 0.55s. Since Pérec only won by 0.38s, Cathy actually ran the last 300m of the race faster than Pérec. But Pérec had already won the race with her start. Perhaps, says Bideau. But if Cathy had held off Pérec better in the first 100m, she may not have run so fast over the next 300m, he says. All debts must be paid.

Cathy still had the 200m and the relays to come, her Olympics weren't yet over, but really they were. Louise McPaul felt sorry for Cathy that night in the common room. 'I can't imagine how hard it must be to win an Olympic medal, and then have to refocus and come back out,' she says.

Cathy soon found out. It was the Olympics so, even though she was physically, mentally and emotionally drained, she ran the 200m, made the semi-final, ran sixth, and out. On the bus to the stadium from the warm-up track for her semi-final, Cathy, no longer spellbound by tension, mouthed to Pérec sitting nearby, 'I'm tired.' Says Cathy, 'I remember distinctly that moment because she didn't laugh with me or anything. She didn't respond and now I know why. She was all geared to go out and win again. You learn a lot, you learn a lot.' Pérec went on to win the 200m gold medal as well, a magnificent performance. But even as she was being acclaimed, and as Cathy was out boogieing with Renee Poetschka in Atlanta's nightspots, back in the condo the backroom boffins, Bideau and Plant, were making their plans against La Magnifique.

21.
WHOOPIN' MARY-JO'S BUTT.
POST-OLYMPICS, 1996

'I do not want to be in the parade. Freeman has been waiting for me,' complained Marie-José Pérec to Wilfried Meert, director of the Van Damme memorial meet in Brussels. Meert had organised a parade of champions and past heroes —Kiwi John Walker to Carl Lewis—in a motorcade around the track to mark the 20th anniversary of the meet, named after a famous Belgian 1500m runner. The parade was at 6 p.m. 23 August and Pérec was racing Freeman at 8.30 p.m. Marie-José wanted to be resting, preparing for the race, not riding around in an open car. Only Olympic champions were invited so Cathy was excused, but it was part of Pérec's meet contract so she had to comply.

It was not quite a month after the epic 400m Olympic final and, displaying extraordinary mental and physical reserves, Cathy had returned to London to complete the 1996 European circuit. Nick and Peter Jess had been re-negotiating Freeman's contract with Nike and they were dealing from a position of strength. Her international potential was now unlimited. Cathy was Pérec's heir-apparent and the rising star can often be as valuable as the star herself. Not only that, Freeman had come to embody Nike's image, her passion, the way she opened herself to the track, bared her heart and soul. She runs with drama and Nike markets the melodrama of sport. If Pérec followed her usual pattern and had a soft year in 1997, Cathy could be world champion within 12 months, Bideau told Nike. Reebok had Pérec, Nike needed Freeman. Not only that. If Pérec's career ended sooner rather than later, then Reebok might come after Cathy. Adidas already were showing interest.

Bideau reasoned that Sydney 2000 being Cathy's home Olympics, the world's media, marketeers and tourism chiefs would adopt her as the recognisable face of the host nation. She could ascend to the rarefied global earnings of golfer Greg Norman and motorcyclist Michael Doohan. Bideau sensed in Europe the same building awareness of the Freeman phenomenon that he detected in Australia just before the 1994 Commonwealth Games.

He told Nike that Freeman had delivered in excess of what the company could have expected. She had even risked Australian Olympic executives' wrath by attending a set-up press conference at Nike headquarters in Atlanta. She was interviewed by Nike man Carl Lewis, with the Nike 'swoosh' logo prominently displayed. Australia's Olympic sponsors were Adidas and Nike's action was publicly criticised as illegal ambush marketing.

Within a month of the Olympics, Bideau and Jess had Cathy's contract signed, for a reported $500,000 a year, taking her through to Sydney 2000. Nike were the biggest, but Bideau then set about clarifying new contracts with her other major sponsors, Ford and Oakley. Then they switched from Telstra to Optus who were sponsoring the Australian grand prix athletic series. They didn't re-sign with Kellogg's and Schweppes but Bideau didn't mind. Less is more, is his creed, as he drip feeds her exposure to an incessant media and eager advertisers. All in all, if Cathy ran to her potential in the next few years, she would be among the highest-paid female athletes in the world before she had even won an

Olympic gold. Peter Jess declines to talk money. 'She is well off,' he concedes, po-faced. Suffice to say that, if she was a rock star, she would be based in an off-shore tax haven by now.

As part of the deal, Nike paid Bideau a management fee on top of Cathy's contract, but Nick had an even bigger vision. He had worked out how to market himself, his knowledge, his contacts, and his obsessive interest in athletics as a tangible asset—the Melbourne Track Club. By wrapping the club around Freeman, and Steve Moneghetti and Tim Forsyth, MTC became a management and marketing vehicle licensed to negotiate increased revenue for other less famous athletes who came under the MTC mantle. MTC enabled Bideau to resign as a journalist to manage the club, and it gave him a powerful base in Australian athletics. He's hooked on helping, is Bideau. 'It gives me a great thrill to see Cathy win,' he says. 'It makes me proud. If another runner loses, I feel disappointed for them. If Cathy loses, I feel partly to blame.'

Bideau told Maurie Plant in Atlanta that he didn't care about the Olympic 200m final, the relays or the closing ceremony, he had targeted one last goal in 1996. He wanted Freeman to register a win over Pérec, so that Marie-José knew that Cathy was still coming after her. In this he had backing from Cathy's stepfather, Bruce Barber. 'Catherine will keep going at her, and going at her, until Pérec cracks,' he said. 'I've seen Catherine break so many other girls' hearts. She is quite ruthless in her own way.' Bideau also had a long-term strategy. He divined in Pérec's personality that she would rather withdraw from the ring gracefully than get knocked out. The first step was to dent her confidence.

Cathy picked up on the Pérec character, too. 'Coming from French society, I think she really cherishes what comes with winning,' she says. 'I think she needs the whole package. I don't think she can live in athletics without success. Whereas I can. I don't like losing but I don't think I need that constant

WHOOPIN' MARY-JO'S BUTT

adulation and praise. Mary-Jo's not interested in anything other than coming first. So if I can beat her a couple of times ... who knows? I'm just not as strong as her, yet. I stress *yet*.'

Flying out of Atlanta, Cathy discovered her heroic loss had made her recognisable everywhere, in airports, shopping centres and cabs. Recognisable, too, to the organisers of the Monte Carlo grand prix, but they offered Cathy peanuts compared to what they outlaid for Pérec. 'Anyway, it's too soon,' Bideau told Plant. 'Let Mary-Jo drink more champagne and eat more caviar.' Pérec duly won Monte Carlo, but rumours emerged that she had threatened not to race on the night if certain conditions regarding the lane draw weren't met. With Mary-Jo, her reputation was such that there was always some gossip surrounding her appearances.

Cathy maintained her great shape with an ideal preparation, designed to resolve any post-Olympic letdown. 'I just trained and ticked over while Mary-Jo gallivanted around the countryside,' says Cathy. First she freshened with a 300m race in London, in 36.43s and then flew to Zurich, the richest grand prix of the European circuit, for a 200m against virtually the Olympic final field, minus Merlene Ottey. Back in Sydney, Australia's Olympic athletes were being given a welcome home dinner. Cathy and javelin silver medallist Louise McPaul were hooked up by satellite from Zurich to speak to Prime Minister Howard at the dinner. It was midday in Zurich and Cathy was due to run against Marie-José Pérec in the 200m that evening. Cathy was relaxed but she's never been one to enjoy waiting around to meet politicians. She does not share their own sense of self-importance. Before he was elected PM, John Howard had sent Cathy a Christmas card. 'What's he sending me a card for? I don't even know him,' Cathy wondered to Nick.

She sat patiently in the Zurich studio for 15 minutes, the satellite link ran out but was extended for another 10 minutes. Cathy, waiting for Howard to come on, could hear his dinner address through her earpiece. 'What's he saying?'

asked Nick Bideau. 'Oh rah rah rah, yapping, nothing really,' says Cathy, fidgeting and becoming restless. 'If he doesn't stop in a few minutes, let's go, I can't wait.' Said Nick, 'No, no, you have to stay. You can't give the Prime Minister the flick!'

When Howard finally came on, he said jovially, 'Cathy, when I watched the Olympic Games and saw you run, I was so proud it left me speechless.' Said Cathy, 'Speechless! I find that hard to believe.' The dinner audience in Australia roared laughing. Howard paused, Cathy giggled and carried it off. Later she asked Bideau, 'Was that funny, was it? Do you think I shouldn't have said that?' No, Bideau reassured her. Australians love that, taking the mickey out of politicians.

That evening Cathy finished sixth in 22.55s, her fastest 200m of the year. Pérec could not reproduce her gold medal form, finishing fifth, her usual zing in the straight absent, a hint that she was beginning to feel the strain. It was in Zurich, back in their hotel room, that Cathy gave Bideau an inkling of what was in her mind about their future. There was no argument, no preamble, just the question. 'If I'm not with you any more, would you still help me with my running?' she asked. 'Yeah,' Nick nodded.

Thence to Brussels, where the Zurich meet director, Andreas Bruegger, called Cathy to his hotel suite and presented her with a very expensive Omega wristwatch. 'I only give them to Olympic gold medallists, but you ran so well, you deserve one,' he told her. Freeman captured people's hearts like that. She duly gave the watch to her mother, Cecelia. At the Brussels hotel where the athletes stayed before the meet, Gwen Torrence said in a quiet aside to Cathy, 'Girl, this is it. Mary-Jo, she's going down tonight.' Cathy smiled wanly. Easy to say. During her warm-up, Nick said the same thing. 'You can beat her tonight.' Normally he'd resist that sort of talk, preferring to just tell her she'd run well. Pérec was given lane four, Cathy five. Ho hum. 'She's always inside me,' says Cathy. 'I decided long ago there

WHOOPIN' MARY-JO'S BUTT

was no point in worrying. I'm just not the type to boss people around, to threaten to pull out. But one day I'll be inside her.' Bideau was not unhappy with the draw. He figured Cathy wouldn't let Pérec get past her this time. Ogunkoya was in lane three—Olympic gold, silver and bronze, right there before a packed house of 40,000. This was what Monte Carlo wouldn't pay Cathy for, a re-run of the Olympic final.

And it was a re-run, except that when it came time for Pérec to pass Cathy into the straight, Pérec couldn't do it. 'I'm not surprised any more when she comes up inside me, I sort of expect it,' says Cathy. 'But when she didn't come with me, I just went for it.' Pérec fought and fought but then, in the last 20m, threw it in, just as Bideau hoped she would in Atlanta. Cathy first in 49.48s, Pérec second in 49.72s. Gwen Torrence and several others gave Cathy a hug.

Cathy rarely does a victory lap, even though it is common among winners on the circuit. Her natural shy nature is the antithesis of the extroverted showbiz mode into which many American sprinters click after any victory. 'Do a victory lap,' Nick urged her, this time. 'The crowd in the back straight paid to see you, too.' It was Nick's droll way of signalling that this was Cathy's biggest win, ever. And that this was only Pérec's second defeat over 400m in six years, each time to Cathy, worth savouring and the crowd knew it too. Pérec took the defeat poorly and snubbed Cathy by shunning the victory ceremony. In the drug test room, Pérec put an ice-pack on her hamstring and then abruptly vomited, a sure sign of intense lactic acid build-up in her bloodstream. Cathy went over to see how she was, but Pérec was having a massage and didn't encourage conversation. As Cathy sat and sipped her drink, she looked up at Bideau and asked quizzically, 'How did you know I was going to beat Mary-Jo tonight?' Nick replied enigmatically, 'Because we drink fox soup. We work things out.'

Not that defeating Pérec was any compensation for

CATHY FREEMAN—A JOURNEY JUST BEGUN

Atlanta for Cathy. 'She'd been here, there and everywhere racing and we knew she'd be tired and frail,' says Cathy. 'I can imagine how tough it was for her because I knew what I'd been through.' Still, it was worth a wake-up call back home to Mum in Brisbane.

Berlin wanted Cathy now, offered her $20,000, but Cathy would not be drawn. Unlike runners from some of the poorer African nations, Cathy's sponsorships, principally Nike, mean she doesn't have to worry about snapping up every offer made to her on the circuit. She can be race oriented rather than business oriented. Athletes without her finances often race indiscriminately, chasing short-term cash rewards, but reducing their career lifespan. Such athletes, in the top 10, might make $150,000 a year for five years and then fade. Cathy, in her fifth year on the circuit, was just coming of age.

Not that Cathy would knock back the money, mind you. Her goal of defeating Pérec in the next race, the grand prix 400m final in Milan, carried with it a $78,000 winner-takes-all incentive. To keep her edge, Cathy flew back to the UK and ran a 200m in Sheffield, defeating Ogunkoya, and stayed to watch Arsenal and Chelsea play a 2–2 draw in London. Tiffany Cherry bobbed up for a Scrabble game and light relief, before Cathy returned to Italy on 8 September. This was the meet for which all the Olympians had kept training, the money meet. Cathy expected Pérec to be fresh, to avenge Brussels.

'Warming up, I was getting really excited, because I do,' says Cathy. 'And I think she could sense that I was hungry that day, you know?' Nick had heard on the circuit grapevine the night before that Pérec was looking for a doctor, and he predicted to Plant, and competitions chief Brian Roe who had flown in for the final, 'She won't run. She likes everything to be just right and if not she won't take on our girl here.' For once it seemed that Bideau's crystal ball had clouded as Pérec did run-throughs for an hour, whizzing around like a million dollars. Nick reassured Cathy during her warm-up that, on Cathy's form, Pérec would have to run sub-49s to beat her, and he didn't think she had it in her. Neither did Pérec. Organisers called the field and, just before they were due to walk out on the track, Pérec abruptly withdrew.

'It really threw me, threw us all,' says Cathy. 'I felt really flat, it took a huge chunk of adrenalin away.' Though disappointed, Cathy raised the energy to hold off Ogunkoya in 49.60s, Freeman's seventh sub-50s run that season. At a function that evening Pérec, when interviewed by the international media, said, 'Ah, I did not feel so good, but I am feeling better now, thank you.' But then she told French journalists, 'Why run? I did not come here to run second or fifth.'

Cathy agreed to one more race, in Tokyo, to wind up the season, though it was plain that already the competitive tension had left the athletes. At grand prix meets, organisers provide three meals a day but, before the major championships, the athletes are guarded when they meet to eat. After the last of the majors they chill out, become more friendly, stay up late talking and go out together. Few athletes can sleep immediately after competing and so they kill the hours together gossiping. Once upon a time they talked about training, then it was drugs, and now money, and as always, a favourite topic, relationships.

In Tokyo the athletes stayed in the Takinawa Prince, the same hotel where, in 1991 at the world championships, Cathy had cried in the lobby at being left out of the Australian relay. Now, five years later, she was an Olympic silver medallist and on top of the world. Relay coach Nancy Atterton had been right back then: the upsetting omission from the Tokyo relay team had kick-started Cathy's marvellous career. She ran her slowest 400m of 1996 in Tokyo, 51.97s, just fast enough to stay unbeaten by Ogunkoya who ran second.

Then it was party time. The athletes dressed up that night, and runners with magnificent physiques, like Pérec, Torrence and Merlene Ottey, blossomed as the beauties they are.

CATHY FREEMAN—A JOURNEY JUST BEGUN

'When Merlene turned up you could see the men turn and notice,' says Cathy. 'She looked stunning, carries herself with such poise. Merlene's a queen.' There were plenty of big stars there and Cathy was one of them, eating hors d'oeuvres with Marie-José Pérec. She was even starting to look like them, with her strong neck-to-collarbone trapezius muscles. 'Gwen has the most amazing upper back,' says Cathy. 'I thought, "I want a back like that." The more time I spent with those top women the more I wanted to be like them, feel like them, look like them.'

'I dress pretty conservatively compared to the others,' says Cathy. 'Mary-Jo is a catwalk model and she had on this really tight mini-dress and she told me my dress was too long. I had on a skirt and top and I thought it was kind of cool. So I said, "No, no, yours is too short!"' They were still bantering when US 400m hurdler Calvin Davis, bronze in Atlanta, grabbed a microphone on a small stage and started wisecracking to the party.

'There's a few things ah don't like about this sport and one is ah don't like to see athletes duckin' one another,' said Davis. 'Which brings me to you Mary-Jo, it's good to see you up the back talkin' to Cathy cause I notice you been runnin' the deuce ever since Cathy put a whoopin' on your butt in Brussels a couple of weeks ago.' The whole party turned and looked at the pair and started laughing. Cathy and Mary-Jo didn't hear what Davis said, but knew they were suddenly the centre of attention. Pérec walked over to British 400m champion, Roger Black, and said, 'What, what did he say?' A friend repeated the comment to Cathy, and she laughed. So now she was known as the girl who was out after Pérec. Calvin Davis was right. In the few meets since Brussels, Pérec had either withdrawn from the 400m or run the 200m. Bideau's strategy was bearing fruit, however temporarily.

As the evening progressed, and the party broke up into various athletes' rooms, people Cathy knew but never talked to congratulated her on her silver medal. 'It's nice to get respect from your peers,' she says. 'You're accepted into the club.' She drank beer with Heike Drechsler, Roger Black, Dennis Mitchell and Carl Lewis's brother Mac, and warded off the amorous advances of vodka-slugging Russian pole vaulter Igor Trandenkov. 'That stuff he was drinking would burn your tongue,' says Cathy, laughing. 'He kept on coming up and saying, "I want to kiss you." And Roger Black was saying, "Her boyfriend's in the room!" It was hilarious.'

Has there ever been a year by an Australian such as Cathy's in 1996? At home she had won the national 100 and 200m double, the Stawell Gift and was grand prix Athlete of the Year. Overseas she won an Olympic silver medal and the 400m grand prix title. She raced in 16 finals in the US and Europe over 200, 300 and 400m and won 12 of them. After Atlanta she cut a swathe through the international ranks, Pérec included, winning five of her six races and her circuit season's earnings topped $200,000.

Australia has some wonderful athletes but nobody, not Gainsford-Taylor, Forsyth, Robinson or Vander-Kuyp, McPaul or Stone, win at the major European grand prix meets as does Freeman. Her performance was unmatched since Ron Clarke's record-breaking spree in the 1960s. They talk it up on the track scene, how Freeman, 'she don't back off'. She wins, they say, anywhere—Australia early season, America mid-year, all over Europe, and finally in Tokyo. On the circuit where there's no place to hide, Freeman has been tested and never found wanting.

Up in Mackay, the *Daily Mercury* had everything in proportion with a headline: MACKAY TRIO ON OLYMPIC MEDAL HUNT linking Cathy with fellow medallists, hockey player Baeden Choppy and basketballer Sandy Brondello, all hometown heroes. Cathy's childhood coach Penny Pollock has a daughter Fiona who was teaching at Woree State High in south Cairns, and for weeks afterwards it seemed every Aboriginal student boasted, 'I'm Cathy Freeman's cousin.' Didn't matter if they weren't, they wanted to be.

CATHY FREEMAN—A JOURNEY JUST BEGUN

Before coming home Cathy and Nick holidayed in Hong Kong, went shopping and later, in a bar, ran into Australian cricketers, Michael Kasprowicz and Greg Blewett, who were there to play the Hong Kong Sixes. At 2 a.m., Kasprowicz was still dancing up a storm when Blewett suddenly addressed Cathy earnestly, 'Cathy, just want to tell you, I like your work.'

Back in Australia, Cathy confronted an avalanche of mail at Australia Post—50,000 letters and 5000 Telstra hero faxes. Only Kieren Perkins approached her popularity. Australia Post's Terry Hearity says they replied to 99 per cent of them with a postcard, with Cathy's printed signature and a little printed heart she had drawn beside it. They briefed extra staff to put aside letters from indigenous writers, or anything judged to be personal, and each day Cathy came in and dealt with them. She sat in a room with half a dozen staffers from 10 a.m.–4 p.m. writing answers. 'Cathy, you should read this,' they'd say. Cathy would and then put a special message on the reply card.

In late 1996, I met Cathy and Nick in the Sunnybank Hills house that Cathy bought her parents in Brisbane. They were visiting before leaving for a holiday on Stradbroke Island. I asked Cathy why it was that she, not Davis, Ogunkoya, Yusuf or Richards, had emerged to challenge Pérec. 'They don't have a Nick Bideau,' she said fondly. Yet within a month they were separated, unhappily, irreconcilably, and within six months each had begun new relationships. Their professional association fracturing, Cathy's immediate athletic future looked bleak. But not her long-term destiny. That September, Freeman was privileged to meet the Dalai Lama, the exiled spiritual leader of Tibet who was visiting Australia. Afterwards the Dalai's aide told her, 'It is considered very lucky to have shaken his hand.' The date was 7.30 p.m., 24 September 1996, four years to the hour from the Sydney Olympic 400m final.

22.
TIME HEALS.
PRE-WORLDS, 1997

On 30 November 1996, Cathy's best friend Peta Powell was all excited, about to pick up her new car, a shiny red BMW, when Cathy rang. 'Can you come and get me?' asked Cathy. She sounded a little upset. Sure, said Peta. She would just go and collect the car and be right over. Minutes later Cathy rang again. 'Peta, can you come and get me ... now?' This time Peta picked up the urgency in the plea. She had been half-expecting it. 'Get your stuff together. You can move in here with me,' she said. Cathy and Nick Bideau had finally split. 'One of us had to go because it was so strained and unpleasant,' says Cathy. So now it was over. When Powell drove into Stanley Street, Richmond, Cathy was waiting outside, leaning against a wall, bag on the ground, hands over her face, eyes filled with tears. It was the saddest sight Powell had seen and she set about being there for her friend.

Cathy was nearly 24. It was almost four months, to the day, since the raptures of that Atlanta final. Four months to plummet to the depths of despair. In fact it was the depression she had to have, the inevitable consequence of putting off a decision about her relationship with Nick to give priority to the Olympics. Now it caught up with them both. Cathy had moved in with Nick in Melbourne in May 1991. Now, five and a half years later, it had ended. After the Olympics and the Euro circuit, it had become plain that persisting together was futile. It was Nick who finally broached the question. He should move out. Cathy agreed. 'There, that wasn't so difficult was it?' she said. 'No, if that's what you want,' he said. But, since all Bideau's business was conducted from a downstairs office, and because Cathy wanted to start afresh rather than live with things that reminded her of the past, they decided it would be easier for Cathy to move, and they would buy her a new house.

But between the decision and the reality lay untold tension, frustration and depression for them both. They were so profoundly entwined in their emotional, professional and financial relationships that untangling it all would have taken a drove of therapists. And is there a marriage counsellor in the land who would have recommended what Cathy and Nick now attempted—to end their personal relationship but maintain their professional relationship as athlete and manager? It would be hard to grieve for one relationship while daily nurturing another.

At first Cathy was angry. 'I wanted to break all ties, be free of Nick,' she says. 'Then I decided not to because it was Nick's livelihood, you know. He really needed me in a professional sense.' He did in as much as he had just resigned as a journalist, but equally Cathy understood his importance to her athletic career. Even so she felt somehow betrayed, by Bideau and Co., by Team Freeman, by the Melbourne Track Club. Her pain embraced everyone and everything. Her parents, Cecelia and Bruce, had her financial affairs with Peter Jess audited. 'Cathy tested me absolutely, she didn't trust any of us,' says Jess. 'I was a mate of Nick's so that meant I couldn't be trusted. I always had a feeling that she and Nick wouldn't last forever because of their volatility. They both have really deep and dark moods. So every property Freeman owned was set up as a distinct company.

If there was ever any drama we could unbundle her and Nick very quickly and neatly.'

Jess gave Cecelia's lawyers binders of documentation, tax returns, bank statements and agreements dating from the day Cathy walked into his office. The lawyers explained to Jess how they had an alternative management system which would enable Cathy to increase her income. But Jess's experience as a sports agent was irrefutable. 'The logic was simple,' he says. 'In the past I'd seen top sportspeople join highly successful management groups and become exhausted by over-commitments. Why does Cathy run fast? Why does she win certain big races at certain times? Because she has a serious program in place, four years in advance and it's regularly updated by Nick Bideau. The reason that Cathy is so successful is because she's still an athlete, not a talking head, racing around the countryside until she's rooted.'

Cecelia is curious about Jess, the tough talker with one eye and a pony-tail. 'I mean, was he a former bikie or a crim or what?' she asks. 'He's a bit rough, isn't he, but it just shows, you can't judge people by their appearance. Our lawyer said everything was above board, couldn't find fault. It was a relief because at the time I'd begun to question Nick, which was natural. But there was nothing to worry about because Cathy was being well looked after.'

Even so the schism left its mark. Jess was hurt that he was doubted. He had always rejoiced that Cathy could look at him, a gubba, and see somebody passionate about social justice for her people. 'I felt I'd always been there as a positive force for her, in some of her darkest moments,' he says. 'I thought she would know me better.' But Cathy was disappointed, too, that Jess argued with her not to withdraw from the MTC. She says, 'Instead of saying, "Well, if you feel that way, I'll respect your wishes ..."' She shrugs. 'I know they've done plenty of good things for me, but when my feelings should have been number one ...' They gave her professional advice.

Cathy stayed with Peta Powell for six weeks until a house she'd bought in Lyndhurst Crescent, Richmond, was ready. During that time she talked and talked to Peta, into the wee hours, night after night, sitting on Peta's balcony. 'She was very withdrawn, didn't eat and was quick to tears,' says Powell. 'She was lost.' Bideau rang Powell, probably the first time in seven years, enlisting her help to restore Cathy's sense of purpose in running. 'You've been around from the start,' said Nick. 'If you weren't genuine, you wouldn't still be here.' Powell felt sympathy for both parties. 'I don't think there's anything wrong with Nick,' she says. 'No-one was to blame. I think they both have so much to offer other people, just not each other any more.'

Nick believed Powell enjoyed the buzz of being seen with Cathy at nightspots, usually accompanied by rich food, alcohol and cigarettes—conduct unbecoming for an aspiring Olympic gold medallist. 'I was a hard head on that and didn't want to encourage it,' says Nick. 'I was probably wrong and I can see now that Peta could probably have been a good influence on Cathy if I hadn't been so guarded.'

Powell says Bideau wouldn't know about her social habits. She says, 'The first time I saw Cathy after Atlanta, yeah we celebrated, just once she let her hair down, and I dropped her off at 5 a.m. But Nick was making the same mistake then that he had all along. Cathy has a mind of her own. They think that if Cathy makes a bad decision, it's me or someone else who's put it into her head. And as for food. I'm fanatical, don't eat chocolate and I have to stop myself from picking on Cathy about her eating habits. What Nick forgets is that she's not 18 any more.'

One day early in 1997, in the courtyard of her new house, Cathy really spooked the horses. She was talking to Maurie, Peter Fortune and Nova Peris-Kneebone, the Aboriginal hockey gold medallist who Cathy had encouraged to move to Melbourne to train as a sprinter with Fortune. 'I want to take the year off,' Cathy announced. Maurie spluttered and pointed out the obvious, 'It will be very hard to come back.' Cathy said, 'Well, what about the domestic season?' Maurie looked doubtful, still not a good idea. Peris-Kneebone, listening, remarked to Cathy later, 'Sometimes I think you're just like a puppet on a string.' Even an experienced Olympic athlete like Nova couldn't relate to how regimented Cathy's life was. 'Yes,' says Cathy. 'But at the same time that discipline was one of the main reasons I achieved what I achieved.'

Cathy pressed her argument with the perfect precedent. Marie-José Pérec herself won the worlds in 1991 and the Olympics in 1992, eased in 1993—enabling Jearl Miles to become world 400m champion—before returning to win the European 400m in 1994, the worlds again in 1995 and the Olympics in 1996. 'So it's quite normal,' said Cathy. But an argument against her was that Pérec took time out, but only after she had ascended the summit, not before.

The whole 1996 Olympic campaign had caught up with Freeman and she wasn't the only one suffering. Damien Marsh, training with Gwen Torrence and Pauline Davis in the US, reported they were all unusually tired after training. 'There's always a lull after the Olympic year,' says Marsh. 'Your body just doesn't want to do it again. So it's not surprising Cathy was feeling burnt out. Everybody else was in the same boat.'

Cathy had just turned 24, yet Australia expected her to keep going and going. 'I had obligations to sponsors and advertisers and meet organisers,' she says. 'Deep down I loved running, but it had become a chore and it showed in my times. I was quite prepared to go back to Brisbane, go fishing with my nephews, and spend time with my mum.'

At that stage, Cathy had also become paranoid about people only wanting to know her because she ran fast. It was ironic that Cathy should start seeing members of Team Freeman as being trophy hunters, basking in her reflected glory. Taking a year off was entering unknown territory in terms of her believing she could then easily resume her former career, I suggested to Cathy. Maurie's advice would have been in the best interests of her career, I said. 'Yeah, but he's also supposed to be my friend,' she says. 'Jess, Maurie and Nick thought that if I took a year off it would stuff up the sponsors. But that was the last thing I would want.' She was unlikely to go off and do something really irrational, she says. 'What upsets me the most is that people don't understand me as well as they think they do. I sensed they were desperate and they should have had more faith in me.'

Her faith in herself was boosted when she rang Alexander Bodecker, the Nike executive who had first shown her how to drink tequilas with Michael Johnson at the end of the 1995 season. He had maintained sporadic contact with Cathy and encouraged her to listen to her own heart. 'He supported me, he understood,' says Cathy. 'I think about what I do. I would have kept training, that was the whole idea.'

Bideau's homes were forever open house to athlete friends, but tensions with Freeman were not helped when Irish athlete, Sonia O'Sullivan, the world 5000m champion, came to board with Nick at Stanley Street. She was recovering from her own personal and form difficulties and benefited from training through the Antipodean summer.

Bideau sought to nurse Freeman's fitness along, taking her to New Zealand where she won the 100 and 200m in the Robin Tait classic. Fortunately Falilat Ogunkoya, who ran second in the 200m, was equally out of shape. Training without verve, Cathy couldn't quarantine her running from her emotions. She didn't want to run in the Victorian championships, and eventually she and training partner Lauren Hewitt agreed to split the sprints between them. On 9 February 1997 Cathy won the state 200m in 24.10s, slower than when she ran 23.59s to win her first national 200m title as a 17-year-old, seven years earlier. A week later in Hobart she ran fifth to Gainsford-Taylor over 100m in 11.89s, again slower than she ran as a junior in 1990. Fifth!

TIME HEALS

It was her worst placing ever in an Australian grand prix. At the Nike Classic on 20 February, she ran better over 200m in 22.98s, though still behind Gainsford-Taylor's 22.84s. Fortunately Emma George's world record-breaking feats in the pole vault kept the spotlight off Freeman's demise.

But news of the split was soon gossip in the media. *New Idea* ran a large break-up story on 1 March, and Peter Fortune earned Bideau's wrath by talking about it to News Ltd journalist Mike Hurst. 'I made a few blunders,' admits Fortune. 'Hurstie's clever, he has a friendly, chummy banter with you, and all the time he's got his bloody little tape running.' Then Cathy received bad press from a visit she had always wanted to make, to talk to Aboriginal children in Redfern, Sydney. The visit was part of her mission to inspire, the side of her which prompts Peta Powell to remark, 'When she looks at Aboriginal children, if she had her way, she'd pick them all up and take them home.' Cathy is related by marriage to Pat O'Shane, Australia's first Aboriginal magistrate, and when Pat's nine-year-old nephew, Tjandamurra O'Shane, was set alight in a Cairns schoolyard, Cathy made a point of visiting him in hospital, no media, no publicity, no interviews.

Cathy had visited Redfern before, informally, just stopped the car near Eveleigh Street and, within 10 minutes, the word had spread—Cathy's here. A crowd of kids swamped her. 'I love kids, and I absolutely love the idea of being able to change the course of their lives,' says Cathy. 'It's not a responsibility or a pressure, it's just a wonderful position to be in.' Cathy's sponsor, John Moriarty of Balarinji designs, organised her next visit and Channel Nine's 'A Current Affair' requested exclusive footage of Cathy's street walk. But media jealousy of 'ACA' soon blew the visit apart, with demands for equal access and interviews from rival television crews. Cathy, together with Aboriginal Olympic hurdler, Kyle Vander-Kuyp, handed out some Nike products but, unexpectedly, hundreds of children gathered, adding to the chaos. 'It was just a media bombardment,' says Cathy. 'All I wanted was to move among the young Aboriginal people of Redfern.' Cathy had no trouble relating to the residents of Eveleigh Street. One of her endearing qualities is that she remains largely unchanged in her essential personality. 'You have to be sensitive to them, to what makes them feel comfortable,' she says. 'I know what makes them feel comfortable, because I was once very much like that myself.' With increasing maturity, Freeman feels more confident about commenting on the conflicts inherent in her upbringing and those besetting the nation. She knows better than most the condition of the Aboriginal nation. She has visited Aboriginal homes where the conditions have shocked her. 'I've seen drunken violence, where everything is a total mess, where the youths get drunk and fight,' she says. 'Where nothing is taken good care of, where there's alcohol abuse and nobody really respects their possessions. They're demoralised, they're used to living with no self-worth, their whole standard of living is low, third world really.

'It makes me sad yet, at the same time, seeing those things empowers me, makes me stronger, more determined. Because I'm black, I'm one of them and every time I win something or am honoured, it could be an example to some young Aboriginal who might think they have no better place to go than down. I want them to feel inspired.'

Vander-Kuyp had moved in to share with Cathy in her new home in Lyndhurst Street, Richmond and that eased her loneliness briefly. Except that Kyle had two differing moods, one being warm, friendly and open, the other being withdrawn and non-communicative. 'He was so nice, a good listener and liked teaching me things,' says Cathy. 'But he had his own demons.'

When the media started hounding Cathy for comments on the Pauline Hanson phenomenon, she rang Peter Fortune late one night and asked him to take her to the airport early the next morning. She took her dog with her which meant nobody else knew, because usually she left Frankie with Bideau's mother when she travelled. She escaped north to Mum in Brisbane. Fortune organised training partners for her there and she stayed for several weeks.

'She's a great mother, she gave me the hugs and kisses and meals I needed,' says Cathy. 'She has her moments, but when it really counts she's the most loving and giving person, just brilliant.' Indeed, Cecelia Barber is a woman around whom much orbits, personally and professionally. Like her mother, Alice Sibley, Cecelia has put aside her own troubled childhood to succour others, through an Aboriginal outreach centre, an Aboriginal teaching committee, and as a justice of the peace. As well as her four children, Gavin, Catherine, Norman and Garth, she brought up her grandson, Gavin, into his teens, and had another young grandson, George—both Gavin senior's sons—living with her.

Cecelia gave her daughter her favourite advice, 'Time heals all wounds.' Nick phoned and told Cecelia that one of Cathy's sponsors, about to renegotiate a contract, was going cold because of the adverse publicity. If Cathy did not intend to run, the company would have to restructure their corporate strategy. Cecelia relayed that to Cathy, who flared. 'I could tell by Mum's voice, money is an issue with her,' says Cathy. 'She'd been brought up in a way where money was really hard to get. Whereas I'd be more than happy to just have enough to live on from day to day.' She pauses and reconsiders. 'I mean, I think I'd be OK. It's hard to know because I'm so used to being able to travel and having money to spend whenever I want to.'

Cecelia backed off after their difference over the endorsement issue. 'I knew then I had to be careful what I said, because Catherine got angry with me over that.' Then Cathy was chosen as Telstra's Sports Personality of the Year, to be awarded by the Prime Minister in Melbourne. She didn't want to go but Cecelia, being more politically aware, felt on safer ground here. 'She was objecting, but I said,

"Catherine, you have to go, if you don't it could become political. It will be seen as a slap in the face for John Howard, and once the black people pick up on that they'll all get on the bandwagon."'

'Mu-u-u-um!' Cathy complained. But she went. 'I went because I'm more than just an athlete, aren't I?' she says exasperatedly. 'And that's what I don't like sometimes, especially at that time. I just hated it. I wasn't in the mood.' Cathy was also paying the price of stardom. 'I used to get frustrated and annoyed at the intrusions on my time,' she says. 'Then I realised that most people are actually part of you, they make you a part of them. I know that I carried on like a spoilt brat sometimes, but it seems that the only thing I do for myself, just for me, is running.'

Raelene Boyle had arrived in Melbourne as the subject of 'This Is Your Life' on television. Cathy appeared on the show and Raelene told how Cathy's funny messages on her answering machine, all giggles and impromptu comments, gave her an enormous kick when she was going through tough times. Boyle met Bideau and quickly sussed the breakdown. 'Well, you knew this was going to happen one day, didn't you?' she told Nick calmly. Yeah. And then she asked him an unusual question. Was he all right? For months people had been warning Bideau, 'Don't you ever hurt Cathy,' as though she was the only injured party. Boyle was only the second person to actually enquire how he was coping. The first? Cathy herself. If Nick ever needed her help, she'd be there straight away, she promised him.

Friends rallied around both of them. Driving back from Falls Creek one day, Chris Wardlaw got a call in his car, Nick wanted to see him. 'He was really down, in a shocking way,' says Wardlaw. 'Needed an hour or so to stand him up.' Peter Jess told Nick, 'Put your helmet on, put your head down and pedal harder.' But however down Nick felt, he was older and knew he was more resilient than Cathy at that time. He believed that Cathy would resolve her sadness more quickly by returning to that which she loved best—running. He sent Peter Fortune and Zoe Jess—Peter Jess's daughter who had joined the MTC—to retrieve Cathy from Brisbane. Bideau told Fortune, 'She'll kick and argue and fight, but don't budge on it. Be tough, say you're her coach, you want her back training.' To which Fortune says, 'That's all very well. I'm the coach. I should tell her this and that—when he's spent five years telling her not to take any notice of the coach, the coach is your enemy and I'm your friend. Talk about irony. Nick ensured I never had that very authority.'

This sparks indignation from Bideau who denies he undermined Fortune's authority. Only when Fortune failed to deliver with Cathy, did he step in and take control, says Nick. 'On training camps I often agreed with Cathy when she complained about his annoying habits,' he says. 'But she threatened to get rid of him regularly and I supported him by telling her that he was her coach, she needed him, and that he wasn't really that hard to put up with.'

For Fortune the facts were that Cathy had taken a two-month break after Atlanta, came back overweight and wasn't training well. 'She doesn't metabolise rich, fatty foods very well,' says Fortune. 'She tends to stack it on.' With Nick communicating with Cathy via Zoe Jess, and scarcely at all with Fortune, Cathy's entire support base was collapsing, but she was gradually finding her own feet. During the early days of her separation from Bideau, Cathy struck up a friendship with Nova Peris-Kneebone. 'We hung out, we were pretty tight, being black and having a bit in common,' says Cathy. But they fell out over a private matter and it became more grist for the media mill because Peris-Kneebone was renting Cathy's house and had to leave. This left Cathy lonely once more for Murri company. She was like an island in Melbourne, grateful for any social outing, even if it meant a few beers as well. Peter Jess had a horror of Cathy drinking. Yet hadn't she drunk red wine with him before the Stawell Gift the previous year? 'She drank that with meals, good for digestion,' he says. 'But to drink for drink's sake, with her finely tuned metabolism, it's like putting low-grade diesel into a high-performance racing engine. Just stuffs it right up.'

Before the national titles in Melbourne in the first week of March 1997, Cathy drummed herself up to be positive and told the media, yes, she thought she could beat Gainsford-Taylor in the 200m. That became a provocative headline for Melinda, and was news to Bideau, but he hadn't been attending training, so maybe she was fitter than he knew. She wasn't. She dawdled through the 400m in 52.09s, but came to life in the 200m, running a fast-closing 22.50s, to Melinda's 22.34s. 'No disgrace being beaten by Melinda,' said Cathy afterwards. 'I didn't say I was going to beat her, I said I could beat her.' Melinda had taken too many past pastings from Cathy to let the moment go without a mild dig at Cathy's prediction. But she also acknowledged what Cathy had been arguing for several seasons, 'Both Cathy and I have bigger fish to fry.' That evening, Atlanta national team manager, Margaret Mahony, noticed Cathy alone in the car park. She rang Nick and said, 'I'm really worried about Cathy. She looked like a lost soul last night.'

Three months into the split, Bideau had hired domestic help to fill his home duties for Cathy. He knew that if good food wasn't provided, Cathy would eat fast food. It was just one of her idiosyncrasies. She didn't cook. Nick flew off to the world indoors in Paris with Tim Forsyth and returned a week later, dismayed to find that Fortune had entered Cathy against a rampant Peris-Kneebone over 100m at an Olympic Park interclub. Cathy lost, Peris-Kneebone was delighted. 'A win's a win,' she said. Cathy couldn't give a stuff. 'OK, so the media make a big deal about me being beaten by Nova, so what?' she says. To Bideau it was bad management, it lacked class to have a runner of Cathy's world standing being defeated by a lesser athlete.

Maurie Plant suggested Cathy go to South Africa where Andy Norman had a few meets. Bideau jumped at the chance to get her out of the country. 'Do you want me to come?' Nick asked her. She thought hard before answering, 'Yes.' Despite everything, this is what she did, running, and Nick helped her run fast. Maurie travelled with Freeman, plus exciting new sprinter Matt Shirvington and 800m runner Paul Byrne. On 28 March she clocked 22.56s to win a 200m in Pietersburg. Nick flew in to join them and in her second race over 400m in Pretoria, she downed Ogunkoya over 400m in 50.70s, a vast improvement on her home form. Cathy's troubled spirits were not lost on Ogunkoya who thought she saw an opportunity to overturn her run of losses to Freeman. In Cape Town she pushed Freeman hard, but Cathy downed her again in 50.96s to Falilat's 51.33s.

The trip had its down moments for both Cathy and Nick. They seemed to take it in turns. One day Bideau would say he couldn't manage her any more, next day Cathy would say she didn't want him to. 'But don't get us wrong, most of the days we were pretty good,' says Cathy. 'It's just occasionally we were tense,' Nick concurred. 'After a while we were OK,' he says. 'She understood I really cared about her.' All this was interspersed with occasions when their surroundings made them forget themselves. 'We visited two wildlife parks, saw lions eating carcasses in the wild, which was cool,' says Cathy. 'And apes on the mountainside.' She also saw the cell in Robben Island prison, 5km off Cape Town, where Nelson Mandela spent 18 of his 27 years in gaol. 'Even the tour guide had been a prisoner there for 22 years,' says Cathy. 'I stood there and just imagined what it would have been like, how small the cells were, and what a colourless, lifeless world it was, and how crazy it would send you. But not him.' Local black groups, seeking to inspire women to get into sport, took her to address meetings. One image remains for Cathy. A small boy on a dirt road in a shanty town practising his golf swing with an old club, for a professional sport which probably has fewer black participants than any other internationally played game.

CATHY FREEMAN—A JOURNEY JUST BEGUN

Cathy trained at the famous cradle of white-dominated rugby union, Stellenbosch university, and then, in Cape Town, she spoke to women's groups, mostly black, in a rundown sports centre. 'We visited the home of the top female marathon runner in South Africa,' says Cathy. 'She was black and she lived in really poor conditions, probably worse than the missions back home.' It was all very salutary for Cathy and threw into sharp relief, by comparison, her own personal problems. All of which she hoped to leave behind as she prepared to train in America for six weeks in the countdown to the world championships in Athens in August. How Cathy hoped to accomplish this, living in the same apartment as Nick, remains one of the mysteries of the universe. They were good at athletics this pair, but not much in touch with the anger from their wounded souls.

23.
CONCHITA IN EL PASO.
PRE-WORLDS, 1997

Cathy's father, Norman Freeman, who could strum the guitar a bit, had a favourite song, the old Marty Robbins song, 'Out in the west Texas town of El Paso ...' It had such nostalgic memories for Cathy that when Maurie Plant said he'd heard the University of Texas, El Paso (UTEP), was a good place in America to spend six weeks training, she readily agreed. But even Plant wasn't prepared for the barren, treeless, dust storm-swept horizon that greeted them. 'This is the moon with oxygen,' joked Plant. 'I wanted few distractions but this is solitary confinement.' Cathy said it reminded her of Hughenden, in western Queensland, where she lived briefly in her childhood. El Paso has a mountain desert climate, freezing cold at night, searing heat in the middle of the day. Cathy told her older brother Gavin, 'That's the last time I make a decision based on one of Dad's favourite songs!' Yet it was here, in this stark, alien environment that Cathy finally faced down her own crippling dependency on Nick Bideau, where she asserted her individuality and began the long, hard road to rehabilitating herself as a fully independent, adult athlete.

Once they settled in to El Paso it took only a few days for

an argument between Cathy and Nick to develop into a crisis. They were asking the impossible of each other. Cathy responded by quitting training. Nick said he was out of there. Plant pleaded with him to wait until Cathy's training partners arrived at the end of the week. Nick said, 'Get Fort, fast!' Maurie knew Cathy and Fortune had grown apart, but by then she wasn't believing in anyone, and at least Fortune was a known figure.

Maurie rang Fortune, 'It's blown up. How quickly can you get here?' Fortune, weary of the Freeman rollercoaster, felt an allegiance to his young Melbourne runner Lauren Hewitt whom he was preparing for the Athens world titles. Then Cathy rang. 'I think I need you over here. Can you come?' she asked. Fortune was ambivalent, felt tugged. 'I didn't want to go, I'd given up on that scene,' he says. 'Well, I hadn't really, because I was still providing them with training schedules, but I'd had enough.' He booked a flight several days ahead, but then a few days later, Cathy rang again. 'Why aren't you here by now?' she asked anxiously. Maurie immediately got him an earlier flight. It was panic in El Paso.

Then, like the cavalry over the hill, came the Melbourne Track Club troops—Jason Richardson, 28, a quick-quipping, 1993 Stawell Gift winner who had converted to 400m; Cameron McKenzie, 28, equally witty, member of the Aussie 4 x 400m relay team in Atlanta; and quiet straight man Mark Moresi, another respected Melbourne 400m dasher. They all had long-range plans for the 1998 Commonwealth Games, and all were laidback, sensitive, cool dudes, who were out to get fit and have a good time.

Some 16 hours after the lads arrived, Nick called in at their apartment 100m from his own and briefed them on events. Richardson left the room to go to the toilet and, when he emerged, a minute or so later, McKenzie and Moresi were sitting glum-faced on the loungeroom floor. 'What's wrong? asked Jason. Nick's gone, off to Philadelphia, they said. Said Jason, 'Gees, I didn't think I was in the toilet that long!' Nick

1997. Athens. World title finish. Cathy just outlasts good friend, Jamaica's Sandie Richards. She won despite personal problems and her lack of absolute top form. (*Photo*: courtesy of Andrew and Peter Loughman)

Peter Fortune, Cathy's coach (left) with Nick Bideau. Though they argued, they balanced each other well in nurturing Cathy's career. (*Photo*: courtesy of *Runner's World*)

Maurie Plant, Cathy's circuit agent. His humour belies a reputation as a shrewd athletics judge. He is invaluable in assisting with Cathy's race schedule.

Peter Jess, Cathy's accountant, sports nut and ardent Freeman supporter with Cathy after her Atlanta silver medal.

1997. Athens. World 400m final. Relief rather than rapture after she won gold by a hair's breadth. Note the lane number on her thigh. Winning from lane one made her victory all the more laudable.
(*Photo:* courtesy of Sporting Pix)

1997. Athens. Now it sinks in, after all her troubles, heartache and pain — world champion. She had endured a 'beep beep beep' of a year, she said.

1997. Athens. World 400m. With two women she greatly admires on the 400m circuit—left, silver medallist and friend, Jamaican Sandie Richards; and right, bronze medallist, American Jearl Miles-Clark.

1997. Athens. On the Acropolis, spending time paying homage to whichever gods smiled upon her the previous evening. The Athenians loved Cathy, because of her friendly nature and because she was from Melbourne. (*Photo:* courtesy of Sporting Pix)

1998. Adelaide. At the Optus grand prix, in her Melbourne Track Club rig. A picture of fitness, she was on track to kick butt in the Commonwealth Games in Kuala Lumpur until injury intervened.
(*Photo:* courtesy of Sporting Pix)

1998. Limbering up before a meet. The whole process of warming up for her sub-minute 400m race takes about an hour. Only the uninitiated would breach her focus during that hour.

1997. Sydney. Cathy and Carl Lewis ham it up at a schools carnival. He helped Cathy deal with media after Aboriginal elders implored her not to run in Sydney 2000.
(*Photo:* courtesy of *The Age*)

1997. Melbourne. Yarra Primary School, Richmond. Cathy has an instant rapport with children, lines them up and patiently signs their autograph books for an hour after meets.
(*Photo:* courtesy of *The Age*)

1998. Perth. Australian of the Year with her award after the ceremony. She said she was more proud of this than the gold medal she won in Athens. (*Photo:* courtesy of *The Age*)

1997. Brisbane. Cathy has never lived at home since she left for boarding school aged 14. Perhaps this is why mother and daughter are so emotionally close.

Left: 1998. Melbourne. New friend, Alexander Bodecker, a US Nike executive from Oregon, plays a supportive role. His presence helped calm Cathy during tumultuous times in Athens.
Right: 1998. Melbourne. With Frankie—not the fine Namibian sprinter, Frankie Fredericks, but his namesake, Frankie Freeman, the chihuahua cross whose mortal enemy is an aggressive Willie wagtail at Olympic Park.

1998. A pensive Freeman. Her future is mapped until Sydney 2000, and maybe until Athens 2004. After that a family is among her plans.

1994. In Kakadu, with her flag and her country, serene in her surrounds. Australian and Aboriginal, one and the same, she says, and proud of it.

flew to Philadelphia, where Sonia O'Sullivan had her training base, and rang Richardson from there, asking him to move into the apartment to keep Cathy company until Fortune arrived. Nick subsequently called Jason for updates on Cathy's training progress but didn't call Cathy once in five weeks. It was his own form of cold turkey. 'It was really tough, but I had to do it,' he says. 'It was the only thing that would work.'

Cathy wanted to go home. 'Running hasn't always been my priority,' she says. 'I don't think it ever will be. It's up there, but it's not as important as a loving relationship.' Or the loss thereof, which so depressed her that she no longer possessed the imagination to make the connection between her actions and their consequences. So Jason provided it for her. 'That's great, you'll go home, see your mum and kiss your nephew,' he said. 'Then you'll sit around and after a few days you'll start thinking about Athens. And after a few weeks you'll be going stir crazy. You might think you're unhappy here, but it won't be anything to how you'll feel back there.'

Fortune arrived and struck Freeman in the same mood. 'The first training session we did she was generally unhappy and I told her we'd have to talk,' says Fortune. 'I told her, "I can't keep pushing if you aren't willing to give it a go." She was actually very reasonable and said, "Look, I don't know why I got you here because I don't think I'm going to keep going."'

In Brisbane, Cathy's mother was the third in line to field Cathy's doubts when she rang and told of her tentative homecoming. Cecelia knew Cathy must be devastated as never before, but encouraged her, 'You've been dreaming about this for years, you've planned this all your life. If you want me to go over there, get me there.' Cathy replied, 'No, Mum. I'll be all right.' To which Cecelia said, 'If that's the case, you stay there and ride this through.'

Fourth in line was sports psychologist Jeff Simons back in Melbourne. 'I rang him from Texas, because he had helped me through the roughest period of my life during the break-up,' says Cathy. 'And he really helped me work things through again. See, deep down I knew that running is such a part of me that I would have regretted watching the world championships on television. In fact I would have hated it. So I guess I had no choice.' Having resolved to stay on, Cathy took to training with a will. Says Fortune, 'She really knuckled down, almost ridiculously so. We trained at 10 a.m. and she'd be at the car at 9.59 a.m. saying, "Where the hell is everybody?"'

The troops called Cathy for a powwow. They told her: forget the landscape, it's medium altitude—about the same as Canberra—useful for building oxygen-carrying haemoglobin cells in the bloodstream; forget the heat, it will help you acclimatise for Athens, venue for the world titles in three months time. They would eat well, but follow a strict diet program from a book called *The Zone*, which determined precisely how many grams of protein and the like they were allowed each day. UTEP's facilities were first class; quite a few Euro-circuit athletes were training there. McKenzie outlined their planned regime to her. Track and gym every day, about 10 sessions a week, of which half were really vital and for which she would need a good night's sleep and a healthy breakfast. The other five were less vital, if she wanted a day off, fine. But Cathy didn't miss a session.

Still, she wasn't sleeping well. Emotional overload, the guys agreed. Until Richo called in at 9.30 one night and there was Cathy mixing herself a strong cup of instant coffee. 'What are you doing?' he asked astounded. 'You can't do that. No wonder you're not sleeping well.' He tipped it down the sink and made her a cup of herbal tea. Of course, said Cathy, she knew that. But she was so engrossed with her thoughts she didn't notice her bad habit.

On the track, Cathy introduced them to the Freeman speciality. 'She'd run pretty much spot-on for the first few repetitions,' says McKenzie. 'Then the last one, you'd come off the bend and she'd be beside you, giving it absolutely everything. And I'm going, "Oh, gees, I don't feel like this," but you'd find yourself having to respond. She was very, very competitive.' Jason Richardson calls her the little perfectionist. 'If we're doing two laps warm-up, she starts on the line and finishes there. I mean it's only jogging, but with her there's no fading in the last 10 metres and walking.'

Off the track she was the same. In six weeks she lost one game of Scrabble. 'She drove us nuts,' says Cameron. 'Take 15 minutes for her to have a go, have us wondering what great word she was going to put down and it would only be a two-letter word, but in a valuable space.' Richardson says the three boys instinctively made it their business to make Cathy laugh. 'Be idiots really, the village clowns,' he says. 'And it worked.' He found her sociable but saw how other women might not. 'She's so big in track and field, a lot of girls are intimidated by her,' he says. 'It's no use her training with girls because they can't push her. So naturally she's going to become mates with the boys she trains with.'

Cathy is eternally grateful. Because of their unwearying friendship and affection, she drew back from the abyss of depression and grew to enjoy one of her happiest ever training camps. 'They made training an absolute pleasure and got me through the season,' she says. 'Especially Jase, but all three. I was a lucky girl.' It was the closest Cathy ever experienced to having a close, young group of peers to enjoy at training, even if they were all male.

UTEP was on the Mexican border and early in their stay the four musketeers ventured into the Mexican border town, Juarez, for a day trip of shopping and sightseeing. They returned as Conchita Freeman, Chilli McKenzie, Two Dogs Moresi and Peluso Richardson. Conchita stuck most; she was called nothing else over there for weeks and still gets it when the boys meet her today.

On another trip McKenzie bought some lapis arrowhead pendants but discovered a little later he had been overcharged on his credit card. When he went back to complain, the excitable owner suddenly whipped a stun-gun from under his counter, held it against McKenzie's chest and started swearing. Cathy, who had not seen the gun, leapt in, pointing at the owner and saying, 'You can't talk to my friend like that.' Says McKenzie, 'I was sweating that he'd get angry with Cathy as well and all I could see was the *Herald Sun* headline, "Freeman Stun-Gunned, McKenzie to Blame."' Cathy retreated to the door, protesting still, until the police arrived. Flattered by the presence of an Atlantan silver medallist, the police ensured Chilli's money was refunded.

Midway through the camp Cathy disappeared for a weekend. She had been telephoning her Nike friend, Alexander Bodecker, who lives in Portland, Oregon. Among his Nike hats, Bodecker was the company's contact with the star Brazilian soccer team. He travelled extensively with them and had met Cathy at various Nike functions around the world. When Cathy finally moved into Lyndhurst Street, Richmond, her friends had urged her: if you want to talk to him, call him. So she did.

And that missing weekend, she spent with Bodecker in Miami watching Brazil play a match. She told Fortune and the boys where she was going and that was cool with them, but privacy is as rare as a precious ointment to Cathy. Sure enough, when she returned to her hotel room after the match, there was the telephone answering machine light blinking. 'Catherine darling, this is your mother here. I hope you're all right. I'm just a bit worried about you.' Oh M-u-u-um! It was 3 April 1997. She was 24.

Back in El Paso, Fortune was no more compatible in the apartment with Cathy than was Nick. Jason Richardson saw it clearly. 'Fort annoyed the living daylights out of her, and she treated him something shocking,' he says flatly. 'It was tough for everyone but I reckon Fort did a good job under trying circumstances.' Cathy believes she and Fortune broke down because Nick was no longer in the equation. She says,

CONCHITA IN EL PASO

'With them both there, everything was secure and in place. They were the opposites yet they balanced each other up. Nick was so confident and dominating, whereas Fort was more sensitive and less gruff. So when Nick was over the top I could always go to Fort, who was a fatherly man.'

Says Fortune, 'Coaching is a difficult game, so interpersonal.' But he believes that El Paso set Cathy up for her approaching European season. 'Nick and I vehemently disagree on this, and we agree to disagree,' he says. 'Nick says she didn't get fit, but Nick wasn't there. All right, she didn't lose weight, and maybe even gained a little. She was eating well, but it wasn't fat.' The boys argue that how could Cathy not be fit when they certainly were? 'She wasn't the Freeman model of Atlanta 1996, wasn't as intense with her diet,' says Jason. 'But look at us. I was in the best shape of my life. I went to Europe and ran six consecutive PB's. Cameron was injured in Europe but the benefit showed in the next Australian season when he ran two PBs.'

The group flew up to Oregon for the Prefontaine meet in Eugene, about 200km south of Portland, Alexander Bodecker's home town. Cathy ran third over 200m to American Inger Miller and Bahamian Chandra Sturrup, in 23.09s, the slowest she has ever run outside Australia. 'I didn't take it seriously,' says Cathy. 'I was just so happy to see Alexander. I was laughing heaps that day. It was so nice to be happy after all the drama I'd been through.' Fortune returned to Australia and Cathy relinquished a little of the work ethic she had employed as a surrogate for absent affection in El Paso. Instead of returning to Texas, the group stayed 10 days in Portland. Maurie didn't like it and rang Nick. 'Maurie, I'm not going to tell her, it's not my area any more,' he said.

How did she train in Portland? 'Oh shithouse!' says Jason Richardson. 'She just went backwards in those 10 days. Unbelievable. She trained with us, but we'd have to wake her at 10 o'clock every morning. Previously Cathy would have been up for a couple of hours, and here she was rubbing sleep from her eyes at the track. It wasn't the same little group that we'd had in El Paso. Actually it was a miracle that we got her to most sessions in Portland.' At first Cathy ruefully agreed. 'I thought I was training well in Portland, but looking back, I wasn't,' she says. 'Nor was I eating so well.' In a later conversation Cathy qualifies this admission. 'It's overstating it to say I lost fitness in Portland,' she says. 'You don't lose fitness in 10 days. I thought I was doing all right at the time. I don't think I went backwards. Or if I did, nobody told me so. I really thought I was doing the right thing.'

So both Nick and Fortune were right. Cathy was fit when she left El Paso, but had lost a little by the time she arrived in London. The finger points straight at Alexander Bodecker. Was he, as was rumoured, wining and dining her, ice-cream and out dancing late at night? Bodecker laughs. 'I know that's the myth, but during her stay I got an emergency call and I was in Europe for five of those 10 days,' he says. 'But that really misses the point. I don't control Catherine, I don't want to. I don't tell her what to eat, when to rise, when to train. That's her responsibility and her coach's.' Bodecker sees Freeman as a self-motivated athlete, who loves to run. 'She needed a little space,' he says. 'Her coach, Fort, and her manager, Nick, had played a significant role since she was 18. But she was now 24, and she was definitely feeling over-protected.'

When I repeated that conversation to Cathy, she clapped her hands and exclaimed, 'Oh, thank you, thank you!' Thank you to Bodecker for treating her as an adult, she meant, even if it meant she lost a little fitness for the world titles. Cathy says she realised she had to take more responsibility for her actions and that in the transition from over-protected environment to independent living, she was bound to err in judgement. Meanwhile the all-male Team Freeman support crew were adapting to the arrival of a new influence in Cathy's life, Alexander Bodecker. After six years of exclusive control of Freeman's life, accepting Bodecker's presence was proving a difficult transition for everyone.

Bideau vehemently defends his protective treatment of Cathy as the only path that he knew for her to realise her potential as an athlete. He was never game to let her float free because he feared that, like her brother Norman who eventually preferred football to athletics, Cathy would find other pursuits in life that were more enjoyable, and required less discipline, than running.

Bideau flew to London to organise another house near Hampton Hill for the crowd of MTC athletes arriving. They arrived in dribs and drabs; Cathy's training partner Pat Seal and hurdler Kyle Vander-Kuyp one day, Jason Richardson and Cathy the next. Nick couldn't believe the athlete who walked through Heathrow arrivals gate—Cathy Freeman, weighing in around 57–58kg, as against her ideal running weight of 51–52kg. She was a stone overweight, a stark contrast to the picture postcard Freeman from Atlanta, so admired by Chris Wardlaw.

Richardson tried to explain, 'Nick, 10 days ago ...' but Bideau said, 'Richo, I've seen her in good shape, and this ain't it!' Richardson is an up-front, candid character and he recognises some of this trait in Cathy too. 'If you ask her if you look like Tom Cruise, she'll say no way, you're plain ugly,' says Jason. 'You've got to love her for it, she's brutally honest. And she was brutal to herself. She knew she was carrying weight. In London she was paranoid about it from then on.'

Bideau organised the arrivals into two houses—Cathy with Tim Forsyth, Pat Seal, Kyle Vander-Kuyp and 1500m champion Margaret Crowley in Cathy's house in Deerhurst Crescent, Hampton Hill. And in another house nearby, he boarded Richardson and McKenzie, 800m runner Paul Byrne, and steepler Chris Unthank. Damien Marsh visited, as well as Peter Jess and masseur Garry Miritis.

Nick stayed with Sonia O'Sullivan, two kilometres away,

put a fax machine in Cathy's house to send messages and ran the houses like a quartermaster, even down to showing Cathy's crowd how to cook low-fat, high-protein meals like stir-fried scallops, fresh vegetables and ginger, served with boiled rice. Surrounded by such familiarity and dedication, Cathy gradually began to focus on the world titles now about nine weeks off. Her training improved from robotically following a program to tough, high-quality sessions.

Pat Seal was an old sparring partner from Melbourne, and he and Cathy went for walks in the park behind their house, among the free-roaming deer. One day they sat in an ancient church graveyard in Kingston talking about their fathers. 'Her dad and my dad both died about the same time,' says Pat. 'My dad was a good athlete and her dad was a good footballer so I suppose, sport-wise, we'd both been inspired by our fathers. She was good to talk to, personal discussions never worried her.'

Bideau had recruited Seal from retirement in 1995, but his PB of about 50s, which was equal to Freeman's then, was now substantially slower. He made up for it with effort. 'I'm a good trainer. I can do a lot of reps at a pretty high rate and I enjoy that, even though at times it's pretty traumatic, putting your body through it,' he says. 'I'm probably half a metre in front of her most of the time, that's me going 110 per cent and her 80 per cent. Nick would come up to me and say in front of her, "OK Pat, I want you to really take this out hard and hammer yourself." She'd hear this and I'd get nervous, and when I do I stop talking. That really agitates her, and she'd respond. We were extremely competitive, but at the end we'd laugh about it.'

Seal believes Freeman trains only as hard as she has to and that if she trained as hard as she is physically capable, she would blow the world record away. 'That's my perception,' he says. 'If she ran 100 per cent at training, she'd run amazing times. But in another way maybe she couldn't, because something would have to give. She'd find it too mentally hard, lose enjoyment and probably lose interest. But physically she has it in her.'

For the first time ever, Nick didn't attend Cathy's first three races in Europe, so Maurie reported from the front. Her first race was over 200m in Helsinki on 20 June, but she was a different-looking athlete by then. One morning, in Camden Town, London, she watched Richardson, Vander-Kuyp and Rohan Robinson have haircuts of varying styles, but all very short. As the day wore on, Cathy said to Richo, 'My day's unfulfilled. I want my hair cut.' In the markets they found a tiny hairdressing booth, but Robinson protested to Cathy, 'You can't do it, you're a role model for kids. Don't do it, you'll thank me later.' It was a red rag to Cathy. But she was still hesitating when, at that moment, a gorgeous young woman with collar-length hair, the same as Cathy's, marched in and said, 'All off, zero length.' Richo, who had been promoting this for Cathy, exclaimed, 'Ah, an angel sent from heaven to show the way.'

Says Cathy, 'This girl looked great afterwards, so I started at No 5 blade, then No 4, and Kyle was saying "No more. No less than 4!" He couldn't watch so he had to go outside, and Rohan was saying "No, no!" and Jase is saying, "Get it off!" It was the funniest scene, people were watching, the boys were going off, and I went right down to 1.5. It felt great.' A little later she went back and got a No 1 for the world championships.

People told Cathy afterwards her haircut must have had something to do with her break-up. I quoted to her Dannii Minogue who said that, after break-ups, women often act rebelliously like colouring their hair outrageously, taking sudden trips, or splurging on expensive clothes. In Dannii's case, she posed for *Playboy*! Cathy laughed. 'I did it to show that I never really care for other people's thoughts or opinions about me,' she says. 'It definitely affected me psychologically. It made me feel heaps more masculine, more aggressive and tougher. But at the same time it made me feel a lot more comfortable with being a woman. Cameron McKenzie said it made a statement like, "I'm gorgeous, but don't f— with me."'

She shocked the circuit, especially when she had her nose pierced as well. That was a shock to her! For an instant, a sharp pain shot down her cheek to her mouth, along her jawline and up to her ear. Her hair was the talk of the competitors' bus to the track in Helsinki. Frankie Fredericks kept muttering, 'What have you done? What have you done?' Cathy says Frankie's grandmother had always told him a woman's beauty resides in her hair, and Cathy's was almost all gone! Cathy ran 22.80s behind Gainsford-Taylor's 22.75s in Helsinki and looked better for the run at her next start in Lucerne, on 26 June, where in wind and rain she defeated two Americans over 400m in 50.99s.

From the outset Nick had broken the weight factor into manageable portions—nine weeks to the worlds, a pound a week, easy to lose that. En route Cathy bombed out in a poor 200m race in Sheffield, going down to Melinda Gainsford. 'Nobody could talk to me on the way home in the train,' says Cathy. 'I was so furious. I was frustrated because I didn't know how fit I was and the world champs were creeping up on me. Even next morning, in the breakfast area at home, Jason asked me innocently what I was doing, and I snapped, "What do you think I'm doing? What Does It Look Like? *I'm getting breakfast!*" I didn't mean to be rude, but I was on edge. Sheffield made me just so determined to go out and give it a good go in Oslo.'

The world championship 400m in Athens was run on 4 August 1997, but for Cathy it was a race in two parts, with the first enacted in Oslo exactly a month earlier. Team Freeman may have been disintegrating but Bideau and Plant reached for the freeze-dried fox soup as they contemplated how to lift a non-super-fit Freeman to the world title. First there was the perennial problem of Marie-José Pérec. Nick consulted a friend from French television, Mark Mauret, on

Pérec's mindset. Mauret thought Mary-Jo would run the 200m, not the 400m, in Athens. He also said he was sorry to hear about Nick and Cathy. 'How did you know?' asked Nick, puzzled. 'Marie-José told me,' said Mark. She had said that Ogunkoya would win in Athens from Jearl Miles, who had run 49.40s in the US trials. 'Didn't rate Cathy, eh?' asked Nick. Mark quoted Pérec, 'No, Freeman is out of shape. She haf lurv problems.'

Cathy invited Alexander Bodecker to Oslo to watch her race, rang Peta Powell in Melbourne and giggled, 'I'm worried how he'll react to my haircut.' Here was further reason to excel in Oslo. It was the first time that Bodecker had seen her run, and, as when she had her parents in the crowd, making others proud of her was a definite motivator for Cathy.

After missing Cathy's early races, Nick had re-entered the fray, flying to Oslo and attending the strawberries and cream party which the Oslo director, Svein-Arne Hansen, threw at his house for athletes on the Thursday afternoon before the Friday night meet.

Nick spotted Cathy talking to Bodecker, marched over, stuck out his hand, and said, 'Welcome to the European circuit, Sandy. Great to see you.' He then gave Cathy her lane number, told her where she could pick up her race numbers, and said he would see her before her race tomorrow night for a talk. And turned and walked away. One small walk for Nick, one giant step towards peace with Cathy. Or so he hoped. That night, in the bar of the Oslo Plaza hotel, Maurie confessed his fears to Nick. 'She's lost it, she's not even going to make the final in Athens,' he said, shaking his head. 'She'll run no better than 50.2s here.' Nick calmed him. 'She still looks a bit heavy, but trust me, she's not going that badly.'

The Oslo 400m was not a scheduled race. Most of the other 400m runners were racing in Lausanne two nights earlier. Having her own home in London meant Cathy didn't have to chase the race meet and accommodation merry-go-round all over Europe. Says Sandie Richards, 'I was in

Lausanne and we didn't even know there was a quarter on in Oslo. I guess they put one on for Cathy at the last minute.' Well, not quite the last minute. A week earlier Maurie and Nick had implemented their shrewd strategy. They needed Cathy to run a fast 400m to boost her own uncertain confidence, and possibly scare Pérec from entering the 400m in Athens. Plant asked Arne Hansen to include a 400m on his race list, but asked him not to advertise it with the agents of any of the circuit stars. Nick wanted an easy field so that Cathy could run a controlled, untrammelled race. Hansen agreed because Freeman had always supported the meet and always ran well for him. There would be no Pérec, Ogunkoya, Miles or Richards.

On race day, Nick chatted with Garry Miritis as he massaged Tim Forsyth. He put the question to the two-man panel: should he use what Pérec had said to motivate Cathy? Yep, they were unanimous, go for it. Thus at the track that evening he sat down with Cathy and explained the scenario. 'Pérec says that you're out of shape, can't win in Athens,' he said. 'She says she's not running the 400m in Athens, but you know what Mary-Jo's like.' Cathy knew. As far as she was concerned, Pérec would be there. Said Nick, 'She's thinking of running all right, but she's scared of you. If you run well tonight, she'll drop off. Okay, you're not in the best shape of your life, but you're not that far out of shape either. It's sunny, it's warm. You've set two Australian records on this track, you like it. You trained well last month and you've already locked down a 50.99s in bad weather. You can run low 50s—50.1s or 50.2s here.' In the last week before Olso, Cathy had put together a couple of sessions which showed Nick she could run sub-50s, but didn't dare say so for fear of setting up false expectations.

It was the most plausible pre-race instruction an athlete could wish for, and Cathy listened intently absorbing the message, just like in the old days. Go out hard in the first 200m, said Nick. 'Are you sure I won't get tired?' said Cathy,

CONCHITA IN EL PASO

faint old Gothenburg fears surfacing. No, said Nick. You'll bring it home, but a fast time requires a fast first 200m. Cathy examined the race field, and asked Nick suspiciously, 'How come the field is so weak?' Nick clicked into dissembling mode to boost the credentials of the hand-picked field. 'Weak? That's Bisi Afolabi there, 50.50s runner, in good shape,' he said. Then gave several other runners false pedigrees. 'It's a tough field, you'll have to concentrate here.' Did Cathy believe him? Didn't need to. It was their game, and it unfailingly motivated Cathy. Nick walked through the infield and stationed himself at the 200m mark. As Cathy sped by in quick time, he called out, 'Yes!' and knew she heard him. She attacked the bend and, under no challenge, held firm down the straight. Nick checked the track clock: 49.39s, the fastest of the season, 1/100th faster than Miles's 49.40s. Nick clenched a fist. It didn't come better than this for the arch-strategist.

When Cathy saw the clock she couldn't believe it. 'I was so happy,' she says. 'It meant I wasn't as unfit as I thought I was.' She ran over and excitedly hugged Maurie, gave her finish flowers to Bodecker and then, when Nick arrived from his 200m posting, gave him a hug too. As Nick climbed the fence, Maurie came over and said mock-earnestly, 'Now, Nick, this will be the last time this year that you will hear me say this: I was wrong.' They both laughed, the co-conspirators were back in town! In Stockholm soon after, Cathy ran second over 200m to US sensation Marion Jones and then moved on to Stuttgart where Ogunkoya was awaiting her. Ogunkoya had defeated Jearl Miles in Lausanne in a sub-50s run and once more thought she had Cathy's measure. Nick saw Pérec in the stadium just before the race, saw her ostentatiously leave, but was informed later that she had stopped and watched the race from a private position. Cathy, tired from heavy training, was sluggish to start and, for the first time, Ogunkoya led her into the straight. 'There are certain people you know you are going to beat,' says Cathy. 'And there are people who are going to be tough. The only person who's tough is Pérec. The others, even if I'm unfit, they're going to have to dig deep to beat me. I don't mean to sound cocky, it's more a comfort thing.' Sure enough, with 50m to go, Cathy lifted and caught the strong Nigerian in the last five strides. Time, 49.86s. Pérec departed the stadium.

After that race Sandie Richards, who finished fourth, fainted, not from the race itself, but through travel exhaustion. She and 400m world record holder, Butch Reynolds, had flown nine hours from California the previous night, plus a two-hour drive from the airport. After 300m in the race she felt her legs go. Richards couldn't take the travelling any more, back and forth from the US, and so enquired from world 800m champion Cuban Ana Quirot if she could train in Spain with the Cubans. Nick overheard and remembered that most of his MTC athletes had departed for an Australian team training camp in Budapest. Only Crowley and Marsh were left. 'You can come to London and train with us, if you like,' said Nick. Sandie recalls the exchange. 'I go, Huh!' she says. 'I was in shock because every quarter-miler wants to train with other quarter-milers, especially if they are faster, so I said, "Are you sure?" Because I was friends with Cathy at that stage and I didn't want a problem where if I happen to beat her, she passes me on the track afterwards and won't say hello.' As Pérec had done to her. So Sandie came to London for three weeks of intensive training. Cathy welcomed female training company. 'We got on famously,' she says. 'Occasionally we'd get on each other's nerves, but who doesn't?' On the track, Cathy thrived with a happy, chatty woman beside her instead of her motley males. 'She's got a great work ethic and a big, strong heart,' says Cathy. 'She hasn't got a lot of speed, but boy, she can certainly keep running.'

Bideau introduced Richards to quality sets she'd never done before in her life. 'One particular session, I still hate it, is six 200m, in around 24–25s with 5, 4, 3, 2, and 1 minute rests in between,' says Sandie. 'When it gets to the last one your legs feel like the whole world is in them. It feels like when you're at 350m in a quarter, when it's real, real bad. And it was funny, because Cathy is used to that work and knows what to expect, but I didn't. We get to the last one and she flew off, so I went too and my God! when I finished, I puked. But I didn't care because I was happy, I was pushing myself. I was in 50.30s shape when I went to London, but I could feel they would get me below that 50s barrier.'

Some 18 months earlier, Richards had been disappointed at being used as Cathy's hare for Freeman to break 50s in Melbourne. Now the friendship between the three so blossomed that Richards was able to say, 'Cathy is a great girl. Sometimes she is mad, but she is a really, really nice person. And I know now Nick is one of the kindest persons I have met, you know. Every day I thank God for my personality for being able to meet good people who mean me well.'

Richards's strength had never converted to speed. In Atlanta, the first six broke 50s, Sandie came in seventh and did not break 50s. 'I was in great shape then so it was disappointing for me because that was the fastest race ever in an Olympic final,' she says. 'And whether I got a medal or not I wanted to run 49s, because people I knew I could beat every day, they went and ran 49s that day. I'm as fast as Jearl Miles and she ran 49.5s in Atlanta. I should have been up there. I was crushed for a while.' Her career was also on the line. Jamaica does not have Australia's advertising wealth and Richards was not as famous at home as Merlene Ottey or Grace Jackson. At 28, she needed a result to secure new sponsorship contracts.

Bideau, watching the pair train, saw Richards's aggression but saw how Cathy had her covered for speed, if not strength. After a hard workout on any given day, the next day Cathy would just go through the motions. Nick approved, he didn't want her to tire. It was a fine balance he sought. 'If Athens had been just one 400m race, she'd have killed them,' he says. The problem would be the four rounds, two heats on one day, and no rest day between the heats, semi-final and final. Four races in three days! Cathy lacked the essential early season fitness to run them all aggressively.

Richards slotted into Cathy's domestic set-up too, readily cooking, cleaning and washing. In return Nick never asked her for rent or any other costs. The eldest of seven children, her mother unmarried, Richards grew up poor in Jamaica, and by 17 was in the US on a track scholarship. 'You need to be street smart in the US, you could be educated, have money, but if you're not street smart, you got problems,' she says. In short, Sandie acquired all the savvy and skills that Cathy, protected by Cecelia and then Nick, did not.

Sandie saw it. 'I tell Nick this every day,' she says. 'Maybe if he had let Cathy do some stuff on her own. But he loved her so much, he wanted to protect her so bad, he did everything, so now there's stuff she can't do. I met Cathy's mother Cecelia and she said to me, "Nick and me, we're part of the problem." And I said, "Well, you all did something wrong along the line." Don't misunderstand me, I love Cathy to death. But sometimes I marvel and think, "Wow, if I had someone like Nick, I'd be a rich person, because I'd be running 49.40 every day just like her." So Cathy's been lucky.'

Before leaving for Athens, Sandie queried Bideau on her chances. 'He never usually says what particular time you're going to run, but he will give you a ball-park figure,' she says. Nick told her, 'The worst you can come is fifth in the final.' Sandie threw her hands up. 'No, no! I don't want to come fifth! I want a medal, I don't care which medal.' Nick came at it another way. 'You're ready to run, you're in 49.5s shape.' At London airport, Nick gave his ticket to Margaret Crowley to accompany Cathy in business class. He walked towards economy and said to Richards, 'Come on, Sandie. I can't help you too much, can't have you beating our girl. She's got to have the comfortable ride.'

24.
First Among Billions. Worlds, Athens 1997

Athens, Olympic city of 2004, is an Aegean metropolis of two million, which bakes in summer in a blistering midday sun, easing to blood-red evening sunsets. The Athenians took Cathy Freeman to their heart once she arrived. She was Australian, most favoured nation with Greeks since everyone seems to have a relative or friend who lives there. Indeed Melbourne, Cathy's home city, is reputed to be the largest centre of Greek population outside Athens itself. Being black gave her a certain exotic cachet and on television her naturally happy nature appealed, aided by her amusing, cheeky hair-fuzz look. To top it off, when some athletes complained that the championships stadium track was too hard, Cathy said she liked it just fine, thank you.

In 480 BC the Spartans of Greece, though heavily outnumbered, heroically defended a narrow pass at Thermopylae, in eastern Greece, against invading Persians. Before the battle they polished their swords, groomed themselves and combed their hair. Cathy's haircut left little to groom, but she soon knew she was in a battle, on and off the track.

She roomed with Margaret Crowley in the Australian team's hotel, while Bideau met up with Peter Jess and his daughter Zoe, who had been his intermediary via fax with Cathy during the troubles in El Paso. Bideau also met Peter Fortune who was attached to the national team for Freeman and Lauren Hewitt. Cathy didn't want Fortune to oversee her preparation. She found, no surprise, that Fortune was no substitute after Bideau defected in El Paso.

A few weeks earlier, in London, Nick had sent an intemperate letter to Fortune, virtually blaming him for Freeman's poor fitness after El Paso and Oregon. He told Fortune he wasn't needed in London, and Bideau obtained accreditation to the warm-up track in Athens to talk to Cathy before her races. Even in his absence, back in Melbourne, Fortune was proving a handy scapegoat for the warring Cathy and Nick show.

Bideau wrote in his trenchant letter to Fortune, 'She [Cathy] tells me that you say it is not your role to tell her what to eat, but as coach I thought it was your role to have her ready to run as well as possible and that is very difficult to do when you are fat.' Nick says he doesn't know what made him write the letter. 'I certainly didn't handle it the best way, but I was angry at the time,' he says. Without Fortune as the fall guy, Bideau was copping the full heat of Cathy's considerable athletic angst. Bideau may also have felt insecure after his long absence from Cathy's side in El Paso and feared Fortune may have been undermining his influence.

The issue of the coach remains an unhappy aspect of the Freeman story. Fortune's continued presence around Freeman was testimony to the mysterious magnetism that Freeman and her running exerted over otherwise rational men. They loved being associated with her—manager, coach, agent, accountant, medico, masseur, officials, training partners. I heard again, in my mind, Peter Jess's inspired remark, 'She's like a sleek panther, you can't hear her, you can't see her, until she's upon you ... and then she's got you.'

The extraordinary aspect of the Fortune affair was the reluctance Freeman felt about actually sacking her coach.

Team Freeman had brought such success that Cathy, who had the ultimate authority, was never sufficiently moved to make the decision to dismiss Fortune. Bideau did, in a roundabout way, in his letter from London, in which he said Fortune wasn't needed in London. Bideau says he would have sacked Fortune as early as 1995, after Gothenburg, when Fortune was not able to intercede to prevent Freeman from blowing her chances in the worlds 400m. As far as Nick was concerned, Fortune showed there he was not up to the job. But athlete, coach and manager are a complex triangle in any sport, as demonstrated by the informal nature of Fortune's financial arrangements with Cathy.

Cathy Freeman Enterprises never paid Fortune to coach. Fortune says that sometimes, money was vaguely offered to him. 'I came to them as an amateur coach, and I think that money does change the relationship with an athlete,' he concedes. 'So I didn't push it. But in this day and age coaching is a profession, and one of my main disagreements with Team Freeman was that others seemed to be encouraged to make a dollar out of Cathy's immense success, but not the coach. I basically had to build my life around her, change all my way of living, write her training program and attend to her every day at the track. I believe Nick had very definite ideas that I shouldn't be paid.'

Few coaches are paid, although some American coaches may take a percentage of their star athlete's track prize money. Fortune always felt that if he'd demanded to be recompensed for coaching Cathy, they would have dispensed with him. Cathy says she didn't have a problem with paying Fortune, though she is unsure whether Nick was similarly inclined. Bideau says if Fortune had asked for a reasonable amount as recognition of his expertise, they'd have paid it. It was never tested. That was the nature of the problem between the three of them. In many ways, Nick had hired Fortune to be his voice, and in accepting these unspoken terms, Fortune lost his.

However, Freeman often funded Fortune's air fares overseas, assisted with accommodation and living costs and in Melbourne, Bideau gave Fortune his own car to use after Bideau and Cathy were provided with a sponsor's car. As Freeman's coach, Fortune also became eligible for various substantial payments from Athletics Australia and the AOC's Olympic incentives scheme. As well, if he wished, Fortune could parlay his substantial fame as Cathy's coach to whatever advantage he could. The *Sunday Age* published some of his Freeman training routines during the world titles. Then, in 1995, his association with Cathy eventually contributed to him obtaining what he had long coveted, a full-time coaching position with the Victorian Institute of Sport. 'Yes,' he nods. 'I'm quite grateful for that. I've learnt massive amounts through being involved with Cathy. I'm a far better coach now than I was six years ago.'

Fortune's dissatisfaction was not so much monetary as a feeling of being unappreciated by Cathy herself. Nobody on Team Freeman was actually paid a stipend. Nick was paid a management fee by Nike, but Maurie Plant was not paid, nor her training partners. Their association with Freeman certainly raised their profile within their own spheres, but it was never the primary reason for their contact. But a coach's platonic attachment to a star athlete is the stuff of novels and Fortune is hurt that he was not allowed to see her through to 2000.

Each side is best summarised by Peter Jess and Chris Wardlaw. Jess backs Bideau. 'The coach, by simple definition, gets someone to do something they have to do,' he says. 'If they won't do it then you aren't a coach. You should go. You should sack yourself, get out of the kitchen.' Jess believes that if Fortune had pulled out of El Paso, Cathy would have been on the phone to Nick quick smart, asking him to come back. And he would have? 'Too right,' says Jess. 'Remember, no matter what anybody says or does, Catherine and Nick had an intangible link, and people who misread it kill themselves.' Chris Wardlaw, a friend of both Fortune and Bideau, is in an equally good position to judge. 'Six years is a long time in a coaching relationship,' he says. 'I know all the arguments, and I think Fort did a terrific job.' Judged by a harsh athletic maxim: 'Never be loyal to your coach; if you haven't improved in a year, get rid of your coach,' Fortune never had a bad year.

By the start of the world titles on 1 August 1997, the brilliance—it is not too strong a word—of Bideau's insistence on Cathy setting herself to defeat Pérec in Brussels the previous year, straight after their epic battle in Atlanta, became evident. Pérec had pulled out of the worlds 400m. Bideau's insight score into Pérec's character now stood at 2–1. He was astray in Atlanta, when Pérec cast her destiny to the gods, but spot-on in Brussels and Athens. If Cathy could run 49.39s out of shape, what could she do with four more weeks' tough training? Pérec had no appetite for the pain she would have to endure in training to match that.

Having accredited himself onto the warm-up track Bideau now had to deliver and Cathy was proving fractious. It wasn't like Oslo. As a diversion, Nick drew Cathy's attention to Jarmila Kratochvilova, the Czech who ran 47.99s in 1983, the second fastest 400m ever. 'Look how small she is,' commented Nick casually. Cathy said dismissively, 'You wouldn't have been a good competitor, Nick. You would have been too worried about the other runners.'

The morning of the first heat, Cathy rose at 5 a.m. to prepare for her 8 a.m. race. So early in fact, her eyes didn't really clear of sleepiness until after her race. She ran 51.53s, the fourth fastest qualifier, in coming second to Jamaica's Lorraine Graham. She ran to conserve energy but succeeded mainly in running slow, fast, slow, fast, depending on her race position. As she said afterwards, 'People are like horses, it's hard to hold back when you want to go at full gallop. I felt like saying, "Slow down, guys. First four through to the next round, it's cool."' An unwanted distraction occurred after the race when Australian team coach, Tudor Bidder, suggested that there was no second heat that day. If true it was a crucial break for Cathy and her uncertain strength of fitness. Bideau was sure there was another heat. Cathy, sitting listening, thought, 'Oh man, what's going on! I don't need to be worrying about this.' She found it unsettling, wondering whether to relax mentally for the rest of the day, or start preparing for an evening race. 'I don't think they should have had those discussions in front of the athletes because we needed to have confidence in those around us,' says Cathy. 'It was a bad reflection on the team coaches.' Bideau was right, there was another heat.

So that evening came the tough call, the second-round heat on the same day, unlike the Olympics where there is just one race per day. As tensions grew, a mini-battle developed at the warm-up between Cathy and Nick. 'Is this my water?' she asked. It is a genuine concern among athletes, drinking unknown water or the fear of having their own drinks spiked. Yes, said Nick. 'Are you sure?' 'Yeah, I'm pretty sure.' 'Are you absolutely sure that's my water?' 'Well, not absolutely sure, because I've taken my eyes off it for a few seconds, but I'm pretty sure.' 'Well, how do you expect me to drink it, I might get poisoned.' 'OK, I'll get you another one.'

In the second round Cathy was faster, 50.75s, second behind Jearl Miles-Clark who ran 50.66s. Cathy says she sensed Jearl wanted to win, so she let her. Nick was not a happy camper. 'Our girl never dominated, never got in a position to threaten, slow and fast, changed gears, just technically not right,' he says. He told her so and she told him off. 'Listen, I don't give a stuff about the heats, I just want to get into the final,' she said. Nick insisted that she needed to get a good lane. 'I don't give a stuff about what lane, I'll run from any lane,' she said. Prophetic words.

In stark contrast was the quarter-final win by Sandie Richards, who ran a PB of 50.08s. Sandie had no idea she had run so fast. She says, 'I'm thinking, "What's going on here?" Because all these cameras and microphones were coming at me. But I love two races in a day, I felt so strong.' Bideau knew Sandie had improved, but consoled himself. He had seen Cathy outsprint Sandie too often in training to be too concerned.

On the way back in the bus to the team hotel, Nick asked if she wanted him to have dinner with her. She agreed. But when the bus pulled in, Alexander Bodecker was there waiting to greet her, so Nick said he would meet her at 11.30 a.m. the next day. Bodecker became Cathy's release valve for all the manifest pressures of the titles. 'He was just the friend I needed, someone who was new,' says Cathy. 'He was a little ray of sunshine.'

Bideau went to Channel 7's studio and watched the replay of her second-round race. Front man Stan Grant asked, 'What do you think?' Bideau replied, 'That girl is not going to win the world championships.' Grant stared at him, astonished, and ventured, 'Well, that's not so bright.' Bideau continued, pointing at the screen, 'But there's another girl in there and if we can get her to run, she might be a chance.'

Next morning he met Cathy and they walked down the street for a coffee. In his mind, for the first time, Nick feared it might be getting away from them. Yet he had arrived in Athens so confident she was going to win. The semi-final was that night. He plunged in, crash or crash through. He told her she was running poorly, that she wasn't listening to him or concentrating on her race plan. Their coffee and hot chocolate sat forlornly, untouched. Cathy became upset. 'I'm not going to run,' she threatened. Nick did not retreat. That was up to her, he said, it was her life. But if she did run she needed to change her attitude. She wouldn't get the job done if she persisted in playing games. Playing games. Suddenly it was not just the semi-final hovering over the table, it was them, and a Force 12 storm brewing.

'All I wanted was for him to give me some race directions, give me some confidence and be solid in his message, to empower me, you know?' says Cathy. 'It was simple, I needed him, and we had to be professional. But every time he tried to give me advice ... Oh, I don't know.' Personal hurts obscured the message? 'Yes and I said to him, "Do you realise I'm favourite for a world championship title and you're running all this other personal stuff at me?" I was furious, it was a terrible argument. So many times I could have lost it. I was crying and I felt like just jumping on a plane and flying out.'

She stormed out of the coffee shop back to her hotel, hiding her angry tears. Nick was alarmed. Maybe he had gone too far, stuffed it up completely. He doesn't know to this day whether he was 100 per cent right to hit as hard as he did. He walked off down the street, defeated, down in the dumps and despairing. Until he looked up and saw Alexander Bodecker approaching.

His last, best hope. He accosted Bodecker. 'Sandy, you might be wondering what the hell is going on, it must seem strange, but we have a problem,' said Nick. 'Cathy has to understand that I'm here to help her, it's worked a lot of times before. It's very important she wins this race. This is her race. It's there for her to take. Atlanta, no, Athens yes. If she does, it will make her life a lot easier over the next few years and if she doesn't she's going to be miserable. If she doesn't get through these next two races and at least run a good final, she'll be unhappy and it won't help anyone.'

Bodecker was amazed, but listened. He'd been through relationship break-ups himself, he knew they were tough times. Nick entreated him, 'Talk to her, don't lecture her—I just have—let her know you believe I'm trying to help her. She's listened to me before.' Bodecker, a man not easily ruffled, nodded calmly. He had stayed well out of the firing line until then, but he believed, in this respect, Bideau's heart was true. They walked back to the hotel and found a downcast Cathy in the lounge. She looked from one to the other, surprised to see them together. 'I met Sandy outside,' announced Nick. 'He knows what I'm about. Enjoy your lunch.'

FIRST AMONG BILLIONS

Cathy and Alexander sat for an hour in a small booth while he sought to repair the onslaught on her sensibilities. The argument had represented the destruction of her focus, of her confidence, of her motivation, of her mental serenity, of her physiological stability—because distress adrenalin had sent her pulse racing—all within a few hours of racing her arch-rivals, Jearl Miles-Clark and Falilat Ogunkoya, in the toughest semi-final of the worlds 400m. The task beggars the imagination. Bideau had hoped to deliver the equivalent of a benign charge of shock therapy, to rearrange the scrambled manner in which Cathy was running her races. Instead he had left her dazed.

Bodecker's first words to Catherine were like balm. 'I believe you can do it,' he said quietly. Cathy harkened. So simply a corner can be turned. Bodecker, experienced in dealing with such world-famous athletes as Michael Jordan and Ronaldo, believed that he saw in Cathy what he knew to be true about those two stellar athletes. That under the toughest circumstances, where others could not, they were able to mentally raise their performance. They took whatever positive energy was available and focused it incredibly to their benefit. Essentially they never beat themselves. Sandy set about gently reinforcing those obvious positives in Cathy, to revive her great fighting spirit.

Bideau returned at 5 p.m. to accompany her to the warm-up track and immediately sensed a change. No challenge, no arguments, listening. It was business as usual, as in Atlanta. She started to ask questions. How would she go? What did he think? Nick relished these summaries. Pauline Davis is in no shape, forget her. Ogunkoya and Miles-Clark? Don't have to beat them both, but best if you beat one. First or second for a good lane draw in the final, that was the rule. 'You have to let them know you can beat them,' he said. 'Get in their ear that you're a problem to them. So run the first 250m like it's the big race, then decide after that what you have to do to run first or second, but don't kill yourself.'

And that's how Cathy, in lane three, ran it. First 250m she showed she was the boss, cruised past Miles-Clark, in four, and Ogunkoya in five, and then conserved energy on the bend, allowing her inside stagger to keep her in the lead. But having switched off somewhat, she was not ready to respond when, in the last 30m, both her fierce rivals squeezed past her on the line. Jearl, 50.05s, Falilat, 50.06s, Cathy, 50.11s. Bideau was confused. She didn't grind it out—not that he wanted her to, but he wondered now whether she could have, had she needed to. But when he watched a slow-mo replay, he saw her face was relaxed, and that she could have run faster.

Problem was, as third fastest in the semis, she went in the draw for lanes one, two, seven and eight. She drew one. Cathy was having a massage when Nick caught up with her. 'I've got lane one,' she said immediately. 'Yeah, that's a good lane, no worries,' said Nick, ever ready. Next morning, Brendan Foster interviewed Cathy on the roof of the Australian team's President hotel for BBC television. Maurie and Nick watched, just like old times, and later that afternoon, at 4 o'clock, Nick roused her from her nap to be at the warm-up track an hour later. The Louis Spyridon Olympic stadium is named after the Greek runner who won the first modern Olympic marathon in Athens in 1896. A crowd of about 50,000 were there when Cathy and Nick arrived for her 8 p.m. race. A westering sun bathed the stadium in an orange glow. Tim Forsyth made a point of seeing her. 'You're the best runner,' he told her, in his quiet, careful manner. 'All you've got to do is go out there and do it.'

Peter Fortune came over to wish Cathy luck, but she was tense and Nick intervened apologetically, asking Fort to attend to her blocks instead. It was a sad contrast to a year ago, when Cathy had appealed to Fortune to hug her before going into battle in Atlanta. But this was no time for personal psychodramas. Cathy was finally grappling with the realities of lane one. When Carl Lewis heard Cathy had drawn lane one he said it was an insult to the Atlanta silver medallist. 'I would have turned that computer over 50 times until it came up with something better than lane one,' he said.

The problems with lane one for Cathy were manifold. Compared to the middle or outer lanes, the two sharp bends in lane one did not suit her long stride. As well, the inside white line marking of lane one is flush with a white timber rail. Running on the lane marking, or over it, in any lane is illegal, risking disqualification. But minor infractions are rarely noticed or penalised in lanes two to eight—witness Pérec in Gothenburg in 1995. Whereas the cost in lane one for stepping beyond the white line is at least a stumble on the rail and possibly a fall. Normally, 400m runners aim to run 10cm from the inside of their lane. To be safe, Cathy would have to run at least 30cm out which, as I have already pointed out in regards to why Pérec so consistently errs, means an extra 0.3s over 400m, in a race which can be won by 0.03s.

As in Atlanta, Nick prepared himself for Cathy's doubts. Out they came during the warm-up. 'People reckon lane one is a tough lane,' she said. Nick: 'Why's that?' And recited his dogma. 'You train in lane one. Michael Johnson ran 42.4s from lane one in a relay once, fastest ever, so it can't be that hard. You set an Australian record from lane one in Monaco.' Well, close to lane one, she was in lane two in that race in 1994, before the Commonwealth Games. Didn't matter, it was his tone, not the content, which was reassuring. Even so, it begs the question: if Bideau had been more straight up with Freeman from the outset of her career, allowed her to suffer the consequences of her mistakes, she might not have been in lane one that night. On the other hand she may not have been there at all. It is never profitable to presume you have the answer to the conundrum of Freeman and Bideau.

Running bends is more tiring than down the straight and Nick wanted Cathy to run only one bend hard, the second one. Since she had been starting badly, he made a virtue out of it. The difficulty with lane one is the perspective. Lanes four and five seem so far in front that the back runner, instead of running their own race, tries too hard to get into the race too quickly. Nick asked her to do some starts. She did one, it was slow. Nick said, 'Great start, do one more.' Next one was worse. 'Best one yet, start like that,' he said. He reasoned her slow starts meant she wouldn't be able to pick up the field too quickly. 'I wanted her to get into her own rhythm, not to go out chasing the field,' said Nick. 'You see, after years of telling her to go like mad for the first 60 metres to reach top speed, I couldn't now say no, no, take it easy.' Nick also wanted to convince Cathy that her starts were hot so that in the race, no matter how she started, she would believe she had already stolen a bit on the field. That way, when she looked up and saw how far she was behind the front runners, she would have the confidence not to panic, to run her own race.

Credit for the final tactic belongs to all those who had Cathy's running at heart. Says distance coach Chris Wardlaw, 'I don't know whether Nick will admit this, but actually Fort mentioned it to me and I passed it on to Nick, who turns sophisticated tactics into three words or, in this case, one beautifully simple image.' Nick is adamant he got it from Maurie but, anyway, it went like this: make sure that with 150m to go, Cathy had something left. At that point, next to the steeplechase water jump, adjacent to lane one, she was to hit the gas.

Thus Nick told Cathy, 'At that water jump, there's a big green light,' he said gesturing an imaginary globe. 'When you see it, go like hell!' said Nick. 'You'll come into the straight in front, because of the stagger. You'll close on them fast in lane one and they won't sense you, they won't even know you're there, you'll catch them off guard.' This was the Michael Johnson/Marie-José Pérec tactic. Be in front entering the straight, and then stay there. Simple.

With 90 minutes to the 8.05 p.m. race start, Nick did two laps jogging with her, weaving their way through the leaping, bounding, sprinting melee of athletes warming up in multi-coloured uniforms and tracksuits. Each time they passed the water jump, Cathy suddenly surged, leaving Bideau five metres behind. It was ambrosia to Nick, to see her rehearse like that. He must have told her 10 times, the Big Green Light, until he began to worry she might actually expect to see one there.

Six of the women in the final were in the Atlanta final, and five had run in the Gothenburg final two years earlier. In the call room Sandie Richards said quietly to Cathy, 'You can do it, you can do it.' But could she? They walked through a tunnel under a road to enter the stadium, single file, footsteps echoing, silent until Sandie Richards burped, momentarily breaking the tension with her apologetic giggle. Cathy didn't laugh. She felt like she was being led to the abattoir.

As always the realities of the race overtook Cathy's insouciance once she was on the track. She *was* in lane one, she could *not* see around the corner, she *did* feel isolated from the other runners. What's more she had spotted the large yellow track clock beside the white rail of her lane and started thinking, 'Gee, that clock's close to me, I hope I don't hit my arm on the edge of it.' Then as Jeff Simons had instructed, she focused on herself and what she could do.

When the field was led onto the track, Tim Forsyth had just missed his first attempt at a qualifying height of 2.28m in the high jump. Just before the 400m start his name was called again and he thought, 'Ohhh, I'm not going to be able to watch her.' The 400m final gun fired, the field raced past. Tim tried to put Cathy out of his mind but, somewhat disturbed, rushed his jump and missed again. One jump left.

Cathy had made a good start but, after 150m, Tatyana Alekseyeva of Russia in lane two had gone so fast she almost caught Ogunkoya in three. As a consequence the gap back to Cathy looked so large she seemed to be out of it, though she wasn't. Peter Jess's heart sank. 'I thought she'd lost, she was so far behind.' Masseur Garry Miritis exclaimed to Jason Richardson, 'What the hell is she doing!'

Cathy says she didn't feel part of the race group until she actually made her move at 150m, when she gave herself the green light. 'I felt really strong then,' she says. 'I knew that I was coming at them. I had this inner feeling.' Richards, Miles-Clark and Ogunkoya ran the bend as though attached by string to each other, in perfect unison, with Cathy sneaking through unnoticed on their inside. They were a contrast, the four chances, line abreast entering the straight, 80m left to run. Richards looked dominant with her big rolling gait; Miles-Clark was a picture of control, her hands cleaving the air in karate chops; Ogunkoya had her body tilted forward, head absolutely steady, powerful legs pumping; only Cathy seemed to be actually sprinting, running for dear life. She was perhaps half a metre in front. And that's what the race became, a race of half-metres, and finally centimetres. Maurie Plant felt a frisson of hope as Cathy surged into the lead. 'They've got their work cut out to run her down now,' he predicted to himself grimly. 'Not too many ever come past her.'

With 50m to go, Ogunkoya dropped back a stride, Miles-Clark gained imperceptibly without ever looking like she would run Cathy down, but Richards was on the charge, tapping unsuspected energy. Cathy now knew they were there. 'Sandie and Jearl pushed it, pushed it and pushed it,' she says. Richards knew she was overtaking Jearl but was so focused she didn't see anybody else. 'I was just in the zone,' she says. She knew Cathy would be there somewhere, but they were so far apart, lane one to lane five, that she couldn't see whether Freeman was in front or behind. Cathy sensed Sandie's late thrust 10m out. 'Even though I was focused, and I couldn't see her, I could feel her,' says Cathy. Just before the finish, Sandie saw Cathy's legs. 'When you see somebody's foot like that it means they are usually a tad ahead or you are right there, and deadheat,' says Sandie. 'I wanted to lean at the line, but I was still in a full sprint and if I did lean I might have fallen or stumbled, and Jearly would have gotten me, because she was close.'

As Richards hurled at the line, Cathy's stride didn't alter or shorten: she drove to the finish in classic style, upright as a figure from a Parthenon relief. On the line she dipped, and won, by 2/100ths of a second from her friend Sandie Richards. Or as McAvaney called it, voice rising in crescendo, hoarse with emotion: 'She's just in front the Aussie ... Cathy's hanging on ... *Yes! She's done it. She's won it! What a run!*' Jane Flemming simply gasped, 'Unbelievable!'

Jearl and Sandie joined Cathy in a three-way hug, and Cathy gave Sandie a peck on the shoulder. Athletes usually know who's placed as they cross the line but it was so close that, in the seconds after the finish, Cathy glanced across at Maurie Plant and raised her eyebrows questioningly. I won? Yes? She'd already seen how Ukrainian Zhanna Pintusevich had mistakenly run half a victory lap after the women's 100m before embarrassedly realising that Marion Jones had pipped her. Maurie, with the benefit of the BBC monitor, and always the first friend Cathy sees, gave her the thumbs up. 'I was not going to celebrate until I was absolutely sure,' says Cathy. 'But I could bet my life on it I'd won.'

Tim Forsyth was so excited he started to walk over to congratulate her but suddenly thought, 'Hang on, hang on, I've got my own things to do here, like make sure I make this final!' He had one jump left and mercifully made it, and then caught up with Cathy. A man in a black cap, white T-shirt and long red baggy shorts whistled Cathy's attention, walked out onto the track, embraced her and handed her an Aboriginal flag attached to a curtain rod. Anyone who has been to an Olympics or a world championship will know the degree of difficulty involved in sliding past gate marshals and security officials. But there he was, Peter Jess, large as life on the track. Hard on his heels came a tearful Kate Plant,

CATHY FREEMAN—A JOURNEY JUST BEGUN

Maurie's wife, carrying the Australian flag. Not only that, they had emerged from the VIP section into which Jess had somehow conned them. They had waved their flags in there until officials sent down minders to warn them, 'Please, please, you do not wave flag in VIP section.'

So once more Cathy paraded her dual love of her nation and country, and no-one blinked an eye. 'It's times like those, that people make into special moments,' says Cathy. 'I'm so proud of who I am, Australian Aborigine, Australian, two and the same.'

Cathy was first in 49.77s, Richards second in 49.79s and Miles-Clark third in 49.90s. Cathy became the first Australian woman to win a world championship track and field gold medal. Channel 7's Pat Welsh, grinning set to bust, reminded her, 'Hey, you're the first!' Cathy smiled and said, 'Yeah, it's kinda nice. Technically it wasn't one of my best runs but you know, I've had a Beep! Beep! Beep! Beep! hard year and there were times when I didn't think I was going to make it. So I'm pretty emotional.' Some journalists, hearing that, mistakenly thought she said a 'big, big, big, big year'. But she meant exactly as she said. It had been so different to Atlanta, where the preparation, the support, the mindset were perfect. 'In Athens, we didn't know what the hell was going to happen,' she says. 'There was the break-up, the fact I didn't get in shape, the fact my heart was in turmoil, then I drew lane one.'

Nick made his way down to the track and was waylaid by McAvaney, who had picked up that, in the lead-up to the titles, Bideau had coached both gold and silver medallists. Nick said on air that he thought Cathy would win by a larger margin, but that Sandie, being big and strong, had held up through the four rounds better than Cathy. In the mixed zone Sandie grabbed him, hugged him and hugged him some more, saying, 'That training was great. I want to marry you!' Even though beaten, she had run a huge PB and under 50s for the first time in her life. 'And still under 30 years old,' she exclaimed happily.

Richards believes she messed up her race by not starting to sprint soon enough. Cathy sprinted from 150m out, Richards waited another 30m. By then Cathy had slid into the lead. 'I'm strong enough to have started from the 150m and I'm not a speedy person so I have to start earlier,' says Sandie. 'When the finish comes I was in a full sprint and I had so much left. I was in 49.5s shape, I just didn't do it.'

Damien Marsh ventures that even though Cathy didn't seem to tire, it was lucky they had only to run 400m not 402m. Cathy disputes this. 'I've been told I have a good nose for the line, like a horse,' she says. 'In that race, I ran fast enough to win. Or as someone said, I ran slow enough to just win. If I'd been pushed earlier I like to think I would have still found more. We all know where the finish line is and if Sandie was going to beat me, she would have, you know what I mean? Because you can feel people beating you even before they've passed you. And when I have to, I compete.' Jane Flemming supported Cathy's view on this when she told McAvaney, 'I've seen Cathy win so many races by 1/100th or 2/100ths of a second. She just has this absolute animal instinct that I'm sure you have to be born with.'

Cathy felt joyous, and sorry for Sandie. 'I would have been really disappointed if I'd been beaten by anybody, but I'd like to say that if I was going to get beaten, Sandie's my friend, that's just the way it is.' Sandie too is philosophical. 'I was happy,' she says. 'It was meant to be that way I think, that's how I see it.' Yet her words are tinged with a sorrow which only becomes explained when Cathy says, 'There's a part of her, she says her heart broke when she was so close to winning. She's so honest and sincere, that's why we get on so well.' Marie-José Pérec was surprised by the slow time. But she told French sports newspaper *L'Equipe* that may have been due to running two heats in one day. 'That was crazy, it is too hard,' she said.

Cathy was drug tested, phoned her mother and, exhausted and relieved, returned to the team hotel where a small group of friends gathered for beers on the President hotel rooftop on a warm summer's night. Athens was just coming to life, as it does for dinner between 10 p.m. and midnight. Gainsford-Taylor's coach, Jackie Byrnes, came over and congratulated Cathy and Nick, acknowledging a great Australian achievement. Then Cathy's clan adjourned for pizzas across the street.

Cathy still had relays to run, but she was physically and emotionally spent. It was down time for her. She had a media conference the next day and posed for photographs beside the Parthenon. Freeman has been criticised as a hesitant media performer but the international press didn't find her so. She put the gold medal into immediate perspective. 'What it means is that I can do it, I can deal with the pressures surrounding it,' she said. And her message to Aboriginal children? 'It doesn't hurt to think highly of yourself, believe in yourself, and never underestimate your own strength.'

She and Bodecker then went exploring and shopping in the ancient Athens precincts. Cathy had, after all, $80,000 prize money to spend from winning her gold medal. Although, by the time all her contract extras were included, the win was worth close to $300,000. Then Cathy went to a Nike party and, afterwards, nightclubbing and dancing. Athens lends itself to the good life because the partygoing populace don't even start roistering until around midnight. Nightclubs open until 6 a.m., people go to work at 8 a.m. and make up their sleep with a siesta between 2 p.m. and 5 p.m. 'I did some serious partying, a heap of dancing, everything was just flushed out of me by dancing,' she says. 'That wasn't smart, but my legs were already so tired from those 400m. I tried to take the relays seriously but there's so little oneness happening, too much ego walking around in those team relay meetings. It's not like the swimming where even though they're individuals, they're great together.' At school, Cathy enjoyed team sports but used to get annoyed when her team didn't perform. 'I'd yell out, "Do this, do that," and get angry if players didn't take it as seriously as I did,' she says. 'So in the end I chose a solitary sport where it's only me to blame.'

Bideau tried to get Cathy interested in the remainder of the grand prix circuit, but he was swimming against the tide. Sandie Richards stayed with them in London again, and was so excited at her breakthrough she ran two more sub-50s 400m in Europe. Cathy ran a slow 200m in Zurich, and 50.61s in winning a 400m for an international team versus Great Britain at Crystal Palace. Then she called it a day. It had been, as Cathy so expressively put it, a beep beep of a year, so much subterranean angst, so much surviving from one day to the next, so much doubt and so much learnt, all disguised by Cathy's cheerful, smiling face. Chris Wardlaw likens Freeman to an artist, and in view of the complexity of her performance he chooses Jackson Pollock and his Blue Poles for his metaphor. He told me, 'Like Pollock, we all have an opinion about the achievement, some of us might even think we could do it too, but she's the one who did it.'

Back in Australia, Cathy attended a Sydney testimonial lunch for Raelene Boyle, whose breast cancer treatment had left her unable to work. It was ostensibly an auction of Raelene's silver medal. Instead it became an occasion to honour Boyle, where friends and admirers bid a total of $350,000 for an assortment of items, including a pair of spikes Cathy contributed.

When the tumult of being back home subsided a little, Cathy awoke one morning and thought, as she does in her disarming way, 'Fancy—little ol' me, world champion.' It was especially gratifying to square the ledger at a world championship after her disappointment in Gothenburg in 1995. Lift it out of its restrictive context. If you took every

CATHY FREEMAN—A JOURNEY JUST BEGUN

woman on earth—from China and India, Africa, the Americas and Europe, the Pacific and Asia—and lined them up to run 400m as fast as they could, Cathy would beat them all. Every woman can run. Athens literally placed Cathy first among billions.

25.
TOWARDS SYDNEY 2000

In late 1997 a white stretch limousine nosed through the morning traffic towards Bondi Junction in Sydney, ferrying Cathy and Carl Lewis to be guests on Andrew Denton and Amanda Keller's 2MMM breakfast show. Cathy and Carl were chauffeured around Sydney all day promoting Nike's new Sydney–Melbourne track tour for 1998. Carl had arrived at Qantas in Los Angeles the day before, his flight departure imminent, but no ticket. 'Ma'am, this is not rocket science,' Lewis told the flustered ticket attendant. 'You got two choices. I'm either on this plane or I'm not.' So she gave him a boarding pass. Olympic gold medallists transcend such minor barriers.

Looking at the two athletes lounging in the limo, I was struck by their unifying unorthodoxy. Lewis, 36, had recently acquired dreadlocks, an earring and a tattoo. Cathy, 25, has a nose-stud, a tattoo but had started growing out her blade cut hairstyle—under her mum Cecelia's begged orders. 'I'm going through an awkward period in my life, the time most people go through in their early 20s,' says Lewis. 'I was too busy running.'

As Cathy's mother, Cecelia, had counselled, time had

healed all wounds and Cathy and Nick Bideau had survived their personal schism to forge a new partnership as manager and athlete, sustained by the enormous respect they have for each other. Nick had a two-year plan to prepare Cathy for the Sydney Olympics, and most of it involved her being away from Australia. After her world title victory in Athens she was sought by writers from the London *Sunday Times*, the *New York Times*, the *Los Angeles Times* and *USA Today*, as well as Japanese, Greek, Swedish and other international newspapers. She was now of universal interest, an indigenous Australian with a demonstrated rebellious spirit, who was a likely Olympic gold medallist.

Bideau has a theory that, similar to racing, the media produces stress on the central nervous system. 'Athletes get tired at the end of a season, but it's not the physical tiredness, it's the adrenalin rush, the anxiety of each race,' he says. 'Physically they can still get themselves up, but it's the head that gets tired. The mind can take care of lots of things, but not if it's tired. And media attention makes Catherine tired.'

Despite Bideau's constant vigil, requests squeeze through the screen to fall into the lap of the good-natured Freeman. 'Catherine quite simply has a very decent philosophy in that she can't say no,' says Peter Jess. 'She doesn't want to lose face or embarrass you. People who don't read that just don't understand. If she says yes, Nick has to come up and say, "Look, I know she said yes, but really she's too tired. She shouldn't do this."'

Her every move becomes news. Reports of a sparkling ring on Cathy's engagement finger in early 1998 sent the media into its usual flurry, but Cathy is now skilled at brushing aside questions about her private life. Often she used the simple device of remaining silent. 'I can't believe the questions, they have such a cheek,' she says. 'They ask and ask. It's like they're looking for a needle in a haystack.'

Freeman now spends at least six months of the year overseas, much of it competing, but about three months is training in America and England away from the Australian winter, and public recognition. At home in Melbourne her car has tinted windows and she wears wraparound dark glasses, but still her motoring is punctuated by calls of 'Good on you, Cathy!' and 'You gonna win gold for us, babe!' from well-meaning drivers or pedestrians. As Cathy drove up to the entrance of Olympic Park for the Nike meet in Melbourne, in February 1998, the gateman said endearingly, 'Bless you, Cathy. Park wherever you like, love. I knew you when you were no good, and now you're a credit to us all.' As Cathy drove through Nick yelled, 'No good?' grinning and laughing. 'Whenever was she that?' As Cathy expertly parked—she is a good driver—two young policemen, 50 metres away, called out 'Cathy, Cathy!' and started running towards the car. What's up now? we wondered. 'Just want to get your autograph,' says one copper, sheepishly shoving his notebook through the window. It's well intentioned, but wearying nevertheless.

In restaurants people stare in the window or, within five minutes of her being seated, will make the first hesitant approach for an autograph. She's unfailingly pleasant, but soon she'll ask her dining companions, 'Can we go now?' For her personal privacy, public transport or flying anything less than business class is out of the question.

Eventually Freeman became sensitised to formal public appearances. She declined invitations to attend dinners for both Princess Diana and Hillary Clinton when they visited Australia because, as she told me, 'I wouldn't have had a chance to really talk to them. It would be all polite chat and media photographs.' Except that now, in the aftermath of Princess Diana's death, Cathy wishes she had accepted for that dinner.

At 2MMM Andrew Denton asks Cathy, 'How many push-ups can you do?' Says Cathy, 'Umm, 50 push-ups in a row and 500 sit-ups.' Denton, incredulous: 'You don't look *that* strong?' Quips Cathy, laughing, 'No point in having a body like Tarzan and running like Jane!' But she is strong and mornings see her at the Victorian Institute of Sport gymnasium, grimacing through exercises painful even to observe. In a purple singlet, maroon sports top, black lycra shorts, track shoes and socks, she bends, bites her lip, and power cleans 72.5kg, well over her body weight of 52kg. 'It's really hard,' she wheezes. During squats with 150kg, pain creases her face. 'My quads are screaming!' she groans. Afterwards she explains, 'I'm one of the smaller athletes on the circuit so I need all the strength I can get.'

Occasionally Nick does the proposed exercise first to see what muscles will be used. Sports physiologist Mark McGrath, with whom Cathy has been training since October 1997, is amused to see Bideau do his exercise test run, rather like watching a food taster for royalty. It's fair enough. Can't have Freeman being accidentally injured.

Her most strenuous exercise is designed to strengthen her torso. She lies with her upper back and shoulders on a huge, unstable air-filled ball, balancing herself with her feet planted on the floor. It's difficult just to lie like that. Then she pumps a 30kg weight into the air with each arm. As soon as she lifts one arm, her whole body is thrown off balance, lurching to one side. Only her tense torso strength stops her from rolling off the ball and crashing to the floor. McGrath hovers, just in case. Her whole body trembles with the effort of maintaining balance. 'This builds core strength,' says McGrath. 'Part of the reason Michael Johnson is so good is that when he runs, every part of his body remains still, except for his arms and legs. All his core strength radiates out to his extremities.'

With coach Peter Fortune no longer part of the team, responsibility for training now rests with Bideau and a more mature, self-determining Freeman. Her inner resolve became evident over Christmas 1997, in Mackay, when a cyclone depression off the Queensland coast brought squalls of rain so heavy that windscreen wipers on double speed couldn't keep up. Cathy peeped out a window and told Alexander Bodecker the weather was abominable, maybe she would train two sessions tomorrow. A moment later she sighed and said, 'No, I'm going to train today.' So around to Melaleuca Park—sorry, the Cathy Freeman Oval—and in swirling rain she jogged two laps warm-up, then ran a few cautious 120m sprints, splashing through the puddles, followed by her sit-up and push-up routines.

Each push-up, her hands were wrist deep in water and her nose almost touched the muddy grass. Bodecker, who has seen the world's best in soccer and athletics train, watched in admiration. 'Here's something an athlete doesn't have to do,' he says. 'To me, she doesn't need anyone to motivate her to train. She's committed.'

She needs to be as Pérec and Co close in on Marita Koch's world record, thought unapproachable without the drugs Koch is suspected of using. In October 1997, the media hounded Cathy for her opinion about Ekkart Arbeit, the East German coach who was first proposed as Australia's athletic chief despite his drug-shrouded background. What did Cathy think? 'I don't,' she told them crisply. Drugs are anathema to Cathy, but to accommodate the likelihood that some records are suspect, she believes that drugs merely accelerate athletes to performances which were going to be achieved with time anyway. 'Drugs are a short-cut,' she says. 'But at the end of the day it doesn't mean, 15 years on, we can't run those 400m times. We're getting there.'

Who will get there first? Small incidents provide large insights. Marie-José Pérec visited Australia in early 1998 but did not run. During the Nike meet in Melbourne, Pérec half-seriously chided Sandie Richards for training with Cathy during the 1997–98 Australian domestic season. 'I'm your agent,' Pérec mock-pretended to Richards. 'Make sure nobody goes squeezing you like a lemon. Make sure nobody uses you.' Says Sandie, 'She was talking a whole lot of noise that night. It was just madness. Mary-Jo was trying to discourage me from coming down here to train with Cathy, because she knows we both got the potential to bust her butt!'

When the circuit moved to Sydney in February 1998, Pérec approached Cathy in the lobby of the Sheraton hotel and asked where she could buy some of the Aboriginal design clothing that Cathy often wears. Of course it was Balarinji. Pérec then asked Cathy where she could buy a didgeridoo. 'You can't,' said Cathy seriously. 'Why not?' said Pérec. 'Because if a woman plays a didgeridoo, it makes her infertile,' said Cathy. Pérec hesitated, uncertain whether Cathy was kidding her, and then laughed nervously. 'Oh, only if you believe it,' she said. Cathy looked at her and shrugged. She couldn't have spooked Pérec more had she been a kadaicha man.

Freeman has acquired a new sense of purpose since Athens. 'That title changed everything,' she says. 'It was so important.' More than her courageous second in Atlanta? 'Yes, Atlanta gave me confidence, but winning is different again.' As the Nike limo swept across the Sydney Harbour Bridge, bound for a morning television appearance, Cathy was deciding how to respond to the call that week by the Perth-based Nyoongah Circle of Elders for her to boycott the Sydney Olympics. Despite her lack of contact with traditional Aboriginal culture, and her trans-world lifestyle, Cathy is respectful of the indigenous nation. 'They're very angry,' she says with a sense of reverence. 'They've experienced a lot more discrimination than today's indigenous generation. So they're probably still bitter.' She did not wish to offend the Elders and so was grateful that loquacious Carl Lewis was on hand to reply.

Lewis has experienced two Olympic boycotts—the Americans refused to go to Moscow in 1980, and the Soviets reciprocated in Los Angeles in 1984. 'Boycotts simply don't work,' Lewis told Steve Leibmann on Channel 9's 'Today' show. 'They're outdated and ineffective. How can you influence something by not being there? You should race and try to make a difference.' Cathy admires Lewis's smooth skill with the media, even though it's not her way. Off the set, Cathy told him, 'When I see you in Europe I'm reluctant to approach you because you're so famous.' Lewis replied, 'Well, not any more, because we've been hanging out together and now we're friends.'

Russian swim coach Gennadi Touretski, who coaches world champions Michael Klim and Alexander Popov, says that to be a true champion, athletes have to be ambassadors for their country. For Cathy, recognition of this came with a call on Bideau's mobile phone one day as she jogged around the football fields opposite Olympic Park. It was a top secret call, but try as he might, Bideau could not disguise the pleasure in his voice. 'It's the Australia Day Council,' he said, handing the phone to Cathy. She had been chosen Australian of the Year. The enormity of it left her breathless. She laughed and gasped. 'Me? Why me? They could have chosen so many other people, yet they chose me,' she exclaims. 'Because you're a great Australian,' says Nick. 'Well, it's an honour,' she says, jumping around with excitement. 'I guess I'm making history.'

A few minutes later she skipped by, grinned and called out mischievously, 'Whoa! Australia Day? Invasion Day!' and jogged off, giggling. Her inference: Hey, what will the bro's think about this! She is the sixth Aboriginal Australian to be so honoured, and the first Australian ever to win both the Young Australian (1990) and the Australian of the Year. A month later, in Perth, she received the award from the Prime Minister, John Howard. She opened her address with two 'Wows!', and told the audience the award made her more proud than winning the 400m world championship. They were not empty words. She had been made an Aboriginal icon, alongside Lionel Rose (1968), Evonne Goolagong-Cawley (1971), Galarrwuy Yunupingu (1978), Lois O'Donoghue (1984) and Mandawuy Yunupingu (1992). Her official speech script read, 'I'm young, female and Aboriginal, which definitely puts me in a minority group in Australia.' But Cathy can't help her sense of irreverence and drew laughter when she said instead, 'I'm young, female, beautiful and sexy … and I'm only joking!'

She may have been joking, but she looked just that in a filmy ankle-length creamy-grey muslin dress with a black slip underneath, held by thin straps over her tanned, well-shaped shoulders. With her hair returning to a bobbed length, she looked as she said, young and beautiful. Says her friend from Australia Post, Mark Pickering, 'When I think about how shy and awkward she was when I first met her, she has grown into a very classy-looking woman. She has wonderful skin, scarcely has to wear make-up. For the Telstra awards, when she was female Athlete of the Year, she wore a Saba dress and I thought, "My God girl, you are looking beautiful."'

Unfortunately, Ipswich politician, Pauline Hanson, rained on the parade by questioning whether the choice of Freeman—and a 20-year-old Vietnamese refugee, Tan Le, as Young Australian—was mere political correctness. Cathy, who heard of the remarks after winning the 400m at the Adelaide grand prix that evening, said, 'I know how I feel. I know I'm very honoured to be Australian of the Year.'

Cathy steadfastly refuses to buy into the whole racism debate, even when sorely provoked. Despite the Aboriginal flag which she carries on significant occasions, she is not seen as an Aboriginal militant. Not for her the raised fist, the boycott or the strident protest. Black activists have tacitly acknowledged this by rarely pressuring her for support. Did she think Prime Minister Howard should have apologised over the Stolen Children generations? It was a loaded question, knowing as I did that her Nanna was a victim. 'I guess it would have been a step in the right direction,' Cathy says, carefully. 'It wouldn't have harmed anyone, would it? If anything it would have shown the Aboriginal people, shown us, that at least they acknowledged they did a wrong back then, that damage had been done.'

Cathy herself is willing to forgive and forget. In January 1998, she agreed to a Bushells tea television commercial with her bête noire Arthur Tunstall. The commercial, which has the theme of bringing antagonists together over a cuppa, scripts Cathy handing Tunstall a cup of tea and asking, 'White, Arthur?' He replies, 'No, black is just fine thanks, Cathy.' It finishes with Tunstall enquiring, 'Like any of the new flags, Cathy?'

The two did not have to be on the film set together the entire time and as Tunstall was doing his scenes, Cathy stood on the verandah of the location, a private home in Melbourne. 'I hadn't seen Cathy since the Games and she was shy at first, naturally,' says Tunstall. 'When she came out after her part of the ad, she was standing about 20 feet away, so I walked up to her and said, "Good morning, Cathy, it's a beautiful day." I could see she was a little bit hesitant. So I said, "You know, I trust we're friends," and then I went on and just spoke to her normally. I wished her well in the future. She's a great Australian and she's brought great credit to the country as an athlete.'

Cathy decided that once she agreed to work with Tunstall, she'd let bygones be bygones. 'Actually, I was sitting next to him and I suddenly remembered about all that, the flag and the jokes, and I started to get really pissed off,' says Cathy, frowning. 'I couldn't work it out, because I got the feeling that he's probably not racist. Then I thought, "Oh, what's the point of causing a scene over bullshit like that." So then I warmed to him a little bit. He's quite funny. He says that every morning he looks in the mirror and reminds himself how handsome he is. And then he says to himself, "I'm going to go out and not give an inch to those bastards." He suggested I do the same.'

Cathy is wistful for knowledge of her people and reads Aboriginal histories avidly. She wishes that in her day all students were taught Aboriginal history, as do many schools now. 'Times have changed,' she says. 'I learnt all about Captain James Cook, Sir Joseph Banks and Governor Macquarie, never the names of the Aboriginal tribes the early settlers hunted and shot. I mean, even now, people my age know more about Malcolm X and Martin Luther King, Geronimo and even Gandhi, than any Aboriginal heroes.'

As a consequence, her own Aboriginal heroes are her contemporaries, like the Yunupingu brothers, Galarrwuy and Mandawuy. She visited them at their home in Gove in late 1997—three indigenous Aussies of the Year together. Cathy and Bodecker were on holidays in the Northern Territory and she saw how the Yunupingus transcended cultures, managed modern Australia yet kept in contact with their traditional ways. One night, sitting around a camp fire, they even performed an impromptu dance for her. A corroboree, she called it. 'Not the full get-up, just the dances, but it was unreal,' she says. 'It was the first time I'd seen it, the closest I've come to experiencing Aboriginal culture. I got a bit emotional watching, it really affected me.'

She knows all the other Aboriginal Aussies of the Year, too. Lionel Rose she met when she attended the launch of a television series about him in Melbourne back in 1991. She took both her young brothers, Norman and Garth, with her and Rose gave them a set of boxing gloves each. They returned to Miller Street, Richmond and, with gloves the size of pillows, joyously and harmlessly punched the living suitcases out of each other. Cathy heard Rose tell Steve Vizard on his television show that although he suffered heart problems, he still had the occasional smoke. When Vizard expressed his surprise, Rose quipped, 'Mate, I'm not here for a long time, I'm here for a good time!' Lionel's devil-may-care attitude reminded Cathy of her father.

Freeman has much in common with Wimbledon winner Evonne Goolagong-Cawley, a shy, graceful athlete who, like Freeman, grew up largely in white company. Like Goolagong-

Cawley, to succeed, Freeman has had to become tunnel-visioned, her life a succession of training, travelling, competing, gymnasium, massage, physiotherapy, media, sponsorship appearances, exhaustion and sleep.

The 1998 domestic season was all that, after which Cathy flew to the US for her usual northern summer training where she soon built her best form since the Atlanta Olympics. She won a 400m in Eugene, Oregon, in 50.02s, her fastest US opening to an international season ever. She flew to Europe and ran 50.35s in Lucerne on 2 July, stretching her winning streak from 23 August 1996, soon after Atlanta, to 21 races.

She was fighting fit in Oslo, on 9 July, for a 400m which included the Nigerians, Falilat Ogunkoya and Charity Opara, and German Grit Breuer. As Cathy put on her flashy new spikes with her name down the side, she pulled the tongue out of her left shoe. It was five minutes to start time, she had no spare pair with her. 'I'll run without the tongue,' she told Nick Bideau, tightening the laces to compensate.

Oslo's track is an unusual shape in that it has two long straights and two quite sharp bends. Cathy ran aggressively down the back straight and then, rounding the curve into the straight, felt a sudden crunch and pain in her left foot. She ran on, finishing fourth, disappointed at her time, 50.92s, when she had promised so much. She iced her foot but didn't blame the injury for her defeat. Neither did Nick Bideau, both of them a little perplexed. They wondered whether the discarded shoe tongue had left her foot unstable in the shoe.

The foot discomfort appeared to settle and Cathy flew to Rome four days later. But when she tried to warm up with some track drills, her foot was definitely worse than before. She told Nick, 'I think it's more serious than we first thought.' In Rome she had an X-ray which showed nothing, and then an MRI (Magnetic Resonance Imaging) scan which did reveal something. A bone bruise, and a small bone cyst, under the end of the first metatarsal, the bone in the foot which joins up with the base of the big toe. The prognosis was that it should repair in a couple of weeks, at worst. They returned to London where an orthopaedic surgeon, Dr Graham Holloway, gave her a cortisone injection into the joint to speed the process. It helped, but didn't cure it. Cathy kept trim, bicycling in the gym, water running and light jogging. But as days stretched into weeks, she became more concerned. The worst aspect was that she was in limbo, resting up with the aim of racing the next week but never quite able to follow through. In succeeding weeks she missed races at the Goodwill Games in New York, followed by meets in Sheffield, Monaco, Zurich, Lausanne and Brussels.

The Commonwealth Games in early September were drawing near and every week, when I rang Cathy in London, her voice sounded a little more flat. She would go out, test the foot on the track, feel the joint still tender, and submit to another frustrating week. Alexander Bodecker flew in from America, Cathy's parents arrived on a European holiday and stayed with her in Deerhurst Crescent, Hampton Hill, as did her best friend Peta Powell. Cathy was glad of their company but nothing could dispel her growing anxiety.

In desperation, Nick Bideau asked Dr Peter Fuller to fly in from Melbourne. In a last ditch effort, Dr Fuller gave her a second cortisone injection. To no avail. Then a CAT scan finally exposed the hidden trauma. 'A second cyst on the metatarsal bone, about 50mm back from where the ligament attaches to the bone, had ruptured,' said Dr Fuller. 'When she was running the Oslo bend, possibly as her toe bent back, the ligament pulled a little flake off the bone. On the scan you can see, what appears to be, a bite out of the bone, only a few millimetres wide. That's created a persistent bruising going into the joint.'

Students of Freeman's running would notice an exaggerated pronation (inward roll) of her feet as she strikes and pivots, putting excessive pressure on her big toe joints. As a consequence, she has bunions at the base of both big toes and Dr Fuller says she probably has wear and tear in these joints. 'The cysts develop due to abnormal pressure and they would have been there for quite a long time,' he says. 'The bunion deformity in her right foot is actually worse than in her left. Yet it is her left foot which is injured because it takes the most pressure on the track, running bends anti-clockwise as athletes do.'

Cathy, 25, had worn spikes and run every season since she was 11. She had raced 14 straight seasons without a break—seven of them with Team Freeman—almost injury-free. Now she was no different to all the injury-stricken athletes who had previously expressed wonderment at her hardiness. It had taken a long time to manifest, but Cathy's running style and foot bone structure had combined to produce a small weakness which had eventually given way. The remedy, says Dr Fuller, may be for her to wear running shoes with a stiffer sole to protect the joint as she comes forward, and the toe as it bends back.

So that was that, for her 1998 season and for the Commonwealth Games. She had wanted to have a big year, to prove that she was a worthy world champion. In some ways the diagnosis was a relief, an end to the uncertainty, but on 26 August, nearly seven weeks after Oslo, as Cathy tearfully announced her withdrawal from the Games, she felt terrible. 'It sucks,' she said succinctly. She loves running for Australia. The Commonwealth Games, particularly, held good memories for her—relay gold medal in 1990, gold medal double in 1994. The latter, in Victoria, Canada, had also catapaulted her, and her Aboriginality, onto the world stage. She was loth to withdraw but it was a learning experience and better to have happened then, in Europe in 1998, then later.

Such as in Sydney 2000, at the Olympic Stadium, Homebush, where, in December 1997, Nike's stretch limousine eventually deposited us. Inside, on the track site, Cathy alights from the limousine near where the 400m will start and gazes about in awe. A giant crane, capable of lifting 1500 tonnes, sways skyward. The field around her is littered with construction equipment. Huge, cavernous concrete grandstands gape emptily on either side. Above the exhausts of heavy machinery, Freeman can hear another noise, the roar of 110,000 voices as she steps on the track for the 400m final.

In her mind's eye, she sees the world's flags streaming on high against the evening sky, sees a sea of Aussie flags held aloft in a mass demonstration of affection, admiration and good wishes. It's a din which fills the imagination and the senses all at once, and sets her heart fluttering excitedly. These are the Olympics for which her heritage has gifted her, this is the race for which her career has prepared her, and this is the moment when a modest young Aboriginal woman can both express her great talent and unite all Australians in an outpouring of national pride.

'This is so weird,' says Cathy, pressing her hands to her stomach to still the butterflies. 'I'm getting all choked up. The crowd will go ballistic. I can't wait to see my family's faces in the crowd.' She has no time pasted on the mirror for the Sydney Olympics: it's a secret, locked in her bank pin number. Carl Lewis, veteran of nine Olympic golds, smiles at his slender friend. 'OK, Cathy, this is your gig,' he says and choreographs her future moment of truth. 'Uniform basket goes there,' he says, pointing to some rubble. 'Starting blocks down here,' near a pile of tools. 'Stretch, warm-up, maybe do a few run-throughs.' Nick adds to the scenario. 'This is where it will be. Right? There'll be crowds and colour and noise, but under all that there will be just this track. And all you have to do is run one lap, fast!' Cathy nods, and then takes off in her black and white Melbourne Track Club tracksuit and Nike shoes, loping off, across the rough, rock-strewn ground which holds her destiny.

SHORT LIST OF HONOURS

1991 Young Australian of the Year.
1996 Telstra's Sports Personality of the Year.
1997 Australian of the Year.
1997 Voted the most admired woman in Australia, ahead of Hazel Hawke, Dawn Fraser and Sara Henderson—Newspoll.
1997 National Trust poll votes her as one of Australia's 100 living national treasures.
1997 Ranked 10th of Australia's top 12 most powerful people.
1997 Ranked in the nation's top 20 most popular personalities, by a survey of 120 advertising agencies.
1997 Ranked fifth in best Australian sportperson of all time, behind Sir Donald Bradman, Dawn Fraser, Greg Norman and Kieren Perkins.
1997 Chosen Australia's top sportswoman—consumer survey.
1997 Telstra's Female Athlete of the Year.
1997 Aboriginal and Torres Strait Island Sportswoman of the Year.
1997 The *Age* newspaper's Sportsperson of the Year.

CATHY FREEMAN—A JOURNEY JUST BEGUN

1997 *Australian Runner and Athlete* magazine's Athlete of the Year.
1997 Ranked No 1, women's 400m by *US Track and Field News*, and fourth overall in their female Athlete of the Year.
1997 Twice been named in the Australian Sporting Hall of Fame's achievement roll.
1997 Modelled in Madam Tussaud's Waxworks; street named after her in Mackay.
1998 Listed in *International Who's Who*.

INDEX

A
AAA titles (UK) 110–11
Aboriginal and Torres Strait Islander Commission 36
Aboriginality: Frank Fisher's rugby 8–9, 11; eugenics movement 15–16; cultural assimilation policy 16–17; Stolen Children 16–17; Human Rights and Equal Opportunity Commission report 17; primary school competitions 33; discrimination 36–37; CF's views on 40–42; at Fairholme College 53; CF's 1990 Commonwealth Games 72–73; her selection as Young Australian of the Year 82–83; CF faces discrimination 95; flag 107–8, 162, 167–73, 176; CF first woman selected for Olympics 113; sport coaching clinics 143–44; lack of athletics opportunity 144–45; her inspiration hopes 162–63; CF's Commonwealth Games reception 189; motifs on running shoes 257; CF visits Redfern 293–94; CF called on to boycott Sydney Olympics 344–45; her attitude to 346; her heroes 347–49
Afolabi, Alabisi 258
Ah Sam, Annie 20
Ah Sam, Tommy 18

Alekseyeva, Tatyana 331
Andrew, Prince 69
Arbeit, Ekkart 343
Assad, Willie 17
Athlete of the Year award (1993) 129
Athletics Australia 66
Atkinson, Sallyanne 78
Atterton, Nancy 67, 70, 90–91, 118, 181, 283
Australia Day Council 88, 345
Australia Post 95, 198, 228, 243, 286
Australian Institute of Sport 32
Australian of the Year 345

B
Backo, Sam 74
Bailey, Bill 212
Balarinji designs 108
Barber, Bruce (CF's step-father): courts Cecilia 27–30; contacts AIS 32; decides to make CF Olympian 33–34; fundraising 34; CF's advocate 39; reacts to sexual assault on CF 47–48; visits CF's school 50–51; negotiates scholarship 59; reaction to Bideau 82, 85; CF's Commonwealth Games win 177; CF buys house for 224; Atlanta 255, 270, 273; CF's goal to beat Pérec 278; CF's breakup with Bideau 288
Barber, Cecilia (CF's mother, earlier

Sibley, then Freeman): early years 15–16, 19–23; marriage 14; married life with Norman 23–26; life with Bruce 27–30; suffers discrimination 36–37; aspirations 40; protectiveness towards CF 42; visits CF's school 50–51; Anne-Marie's death 73–74; reaction to Bideau 82, 85–86; Barcelona 109, 116–17; Norman's death 140–41; CF's victory lap 168; CF's Commonwealth Games win 177; Gothenburg world titles 214; CF buys house for 224; Atlanta 255, 270, 273; CF's breakup with Bideau 288–89; comforts CF 295–96; CF's troubles in El Paso 303
Barkley, Charles 115
Bartlam, R.H. 21–22
Bauldry, Bessie 5
Becker, Boris 115
Bidder, Tudor 324
Bideau, Nick
  early years: youth 130, 134; meets CF 64; interviews her 67; attends 1990 Commonwealth Games 71; Anne-Marie's death 74; Bulgaria tour (1990) 77; buys CF dress 77
  life with CF: starts going out with CF 78; invites her to Melbourne 81–82; influence on her 84, 85; CF's move to Melbourne 86; Truth story 87–88; becomes CF's benefactor 89; CF dropped from Tokyo relay team 90; persuades Fortune to coach CF 92; life with CF 92–97; persuades Roe to accept CF for Hobart 97–98
  Barcelona Olympics: CF's preparations for Olympics 99–100, 106; sponsorships 108; British AAA titles 110; at Oslo 112; in Barcelona 114–15
  Stuttgart worlds: CF's training regime 122; CF's Adelaide sprints 124–25; negotiates with Nike 126–27; Brisbane nationals 127; in Toronto 134; suffers racism 134–35; California holiday 134–35; in England and Italy 135–36; Stuttgart world titles 136–38; CF's father dies 138–40
  Commonwealth Games (1994): Doomadgee sport clinic 143–44; in America 150–52; European tour 153, 155, 160; at the Games 164–65; advice 166; CF's victory 169, 171; media frenzy 172; CF's 200m 173; her second gold 176, 177; relay 181, 184
  after the Games: Paris grand prix 185–88; holiday 190; senses change in relationship with CF 190–92; accident 194; CF loses motivation 194; domestic life 194–96; CF's signing sessions 197; CF's losses 202; to LA 202–5; visits Atlanta 206
  Gothenburg (1995): buys house in UK with CF and Jess 209; European season 209–11; arrives in Gothenburg 208; Pérec's lane violation 212–13; CF's pre-race stress 213; her 400m loss 216–17; congratulates Gainsford 218; Nike promotion meeting 221–22; CF moves out 223–24; arranges for CF to buy house for parents 224
  preparation for Atlanta: plan for Atlanta 226–27; tries to withdraw control 227–28; 1995–96 domestic season 229–30, 231; CF's Stawell Gift win 235; in Atlanta for training 236–42; threatens to walk out 238–40; runs in local races 240; CF's Olympic plan 245
  Atlanta Olympics (1996): composes winning strategies 252–54; Hurst's newspaper article on CF 254–55; arrives in Atlanta 255; prepares 256–62; the day 262–65; the race 267–70; CF's tribute 272
  after Atlanta: renegotiates Nike contract 276–78; Melbourne Track Club 278; goal for CF to beat Pérec 278–79, 282; breaks up with CF 287–88, 296–97, 298, 290; O'Sullivan comes to stay 292; persuades CF to go to South Africa 298–99; walks out in El Paso 302–3; London 309–10; Oslo 313–15; invites Richards to train with CF 316–18; blames Fortune 320–21
  Athens (1997): CF's heats 323, 324;

INDEX

chides CF 325–26; seeks Bodecker's help 326; prepares CF for the finals 328–31; CF's win 334, 336
after Athens: re-forges business partnership with CF 340; tests CF's exercises 342; CF chosen Australian of the Year 345
Black, Roger 285
Blair, Fiona 76
Blewett, Greg 286
Bodecker, Alexander (Sandy): meets CF 223; CF's breakup with Bideau 292; CF stays with 306, 308–9; Oslo 313; Athens 325–27, 336; intercedes for Bideau 326–27; Queensland 343, 350
Boegman, Nicole 138, 151
Bowlen, Kathy 148
Boyle, Raelene 77, 88–90, 104, 131, 250, 273, 296, 337
Bradman, Donald 11
Breuer, Grit 219–20, 260, 265, 349
Brondello, Sandy 285
Brook, Dora 17
Brooks, Neil 177
Bruce Jenner Classic (San Jose, 1995) 206
Bruegger, Andreas 280
Bryzgina, Olga 114
Bubka, Sergey 211
Burke, Don 198–99
Byrne, Paul 299, 309
Byrnes, Jackie 126, 156, 336

C
Campbell, Juliet 206, 245
Campbell Miles trophy 37
Capobianca, Dean 262
Catherine Freeman Sports 96
Cherry, Tiffany 166, 176, 224, 282
Choppy, Baeden 285
Christie, Linford 68, 104–5, 123, 140, 199
Clark, Darren 68, 102, 133, 134, 250–51
Clarke, Ron 104, 112
Coates, John 66–67, 257
Cockatoo, John 19
Coe, Sebastian 104, 175–76
Coleman, David 169, 176–77
Commonwealth Athlete of the Year (1994) 176

Commonwealth Games: 1990 65–74; 1994 162–84
Commonwealth Games Association 66
Connor, Keith 180, 184
Corowa, Larry 143–44
Coutts, Shanie 234
CRA 143
Crowley, Margaret 309, 319
Culbert, David 94, 110, 118, 128, 158, 270, 272
'Current Affair, A' 128
Cuthbert, Betty 250
Cuthbert, Juliet 153

D
Dalai Lama 286
Daniel, Lyle 37
Danila, Mike 50, 59, 60–63, 68, 69, 74–75, 79–80, 83–84, 85
Davies, Judy-Joy 132
Davis, Calvin 284
Davis, Pauline: Oslo (1992) 111–12, 113; 1994: Gateshead 155; Commonwealth Games 174; Paris grand prix 186; 1995: San Jose 206; European season 216, 219; Atlanta (1996) 265
de Castella, Rob 68, 104
Denton, Andrew 339, 341
Devers, Gail 211
Donegan, Peter 166–67, 175
Douglas, Sandra 117
Downer, Alexander 170
Dream Team (basketball team) 115
Drechsler, Heike 285
Dunstan, Monique 64, 67, 71–72, 84, 86, 90, 180–81
Dynevor, Jeffrey 74

E
Erixon, Mats 213
Evetts, Sue 170
Ezinwa, Davidson and Osmond 68, 196–97

F
Fairholme College 51–55, 61
Faithful, Paul 51, 59
Faulkner, John 170
Featherstone, Sue 46–47
Fisher, Frank 8–12
Fisher, Norman Tolibah (Tolly) 9, 11, 141

CATHY FREEMAN—A JOURNEY JUST BEGUN

Fisher, Swampy 10–11
Flemming, Jane 69–70, 73, 76, 124–25, 127–29, 137–38, 335
Flintoff-King, Debbie 68, 146, 270
Ford, Michelle 78, 79
Ford (firm) 150
Forsyth, Tim: 1990 Australian junior team 77; meets CF 111; Nike press conference 115; captains junior team for Seoul 119; 1994: New York 150–51; Commonwealth Games 168; Gothenburg (1995) 215, 218; Atlanta 268; Melbourne Track Club 278; 1997: London 309; Oslo 314; Athens 328, 331, 333
Fortune, Peter: agrees to coach CF 92; Olympic trials 99, 102–3; CF trains for Olympics 105; CF at the AAA titles 110; CF's training regime 122; CF challenges Gainsford 125; in London 136; Stuttgart world titles 137; CF's character 147; CF in America 150; 1994 European season 153, 157–58, 158–59; Commonwealth Games 164, 166, 185; CF's loss of motivation 194; changes training methods 200; 1995 European season 210; Gothenburg 214–16; Bideau's plan for Atlanta 226; Atlanta 236, 237–39, 241, 256, 262, 264, 270, 273, 274; CF's breakup with Bideau 293, 297; El Paso 302, 306–7; returns to Australia 307; blamed by Bideau 320; role 320–22; Athens 328, 320
Foster, Brendan 164, 213, 244, 256, 328
Fraser, Dawn 170
Fredericks, Frankie 312
Freeman, Anne-Marie 23–25, 73–74
Freeman, Cathy
early years: birth 14, 25; father's departure 26–27; childhood 28; mother's marriage to Barber 28–29
primary school: moves to Hughendon 32; first national titles 31–32; attends AIS 32; joins Slade Point athletic club 37; misses 1986 season through poor health 38; home life 39; Aboriginality 40–42; sexually assaulted 44–48
high school: Fairholme College 51–57, 62; International Athletics Exchange tour (1989) 57; runs at Pacific School Games (1988) 59; attends Kooralbyn 60, 62–64; working relationship with Danila 61; improves 63–64; meets Bideau 64
Commonwealth Games (1990): relay 71–72; Anne-Marie's death 73–74; honoured with dot painting gift 74; asthma 75; learns to hurdle 75; Guiver becomes manager 75–76; first Aboriginal to win open Australian track title 76; receives Mobil prize 76–77; Bulgaria championships 77–78; Melbourne's Olympic bid 78–79; graduates from school 79; transfers to Kooralbyn Valley Resort 80
Melbourne (1991): Bideau's influence 81–82, 84; Young Australian of the Year 82–83; meets Hollows 83; Queensland titles 84; nationals in Sydney 84–85; moves to Melbourne 85–86, 87; Mt Sac relays 86–87; Truth story 87; appears on 'Sportsworld' 88; trains for Tokyo under Boyle 88; health collapses 89; Boyle's hard advice 89–90; dropped from relay team 90–91; in Tokyo 90–93; life with Bideau 92–97; spirituality 93; meets Powell 94; learns to drive 94–95; works for Australia Post 95; impresses Roe 97–98
pre-Olympics (1992): trials 99–101; trains for Olympics 103–4; wins Victoria 100m and 200m 105–6; injures ankle 106; qualifies for Barcelona 106; selection trials 107; enrols at Melbourne University 107; acquires Aboriginal flag 107–8; sponsorships 108
Barcelona Olympics (1992): British AAA titles 111; meets Forsyth 111; at Oslo 111–13; in London 113; selected for Barcelona 113–14; runs at Gateshead 114; in Barcelona 114–15; opening ceremony 116; heats 116; misses the semi-finals 117; Australian

INDEX

reception 118–19; captains Seoul team 119; performance at Seoul 119

Stuttgart (1993–94): training regime 122; concentrates on 200m 123; Hobart championship 123; Australia Day grand prix 123–24; Adelaide sprints 124–25; competition with Gainsford 125–29; Nike sponsorship 126–27; Brisbane nationals 127; Toronto world indoor titles 133–34; California holiday 134–35; in England and Italy 135–36; Stuttgart world titles 136–38; Sheffield 138; father's death 138–41; to Italy and back to Australia 140; self-assessment 141–42

pre-Commonwealth Games (1993–94): Doomadgee sport clinic 143–44; ranked eighth in the world 145; speaks out on AFL policy 145; further competition with Gainsford 146–49; sponsorships 150; in America 150–52; European tour 152, 154–61; runs at Gateshead 154–55; in Scandinavia 155–57; Monte Carlo 159–61; and Zurich 161

Commonwealth Games (1994): Aboriginal flag 162, 163; motives for running 162–63; runs the heats 163, 164–65, 166–67; the 400m 166–67; wins Gold 167; victory lap with the Aboriginal flag 167–68; officials' reaction 169–70; and the public's 170–71; media frenzy 171–72; runs 200m race 173–76; wins second Gold 175–76; Commonwealth Athlete of the Year 176; second victory lap 176; the aftermath 177; celebrates 177–78; loses relay 180–84

after the Games: Paris grand prix 185–87; World Cup 200m in London 188; Australian reception 188–89; holiday 190; senses change in relationship with Bideau 190–92; loses motivation 193–94; domestic life 194–96; resumes training 196; signing sessions 197; suffers fame 198–200; loses to Gainsford 200–201; public reaction to losses 201–2; trains in LA 202–5; Tunstall's joke 203–4; races in New York and San Jose 206; visits Atlanta 206; returns to Australia 206–7; calf injury 207

Gothenburg (1995): buys house in UK 209; European season 209–11; arrives in Gothenburg 208; under stress before title race 213–16; loses the 400m title 216–18; relay 218; continues European season 219–20; on drugs in sport 220; holidays in Ireland 221; Nike promotion meeting 221–23; meets Bodecker 223; returns to Australia 223; moves out from relationship with Bideau 223–24; buys house for parents 224; moves back in with Bideau 224

preparation for Atlanta: Bideau's Atlanta plan 226–27; increases training 227; works as journalist's assistant at Australia Post 228–29; trains with Simons 229; 1995–96 domestic season 230–35; races against Richards 231–32; breaks 50s barrier 231; female Athlete of the Year 232; Stawell Gift pro 233–35; in Atlanta to train 235–42; Bideau's threat to leave 238–39; Olympics preview race 241; feels lack of friends 241–42; runs in Eugene, Oregon 242; superfit 243; style 243–44; preparatory races in England 244–46; Gateshead 244–45; food poisoning 245; Olympic plan 245; Pérec attempts to psych her 246; nervous 251

Atlanta Olympics (1996): composes winning strategies 252–54; Games diary 254; Hurst's newspaper article 254–55; arrives in Atlanta 255; prepares for the 400m 256–62; runs heats 258; semis 260; the day 262–66; the race 267–70; after the race 270–75; medal ceremony 271

after Atlanta: 1996 European circuit 276, 279–83; Nike sponsorship

359

276–78; determined to beat Pérec 278–79; interview with PM 279–80; gift from Bruegger 280; beats Pérec 281; in the UK 282; Pérec's withdrawal 283, 284; Tokyo 283–85; back in Australia 286; meets the Dalai Lama 286; breaks up with Bideau 287–90; considers taking the year off 290–92; the stress shows in her running 292–93; visits Redfern 293–94; escapes north 294–95; Telstra's Sports Personality of the Year 295–96; appears on Boyle's 'This is Your Life' 296; loses to Gainsford 298; and to Peris-Kneebone 298; visits South Africa 299–300

preparation for Athens: El Paso 301–7; Bideau walks out 302; pulls through 303–6; visits Mexico 305–6; stays with Bodecker 306; to Oregon 307–8; loses condition 308–9, 312–15; London 309; European season 311–16; has hair cut off 311–12; and nose pierced 312; trains with Richards 316–18

Athens (1997): arrives in Athens 319; heats 323–24; row with Bideau 325–27; semi-finals 328; prepares for the finals 328–31; the race 331–33, 335; wins 333–34; first Australian woman to win world championship track and field medal 334; victory lap with both flags 334; after the race 336; continues the Eruopean circuit 337; tribute to Boyle 337

towards 2000: engagement 340; re-forges business partnership with Bideau 340; suffers public adulation 340–41; exercises 342; training schedule 342–43; on drugs in sport 343; called on to boycott Sydney Olympics 344; spooks Pérec 344; Australian of the Year 345–46; response to Hanson 346; attitude to racism debate 346–47; and to Tunstall 347; Aboriginal heroes 347–49; US and European 1998 season 349; long-term foot injury 349–51; forced to retire from 1998 Commonwealth Games 351; prepares for Olympics 2000 351–52

Freeman, Cecelia (CF's mother) *see* Barber, Cecelia
Freeman, Claude 'Charlie' 12
Freeman, Garth (CF's brother) 25, 140
Freeman, Gavin (CF's brother) 23, 27, 82, 140
Freeman, Norman (CF's brother) 25, 34, 59, 76, 105, 140–41, 206–7
Freeman, Norman (CF's father): early life 12–14; courts Cecelia 23; fatherhood 25–26; leaves home 26; divorce 29; Anne-Marie's death 73–74; sees CF run in Brisbane 76; death 138–39, 140–41
Fuller, Dr Peter 107, 243–44, 350

G
Gainsford, Melinda: 1991 relay team 91; qualifies for Barcelona 106, 107; Barcelona Olympics 118; at Seoul 119–20; tussle with CF for supremacy 123–29; in Toronto 133; kindness to CF 137–38; 1994: grand prix circuit 145–49; European season 155–56, 157, 158; Commonwealth Games 173–76, 180–81; 1995: beats CF 200–201, 202; European season 209–10; Gothenburg 218–19; beats CF again 292, 298; 1997 European season 312
Gibson, Mike 170
Gilbert, Eddie 10–11
Giles, Kelvin 108, 110
Goolagong-Cawley, Evonne 168, 170, 348–49
Gosper, Kevan 78
Graham, Lorraine 323–24
Grant, Stan 325
Gray, Lyn 7, 32, 56
Gray, Vanessa 6–7, 31–32, 53, 54–56, 60
Griffith-Joyner, Florence 57
Grogan, Brett 83
Grogan, Clarrie 83
Guidry-White, Carlette 206
Guiver, Ian 75, 78, 80, 85, 86, 96
Gunnell, Sally 176, 182–83, 244

INDEX

H
Hansen, Arne 314
Hanson, Ian 169
Hanson, Pauline 346
Hassen, Jack 19
Hawke, Bob 78, 79, 170
Hayes, Terry 13
Healy, Ian 76
Hearity, Terry 286
Henry, Garry 94
Hewitt, Lauren 146, 257, 262, 270, 292–93, 320
Hilliard, Craig 70
Holcombe, Mark 203, 236–37, 240, 251, 271
Holding, Clyde 170–71
Holloway, Dr Graham 350
Hollows, Fred 83
Hollows, Gabi 83
Honey, Gary 87
Houston, Gar 12, 14
Howard, John 279–80, 296, 345, 346
Hudson, David 165
Hurst, Mike 254–55, 293

I
International Athletics Exchange tour (1988) 57
Iszlaub, Percy 8–10

J
Jackson, Colin 68
Jackson, Grace 114
Jagger, Mick 199
James, Glenn 88
Jayasinghe, Susanthika 196
Jess, Peter: character 96; provides advice about Truth story 87; caught in the cross-fire 94; sponsorships 108; New York (1994) 150–51; CF's dream of victory lap with Aboriginal flag 162–63; Commonwealth Games (1994) 165–66, 167, 169, 171, 177–78; 1995 European season 209; Gothenburg 208–9, 215, 217, 218; runs at Stawell 232–33; in Atlanta 258, 261–62, 271, 273; renegotiates Nike contract 276; CF's breakup with Bideau 288–89, 296; 1997: London 309; Athens 319, 332, 333; backs Fortune 322
Jess, Zoe 297, 320

Johnson, Kerry 64, 65, 67–68, 69–73, 76, 90, 166–67
Johnson, Len 217
Johnson, Michael 148, 211, 222, 227, 270
Jones, Marion 315
Joyner-Kersee, Jackie 211

K
Kaiser-Brown, Natasha 150–51, 154, 155
Kasprowicz, Michael 286
Keating, Paul 171, 189–90
Kennett, Jeff 170, 199
Keter, Erick 151
Kibet, Sammy 244
King, Neil 66, 127, 173, 178–79, 201, 203
King, Phil 212, 270
Kirner, Joan 78
Knight, Phil 221
Koch, Marita 131
Kooralbyn International School 50, 59–60, 74–75
Kowalski, Daniel 256, 271
Kratochvilova, Jarmila 323
Kring, Ray 130
Kulawansa, Sriyani 196

L
Landy, John 100–101, 104, 112
Lane, Tim 173
Langat, Sammy 244
Lewis, Carl 57, 92, 211, 222, 268, 277, 328–29, 339, 344–45
Lewis, Chris 145
Lewis, Hayley 73
Lewis, Jackie 234
Lewis, Mac 285
Lewis, Wally 143–44
Lock, Michelle 99, 100, 108, 110, 113, 117
Loggins, Leroy 76
Lynagh, Michael 76

M
McAvaney, Bruce 88, 100, 132, 135, 137, 172, 268, 333
McCarthy, Darby 34–35, 53
McDermott, Craig 76
McDonald, Kim 225
McEwen, Fletcher 63
McGrath, Mark 342

McKenzie 309
McMullen, Jeff 83
McPaul, Louise 273, 275, 279
Madden, Chris 59
Maellett, Cliff 180
Magnay, Jacquelin 184
Mahony, Margaret 70, 91, 169, 172–73, 178–79, 217, 256–57, 298
MKenzie, Cameron 302, 305–6
Malone, Maicel 155, 186, 211, 260
Marsh, Damien 77, 133, 206, 220–21, 240, 291, 309, 335
Masur, Wally 135
Mauret, Mark 312–13
McDonald, Kim 209
Melbourne Track Club 278
Melbourne University 107
Merton, Dickie 95–96
Miles, Jearl: Oslo (1992) 111, 113; Sheffield (1993) 138; 1994: New York 150–51; European season 154, 155; Paris grand prix 186; 1995: New York Grand Prix 206; European season 211, 219; Gothenburg 216; 1996: UK 245; Athens 324, 328, 332–33, 334
Miller, Scott 258
Minogue, Kylie 198
Miritis, Garry 96, 256, 263, 309, 314, 332
Mitchell, Dennis 285
Mitchell, Neil 202
Mobil grand prix series 76–77
Moneghetti, Steve 130, 132, 178, 235, 278
Moore, Melissa 90–91, 106
Moresi, Mark 302, 305
Moriarty, John 108, 143, 293
Moriarty, Ros 108, 241
Mundine, Tony 170
Mutola, Maria 160, 212

N
National Indigenous Sports Award board 34–35
Naylor, Lee 181, 184, 218, 258
Naylor, Shane 105
NEC Classic (1996) 231
Nike (firm): approaches CF 77; sponsors her 108; press conference 'Men Who Fly' 115; renegotiates CF's contract 126–27; CF's victory lap with the Aboriginal flag 171; welcomes CF 205; pre-Gothenburg press conference 211; promotion meeting 221–22; provides running shoes with Aboriginal motif 257; Atlanta 272–73; renegotiates CF's contract again 276–77; 1998 promotion 339
Norman, Andy 112–13, 153, 157
Nunn, Glynis 51, 69, 128–29

O
Oakley, Ross 145
Oakley sunglasses 108
O'Brien, Dan 211
Ogunkoya, Falilat: Atlanta 266, 268, 269, 271; 1996 European season 281, 282, 283; 1997: New Zealand 292; South Africa 299; Stockholm 315; Athens 328, 332; 1998 European season 349
Olympic Games: Barcelona (1992) 110–20; Atlanta (1996) 78, 252–71
Olympic Job Opportunities Program 95
O'Mara, Frank 221
O'Neill, Susie 258
Onyali, Mary 3, 164, 173–76, 188, 206
Opara, Charity 349
Osborne, Norm 32, 105
O'Shane, Pat 170
O'Shane, Tjandamurra 293
O'Sullivan, Sonia 292, 309
Ottey, Merlene 68, 136, 137, 153, 161, 188, 283–84
Ovett, Steve 104, 270

P
Pacific Schools Games: 1984 31–32; 1988 59
Paynter, Julian 259
Pérec, Marie-José 246–49; Barcelona 116, 118; 1993 European season 137; 1994: New York 151; Monte Carlo 159–61; European season 161; Paris grand prix 186–87; attitude to CF 205; 1995 European season 209; Gothenburg worlds 212–13, 216, 217; Olympics preview race 241; tries to psych CF 246; Atlanta 260, 264, 265–66, 267–69, 271, 274–75; Bideau's hopes 278–79; 1996 season 280–84; beaten by CF 281; withdraws 282; assesses CF's

INDEX

problems 312–13, 314; tries to dissuade Richards from training with CF 343–44; CF spooks 344
Peris-Kneebone, Nova 297, 298
Perkins, Charlie 35, 255, 270
Perkins, Kieren 115
Perpoli, Danielle 98
Pickering, Mark 197, 228–29, 234, 346
Plant, Kate 147, 333–34
Plant, Maurie: early years 153–54; Koch's 1985 run 131; observes CF 104, 111; Oslo 112–13; Gateshead 114; observes CF 123; on Australians overseas 133; father's death 138; CF's character 147–48; in America 150; 1994: European season 153, 156, 158, 161; Commonwealth Games 164, 167, 174, 176; CF's loss of motivation 194; 1995 European season 210; Gothenburg 212; CF's 1996 Gateshead run 244; Atlanta 240, 272, 273, 274; CF's decision to take a year off 290–91; South Africa 298–99; El Paso 301–2; CF's loss of condition 313; Oslo 314, 315; CF's win 333
Plant, Maurie, Atlanta 236
Poetschka, Renee: CF's main Australian rival 4; 1990 Commonwealth Games relay 78; trials for Barcelona 99, 102, 110; explains lactic acid pain 100; British AAAs 111; Barcelona 113, 117; 1993: Brisbane nationals 129; Toronto 133; 1994: grand prix circuit 149–50; Australian record 152; Monte Carlo 159–60; Commonwealth Games 164, 167, 181–82, 184, 185; after the Games 202; 1995 European season 211; Gothenburg 218; 1996: NEC classic 231, 232; Atlanta 258
Pollock, Penny 38, 170, 285
Pope, Kym 75
Postle, Arthur 10
Powell, Mike 92, 127
Powell, Peta 94, 202, 256–57, 265, 287, 290, 350
Prefontaine meet (Eugene, Oregon) 307
Privalova, Irina 137, 156–57, 161, 188, 211

Q
Quarrie, Don 151–52

R
Rashad, Phylicia 115
Regis, John 140
Reynolds, Henry 16
Richards, Keith 199
Richards, Sandie: Barcelona 118; San Jose (1993) 151–52; 1994: European season 155, 160; Commonwealth Games 164, 165, 166–67, 182–83; 1995 European season 211; invited to Australia for 1995–96 season 230–32; friendship with Pérec 248; Atlanta 260, 264, 266; 1997: Oslo 313–14; Stockholm 316; trains with CF 316–18; Athens 324–25, 331–32, 332–35; stays with CF in London 337; trains with her 343–44
Richardson, Carol and Graham (London residents) 114
Richardson, Graham (Minister for Sport) 66
Richardson, Jason 302–3, 305, 306, 307–8, 309, 311
Riley, Samantha 258
Risman, A. J. (Gus) 8–9
Robilliard, Steve 234
Robinson, Rohan 77, 311
Roe, Brian 97–98, 106–7, 230, 273, 282
Rolling Stones 199
Rose, Lionel 348
Rowe, Geoff 173, 176, 203
Roy, Geraldine 12
Ruckle, Tani 178

S
Sambell, Kathy 64, 66, 68, 71–73, 87, 90, 180–81
Saunders, Janice 38, 170, 265
Saxby, Kerry 116, 133
Schobel, Jean Pierre 161
Schuwalow, Carolyn 218
Scott, Denny and Beverly 134
Seal, Pat 3–4, 309, 310
Seegobin, Cubie 151–52
Sessarago, John 53, 54, 56–57, 58
Sharman, Jimmy 18
Shirvington, Matt 299
Sibley, Alice (Mero) 16–18, 22–23, 86
Sibley, Cecelia see Barber, Cecelia

Sibley, George 16–18, 18–19, 23, 109
Sibley, George Charles 18
Sibley, Sonny 18, 21–23
Silcock, Nat 8
Simons, Jeff 229, 263, 303–4
Smith, John 203, 205, 266
Stafford, Ken 59
Stafford, Kylie 54–55, 59
Stawell Gift pro (1996) 232–35
Stephens, Brett 93, 96–97
Stewart, Sharon 99, 100, 105, 110, 113–14
Stone, Joanna 77
Svensson, Eva 213

T
Talbot, John 13, 141
Tannock, John 235
Telstra 150
Telstra's Sports Personality of the Year 295–96
Thaiday, Willie 21–22
Tighe, Karen 234
Toleman, John 95
Torrence, Gwen: Barcelona 113; 1993: Stuttgart world titles 137; invited to Australia 148; 1994 European season 156–57, 161; 1995: New York Grand Prix 206; Gothenburg 212; 1996: Atlanta 237; European season 280, 281; Tokyo 283–84
Touretski, Gennadi 345
Trandenkov, Igor 285

Truth newspaper 87
Tunstall, Arthur 66, 169, 170, 172–73, 178–79, 203–4, 347
2MMM 339, 341

U
Univerity of Texas, El Paso (UTEP) 301
Unthank, Paul 309

V
Vander-Kuyp, Kyle 77, 293, 294, 309, 311
Vizanari, Lisa-Marie 77
Voronova, Natalya 133

W
Walford, Ricky 143
Walker, John 96–97, 104, 130–32
Waller, Manly 206
Wardlaw, Carmel 100
Wardlaw, Chris 92, 100, 213, 235, 243, 260, 322–23, 330, 337
Welsh, Pat 270, 334
Wilkinson, Peter 128
Winmar, Nicky 145

Y
Young Australian of the Year award 82–83
Yunupingu, Galarrwuy and Mandawuy 348
Yusuf, Fatima 78, 164, 166–67, 183–84, 260, 266